For Mari…

With every good birthday wishes -

David Patterson

18 February 1996

A Phoenix in Fetters

OTHER BOOKS IN THE OXFORD CENTRE SERIES

Monotheism: A Philosophic Inquiry into the Foundations of Theology and Ethics
Lenn E. Goodman

Divine Name and Presence: The Memra
Robert Hayward

A Jewish Life Under the Tsars: The Autobiography of Chaim Aronson, 1825–1888
Translated from the original Hebrew and edited by Norman Marsden

Essays in Honour of Yigael Yadin
Edited by Geza Vermes and Jacob Neusner

State and Society in Roman Galilee, AD 132–212
Martin Goodman

The Great Transition: The Recovery of the Lost Centers of Modern Hebrew Literature
Edited by Glenda Abramson and Tudor Parfitt

Oxford Centre for Postgraduate Hebrew Studies

A PHOENIX IN FETTERS

Studies in Nineteenth and Early Twentieth Century Hebrew Fiction

David Patterson

ROWMAN & LITTLEFIELD PUBLISHERS, INC.

ROWMAN & LITTLEFIELD PUBLISHERS, INC.

Published in the United States of America
by Rowman & Littlefield Publishers, Inc.
8705 Bollman Place, Savage, Maryland 20763

British Cataloging in Publication Information Available

Library of Congress Cataloging in Publication Data

Patterson, David.
A phoenix in fetters.

Bibliography: p.8
Includes index.
1. Hebrew fiction—History and criticism. I. Title.
PJ5029.P37 1987 892.4'3'009 86–33921
ISBN O–8476–7564–5

Typeset on a Lasercomp
at Oxford University Computing Service

∞™ The paper used in this publication meets the minimum requirements of American National Standard for Information Sciences—Permanence of Paper for Printed Library Materials, ANSI Z39.48–1984.

For Jose

Contents

Preface ix
Acknowledgments xi

1 Introduction: The Emergence of Modern Hebrew Literature 1
2 Epistolary Elements in the Novels of Abraham Mapu 21
3 Epistolary Elements in the Novels of Mapu's Successors 34
4 Sickness and Death 44
5 Religion and Life 53
6 A Portrait of Hasidism 66
7 A Portrait of the "Ṣaddiq" 79
8 Aspects of Language 93
9 Israel Weisbrem 102
10 Ancient Hebrew Law in Modern Hebrew Literature 118
11 From Mapu to Mendele: In Search of Artistry 127
12 Epilog: The Transference of Hebrew Literature from Eastern Europe to *'Ereṣ Yisra'el* 144

Abbreviations 157
Notes 159
Bibliography 193
Index 203

Preface

THE FLOWERING of modern Hebrew literature and the rebirth of Hebrew as a living language provide striking testimony to the vitality of the Jewish people in the nineteenth and twentieth centuries. As late as 1881 it is highly improbable that Hebrew could have been the sole language of any single individual anywhere in the world. Today, there are more than a million people for whom Hebrew is the only language, a further million for whom it is the first language, and an additional million for whom it is an important second language. The progression from zero to more than three million speakers of Hebrew in the course of a century is, perhaps, a linguistic phenomenon without parallel, and certainly one that is worthy of considerable remark.

Between the French Revolution and World War I, first in Central and then increasingly in Eastern Europe, Hebrew literature experienced a veritable renaissance, and proceeded to mirror, whether realistically or satirically, the social, religious, economic, and political aspects of Jewish life, particularly in the Russian "Pale of Settlement." During its first hundred years of renewed creativity, however, the literature was severely hampered by an artificial theory of literature to which most of its practitioners adhered. Hence the image of a Phoenix in fetters conveys the sense of renewal and restriction that informs much of the literature considered in this volume.

The twelve chapters of the book were originally conceived as self-contained studies, and so a certain amount of overlapping remains, although this has been kept to a minimum. The bulk of the work is concerned with the Hebrew novel in the thirty five years following its inception in 1853, but the Introduction and the Epilog considerably extend the boundaries in both directions, while part of Chapter 10 deals with a novel published in the first decade of the State of Israel. Chapter 2 presents supplementary material to my book *Abraham Mapu, The Creator of the Hebrew Novel*, London, 1964, Ithaca, 1968. Chapters 3–9 and parts of Chapters 10 and 11 are complementary to my book *The Hebrew Novel in Czarist Russia*, Edinburgh, 1964. The reader is advised to refer to the Preface and the Introduction to that volume for background information, as well as for short biographies of the authors and brief summaries of the plots of the novels under review.

Except in the case of familiar names, the following system of transliteration has been adopted:

א	’	בּ	b	ב	bh	גּ	g	ג	gh
דּ	d	ד	dh	ה	h	ו	w	ז	z
ח	ḥ	ט	ṭ	י	y	כּ	k	כ	kh
ל	l	מ	m	נ	n	ס	s	ע	‘
פּ	p	פ	ph	צ	ṣ	ק	q	ר	r
שׂ	s	שׁ	š	תּ	t	ת	th		

David Patterson
Oxford Centre for Postgraduate Hebrew Studies, 1989

Acknowledgments

THE STUDIES included in this work were published in first form in a variety of books and journals. My grateful thanks are due to the following publishers and editors for permission to make use of the materials for this volume:

Chapter 1. D. Daiches and A. Thorlby, eds., *Literature and Western Civilisation*, vol. 5, *The Modern World ii: Realities*, London, 1972.
Chapter 2. *Bulletin of the Leeds Oriental Society*, vol. 4, 1962/3.
Chapter 3. *Ibid.*, vol. 5, 1963/5.
Chapter 4. *Jewish Journal of Sociology*, vol. v, no. 1, 1963.
Chapter 5. *Bulletin of the John Rylands Library*, vol. xlii, no. 2, 1959–60.
Chapter 6. *Journal of Semitic Studies*, vol. 5, no. 4, 1960.
Chapter 7. *Ibid.*, vol. 8, no. 2, 1963.
Chapter 8. *Ibid.*, vol. 7, no. 2, 1962.
Chapter 9. *Ibid.*, vol. 4, no. 1, 1959.
Chapter 10. *Journal of Jewish Studies*, vol. xxv, no. 1, 1974.
Chapter 11. *Modern Judaism*, vol. 1, no. 3, 1982, and *Proceedings of the Fifth World Congress of Jewish Studies*, vol. iii, Division iii, Jerusalem, 1972.
Chapter 12. *Journal of Jewish Studies*, vol. xxix, no. 1, 1978, and C. Rabin, D. Patterson, B. Z. Luria, and Y. Avisher, eds., *Studies in the Bible and the Hebrew Language offered to Meir Wallenstein*, Jerusalem, 1979.

Over the three decades which span the studies in this volume, I have benefited from the generous advice of many friends and colleagues and the help of a number of institutions. I am grateful for the kind assistance of Mr. R. Judd and especially Mr. R. A. May of the Bodleian Library, Oxford, Mrs. C. M. Griffin and Ms. D. Holl of the University Computing Service, and Mr. S. V. Cope. Dr. D. Aberbach and Mr. M. Moseley have read the manuscript closely and supplied many valuable comments. Invitations to spend periods of time at Mishkenot Shaananim, Jerusalem, The Humanities Research

Centre, Canberra, The Society for the Humanities, Cornell University, Hebrew Union College, Cincinnati, and the Ben Gurion Institute at Sde Boker, Israel, have greatly facilitated the composition of this book, and sincere thanks are due to their principals and staffs. It is a pleasure to acknowledge my debt to my colleagues and the library and office staffs at the Oxford Centre for Postgraduate Hebrew Studies, and at the Oriental Institute, Oxford.

I am grateful to Dr Richard White who has kindly prepared the index.

Finally, I would like to express my gratitude to my wife who has been a constant source of encouragement and help for thirty eight years. This volume is dedicated to her as a token of appreciation.

I

Introduction: The Emergence of Modern Hebrew Literature

MODERN HEBREW literature[1] is of more than parochial interest for a number of reasons. Quite apart from its considerable literary worth, the close links that it displays variously with Italian, French, German, Yiddish, Russian, English, and American writing can prove highly instructive to the student of comparative literature. Its vigorous search for new modes of expression played a major role in the revival of Hebrew as a living language. Hebrew appears to be the sole example of an entirely successful resurrection of a "dead" language, and thus the laboratory situation it offers in the field of linguistics may well be unique. Hebrew literature, moreover, reflects the complex of social forces and pressures that underlay European anti-Semitism and led to the horror of the Holocaust during World War II. That nightmare episode must be regarded as a yardstick for European civilization, and any literature that illuminates the background from which it evolved deserves the closest scrutiny. No less importantly, Hebrew literature served as midwife to the birth of modern Jewish nationalism, which in turn produced the Zionist movement and culminated in the State of Israel.

The period covered in this chapter extends roughly from the French Revolution to World War I. Although it has been argued that modern Hebrew literature may be traced back to the first half of the eighteenth century, and indeed even earlier,[2] in Italy and Holland, perhaps a better starting point is its appearance in Germany at the end of the eighteenth century. But whichever view is held, the principal difference between modern Hebrew literature and the Hebrew literature that preceded it is one of spirit. The previous strata of Hebrew literature—namely the Bible, Mishnah, Talmud, Midrash, and the vast collection covered by the term "medieval"—reflect a mainly Jewish creativity. For the most part the literature serves as a medium for expressing and transmitting specifically Jewish values, and for that reason form and content appear welded together in harmony, with the language admirably suited to the themes. For modern

Hebrew literature, particularly in the hundred years following the French Revolution, this is no longer true. For a century the literature is largely concerned with the expression of other values in Hebrew guise; the language and form remain the same, but the content is vastly different. Instead of suiting the content, the form is imposed upon it artificially, and attempts are made to cover a wide range of ideas in Hebrew before the language is properly able to express them. It is important to consider why this should have been so, because there can be few periods of literature when social motivations are more clearly discernible than during the century and a quarter under review. The historical processes may also help to explain the remarkable improvement in quality that characterizes Hebrew literature during the twenty five years before World War I.

In Western Europe the Jewish people entered the modern world some 250 years late, although still well in advance of the Jewish communities in Eastern Europe. This painful retardation stems from the institution of the ghetto in the middle of the sixteenth century, first in Italy and then with great rapidity in many other parts of Europe. Before the ghetto period the Jews, although scattered throughout many lands and without title to any particular territory, had managed to maintain their integrity as a people. The nature of Judaism, which combined an element of nationalism sufficient to fashion a self-contained and self-sustaining pattern of life with an admixture of universality, accorded well with medieval concepts. Their confidence was buoyed, moreover, by a sincere and absolute belief in the imminent coming of the Messiah. The tenacity of that faith is witnessed by the succession of false "messiahs" throughout the medieval period, each of whom received enthusiastic support in spite of all previous disappointments. Glückel of Hameln relates, for example, how hard-headed Jewish businessmen sold their possessions and flocked to the Hanseatic ports waiting to be transferred to the Holy Land in the wake of Sabbatai Zevi, the most celebrated pretender to the messianic throne.[3] Again, medieval Jewish communities drew comfort from a sense of cultural superiority, in keeping with the "chosen people" concept, that was nourished by a high level of literacy and by strict rules concerning hygiene and morality at a time when such practices were held in scant esteem within the host societies. Such feelings of pride, however, were due for a sobering reappraisal.

The period of the ghetto, which extends from the middle of the sixteenth to the end of the eighteenth century, is one of the most degrading in Jewish history, and one that led to a narrowing of intellectual horizons no less severe than the ugly limitations to physical freedom. Confined behind walls and gates in cramped and insalubrious quarters, securely insulated from the outside world, Jews suffered overcrowding, squalor, and occupational diseases of lung and eye, as well as intellectual atrophy. Even the ancient tradition of scholarship became increasingly geared to a barren casuistry concerned with peripheral and minor issues, while the real springs of intellectual activity ran dry. The ever-narrowing circle of ideas is reflected in the pettiness of what were considered issues. Toward the end of the period a dispute over the proper pronunciation of the half-vowels in Hebrew split the ghetto in Rome for almost thirty years![4]

It is important to recall that the two and a half centuries of ghetto life coincide with the great flowering of the spirit in Western Europe in almost every intellectual and artistic realm. In music and architecture, in art and literature, in mathematics, science, philosophy, and law, the Renaissance ushered in an era of splendid creativity, widening the intellectual horizons of Europe even as its physical horizons were being widened by the great voyages of discovery. Navigators and scientists, soldiers and philosophers, were pushing back frontiers, voyaging strange seas, and exploring unknown regions, both in the physical world and in the realm of the intellect. A revolution in economics went hand in hand with a change in the whole method of scholarship from medieval scholasticism to experimental science. And during the whole of this formative era, Jewish life was more and more turned in upon itself.

Thus, when the Napoleonic armies swept across Europe and broke down the ghetto gates, the Jews emerged into a world that had changed beyond all recognition. The bitter truth was all too evident. Far from occupying a comforting role of superiority, they had become cultural laggards. The relative positions had altered so drastically that if the glittering prizes of European culture were to be won, some radical adjustment was unavoidable. The impact of the outside world on the Jews released from the confines of the ghetto is one of the main formative factors in modern Jewish history. Within the space of a few years a generation attempted to catapult itself through a process of intellectual and cultural development that Western Europe had undergone slowly and painfully in no less than two and a half centuries. That Jewish life was thrown into confusion, that the task of grappling with the modern world and adapting the old beliefs to European concepts became the overriding problem, need occasion little surprise. Indeed, the subsequent major movements within Judaism may largely be regarded as attempts to answer a single but compelling question: how to harmonize the old traditions with the newly discovered, enticing, but still elusive blandishments of Western European civilization.

The struggle for political emancipation and social acceptance gave rise to two far-reaching changes that permeated Jewish life in the course of the nineteenth century. It was also responsible for a monumental self-delusion that was finally shaken off only in the traumatic events of the twentieth century. In the first place, the process of integration into the wider society seemed to be impeded by two important elements in Judaism. One was the still unimpaired strength of the belief in a messianic restoration of the people to its ancient homeland. The second lay in the great complex of Jewish law, which served as a barrier to participation of the Jew in the broad activities of the society in which he lived. Opponents of Jewish emancipation argued repeatedly that the Jews could scarcely claim the rights and duties of citizenship when they lived by different laws and deliberately fostered a sense of national unity with their brethren in other lands. To refute these charges a movement of religious reform arose, which attempted to purge Judaism of its national element, especially the belief in the coming of a personal messiah and the return of the exiles. At the same time, it called upon Jews to abrogate the injunctions and prohibitions that inhibited Jewish participation in wider society on equal terms.

The second major change arising from the attempt to forge an outlook compatible with contemporary European society, while still maintaining Jewish identity and traditional values, was embodied in the Hebrew movement of enlightenment, known as *Haskalah.* The belief that a knowledge of at least the rudiments of European culture was an essential step toward social acceptance led to a radical modification of the patterns of Jewish education. For centuries the Jewish child had received a traditional Hebrew education devoted almost entirely to rabbinical studies. But now a demand arose to widen the syllabus, to introduce, side by side with religious instruction, the elements of secular studies: a little geography, history, and mathematics, and even some knowledge of a European language. In Germany, for example, German was introduced into the syllabus of some Jewish schools, so that instead of being able to speak only Yiddish, the Jewish child began to make his first acquaintance with the language of the country in which he lived! The aim of education was focused on enlightenment: the triumph of knowledge over ignorance, reason over superstition, modern light over medieval darkness.

Jewish self-delusion in the nineteenth century springs largely from the time lag in the movement of formative ideas from the outside world into Jewish thinking.[5] The appeal to reason and enlightenment, which had so powerful an impact on Western European society in the eighteenth century, penetrated Jewish circles in full measure only in the nineteenth. By then, however, other powerful movements that were destined to play a decisive role in shaping the face of Europe, such as nationalism and socialism, were already gathering force in the outside world. But, again, a similar time lag delayed any effective penetration by these two main currents of European thought into Jewish life until the last quarter of the nineteenth century. Hence the call for enlightenment—which exerted an almost hypnotic appeal in Jewish intellectual circles, first in Western Europe and later in the much more numerous settlements in Eastern Europe, for a century following the French Revolution—seems curiously unreal. Jews became persuaded of the efficacy of reason as a panacea for all their difficulties almost as Europe was becoming soberly aware of the limitations of reason as a guide to the understanding of human conduct. For most of the nineteenth century the Jews of Europe hitched their aspirations to an eighteenth-century star.

The yearning for equality of opportunity, intellectual excitement, and social acceptance persuaded many Jews to believe that with the spread of enlightenment prejudice would vanish, and all would be "sweetness and light." All the persecution and segregation, it was agreed, must surely have been some ghastly mistake. Once the peoples of Europe had been shown that hatred of the Jews was illogical, unfounded, and contrary to the principles of brotherly love, they would welcome them into their ranks, provided only—and the proviso was important—that the Jews could prove their readiness to appreciate the benefits of European culture. The spread of enlightenment demanded a process of self-enlightenment, which in turn required changes in education. The resulting shift in perspectives gave rise to a new kind of literature.

The growth of modern Hebrew literature clearly mirrors the broad aim of Jewish self-enlightenment, and was regarded as a major instrument for its fulfillment. Side by side with the attempt to widen the school syllabus, the exponents of the Hebrew movement of enlightenment, known as *Maskilim*, tried to expand the horizons of Jewish life by introducing a whole range of new ideas into Hebrew literature. Hebrew, after all, was then the only literary language at their disposal, because no other was taught in their schools. The *Maskilim*'s new ideas required the translation of a large number of standard works into Hebrew—including textbooks on philosophy, mathematics, grammar, geography, and history—as well as the composition of comparable original works. Thus a wide range of knowledge was squeezed into linguistic molds that were largely alien to its nature.

The *Maskilim* were convinced that one of the principal obstacles to the harmonization of Jewish life with the modern world arose from the fact that the Jews in the ghetto had been so cut off from the sources of nature that their esthetic appreciation of the world had atrophied. The belief was bolstered by the prevailing concept of the link between esthetics and ethics, so that any attempt to improve the ethical standards of the Jewish people seemed to demand a prior refinement of the esthetic sense. An examination of the various strata of Hebrew that might prove most suitable for the achievement of such aims persuaded the *Maskilim* to concentrate upon the Hebrew of the Bible, first because the language of the Bible is full of simile and metaphor drawn from the springs of nature, and second because of the quality and quantity of biblical Hebrew poetry which, it was felt, would help to awaken the esthetic sense regarded as so important for Jewish regeneration.

The vocabulary of the Bible, however, contains less than 6,000 words, and although it is admirably suited to certain categories of expression—such as historical narrative, wisdom literature, nature poetry, and especially prophecy—it remains a very clumsy instrument for the expression of modern concepts. For psychology, philology, mathematics, or any of the wide range of modern disciplines, its vocabulary is simply not adequate. Any attempt to express such concepts in biblical language must resort to circumlocution.

The writer is forced to employ a biblical phrase that seems to approximate to the required meaning, and then try to foster a general convention among his readers that, when such and such a phrase is used, what is actually meant is something else.[6] This proved to be one of the most serious difficulties encountered by early writers of modern Hebrew literature. Their very attempt to widen the scope of Jewish interests to include the range of modern knowledge conflicted with their second ideal, namely the expression of those ideas in a revived biblical Hebrew.

It was a fundamental dichotomy, and because of it the growth of Hebrew literature remained stunted for almost a century. With a few notable exceptions, the *Maskilim* deliberately avoided the vocabulary of the whole range of post-biblical Hebrew—the Mishnah, Talmud, Midrash, and medieval Hebrew literature—in spite of its richness of vocabulary, its flexibility of syntax, and its much greater suitability, in many ways, for the expression of modern ideas; instead, they fixed their eyes firmly on the basic stratum of the language. It was a quixotic attitude to literature, a combination of idealism and naivety that, in spite of its quaintness, can still exert a certain fascination.

For almost one hundred years, the character of modern Hebrew literature was mainly experimental. Although the regeneration of Hebrew was fostered in Königsberg (East Prussia) and Berlin in the last decades of the eighteenth century, the movement derived its impetus from Germany for no more than twenty or thirty years. During that time a modest quantity of interesting literature was produced by a group of writers who were the main contributors to a literary journal, *Ha-Me'asseph* (The Gatherer); the best of them were Isaac Satanow, Judah Lev Ben-Zeev, Joel Brill, Baruch Lindau, and Isaac Euchel. The literature includes much high-flown poetry, wisdom literature, proverbs, fables, and the like, as well as numerous works on history, geography, natural science, education, ethics, grammar, and criticism.[7]

The period also produced a poet of some stature, Naphtali Hartwig Wessely, who—convinced that it should be the task of poetry to elevate the spirit—devoted his energies to the search for lofty themes. He was particularly impressed by the German poet F. G. Klopstock's epic *Messias* (1748), and resolved to compose a Hebrew epic in a similar vein, using the story of the Exodus as his theme and Moses as his hero. The work was planned to extend to no less than eighteen cantos divided into six parts, of which all but the final section were completed. The achievement remains impressive, mainly because of the author's skill in tackling the formidable linguistic problems arising from so grandiose a project. In its day Wessely's *Širei Tiph'ereth* (the title means "Songs of Glory") was loudly acclaimed, but today it is regarded as a museum piece. Few readers will have the stamina to struggle through so lengthy and labored a work. Yet Wessely's poetry exerted a dominating influence on his successors for more than half a century. He is also responsible for the fact that a large proportion of Hebrew poetry composed during the first sixty years of the nineteenth century was written in heavy six-line stanzas with the rhyme-scheme: a a b c c b. His influence may also be discerned in the reflective, philosophic themes favored by his immediate successors.

But life ran ahead of the exponents of enlightenment. The *Maskilim* had undertaken the formidable task of producing a new kind of Hebrew literature in the firm belief that their labors would enable a rising generation to acquire at least a modicum of modern knowledge while remaining faithful to Hebrew. In practice, the young generation soon found that it was far easier to learn German and approach the sources in the original, rather than attempt to grasp their meaning through the veil of a stilted and artificial Hebrew. Within the space of one generation, Jewish youth in Germany largely abandoned Hebrew as a mode of obtaining the kinds of knowledge they felt they needed in the modern world, and turned to German as a much more flexible and satisfactory instrument for its acquisition.[8] Indeed, had modern Hebrew literature been limited solely to Germany, it is likely that it would have been short-lived and without lasting importance.

Seeds of the new kind of Hebrew literature, however, were soon planted in the more fertile soil of Eastern Europe, where the great majority of Jews lived during the nineteenth century. The ideas were carried by wandering scholars, most of whom traveled from Galicia and the Russian Pale of Settlement, the area in which the Jews of Russia were compelled to reside, to Berlin or one of the other centers of enlightenment in Western Europe. There they would acquire the ideas of *Haskalah* before returning to propagate the new learning in the *Yešibhoth*, the great centers of Jewish study in Eastern Europe. Because many of the new tenets seemed to conflict sharply with orthodox Judaism, the scholars frequently encountered rigorous opposition, and were compelled to spread their teachings by stealth. Henceforth, their disciples in the *Yešibhoth* would often sit, ostensibly studying the Talmud, but actually reading some new Hebrew work on mathematics, philosophy, or grammar, or even some recent literary composition.[9] Discovery often resulted in expulsion, which was a double misfortune, because not only the student's studies but also his source of livelihood were put in jeopardy.

Stealthily, from cellars and attics, the new learning gradually spread among the Jews of Eastern Europe, gaining a surer foothold than it had ever won in Germany. In the great Jewish preserve of Eastern Europe the real foundations of modern Hebrew literature were firmly established, and it was there that the main lines of its subsequent development were determined. In addition to the forms and themes that had appeared in Germany, new literary genres arose, reflecting an entirely different social and political situation. The Jewries of Eastern Europe were much more concentrated than was that of Germany, and they formed a more compact and self-contained stratum of the population. Russian Jewry, in particular, was far less able to channel its energies through the medium of a language other than Hebrew. In Eastern Europe generally, Hebrew continued for many decades to be the language through which Jews could hope to gain a knowledge of the modern world. For that reason it was cultivated far more seriously than in Germany. The number of translations increased dramatically, while the amount of original writing in Hebrew grew even more rapidly in the vigorous attempt to mirror the social struggles of the day.

The acute conflict between the Jews of Russia and the Czarist administration in the nineteenth century may be traced to the partitions of Poland at the end of the eighteenth century, when an area containing approximately one million Jews was absorbed into the Russian Empire. With their own customs, mores, modes of dress, and dietary laws, their own distinctive religion, language, and system of education, the Jews clearly constituted an alien element in Russia at a time when the government was attempting to weld the various elements in the population into a homogeneous nation. The resulting confrontation is one of the keys to the understanding of modern Jewish history. Indeed, the growth of Jewish nationalism in the second half of the nineteenth century may be viewed as a by-product of Russian nationalist policies.[10]

The accession of Nicholas I marks the beginning of the struggle. Bigot, fanatic, and tyrant, Nicholas (1825–55) embarked upon a ruthless oppression of the Jews in an attempt to eradicate their alien identity. Economic pressure was applied by reducing the area of the Pale of Settlement at a time of population explosion. By the middle of the century the Jewish economic plight had become so acute that a man with a barrel of herrings was deemed a merchant! The misery was exacerbated by the introduction of military service for twenty five years, with the recruits sent to areas remote from any Jewish contact.[11] To ensure the necessary quota of conscripts, kidnapers were hired to impress mere children from the streets and schools and dispatch them to so-called pre-military training establishments, where they remained until they became old enough to begin their military service. Hebrew literature abounds with agonized descriptions of this reign of terror, which haunted Jewish life for more than a generation.[12]

To wean the Jews from their ancestral faith, Nicholas established some 2,000 elementary schools in the Pale of Settlement and made attendance compulsory. In their anxiety to protect their young from missionary influences, Jewish parents resorted to every possible method to prevent their children attending government schools. Frequently they bribed the underpaid teachers to mark the registers as full while the classrooms remained empty.[13] The compulsory teaching of Russian in the *Yešibhoth*, intended by the government as a means of undermining Jewish cultural insularity, was largely evaded by limiting the study of Russian to such pupils as were considered not bright enough to study the Talmud![14] This method ensured a number of pupils being able to answer the questions of government inspectors, so as to give the impression that Russian was being widely taught. In many cases, the children who did learn Russian derived great benefit from it in later life, but that is by the way.

The communities suffered from internal strife no less than from outside pressure. For many decades, orthodox Jewry in Eastern Europe had been divided into two hostile camps: the old orthodox believers, known as *Mithnaggedhim*, and the followers of a more recent religious movement, called *Ḥasidhim*. So bitter was the factionalism that even intermarriage was rare and strenuously discouraged. Once the exponents of enlightenment entered the fray, a fierce three-cornered "free-for-all" ensued, with each of the factions bitterly denouncing and even persecuting the other two. The question of religious reform, which the *Maskilim* advocated, aroused much passion and personal animosity, even though the proposed reforms were mild compared with what had previously taken place in Germany.

The *Maskilim* aroused even greater resentment, however, for taking the educational experiments of the Czarist administration at their face value as a serious attempt to alleviate Jewish disabilities. Whereas the government was interested primarily in the disappearance of a specifically Jewish section of its population, the *Maskilim* were anxious to integrate the Jewish population into the broad framework of Russian society, without sacrificing its Jewish identity. Although fundamentally incompatible, the aims of both parties seemed initially to coincide. Indeed, the exponents of enlightenment scored some considerable success, not during the bitter years of Nicholas, but in the more enlightened early years of his successor, Alexander II (1855–81). Alexander's policies included alleviation of some of the severest hardships inflicted by his predecessor. Permission to attend high schools and universities, and even on certain terms to reside outside the Pale of Settlement, encouraged large numbers of Jewish students to avail themselves of the new educational and professional opportunities. They hoped that emancipation would follow hard upon the heels of education, and that real equality would ensue as soon as a sufficient number of Jews had reached the level of education enjoyed by cultivated Russian society. A wave of enthusiasm for secular learning, which the repressive measures of Nicholas I had been powerless to arouse, swept through the Jewish community following the more enlightened policies of his successor.

From about 1870, however, the Russian government became increasingly concerned with the growth of revolutionary movements, and embarked upon a policy of renewed oppression, which the Jews shared in full measure. As the dream of emancipation faded, the *Maskilim* discovered that they had helped to rear a generation of young Jews who were turning their backs on Judaism in search of success and satisfaction in wider Russian circles. No less than in Germany more than half a century previously, the sad equation governing Jewish life became only too clear, namely that secular education without emancipation leads to apostasy. After decades of preaching the ideals of universalism and integration into Russian society, the *Maskilim* suddenly found their aspirations shattered, and a reverse process gradually set in, aimed at retrenchment. The problem now was how to strengthen Judaism internally and to create a renewed interest in specifically national ideals.

This new tendency received a sudden and dramatic spur from the wave of pogroms that swept over the Jewish communities of Russia following the assassination of Alexander II in 1881. The fact that the pogroms were believed to have been deliberately fomented by the Russian government put an end, once and for all, to any Jewish hope of emancipation or equality of citizenship in Czarist Russia. The reality of the Jewish situation was suddenly revealed in all its horror. Mass emigration westwards, and particularly to the United States, an uncritical adherence to the revolutionary movements, and the first trickle of Jewish pioneers to Palestine were three of the more important reactions to the catastrophe. By the end of the 1880s the naive and self-deluding ideology of enlightenment had largely vanished, to be replaced by a more sober, if unflattering, self-awareness.[15]

It is against this background—of crushing poverty, communal strife, and government oppression, followed first by a short span of comparative alleviation and dawning hope, and then by a new and even more ferocious period of oppression—that the movement of *Haskalah* in Russia set the patterns of modern Hebrew literature. It was primarily polemical, engaged in a battle to change not only the course of Jewish education, but also, ultimately, the forms of Jewish life. It attempted not merely to broaden the scope of economic activity, but in addition to introduce new attitudes toward Judaism itself. Anxiously it sought solutions, ready to pounce upon scapegoats within the community who were considered to be the causes of the general distress. It was a highly motivated literature.

The literary forms used for the attainment of its ends include satire, story, novel, essay, and even poetry. The early satirists Joseph Perl (1773–1839) and Isaac Erter (1792–1851) had already proved the effectiveness of their weapons in Galicia, where the Jewish community—a prey to poverty, ignorance, and superstition—seemed ripe for the introduction of social and educational reform. Joseph Perl had launched a devastating attack on what he regarded as a debased and degrading religiosity in two quasi-novels in epistolary form. *Megalleh Ṭemirin* (1819; The Revealer of Secrets) and *Boḥan Ṣaddiq* (1838; The Test of the Righteous) employ the methods of Rubianus' *Epistolae Obscurorum Virorum* to expose the alleged abuses of Hasidism from within, while pretending that the writer's aim is to glorify the sect! At the same time the author indirectly attempts to advance the cause of *Haskalah* by pouring ridicule on its opponents.[16]

Not only Hasidism but the whole spectrum of Jewish society in Galicia came under Erter's fire. A slender volume of his collected satires, *Ha-Ṣopheh le-Bheith Yisrael* (1858; The Watchman of the House of Israel), although somewhat dated, represents a real contribution to literature in addition to having considerable historical interest. Erter's insight and passion for truth were combined with artistic economy and literary skill. In the realm of satire he was a master. But quite apart from their intrinsic worth, the writings of the Galician satirists served as a valuable preliminary exercise for the Hebrew novelists in Russia. The handling of plot, narrative, characterization, and dialog together with the satirical and didactic elements proved very instructive for their successors. The constant resort to letters and dreams as major plot devices for nearly forty years, which stems partly from the work of Perl and Erter, is a measure of their influence on the early Hebrew novel.[17]

The novel proper, however, begins with the publication of *'Ahabhath Ṣiyyon* (1853; The Love of Zion) by Abraham Mapu (1808–67), which is the first novel in a biblical setting in any language, as far as the writer is aware.[18] Mapu also wrote a second novel depicting life in ancient Israel, entitled *'Ašmath Šomron* (1865–6; The Guilt of Samaria), and a third novel, *'Ayiṭ Ṣabhua'* (1858–69; The Hypocrite), that describes contemporary Jewish life in Lithuania. The appearance of this third novel opened up a whole new realm in Hebrew literature. Although poor in structure, rambling, and inadequate, *The Hypocrite* became a literary signpost for no less than a generation. This was due, at least in part, to the fact that the social and didactic aspects of Mapu's work were regarded as immediately relevant to the Jewish situation in Russia. In any case they were more susceptible to imitation than the impressive esthetic qualities of his historical novels.

Mapu's originality stems from overall conception rather than from forms and details. Apart from the direct influence of the Bible and of such Hebrew authors as Moses Chaim Luzzatto (1707–47) and the aforementioned Perl and Erter on his writings, Mapu leaned heavily on the French Romantic novelists, particularly Dumas *père* and Eugène Sue.[19] His stories also reflect a more than passing acquaintance with German literature and literary theory. His debt to European writing is most obvious in plot, dramatic technique, and characterization, all of which display serious limitations. As a story-teller Mapu resembles an apprentice rather than a polished craftsman, and he never mastered the art of weaving a successful plot. Nevertheless his writings contain elements of freshness and originality that reveal a touch of genius.

Mapu possessed a power of imagination that could resurrect dead bones. In his historical romances the Bible came to life, and the period of Isaiah was depicted with vividness and freshness of appeal. His strength lay in the portrayal of setting, in smoothness of style, and in an unrivaled mastery of language. Above all, he opened a channel for the free expression of emotion, transfusing a somewhat dry and intellectual literature with feelings of heroism and love. By fostering a sense of pride in the national past and focusing attention on ancient Israel, he played a considerable part in preparing the ground for the nationalist movement from which Zionism later emerged. His novels must be regarded as a factor in modern Jewish history.

In this respect his instinct proved to be more soundly based than his ideals. His adherence to enlightenment as the panacea for the Jewish plight in Russia, and his self-deluding pursuit of emancipation, lend an air of unreality to his novel of contemporary life. The heroes and heroines, who combine a loyalty to their own tradition with the grace and culture of European society, remain curiously unconvincing within the brutal and bigoted framework of Czarist Russia. Yet a quarter of a century was to pass before the lingering traces of such wishful thinking largely disappeared from Hebrew literature. A similar inhibiting effect may be traced to his mastery of language. Mapu's writing represents the consummation of the neo-biblical style so warmly advocated by the *Maskilim.* The style is perhaps the most remarkable, attractive, and yet limiting feature of his novels. In the historical romances the suitability of form and content engenders a feeling of cohesion. But the social novel demonstrates the inadequacy of biblical Hebrew as a means of depicting the complex phenomena of the modern world. In spite of Mapu's own considered advice to his successors to utilize the rich linguistic resources of the later strata of Hebrew literature,[20] the Hebrew novel continued to struggle inside a strait-jacket of biblical vocabulary for another two decades.

The most illustrious of Mapu's immediate successors, Peretz Smolenskin (1842?–85) and Reuben Asher Braudes (1851–1902), are interesting for other reasons.[21] Both writers inherited Mapu's involvement with social problems and his reforming zeal, and both gave them expression in more telling and effective forms. Smolenskin was even more concerned than Mapu with Jewish disabilities, whether caused by external oppression or by communal strife. But his novels display a sober recognition of the absurdity of applying the kinds of remedy suggested for the Jewish communities of Western Europe at the end of the eighteenth century to alleviate the Jewish plight in Russia almost a century later. Whereas the Jewish community in Berlin had found a natural center for imitation in the intellectual and cultural life of a capital city, the Russian Jewish communities were surrounded by illiterate peasants. The channels through which enlightenment was conveyed were so restricted that only a trickle of secular culture could be drawn through them. Hence sprang the gulf between the grandiose ideals of *Haskalah* and the pettiness of their application in practice. Again, Smolenskin demonstrates a healthy disdain for the stock proposals suggested by the *Maskilim* for the alleviation of the dire economic conditions; he argues conclusively that the changes in occupation that they advocated, far from improving the situation, would only aggravate it.[22] His penetrating analysis of the realities of Jewish life added a new and powerful dimension to the Hebrew novel, and some of his predictions proved chillingly accurate.

Yet side by side with serious purpose, cutting social satire, and reforming zeal, a persistent thread of melodrama runs through his novels, forming a strange juxtaposition of bitter realism and escapist fantasy. The influence of

Dickens is clearly recognizable, although Smolenskin lacked the English novelist's ability to sustain a cohesive plot. But even the grotesque elements take on an entertaining and at times hilarious quality. However undisciplined, Smolenskin's talent was immense.[23] Time and again he broke the fetters of a restricted vocabulary and contrived phraseology to fashion a powerful prose. It is the easier to forgive the artistic lapses, frequently caused by the exigencies of over-hasty composition, because of his sincerity and moral earnestness.[24]

Hebrew fiction still required a more vigorous concern with artistry and detail, and the stories of Reuben Asher Braudes represent a step forward along the road to maturity. His novels display a restraint and self-control that compare favorably with the extravagance and fantasy of contemporary Hebrew fiction. But the didactic quality of his writing, and the strong flavor of Russian positivism (which first began to penetrate Hebrew literature at the end of the 1860s), permeate his most important but unfinished novel, *Ha-Dath we-ha-Ḥayyim* (1876–7; Religion and Life).[25]

Braudes' view of literature as a means of encouraging social and religious reform was counterbalanced by an instinctive artistry. A second novel, *Šetei ha-Qeṣawoth* (1888; The Two Extremes), enjoys a much improved structure, with social and religious criticism integrated into the mainstream of the story with considerable skill. In this respect the novel contrasts sharply with most of the Hebrew fiction produced in the period of *Haskalah*, in which the didactic elements obtrude painfully from the course of the narrative. Braudes deserves credit for demonstrating that hyperbole and exaggeration, whether in phraseology or in dramatic device, are by no means the most effective methods of sustaining interest. By avoiding the flamboyant tendencies of contemporary Hebrew writing and by subjecting his material to a more rigorous discipline, Braudes helped to stabilize the Hebrew novel.

It was with Mendele,[26] however, that modern Hebrew literature came of age. A virtuosity that spanned both Yiddish and Hebrew was responsible for his unusual distinction as the "grandfather" of two modern literatures. The translation, or rather transmutation, of his Yiddish novels into Hebrew from the 1890s made Hebrew fiction esthetically viable. The relationship between the two versions of each work is very complex, and serious investigation of the problem—as stated above—is still in its infancy.[27] But there can be no doubt but that the experience of working in the rich and varied idiom of a spoken language made Mendele impatient with the artificial shackles that Hebrew writers had lovingly imposed upon themselves for more than a century.

The difference between Mendele and his predecessors lies in his power of exact expression. Determined to fashion an instrument sufficiently flexible and idiomatic to cope with the language requirements of the modern novel, Mendele utilized not only biblical Hebrew but the whole range of post-biblical vocabulary. In this respect he was firmly in the mainstream of traditional rabbinic writing. The great advance lay in his sensitive and artistic treatment of narrative and dialog. Aramaic, too, was made to yield elements of racy conversation. All the various strata were fused together to form a smooth and convincing idiom. For the first time in modern Hebrew literature the reader feels that the author is completely master of his material, and that he is making the language express exactly what he wishes to say, instead of having to confine his expression to the linguistic limitations of his medium. This rejection of an outworn and inhibiting theory of literature was crucial for the development of Hebrew literature. The benefit is most immediately recognizable in his descriptive passages, which are often touched with humor.

> Alter Yoknehaz is a plump, well-padded, pot-bellied Jew, with a face submerged in a sea of muddy yellow hair in sufficient profusion to supply beard, mustache, and sidelocks for himself and any number of Jews besides. Out of this sea of hair a thick, broad nose protrudes like an island—an object worthy of respect, which for most of the year is stopped up and idle; but at the changing of the seasons, as for example with the approach of the Passover when the snows begin to melt, its owner grasps it firmly and blows it with enthusiasm, at which it emits a series of trumpet-like blasts, mingling its chorus with the swans being prepared for the festival—and the whole town of Bitalon is in uproar. The citizens offer him pinches of snuff amid cries of "Bless you! Bless you!"
>
> Alter Yoknehaz of Bitalon is a bookseller, too, and my acquaintance of many a year. He is not overbright nor given to conversation. But he is a character.[28]

Whereas the novels of Mendele's predecessors suffer from the uncomfortable juxtaposition of serious social criticism and widely improbable melodrama, Mendele's strength lies in the harmonization of his material. Although no less concerned with the misery and degradation of his environment, he approaches his subject with restraint. By means of carefully selected description, he enables the reader to glimpse the ghastly milieu without belaboring him with exhortations. In allowing the lessons to speak for themselves, Mendele lifted the Hebrew novel from the arena of polemics to the realm of artistry.[29] He had grasped the basic truth that art itself is a most potent instrument of education, and in so doing he performed a service of prime importance for Hebrew writing. The ability to couch devastating satire in a light, bantering, matter-of-fact tone earns him a place among the masters.

His art stems partly from his ambivalent attitude toward his characters. Behind their unattractive and indeed grotesque façade, Mendele recognized a certain nobility and gentleness of spirit. The self-deprecating humor that derives from the absurdity of a God-intoxicated people wallowing in mire is delicately balanced by the shame of their constant subjection to humiliation and contempt. The warm attachment to a culture that sees a universe tinged with the divine, with all nature, animate and inanimate alike, endowed with Jewish characteristics, is tempered by the bitter recognition of its wretched plight. In contrast to the self-delusion of the exponents of enlightenment, Mendele's work is permeated with an artistic self-awareness. Jewish life is stripped of its pretensions, but the nakedness is clothed in a web of artistry. Art and reality had at last made contact, and Hebrew literature had come of age.

Although Mendele's world is largely self-contained and self-sustaining, much of the literature written during the twenty five years before World War I is concerned with the disintegration of traditional Jewish life in Eastern Europe and the struggle of the individual to escape from the toils of a decaying society. As awareness ousted self-delusion, and artistry took the place of verbiage, the emergence of writers of real talent led to a dramatic improvement in the quality of Hebrew literature. The new trends reflect a period of bitter conflict. The crisis of faith that accompanied the disintegration of traditional Jewish life produced a number of "angry young men," in hot revolt against diaspora Judaism in all its manifestations. Whereas the traditionalist authors thought in reasoned terms of the continuity of the Jewish spirit, cultural evolution, and the regeneration of Jewish values, with a strong emphasis on the sense of community, their young opponents demanded revolution, a complete break with the past, and the right of the individual to lead a rich, unfettered emotional life. Despite their differences, however, the writers of the period demonstrated a remarkable loyalty to the Hebrew language and Hebrew literature in the face of all obstacles. Their insistence on the revival of Hebrew as the national language was largely responsible for its successful resurrection.

A dominant theme in the fiction of the period is the erosion of the close community life of the little Jewish townships in Poland, Lithuania, and the Ukraine. As the spiritual and psychological security that they afforded was gradually whittled away, a feeling of loneliness and isolation became increasingly apparent. In literature this was reflected in a longing for the certainties of the past counterbalanced by a yearning to escape into the wider world. This ambivalence tends to inhibit action, and the characters—many of them discontented intellectuals—yield more and more to introspection and self-analysis. A greater subtlety and depth of understanding distinguish the characterizations of such talented writers as M. J. Berdichevsky (1865–1921) and M. Z. Feierberg (1874–99), and later of U. N. Gnessin (1879–1913), G. Shofman (1880–1972), and particularly J. H. Brenner (1881–1921), from those of their predecessors. Individuation endows their work with greater conviction and intensity. They are concerned with the inner life and the dark recesses of the mind.

Their psychological probings and—for the first time in modern Hebrew literature—the inclusion of markedly erotic elements considerably strengthen the affinities with contemporary European writing. The time lag separating Hebrew literature from the great literatures of Europe was rapidly closing. Far from trailing behind the movements in Russian, French, German, and

English literature at the end of the nineteenth and the beginning of the twentieth century, Hebrew writers demonstrate a close familiarity with contemporary literary tendencies and techniques, including stream-of-consciousness writing, even before World War I. The major writers had learnt the secret of artistic economy and the loading of sentences to convey different levels of meaning. The use of language is much more flexible, combining clarity with subtlety. Although still inhibited to some degree, Hebrew prose was gradually acquiring the power to come to terms with modern life. The process was accelerated particularly by Brenner, who broke away from the trammels of a stilted vocabulary and clumsy syntax by evolving a direct and uninhibited style. His frequent resort to European vocabulary and his dramatic use of punctuation irritated the purists beyond measure. But, however painful, the impact of his vivid, unconventional style on Hebrew literature was to prove highly salutary.

The sturdy growth of Hebrew prose from the last decade of the nineteenth century was matched by a parallel development in poetry. For much of the century the heavy hand of N. H. Wessely had been all too pervasive. Convinced of the importance of poetry as an instrument for raising the level of esthetic appreciation and reawakening the emotions, almost every Hebrew writer during the period of *Haskalah* considered the publication of at least one poem, if not a collection, as an essential preliminary to a literary career. Much of the Hebrew poetry of the period, therefore, appears the product more of a sense of duty than of inspiration.[30] Its impact was limited to a self-conscious, intellectual appreciation of the esthetic values of poetry, but it did little to evoke the serious deepening of awareness that stems from the real poet's attitude to his experience.

Apart from Wessely, Hebrew literature in the century following the French Revolution was graced with only three poets of any stature, two of whom—Solomon Löwisohn and M. J. Lebensohn—suffered tragic early death. Their slender works are full of promise. The third, Yehudah Leib Gordon (1830–92), succeeded in weaning Hebrew poetry from its devotion to lofty and philosophical themes and in forging it into an instrument for the expression of social and religious problems. But in spite of his reputation as the poet-champion of reform, Gordon wrote poetry that is sometimes wooden, often labored, and which lacks sensitivity; it is more convincing as social commentary than as art.

Gordon deserves credit, however, for one important contribution to modern Hebrew poetry. Far from confining his language to the vocabulary of the Bible, he utilized a wide range of biblical and later Hebrew for the exposition of his ideas. In so doing, he performed a service for Hebrew poetry not unlike Mendele's achievement in the realm of the novel. But although Gordon displayed considerable skill and ingenuity in the employment of post-biblical idiom, he lacked Mendele's artistry. As a result, even his linguistic contribution must be regarded as experimental. The fusion of the various strata of Hebrew into a sufficiently flexible medium for the composition of great poetry was accomplished only by Gordon's more illustrious successor, Chaim Nachman Bialik (1873–1934), who was born in Russia but spent his last years in Palestine.

Prior to Bialik, then, modern Hebrew poetry lacked the originality of ideas and expression that can evoke a truly creative response in the reader. This inability to find the magic combination of words is partly accidental. In every literature there are periods that can boast of no great poet, and nineteenth-century Hebrew letters simply lacked a writer of sufficient talent. But the power to express truth springs from a different source. The inadequacy of Hebrew poetry in the nineteenth century is due at least partly to the fact that even the most ardent exponents of enlightenment lacked a sufficiently profound understanding of the values and ideals of the European civilization they were attempting to graft onto Hebrew culture. Time and again they stress that life must be felt as well as thought, that it is essential to develop the emotional aspect of personality in order to live richly and to the full, but they were themselves unable to do so. Whether they write of nature, therefore, or of love, or of any other of the great themes of lyric poetry, it is as if their feelings are experienced only at second hand, as though their inspiration arises from an intellectual conviction that such feelings *ought* to be expressed, rather than from an inner compulsion that *demands* expression of particular feelings in a particular way.

Bialik raised the level of Hebrew poetry to a new plane. He succeeded partly because he wrote from personal experience and an inner compulsion, and partly because he was able to lay his finger unerringly on the magic spring of language. This facility derived from a mastery of the range of Hebrew sources, together with a powerfully inventive imagination: he molded his material into shapes of his own choosing, instead of limiting himself to artificial patterns laid down by others.

Bialik's inspiration draws continually on his childhood experience, and the impressions of his earliest years recur throughout his poetry. In his delightfully sensitive autobiographical story, *Saphiaḥ*, Bialik reveals an intense awareness of nature and a sense of the closeness and intimacy of God, in his attempt to comprehend the essence of things in greater depth than is ever possible by the exercise of intellect.

> Hardly had I bared to the heavens the little windows of my soul, my two eyes, when the visions of God came streaming unsummoned from the four winds. Sometimes they would well up to me from the depths of silence, in shapes such as appear in dreams or in the waters of a clear pool. There was no speech and no words—only a vision. Such utterance as there was came without words or even sounds. It was a mystic utterance especially created, from which all sound had evaporated, yet which still remained ... And there were times when I heard the silence and saw the voices, for as yet my senses had neither bounds nor limits, but each encroached upon the other. Sound drew sight after it and

> sight sound, and scent—both of them. As yet I knew neither rhythm nor measure. The little mound in the field was a mountain, the pond—an ocean, the end of the village—the horizon of the earth.[31]

Over and above his personal experience, however, Bialik's poetry is a distillation of Jewish experience in Eastern Europe. By the end of the nineteenth century, external and internal pressures were causing a process of fragmentation and disintegration, with the erosion of ancient Hebrew traditions and institutions, mass emigration, and a wholesale flight from Judaism. Even more tragic for Bialik was the disintegration of the spirit, in which he saw the real pathos of the Jewish condition. He suggested no remedies, nor did he attempt to formulate a policy. All he did was to identify himself with the deepest sources of Jewish tradition and to lament its fate. His creative strength derived from a combination of private and public experience. However individual, he was regarded as the mouthpiece of the people in all its moods: hope, aspiration, sorrow, disappointment, and defeat. His poetry reflects the people's vicissitudes in a manner reminiscent of the Psalms: it is a fusion of national and individual emotion. He described a milieu that he had experienced to the core of his being, a society whose values he could appreciate at their highest level, but one that was rapidly crumbling for reasons he knew only too well. His intensity of expression struck a new chord in Hebrew poetry. By liberating it from alien and artificial themes, and by restoring its ancient integrity, Bialik raised the stature of Hebrew poetry to a level scarcely equaled for almost a millennium.[32]

The emancipation of Hebrew poetry, however, was not yet complete. The notion that the Jew was not merely a member of a religious or national group, but equally—if not primarily—a member of the commonwealth of mankind, a human being in the broadest sense, still required demonstration. An awareness that life must be enriched, that the emotions are something to be developed rather than stifled, that beauty and love are precious things rather than temptations to be thrust aside, needed a poet whose roots had drawn nourishment from a more promising soil and whose personality had flowered in a more liberal atmosphere. And insofar as the portrayal of love, beauty, and uninhibited emotion is a legitimate preserve of poetry, modern Hebrew literature owes much to Saul Tschernichowsky (1875–1943).[33]

In his native village in the Crimea, the poet grew up close to nature, with gentile urchins for companions. Third-generation village dwellers, his parents were pious but not rigorously so, and the home atmosphere was happy. Hence his formative years differed greatly from those of most other Hebrew writers. His childhood memories were not clouded by the misery and fear—the dirty crooked streets, the squalid classrooms, and the beatings at the hands of despised, frustrated teachers—that were the normal lot of Jewish children in the towns. His first impressions were of golden fields, blue skies, and the joy of freedom. He combined a flair for languages and literature with a lifelong interest in science and medicine. At the same time his natural exuberance and zest for life were fed upon romantic love. One affair was followed by the next, as he found himself enchanted by a whole series of attractive maidens. The love lyrics that resulted form a striking contrast with the deliberate, self-conscious, and unconvincing presentations of love in the Hebrew literature preceding them. They are spontaneous, natural, and fresh, the genuine outpourings of an enraptured soul.

A passion for Greek literature turned natural inclination into an almost pagan worship of beauty for its own sake. His ideas unfolded in a series of poems decrying a Judaism that had emasculated the people and stifled their ability to live a full, rich life, and celebrating the springs of vitality and the pristine God of valor. Such notes had never been sounded in Hebrew poetry;[34] they were shocking and painful, but were also strangely compelling.

In spite of his awareness of tragedy and pathos, beauty remained the central pillar of his universe:

> The priests of beauty and the artists' throng
> followers of poesy who hold her dear
> will save the world with music and with song.[35]

Above all, he stressed man's unity with nature to the point of pantheism, an approach that endowed his poetry with a broad humanism of a kind that modern Hebrew literature had sought but never found before. Both in form and in content his contribution to Hebrew poetry was profound. The wide variety of meters he employed is equaled only by the range of daring linguistic coinages.[36]

Any appreciation of the striking improvement in the quality of Hebrew literature in the quarter of a century before World War I would be incomplete unless it mentioned, however briefly, the work of the literary critics. Throughout most of the period of *Haskalah*, writers indulged heavily in mutual admiration or resorted to self-praise for daring to compose in Hebrew at all. From the 1860s onward, however, the rapid spread of Hebrew periodicals, together with the appearance of a number of talented critics, such as S. J. Abramowitz (Mendele), A. U. Kovner, A. J. Papirna, and M. L. Lilienblum, exerted a salutary influence. Condemning the amateur quality of Hebrew writing, the hollow phraseology, its inconsistencies, its displays of ignorance and smugness, critics demanded more content, a more positive and practical spirit, a greater depth of feeling, and felicity of expression. Once the initial wave of outraged indignation in the wake of this critical onslaught had subsided, vapid writings gradually gave way to compositions of greater substance and artistry began to take the place of verbiage.

It is curious, however, that in the period extending from 1890 to 1914—which is marked by the emergence of a galaxy of talented writers, and which witnessed a veritable renaissance in Hebrew literature—literary criticism was plunged into despair. Most critics were themselves creative writers, and almost all regarded their colleagues as worthless scribblers.[37] They accused each other of plagiarism, hypocrisy, insincerity, and self-aggrandizement. The literature was dubbed artificial, exaggerated, stupid, empty, and unreal. Writers were blamed for jumbling various styles into an unpalatable mess. Criticism itself was regarded as deplorable, and personal abuse went hand in hand with literary denigration. Criticism was likened to a broomstick, whose task was to sweep Hebrew literature clean, regardless of the casualties en route. Amid this welter of attack and counterattack, a certain stability was finally achieved through the efforts of Asher Ginzberg (1856–1927)—known by his pseudonym Ahad Ha-Am—in his capacity as the first editor of the important literary journal *Ha-Šiloaḥ*.[38] By sheer determination and personal authority, he was able to raise the sights and standards of Hebrew literature, and to banish many of the meretricious literary habits that lingered on from the previous era. His refusal to countenance any contribution to his journal that failed to satisfy his own rigorous standards helped to raise the Hebrew essay to a higher level of craftsmanship.

World War I is a watershed in modern Hebrew literature. After 1918 the main literary center shifted from Eastern Europe to Palestine, where Hebrew writers were faced with a new environment and the formidable problems of adaptation to a very different social setting.[39] In Palestine between the two world wars, a very considerable body of literature that reflects the process of transition appeared in Hebrew. Since the creation of the State of Israel in 1948, a new kind of Hebrew literature has emerged, written by native-born authors whose mother tongue is Hebrew. At its best, the range and quality of their work is striking and worthy of detailed investigation, but that, for the most part, lies well beyond the confines of this study, which is concerned primarily with Hebrew literature in the nineteenth and early twentieth centuries.

2

Epistolary Elements in the Novels of Abraham Mapu

THE TEXT of Abraham Mapu's novel[1] *The Hypocrite*[2] makes reference to more than sixty letters,[3] of which the great majority are quoted in full.[4] Many of the letters are substantial, more than half exceeding 500 words with a few even approaching 5,000 words.[5] Indeed, the sum total of the various sections of the novel written in letter-form amounts to more than 42,000 words, a figure equaling the length of an entire novel of small compass. Admittedly, *The Hypocrite* is a very long story, whose five parts embrace almost a quarter of a million words. Nevertheless the epistolary elements comprise no less than one sixth of the whole so that their place in the overall scheme of the novel deserves serious consideration. *The Hypocrite*, indeed, shares a number of features in common with the class of epistolary novels exemplified by Richardson's *Pamela*.[6] Mapu's adoption of a hybrid form, with the epistolary element comprising only about one sixth of the whole, while nevertheless employing a far greater number of letters than one might expect to find in a non-epistolary novel published in the second half of the nineteenth century, provides an interesting example of the time lag separating much of the Hebrew literature of the period from the European models which influenced its development.

In European literature, epistolary fiction progressed along two fairly distinct paths, although the dividing line is sometimes blurred. In the first place there was the approach of the "outsider," whereby society was subjected to the observation of a visitor from abroad, who was thus enabled to assume the role of onlooker and comment on the rough and tumble of society while safely standing on the sidelines. The first great European vogue for this genre of pseudo-foreign letters dates from Marana's *Letters of a Turkish Spy* some thirty years before it culminated in Montesquieu's *Persian Letters* in 1721. Marana's example led to numerous imitations particularly in England, although at first the element of social criticism was almost smothered by historical detail. During the following decades, however, a more detailed image of contemporary life and customs emerged, frequently expressed in sharply satirical terms. These epistles, purporting to have come from the pen of an observant Oriental, "presented all the advantages of a transparent disguise, which on the one hand, justified the aloofness of the critic's point of view, and on the other, softened the bitterness of the utterances by laying them at the door of a man of different clime and civilization."[7] With Montesquieu, however, the method was raised to a higher plane. In spite of their apparent lightheartedness, *Persian Letters* represented a great advance in social perspective and self-consciousness.[8] Of the numerous imitations in many languages which were published during the eighteenth century, Goldsmith's *Citizen of the World*, in which contemporary English life is subjected to the gentle but devastating scrutiny of a highly civilized visitor from China, displays perhaps the most consummate artistry.

The second major division of epistolary fiction adopts the approach of the "insider," with the correspondent or correspondents forming an integral element in the events they describe or the pattern of society they portray. Far from remaining a detached observer, the correspondent is generally characterized by a deep and often passionate commitment to the narrative, which thus provides an admirable backcloth for the detailed expression and analysis of emotion. "Throughout its history," F. G. Black observes,[9] "the epistolary novel has lived upon sentiment. Letters are sentimental documents designed to convey opinion and feeling rather than fact and action.[10] They naturally encourage self-analysis and reflection; and from self-analysis and reflection it is but a step to dalliance with sentiment."

Following the publication in 1669 of the *Lettres Portugaises*, which was regarded as fiction for a time, although the work was later shown to consist of real letters written by Mariana d'Alcoforado, the letter-novel rapidly became a recognized sub-species.[11] But it was only toward the end of the eighteenth century that the popular taste for epistolary fiction gave rise to a veritable spate of novels in letter-form. In English literature, for example, the vogue of the novel of manners following the publication of Richardson's epistolary *Pamela* in 1741 lasted for almost a century before the form dropped into virtual disuse, and a list of over eight hundred epistolary novels has been recorded for those years.[12]

The ingenuity displayed by Richardson in exploring the possible variations within the type of novel he popularized compelled his immediate successors to resort mainly to imitation. But shortly before Richardson's death Rousseau adopted *Clarissa* as a model for his *Nouvelle Héloïse* (1760), with the addition of a warmth of passion and a poetic exaltation foreign to Richardson and new to the novel. Intensity of passion took a morbidly romantic turn in Goethe's novel of his *Sturm-und-Drang* period, *Die Leiden des jungen Werthers* published in 1774, which infused a note of melodrama and tragedy into the genre. Certainly the principal ingredients of the epistolary novel had all been given powerful expression in European literature before 1780, even though it reached the heights of its popularity only during the following two decades. Gradually, however, a new kind of novel made its appearance that relied only partially on letters. Conscious of the fetters of the epistolary device, writers attempted to retain some of its advantages while making use of the greater freedom of ordinary prose narrative. During the first quarter of the nineteenth century such hybrid forms continued to appear in abundance, with the average non-epistolary novel still containing a surprisingly large number of letters.[13] The pattern, as has been noted above, was utilized by Mapu for the structure of *The Hypocrite* some forty years later than the halcyon period of its European predecessor, although Mapu was by no means the first writer in modern Hebrew literature to adopt epistolary techniques.

In proceeding to a closer survey of the methods favored by the Hebrew authors in the nineteenth century in adapting the letter-form for their own purposes, two further aspects of epistolary technique require brief consideration. One of the devices employed in epistolary fiction of the satirical type consisted of the introduction of a cumbersome footnote apparatus[14] as an accompaniment to the text, partly to generate an aura of authenticity and trustworthiness and partly as a grotesque parody of the object of attack. The adoption of a scholarly footnote apparatus for satirical purposes—in the line of Rabelais, Swift, Sterne, Wieland, and Jean Paul—constitutes a striking feature of the two epistolary satires of the Hebrew writer Joseph Perl, namely *The Revealer of Secrets* and *The Test of the Righteous.*[15]

In a perceptive article, S. Werses has demonstrated the various aspects of the satirical epistolary tradition—including the use of footnotes—to be found in Perl's writings.[16] Admittedly J. L. Landau had previously suggested the possibility of Perl's dependence on d'Argens' *Lettres juives* (1730–6),[17] which makes copious use of footnotes, usually for satirical purposes, and which was well known in the circles of Galician exponents of enlightenment to which Perl belonged. But to Werses belongs the credit of recognizing the real relationship of the footnotes to the structure and ideas of Perl's *The Revealer of Secrets* in particular. Far from introducing them merely as a device to parody Hasidic literature, Perl apparently resorted to footnotes as a well-tried stratagem for the creation of an atmosphere of ironic hocus-pocus. The device, moreover, offered him an additional means of discursive digression for the propagation of his ideas.[18] Werses, in addition, makes the very feasible suggestion that Menahem Lefin (1749–1826) may well be regarded as the link between the European satirical epistolary tradition and his friend and pupil, Perl. Lefin's familiarity with the *Persian Letters* genre may be gauged from an unpublished satire against the Hasidic sect in the form of an exchange of correspondence between a young Italian who has traveled to Poland and his father.[19] As noted above, a framework in which a foreign observer is enabled to describe society in bitterly satirical terms constitutes one of the major categories of epistolary fiction.

The second aspect of epistolary technique which deserves consideration has a far wider application and concerns the role of the letter itself. The epistolary element of a novel is by no means confined to the form. "The writing of the letters is only the beginning; they are copied, sent, received, shown about, discussed, answered, even perhaps hidden, intercepted, stolen, altered or forged. The relation of the earlier letters in an epistolary novel to the later may thus be quite different from the relation of the earlier chapters of a novel to the later."[20]

The letter, therefore, may both be used as a factor in the plot and serve as a framework for the narrative. But the more that letters are introduced as factors in the plot—particularly where the plot is in any case tortuous or complex—the more likely are they to take a melodramatic form and serve as little more than crude fictional devices. Whenever the reader is able to accept the epistolary method unquestioningly without feeling any improbability in its use and without any awareness of artificial stratagems on the author's part, the more likely is that method to be successfully employed. On the whole, it would appear that the letter lends itself to the novel more naturally as a means of presentation than as an agent forcibly dragged into the narrative.[21] But where the author has in any case deliberately adopted a grotesque framework for satirical purposes, the extravagant use of letters for melodramatic effect may be regarded with a certain indulgence. Such, indeed, is the effect of their usage in Perl's satires.[22]

An examination of the influences of the European epistolary tradition upon Hebrew literature in the nineteenth century leads inevitably to the conclusion that while the satirical genre in the tradition of Montesquieu's *Persian Letters* eventually finds its way into Hebrew literature in the fully fledged guise of Perl's *The Revealer of Secrets* and *The Test of the Righteous*, which take advantage of the principal techniques of a long literary chain, the epistolary novel of manners, in the tradition of Richardson's *Pamela*, has no real counterpart in Hebrew. Due to the long time lag separating European and Hebrew literature,[23] the Hebrew novel makes its appearance not merely long after the classical form of the epistolary novel has disappeared but at a time when even the hybrid novel has spent its force. As a result the full epistolary form, with all the subtleties of construction and shifting points of view that it can offer,[24] was restricted in Hebrew literature to satirical writing; and although Mapu and his successors throughout the period of enlightenment endow their novels with a copious supply of letters, their function largely consists of introducing improbable or melodramatic turns into the plot, sometimes of a baffling nature. In addition, as will be seen, they serve as a medium for sketching character, as well as for conveying information either relevant to the plot or of a generally didactic nature.

Although the epistolary element assumes quantitative importance only in Mapu's novel of contemporary life *The Hypocrite*, letters occur or are mentioned in both his historical romances, *The Love of Zion* and *The Guilt of Samaria*.[25] In the former they are used for the advancement of the plot and as vehicles for description or reflection.[26] Their comparative infrequency in the historical romances reflects a similar phenomenon in European literature. It would appear that an atmosphere of intimacy, which the familiar letter can create so well in a contemporary setting, is more difficult to effect within the framework of a remote period. Certainly the historical and Gothic fiction which became so popular in English literature in the first half of the nineteenth century had little resort to the letter.[27]

In spite of their infrequency, however, the letters in *The Love of Zion* play an important role in the somewhat tortuous plot. Early in the story the wicked Zimri escapes from captivity after the fall of Samaria and brings a letter from a fellow captive Hananeel, describing a dream according to which a young man, who claims to be the lover of his granddaughter, Tamar, appears to Hananeel and promises to rescue him. But Hananeel has also entrusted his personal seal to Zimri, who later uses it to send a false message from Hananeel, stating that the latter is dying and thereby destroying confidence in the dream with its description of a youth resembling the hero Amnon.[28] In a further attempt to alienate Tamar's affections from Amnon after first arousing her suspicions that he loves another, Zimri advises the hero to send Tamar a letter seeking reconciliation together with a bottle of wine which Zimri promptly poisons, and then informs the heroine of Amnon's "treachery."

The letter serves as a twofold source of dramatic irony. In the first instance Amnon writes it at the suggestion of Zimri whose advice he has sought in order to win back Tamar's affection, unaware of Zimri's villainous resolve to achieve exactly the opposite result. Secondly Amnon includes the following ironic statement in his letter: "I am sending a bottle of wine as usual. If you accept it from me as wine of love, then all is well and I shall again hold up my head. But if it rebounds on me like treacherous wine, then it will be a sign that God has decreed that I must become a wanderer in a foreign land."[29] It is hardly surprising that the heroine returns the bottle of wine together with a letter written in biting if somewhat euphuistic terms telling him literally to go to hell. The letter concludes:

> Fly for your life, why let me witness your blood being spilled over the ground like water? For my kinsmen burn with anger, and should they catch you they will rend your soul in their rage and show no mercy in the day of wrath. Perhaps you will ask: Whither can I flee from them? Surely you know the path that leads to hell. No pure-minded man would traverse it, but it is yours. You have taken your stand astride it and you shall walk upon it until you find yourself in mourning for your soul, and then you will regret your end.[30]

The dramatic effect is heightened further by the fact that the letter does not specifically mention the reason for Amnon's rejection. The hero is utterly baffled, although he begins to suspect that he may have been slandered!

The remaining correspondence in *The Love of Zion* comprises a number of love letters. A daring innovation at the time, these letters are important not so much because of their role in the plot, which is in any case slight, but because they reflect one of the principal aims of the exponents of enlightenment in the Hebrew literature of the period, namely the free expression of romantic love in the attempt to awaken the emotional aspect of personality in the pursuit of a wider and more meaningful life.[31] As poetry was considered a most helpful means toward the attainment of that end, it is perhaps only to be expected that one of these love letters should be written in the form of a poem, in which the hero pours out his heart to his beloved in very stilted verse.[32] The heroine is suitably impressed. Similar in tone, if not in form, is a letter from the second heroine, Shoshanah, in which she too pours out her hopeless love for her darling Teman. Her final plea to him may serve to illustrate the nature of the missive: "Take pity on a wretched soul, and forget her as though she had never been, and give your love to one more fortunate than she."[33] One further love letter, however, belongs to a somewhat different category. The lengthy epistle encompassing almost an entire chapter which Amnon despatches to Tamar from Nineveh ranks partly as a love letter, but also contains an historico-political survey of the Near East in Isaiah's time as well as a wealth of natural description.[34] Highly romantic in tone and written in characteristic, high-flown style the letter serves as a refreshing interlude after the tortuous machinations of the previous chapter. This particular epistolary stratagem occurs again in *The Hypocrite* in more developed form.

Mapu's second historical novel, *The Guilt of Samaria*, although twice the length of the *Love of Zion*, makes less resort to the letter-form. In four cases the letters are not even quoted, although the contents of all but one are revealed. Nor, for the most part, do they seem to play any significant role in the story.[35] Only one of them has some importance for the plot. Unaware that Uzziel is his father, Eliphelet discovers him making love to his mother Miriam, and departs in high dudgeon, leaving behind a letter for Miriam full of reproaches, but fortunately not quoted. One substantial letter, however, is worthy of comment, for it represents Mapu's writing at its best.[36] Jehosheba's letter to Miriam contains a self-revelation by one mature matron to another, unfolded with sensitive insight and poignant irony. In the course of her narrative the widowed Jehosheba outlines in stately language the affection she has conceived for Eliada, whom she commends to Miriam's care, advising her to employ him as her agent, while confessing that she herself may marry him. But the name Eliada is, in fact, a symbolic pseudonym for Uzziel, Miriam's husband, who has been forced into hiding for many years because of the anger of the wicked King Ahaz. The letter concludes as follows:

> Why should I conceal from you, my dear, what I have in mind? Elkanah for all the glory that surrounded him will never return, and my grief and sorrow will pass eventually, and then I shall want to resume the threads of life. How nice it

> would be to settle down under the protection of this splendid man. I know you will understand me, my dear. If it is bad for a man to live alone, how much worse is the fate of a woman who has to live alone. You know that only too well. So tell Manoah of your decision so that dear Eliada may know where he stands, and may God bring your husband back from exile, and may you have the joy of seeing him return at a propitious hour. You may be sure that your friend Jehosheba will share your joy.

In the event it is comforting to learn that with Miriam's consent Uzziel finally takes the unhappy Jehosheba as a second wife.[37]

While the role performed by letters in the historical novels is clearly limited, the sheer volume of correspondence scattered throughout *The Hypocrite* inevitably gives the novel a certain epistolary flavor. For all their weight of numbers and widespread distribution, however, the letters do not constitute an integral and well-planned element in the overall structure. With the important exception of one series, which will be examined later, the arrangement of the letters makes an haphazard impression, and for all the variety of device which they are made to serve, the letters fail to exert the cohesive force which their number might have warranted. So much so, that apart from the one series mentioned above, the critics seem to have overlooked them altogether.[38] This seemingly haphazard introduction of letters into the novel, however, is readily understandable in view of Mapu's inability to weave a convincing plot. The structure of his novels is reminiscent rather of a clumsy amateur than of a polished craftsman.[39]

Nevertheless, as individual units the letters are important in the novel, and the sum total of units embraces or determines in great measure the numerous twists and turns of a long and complex narrative. The letters may be divided broadly into three main categories, although a number of letters contain elements pertaining to all three. To the first category belong all those which have some bearing on the plot, whether in the form of a dramatic device or as a vehicle for supplying the reader with information not previously known; they are also used to effect an interruption of the narrative or for purposes of dramatic irony. The second category embraces such letters as are included primarily for characterization, and which serve to throw additional light upon the *dramatis personae*, apart from the information which the reader may glean by direct observation. In the third category may be included all the letters used by the author for reflection on or criticism of various aspects of society, or for the propagation of certain ideas or the advocacy of particular policies.[40]

A closer examination of these three main categories may serve to illustrate Mapu's success in exploiting a wide range of the techniques associated with the epistolary novel and at the same time his failure to take advantage of the more subtle aspects of the genre. As far as the plot is concerned, the letter is most frequently encountered in the guise of melodramatic device or as a vehicle for the portrayal of melodramatic action. As a device the letter furnished Mapu with a wide range of application in the classical manner. Letters are regularly forged by the arch-villain Zadok, a master of the art, in order to direct events to his own advantage.[41] They are cunningly planted on virtuous but unsuspecting heroes, who are dragged off to jail in consequence.[42] The heroes also suffer misfortune and distress by having their letters either stolen[43] or intercepted,[44] a device which affords the villains access to the private plans and activities of their enemies, and facilitates their machinations to harm their innocent victims by means of scandal, slander, or persecution.

Many of the letters[45] contain warnings about the nefarious activities of villains masquerading in the guise of righteousness, although the warnings usually go unheeded! One letter, in particular, is worthy of note. After betrothing his sister to the rich old moneylender Achbor,[46] Eliab receives a letter from a friend warning him against the old man's meanness, wickedness, and hypocrisy in the strongest possible terms. The writer approaches his theme without any preliminary niceties:

> I have heard a rumor which makes my blood boil, that you are selling your poor sister to the devil; and I feel constrained to outline for you without delay the sort of man he is and the kind of life he leads.

After a prolonged and vehement exposure of the old man's thorough nastiness the writer concludes:

> You see, my dear Eliab, that I have let you know something of Achbor's wiles, and I warn you not to give your gentle sister to him. Be sure to take my words of warning seriously, and you will have cause to be grateful for my advice.[47]

Fortunately, on this occasion the warning achieves its desired effect.

Apart from such admonitory letters addressed to individuals, the novel contains two interesting examples of what may be termed warning circulars.[48] Both letters describe the villainous past of Zadok alias Alkum alias Hophni—and incidentally, a pirate's son—and unfold a melodramatic sequence of murder, forgery, and theft. In the earlier letter Heman recounts how he had previously placed implicit trust in Alkum, unaware that the villain was responsible for the death by poisoning of Heman's wife. While together on a business trip, however, Heman is startled by a murderous attack launched upon him in the night, which shakes his confidence in the trustworthiness of his associate:

> One day I was making my way to a market town, well supplied with money, and with Alkum accompanying me as usual. We reached an inn where Alkum and I shared a room. The candle was still alight, and I was sleeping restlessly, troubled by all sorts of nightmares. Suddenly I half awoke only to feel blood trickling down my neck. I tried to pull myself together and tell myself that it was only a bad dream. Then I woke up properly and found—O horrible sight!—Alkum the pirate's son standing over me brandishing a razor to slit my

> throat from ear to ear, his face aflame, his eyes bulging terrifyingly in their sockets. Bracing myself I sprang out of bed to defend my life, with only my bare fists to ward off the forces of evil. I wanted to scream: Help, murder! But I realized that if I shouted with such a wound in my throat, the veins would burst and all would be lost. Seeing my end in sight, I summoned all my reserves of strength . . .[49]

The narrative is continued for some time in similar strain, both letters concluding with the information that they are being circulated through the Jewish communities far and wide as a warning, and in an attempt to trace the culprit. The suitability of the device as a medium for the introduction of crude melodrama scarcely requires further demonstration.[50]

The examples furnished above, however, by no means exhaust the dramatic possibilities of the letter utilized by Mapu in *The Hypocrite*. Letters are conveniently found in books, whether deliberately planted there or by sheer accident, as when Hamul discovers a letter in Othniel's book just as he is about to burn it![51] They may be deliberately anonymous, in which form they serve excellently for spreading slander or conveying bad news.[52] The arrival of a letter may produce consternation or result in the recipient's fainting away.[53] Again, when the young Zerah's clothes are discovered on a river bank, they contain a letter explaining that the cause of his suicide is unrequited love.[54] The cloying self-pity and stilted expression of the letter may be seen from the following extract:

> The joy of living has been taken from me, so why should I face a life of bitterness when death is preferable? That is why I have composed this document, which contains my last words. Perhaps Elisheba, too, will read them and realize that my death is due to her, so that my memory will remain embedded in her heart, to embitter all her happiness and joy . . .[55]

Apart from melodramatic devices, letters are employed extensively as a means of conveying information, and as such constitute an important element in the plot. To effect an introduction of these letters, Mapu frequently utilizes the technique of allowing one character to hand over a letter written by a second for the perusal of a third. The events prior to the opening of this story, for example, are described in a series of letters which Jeroham has received from his grandson Naaman, and which he allows Saul his grandson's benefactor to read. These three letters, which together comprise an entire chapter,[56] supply both Saul and the reader with much important information. Saul returns the compliment by reading to Jeroham a further series of letters from or via Naaman of even greater length and of no less importance for the understanding of the plot.[57] A similar purpose is achieved when the wicked Zaphnath shows her paramour Levi a letter which she has abstracted from her husband's bag, and which contains an account of Alkum's villainous exploits.[58] The technique is taken one step further when Zibiah asks Hogeh—one of the good characters—to read her a letter written by Elisheba to Othniel which she, Zibiah, has intercepted but cannot read. She blandly pretends that the letter must have been lost![59]

Elsewhere, however, letters are used to convey information directly to the intended recipient. This straightforward procedure is the more acceptable insofar as it obviates the second-hand flavor inherent in the technique of using two third parties. This is particularly the case, for example, in the letter describing Eden's dramatic nocturnal encounter with a band of robbers and his timely deliverance,[60] or when Naaman receives a letter sent to him in London by his grandfather to acquaint him with news of all the latest intrigues since his departure.[61] Nevertheless, the substantial proportion of the plot presented in letter-form inevitably tends to deaden its impact, so that at times it appears as if the action were being unfolded in reported speech. This unfortunate impression is further strengthened where the letter depicts a minimum of action while consisting largely of inconsequential gossip[62]—an unhappy combination to which *The Hypocrite* is in any case only too prone.

More successful, structurally, is the insertion of letters which interrupt the narrative at moments of tension, and allow the reader's emotions to subside in readiness for the next crisis. Azriel's letters from the Holy Land,[63] which comprise perhaps the most refreshing element in the story and form a natural connecting link with the historical novels,[64] virtually constitute a self-contained frame-story.[65] Interspersed in segments throughout the novel, they represent a valuable cohesive force in a sprawling and somewhat shapeless work. The technique of interruption is sometimes applied even to the letters themselves. While reading an exciting episode in Azriel's letters, for example, Elisheba is handed an impassioned love letter from Zerah which she reads before returning to Azriel's narrative.[66] The same lengthy missive—almost 5,000 words in all—itself quotes another letter, which attempts to account for the real Zadok's renunciation of Shiphrah. It is, of course, a forgery from the pen of pseudo-Zadok![67] Again, a letter may be interrupted while the reader comments on it[68] or in another case by the sounds of the Passover *Haggadah* being recited in the next room and skillfully illustrating the situation described in the letter.[69]

Among the more attractive of the dramatic devices is Mapu's employment of the letter-form for dramatic irony. On two occasions the wicked Zadok (alias Hophni alias Alkum) receives letters attempting to enlist his aid in bringing Hophni or Alkum to justice for their many crimes![70] On another occasion a marriage broker who is anxious to prevent the hero from marrying the heroine, so as to further his own ends, shows the heroine's grandfather Obadiah a letter written by the hero to a friend, in which he confesses his passionate love for Elisheba in spite of her grandfather's opposition, and bluntly declares: "After all Obadiah will not live for ever." Not unnaturally, the old man finds the sentiment less than endearing![71]

Quite apart from their role in the plot, letters are frequently employed for the delineation of character. The direct method is normally followed, with the characterization confined to a narrow canvas and a single plane. In the early part of the story, for example, the characteristics of Jeroham's enemies are cataloged by Naaman and his friend Ahitub in letters that constitute a kind of dossier, and seem at times more suitable for a record office than a novel.[72] Although the descriptions are, on occasion, quite powerful, the characterization is almost entirely of the black and white variety,[73] which leaves little scope for development. The subtlety to be derived from varying viewpoints, which constitutes one of the great advantages of the epistolary genre, is conspicuously absent.

This failure to make use of so successful a technique is all the more surprising in view of Perl's skillful employment of multiple perspectives.[74] But it is not the only aspect of characterization in which Mapu falls short of his predecessor. Through his total command of language Perl establishes whether his characters are committed to the movement of enlightenment *Haskalah* or to Hasidism and even marks the gradual transition of his main character from support for the latter movement to the former by a marked change in his literary style.[75] Mapu's characterizations, on the other hand, suffer from a uniformity of style, which tends to make their rigid stratification into black and white still less convincing. Indeed, when Mapu does attempt to differentiate, the result scarcely reflects the author's intention. Whereas the virtuous characters are apt to write their epistles in the euphuistic and over-florid style which was regarded as "good taste" by most of the Hebrew writers of the period, the wicked characters—except when they are deliberately forging letters in the manner of their opponents—adopt a rather more straightforward and hence more pleasing style.[76] It may well be that Mapu was temperamentally incapable of writing the barbarous jargon which Perl foists upon the opponents of enlightenment in his stories.[77] Certainly, the obscurantism of many of Mapu's villains is not noticeably reflected in their choice of words.

Letters, however, do provide Mapu with one additional means of characterization. On occasion, the author chooses the letter-form to furnish a character with a medium for self-portraiture. Unlike the more frequent use of letters, already noticed, in which one character describes a second for the benefit of a third, the reader in this case is able to form an estimate of personality as it unfolds in the letter. Such is the case, for example, when Elisheba writes a letter to Naaman, in which the generosity of her nature becomes immediately apparent.[78] Indeed, it is this very generosity which the villains, who have intercepted the letter, plan to exploit for their own nefarious purposes. It is a pity that Mapu did not make greater use of this effective method of characterization.

In spite of the serious shortcomings in Mapu's copious use of letters for the construction of the plot of *The Hypocrite* and the depiction of its characters, a third epistolary category plays a more successful role. Those letters which are employed for reflections on contemporary life and social criticism or for the propagation of the author's pet ideas constitute a far more satisfactory element in the novel. The suitability of the letter-form for such purposes has been pointed out above, but in the context of *The Hypocrite* it possesses the additional advantage of directness of approach, in contrast to the letters which relegate the action and characterization of the novel to the third person. Indeed, for Mapu, the exponent of enlightenment and advocate of social reform,[79] the letter served as an excellent medium for expounding his views, without appearing to emphasize the author's didactic aims too blatantly.

A lifelong pedagogue, Mapu lost no opportunity of pointing out what he considered to be the shortcomings of the old traditional type of education, with its narrow horizons and inefficient methods. Time and again the letters sing the praises of a secular education, and a training which will enable the student to earn a dignified livelihood, and at the same time develop his esthetic appreciation of the beauties of the world. They might almost be regarded as tracts for the propagation of the movement of *Haskalah*.[80] Of particular interest is his support for equal educational opportunities for women, and Elisheba's letter to her grandfather, in which she defends her right to study, represents an important advance in the struggle for emancipation.[81] Again, his enthusiasm for the learning of foreign languages appears in Elisheba's ability to cope with a letter of invitation written in French[82]—an unusual accomplishment in her environment. The frequent insertion of arguments advocating the development of a refined literary taste belongs to the same category.[83]

Finally, the letters afforded Mapu ample scope for the free expression of romantic love, which the exponents of enlightenment considered so important a step toward Jewish regeneration.[84] Many of the letters written by the hero and the heroine of the novel display a tenderness and sensitivity of considerable charm.[85] In the mental climate of Mapu's environment the portrayal of such outright declarations of love was an act of considerable daring, and it is a little difficult to realize quite how revolutionary Zerah's impassioned letter to Elisheba must have appeared to Mapu's contemporaries. After praising her beauty and charm in somewhat elegant style Zerah continues:

> From that time [when I first saw you] I became conscious of a new world, a world which God had planted in my heart to plague and delight me by turns, as successive waves of hope and fear swept over me. From the day when I beheld the symbol of love in your beautiful face and felt the pangs of jealousy—from that day I have been mad for love of you, and I am terrified lest you might not feel well disposed toward me.[86]

Mild as such sentiments may appear to a modern reader of sophisticated tastes, their impact upon a society in which it was customary for young couples to see each other for the first time on their wedding day was startling, and it is scarcely surprising that Mapu's stories were read with such avidity.

It is, indeed, in the realm of sentiment that Mapu's use of letters proved most satisfactory.[87] The less effective features of the European epistolary tradition are discernible in his use of the device for the mechanics of characterisation and plot. Only too often, Mapu resorts to third-party account or crude melodrama, while the more subtle benefits inherent in a skillful employment of epistolary techniques are frequently overlooked. The introduction of letters, however, for the propagation of his own ideas, or for the dissemination of his views on contemporary social conditions proved to be more efficacious. In particular, by using letters as a vehicle for the injection of sentiment into his novels, Mapu provided a real service for Hebrew literarure comparable with Perl's use of epistolary elements for satirical purposes. The importance of that service may be perceived in the copious supply of letters included in most of the Hebrew novels composed during the twenty years following Abraham Mapu's death; including a number of interesting new developments in epistolary technique.[88] But that must remain the subject of the next chapter.

3

Epistolary Elements in the Novels of Mapu's Successors[1]

OF ALL the Hebrew novels composed during the period of enlightenment, only the fourth part of Smolenskin's *The Wanderer in the Paths of Life* is written in epistolary form.[2] Nevertheless, during the two decades following the death of Abraham Mapu in 1867, the majority of Hebrew novels conform to the pattern of Mapu's novel of contemporary life, *The Hypocrite*, which quotes or makes reference to more than sixty letters.[3] Although these letters comprise only about one sixth of the total length of *The Hypocrite*, their number is certainly far greater than might be expected in a non-epistolary novel published in the second half of the nineteenth century. The fact that Mapu's successors continued to use this hybrid form clearly illustrates the almost hypnotic influence exerted by the first Hebrew novelist; it also emphasizes still further the time lag separating much of the Hebrew literature of the period from the European models which shaped its development.[4]

In estimating the influence of the two main currents of the European epistolary tradition upon Hebrew literature in the nineteenth century, it is important to recall that while the satirical genre in the tradition of Montesquieu's *Persian Letters* eventually found its way into Hebrew literature in the fully fledged form in Perl's *The Revealer of Secrets* and *The Test of the Righteous*,[5] the epistolary novel of manners, in the tradition of Richardson's *Pamela*, had no real counterpart in Hebrew. The full epistolary form, with all its subtleties of construction and shifting points of view, was restricted in Hebrew literature to satirical writing, while the elements of the epistolary novel of manners may be discovered in the stories of Mapu and his successors only in hybrid form. Indeed, Mapu's employment of the epistolary device for the mechanics of plot and characterization reflects the less satisfactory aspects of the European tradition. Only too often he resorts to crude melodrama or third-party account, while neglecting the subtle advantages which may accrue from a more skillful use of epistolary techniques. Nevertheless, in utilizing the letter-form for the exposition of ideas, for reflections on the social conditions of his time, and, in particular, for the introduction of sentiment, Mapu performed a service for Hebrew literature comparable with Joseph Perl's masterly exploitation of the letter-form for satirical purposes.[6]

The epistolary techniques abounding in Mapu's novels were adopted by his successors with enthusiasm. In addition, however, they employed some of the satirical devices previously utilized by Perl, at the same time adding a number of fresh techniques with respect to structure and mode of expression.[7] The mechanical aspects of the epistolary method continued, nevertheless, to play a dominant role. As formative elements in the plot letters performed three main functions, serving as a convenient method of conveying fresh information, as a dramatic device, and as a means of interrupting the narrative. All three aspects require further examination.

For conveying information the letter clearly represents an admirable instrument. It may describe events which have occurred prior to the opening of the story, or developments within the framework of the plot for the benefit of one or other of the characters—and, of course, the reader. Again, a letter may conveniently serve as a means of tying up loose ends or engineering the *dénouement* of the story. The whole complex plot of Smolenskin's *The Wanderer in the Paths of Life* revolves about the letters given to the young hero early in the story by his mother and an old benefactor just before their deaths, of which the contents are revealed only much later in the story.[8] In a later novel, *The Inheritance*, the arrival of a letter acquaints the reader, although not the hero for whom it is intended, with information essential for an understanding of the plot.[9] Again, many of the facts and much of the background information necessary to follow the complicated narrative of Abramowitz's *Fathers and Sons* are conveyed by means of letters.[10] In Braudes' *Religion and Life*, the letters sent by Shraga describing the growing opposition to rabbinical stringencies largely determine the course of action adopted by the hero Samuel.[11] In a second novel, a short letter containing the information that the hero Jacob Hetzron is already married somewhat disconcerts his prospective bride:[12]

> Dear Barzillai,
> With regard to your question concerning Hetzron, he is indeed content, for he is wealthy, and his wife, the lady of his household, is a woman of much good sense. He has two beautiful children and his wife looks forward to his coming home each day . . .

Indeed, no sooner has she read the first few lines than she faints![13] The minor novelists of the period, such as Leinwand, Meinkin, Manassewitz, Sheikewitz, and Weisbrem, as might be expected, all use the letter-form to convey information.[14]

Although such letters usually serve as a direct link between the sender and recipient, some authors follow Mapu's favorite technique of allowing one character to hand over a letter written by a second for the perusal of a third,[15] in spite of the inherent disadvantage in lending the narrative a second-hand flavor.[16] A variant technique, reserved for very lengthy missives of fifteen, eighteen, or even twenty pages, utilizes letters in the form of diaries, which readily lend themselves to the expression of intimate feelings as well as personal reminiscences.[17] But apart from supplying information, letters are used to elicit information[18] or to convey a warning.[19] A letter, for example, from his *Ṣaddiq* warning him that his present behavior is endangering his soul, immediately reduces the hero of *The Two Extremes* to a state of panic.[20] In similar vein letters may advise a certain course of action, as when the captive heroine of Meinkin's novel, *The Love of the Righteous*, receives the following cryptic note:[21]

> Be prepared, for with God's help you shall be free tonight, for the heavens are black with clouds and the night will surely be dark; if such be the case with the night, the darkness will lighten our way.

For all its brevity, this note is not without significance. Not only is the information it contains important for the heroine, but the mode of expression and the fact that it is imbedded in the narrative without any distinguishing punctuation throw interesting light on the literary climate of the period.[22] For the present discussion, it may also be regarded as a characteristic example of a letter used as a dramatic device.

The melodramatic flavor of most of the novels under review proved highly conducive to the introduction of a wide variety of epistolary devices, once again in the manner of Mapu.[23] Such letters are liberally sprinkled with double or even triple exclamation marks following such expressions as:—"But no, no, no!!!" or "My last moment has come!!!" (the writer is insisting that he is just about to cut his throat, although in the event he does not do so![24]), or with pregnant rows of dots, or with cries of despair, hatred, or revenge, or passionate pleas for forgiveness, or violent descriptions of madness, or heinous examples of villainy in a variety of forms.[25] In classical melodramatic style, letters are forged or used to slander or incriminate innocent victims.[26] They are frequently intercepted, usually deliberately[27] but, on occasion, by accident,[28] or found unexpectedly among papers or in less likely places.[29] They may be anonymous or threatening[30] or deliberately misleading.[31] They are used for all manner of trickery and subterfuge.[32] The hero of *For Love of Ṣaddiqim*, for example, who has been wrongfully conscripted into the Russian army because of a lying letter instigated by his enemies,[33] later receives a note informing him that his beloved has been betrothed to another, which causes him considerable distress:[34]

> In rage and anger he flung it [the letter] contemptuously aside, tearing his hair, foaming at the mouth, his nostrils steaming and his eyes burning with rage! Like a lion deprived of its prey he roared in a strange and terrible voice: Hadassah! Hadassah! . . .—Where is my gun? I shall put an end to my life, for I have no further want of it now that Hadassah has betrayed me! . . .

It transpires that this letter is the work of the heroine's mother, who has also successfully intercepted all correspondence between the lovers during the three years of the hero's military service.[35] Happily, the young couple display commendable fidelity.

The reaction just described is far from unusual. Reference has already been made to one of the instances in which the reading of a letter produces an attack of fainting.[36] But such are by no means the sole reactions. The receipt of a letter may arouse dismay, agitation, or devastation of spirit; it may equally well result in sickness, total ruin, or even death.[37] Letters, again, are written from prison,[38] from death-beds,[39] and, as previously mentioned, before cases of actual or threatened suicide. The following letter, for example, is addressed to a father by his son on the eve of his execution, when he decides to commit suicide instead:[40]

> My father! The last moment has come!!! Now I lift the knife ... Now I put it to my throat! ... Forgive the sins of your unfortunate son ... Forgive me, O my sister! ... For the last time I speak the name that is so dear to me ... I feared until now to mention your name lest the bonds of love should hold me back and bind me to life, but now I fear no longer because I am dying ... My sister, my sister, my sister! ...
>
> Drops of blood covered the last words, and the letters could hardly be read.

On reading this letter, the father collapses and dies. Letters of farewell are left before a sudden departure or elopement,[41] while the arrival of a letter may result in the disappearance of its recipient.[42] Indeed, the postal service is made to bear a heavy responsibility in the novels of the period.

Apart from their melodramatic qualities, letters are frequently utilized as a convenient method of interrupting the narrative either by way of an artistic pause—although nowhere as effectively as Azriel's missives from the Holy Land in Mapu's *The Hypocrite*[43]—or in order to inject fresh interest into a flagging narrative in the manner of a frame-story.[44] The form is frequently employed to outline the previous history or experiences of one or other of the characters,[45] although the reading of the letter may, itself, be interrupted for dramatic purposes and not resumed,[46] while on occasion a letter may contain one or several additional letters.[47] Again, the reading of a letter may be interrupted to enable the recipient to comment on it[48] or, more effectively, to allow the author himself to intervene directly. When the hero of *Religion and Life* replies to Shraga's letter explaining the need for religious reform but expressing the fervent hope that an understanding with the rabbis may be reached, Braudes expresses his surprise at the naivety of his own hero in supposing that the rabbis might prove amenable to his views:[49]

> Samuel! Can this be you expressing such sentiments? Can it be your pen which has written words like these? Do you not know the rabbis and their meetings, and the sort of replies you can expect? How can you pin your hopes on a rabbinical assembly?

As an instrument of dramatic irony letters may sometimes play a poignant role. In *The Reward of the Righteous*, for example, a letter from Miriam thanks the dying Bathsheba for helping her break the yoke of parental discipline and escape to a convent, little knowing that Bathsheba had engineered her flight in order to get rid of a rival for Emil's love.[50] Similarly in *The Artful Villain* the aging hero, Abihail, writes to his lawyer describing how his wife's advice to offer his captors a heavy bribe has saved him from disaster, while all the time the reader is aware that the old man's wife had herself instigated his arrest.[51] Again, the heroine of *The Outcast* receives a letter informing her of her obstinate father's change of heart and his consequent willingness to allow her to return home, just after she has finally severed all possible ties by her conversion to Christianity.[52] It would appear that the letter-form is particularly suitable for such usage.

Some reference has already been made to the startling behavioral effects which the receipt of a letter may engender.[53] But letters are also frequently employed for a more conventional delineation of character. As in Mapu's novel *The Hypocrite*, the direct method is normally followed, whereby a letter from one character to another contains a description of some other person or persons, usually of the black and white variety and again confined to a narrow canvas and a single plane.[54] More successful is the use of the letter-form to furnish a character with a medium of self-portraiture, which enables the reader to form his own estimate of the personality of the writer.[55] In *The Reward of the Righteous*, for example, Gabriel's fine character becomes apparent in his letter to Shemaiah describing his experiences in the first Polish revolt,[56] just as Emil, Shemaiah's son, displays his real nobility of spirit in a letter to his father prior to joining the second:[57]

> Since the conspiracy first began, I have been a member of it; but I hid it from you lest I cause you grief, particularly after I heard your categorical statement that you regard them all as criminals and sinners, while to me they are as brothers and loyal comrades, in life and even unto death. We shall march together in war and peace, nor shall any adversary divide us. For even our respective faiths shall not prove an obstacle, since the kingdom will not be founded on religions, nor its statutes fashioned by their teachings; but justice shall sit on the throne of righteousness, and the upright of heart will be drawn thereafter in probity and truth.

Similarly, the hero of *The Two Extremes* is profoundly moved by the tenderness and generosity of a letter from his wife, in spite of the fact that he has treated her so shamefully.[58]

Regrettably, no attempt is made to exploit the technique of varying viewpoints which is so well suited to the epistolary genre, in spite of the lesson which might have been learned from Perl's skillful employment of multiple perspective.[59] In one respect, however, the influence of Perl proved beneficial for the delineation of character in some of the novels under review, although rather, perhaps, by accident than design. Characterization in fiction largely depends upon the mode of expression which the author attributes to the character concerned.[60] Perl deliberately foists a barbarous jargon upon the opponents of enlightenment partly as a means of determining character, at the same time marking the gradual ideological transition of his main character by a change in literary style.[61] Mapu's characterizations, on the other hand, suffer from a uniformity of style, which renders their rigid stratification into black and white still less convincing.[62] In following Perl's technique of concocting a barbaric style for the letters written by the opponents of enlightenment, or at least indicating that they were written in such a style before correction, Abramowitz and particularly Weisbrem improve the quality of their characterizations, even though their purpose is primarily satirical.[63] The clumsy rabbinical style of a letter despatched by one of the characters in *Religion and Life*,[64] and the kabbalistic terminology of the warning letter which so terrifies the hero of *The Two Extremes*, illustrate Braudes' appreciation of the device.[65] Again, Smolenskin successfully employs a pseudo-rabbinical style in a letter left by a wealthy lady's business manager before his hasty departure, explaining why he cannot furnish the capital sum she has requested. The style of the letter may be judged from the narrator's comments:[66]

> This is what he wrote to her, and I have read it out to you, gentlemen, verbatim. The lady read it out in just the same way, for she was used to reading letters of this sort, and anything she couldn't understand she puzzled out for herself, or the teacher helped her make sense of it.

Apart from their application as elements in the plot or for the delineation of character, letters play an important role in the novels under review as a means of commenting on and criticizing various aspects of contemporary life, or propagating the favorite ideas of the various authors. The European tradition of epistolary fiction bears ample testimony to the suitability of the novel-form for such purposes.[67] Moreover, the many letter-manuals published in Hebrew during the nineteenth century, which frequently include expositions of the ideas of the movement of enlightenment, also reflect similar tendencies.[68] Mapu had used the device with considerable success in *The Hypocrite* to advocate his views on social reform,[69] and his successors followed eagerly in his footsteps. In *Religion and Life* Braudes lays great stress on the despatch of letters far and wide as a method of propagating ideas, and adds a note of authenticity by testifying to the feverish spate of letters written by both parties in the struggle for religious reform in Lithuania which comprises the principal theme of his novel.[70] It is of interest, however, that whereas Mapu uses letters in support of the movement of enlightenment, Smolenskin employs the weight of his epistolary armory in the fourth part of *The Wanderer in the Paths of Life* to launch a scathing attack upon that movement.[71] The same series of letters contains a shrewd assessment of the European political situation,[72] as well as heartfelt descriptions of the deplorable plight of the Jewish communities of Eastern Europe:[73]

> The appearance of these towns has so changed that I scarcely recognized them. The town of Shekhulah [Shklov] was the first in which I thought to spend a few days, but I derived little satisfaction from it. That town, which far surpassed its neighbors in wealthy citizens and places of learning, in persons well versed in Torah and those that feared the Lord, that town had declined in an extraordinary manner. Want and poverty could be seen on every face; its prominent citizens were brought low, its wealthy circles ground into the dust, and all its glory had departed. Only faces filled with anxiety, eyes sunk in their sockets, lips parched and dry from hunger and thirst, faltering legs and bowed backs were all that met the gaze of passers-by.

They also include some interesting observations on new trends in Jewish education.[74] In *Fathers and Sons* Abramowitz utilizes letters for didactic purposes, but with a characteristic gleam of humor. When Ephraim attempts to translate for his wife a letter written by their son prior to his departure, in which he expounds the ideas of enlightenment, Ephraim can only declare that it is all nonsense, and all he can translate for his wife is the word "farewell:"[75]

> Greetings to you my dear parents!
>
> I write this letter in tears before leaving your house! With many sighs and a heavy heart I leave my birthplace and my parents' house to wander far away like a bird; but I have considered the matter carefully and I realize that no good will come from my remaining here.
>
> "Quiet, Ephraim!" said Sarah, "tell me what it means."
>
> "Simon writes ... Simon says ..." Ephraim tried to relate the substance of the letter, but when he saw he could not do it, he quickly changed his manner and said: "Simon writes stuff and nonsense, that it is not good for him to remain in his parents' house."
>
> "Woe is me," sighed Sarah.
>
> Ephraim continued to read while his wife asked questions.
>
> "That's enough, Ephraim," said Sarah. "You've wearied yourself with reading and still told me nothing at all."
>
> "What can I say?" replied Ephraim. "Simon writes nonsense. Believe me, I, too, do not understand his silly dreams and the words which in his ignorance he makes so important."
>
> "Why should I not believe you," rejoined Sarah, "when you read the letter with such difficulty, with your tongue stumbling over the words, like someone avoiding pitfalls! When you were as young as Simon, you could not write either, and it was hard to read your letters and understand them; and when Simon reaches your age, he too will be able to write ..." Ephraim continued to read, uncomprehendingly, as Simon tried to explain in his letter why he had run away from home, concluding as follows: "Once more your son bids you farewell, as he goes into exile from his father's table, Simon."

"Here, too, there is only a lot of nonsense," said Ephraim, "and I find no merit in it, only a farewell to us."

"A farewell to me!" cried Sarah, sighing. "Woe to the desolate mother! ... Why should I live if my son, my heart's delight, is no longer here but goes wandering about the earth! You, Ephraim, you are the cause of it all, for always dealing with him with a heavy hand and slapping his cheeks so shamefully. You were always heaping insults on him and you could never speak to him as a father to a son."

As a device for demonstrating the complete inability of the two generations to communicate, the letter proves highly effective. Weisbrem uses the stratagem of incorrectly addressed envelopes in order to launch a still more devastating assault on the secular ignorance of the older generation in one of the most amusing and successful episodes in the whole range of novels under consideration.[76] Both Braudes and Manassewitz use letters to attack the traditional method of arranging marriages without reference to the wishes of the young couple concerned.[77] Again, the ability to cope with letters written in foreign languages illustrates one further aspiration of the advocates of enlightenment.[78] The letter in Sheikewitz's *The Outcast*, however, in which a young man writes to his teacher promising to support him for the rest of his life because he has opened his eyes to the movement of enlightenment seems, perhaps, a little excessive.[79]

Mapu's example in using letters for the free expression of romantic love, which in his environment constituted an act of considerable daring, is repeated in the novels of his successors. The letter-form lends itself naturally to tenderness, sensitivity, and the analysis of emotion, and allows a less inhibited expression of sentiment than dialog with its direct confrontations of personality.[80] On the other hand, it can all too easily engender a high-flown, euphuistic style—a disability which also affects many of the letters within these novels.[81] Mapu's daring, however, is overshadowed by the boldness of both Smolenskin and Braudes in portraying love letters where one of the parties concerned is already married.[82]

Dearest Shifrah

I love you with an eternal love; for the first time I experience love with all its power. I saw you and I loved you, and since then I have become a different man. From the moment I saw your pure eyes I began to have tender, exalted feelings, and when I thought of you I walked among the stars forgetting the earth and the fullness thereof. I forgot the bonds with which my parents tied me as a child when they married me off before my heart became aware of what love is ...

Smolenskin, indeed, goes much further, and in a series of letters allows the hero of *The Wanderer in the Paths of Life* to discuss his incestuous passion for his stepsister, and his attempts to overcome it.[83] This precedent may have emboldened Manassewitz, who includes in his novel, *The Parents' Sin*, a letter to a father from the long-lost son he had driven from home at the age of ten, revealing that it was he who, all unrecognized, had married the man's daughter, that is the bridegroom's own sister, and disappeared with the dowry immediately following the ceremony! This novel, however, is nowhere characterized by dramatic restraint.[84]

In estimating the role of the epistolary elements in the novels under review, the utilization of techniques not found in Mapu's novels may serve to indicate the lines of change. Apart from a number of additional melodramatic devices such as tear-stained letters[85] or the attempt by double spacing to indicate the trembling signature of a heroine forced to sign three letters before abduction,[86] the novels contain a number of interesting new features. As in Mapu's stories, letters are frequently mentioned without being quoted, whether or not the contents are actually described.[87] A new element, however, is introduced by Braudes in the partial quotation of letters:[88]

> Soon after, Shraga received a long letter from Samuel . . . a letter containing a complete and honest answer to the questions which he had asked in the name of those young men "embittered of soul, bent beneath the Talmud and a distorted education" and who "were prepared to fight as long as there was breath in them" and who "would sacrifice themselves for the holiness of the cause—the reforms needed by the Jews."

This technique was later adopted and developed with considerable effect by among others J. H. Brenner. Again, the letters which comprise almost the entire fourth section of *The Wanderer in the Paths of Life*, taking the form of a one-sided correspondence written by the hero, make frequent reference to the answers received in the interests of continuity.[89] A variant technique adopted by Braudes is the reference to a series of letters in the narration of a past episode, of which the contents are given in each case although none is actually quoted.[90]

Braudes, indeed, displays considerable inventiveness. Reference has already been made to his resort to author-intervention,[91] but his skill may also be recognized in a further device. While composing a short letter to her brother describing the very favorable impression that Samuel has made upon her, the heroine of *Religion and Life* suddenly has second thoughts and "before putting down the word 'love' as she had been just about to do, she stopped writing . . ." A few lines further on, the reader learns that after giving the matter deep thought, she has crossed out the last few lines of her letter.[92] The same author frequently adds postscripts to his letters, using the abbreviation "P.S."[93] This usage is adopted by Weisbrem,[94] whereas on the one occasion where it is required, Smolenskin employs the Hebrew phrase *'aḥarei kothbi.*[95] Both Leinwand and Sheikewitz append an additional paragraph to a letter without any initial formula.[96]

The main contribution of Braudes' use of letters, however, may be discerned in the structural aspects of *The Two Extremes.* Admittedly both

Smolenskin and Abramowitz use letters for tying together a number of sections in *The Wanderer in the Paths of Life* and *Fathers and Sons* respectively, while Braudes employs the same straightfoward device in *Religion and Life.*[97] The obvious method of employing letters which have been mentioned at an earlier stage for the unraveling of the plot has been indicated above.[98] *The Two Extremes,* however, contains examples of much greater structural significance. In part one of the story, Barzillai writes an unquoted letter to Solomon asking him to inquire whether Jacob Hetzron is married or not, and later receives a reply, which is quoted in full, definitely affirming Hetzron's married status.[99] But only in part two of the story is there an account of Solomon receiving Barzillai's letter which is then quoted in full, while the fact of his reply is mentioned some time later, although the actual reply has already been fully revealed some seventy pages previously.[100] A further example of the balance maintained in this carefully constructed novel may be discerned in a comparison of the three letters received by Jacob in the second part of the story with the three addressed to Solomon in the third.[101] The artistic superiority of *The Two Extremes* over all the Hebrew novels of the twenty years under review stems largely from Braudes' sense of structure.[102]

The most striking difference in epistolary technique which distinguishes these novels from those of Mapu, however, lies in the use of letters for satirical purposes. Here the powerful influence of Joseph Perl, and beyond him the European satirical tradition of the epistolary genre, is clearly recognizable partly in the explanatory footnotes employed by Abramowitz, Meinkin, Zobeizensky, and Weisbrem,[103] and partly in the parody on the literary style of their opponents, to which Smolenskin, Abramowitz, Braudes, and Weisbrem resort.[104] As mentioned above, the most devastating as well as amusing attack on ignorance and bigotry occurs in Weisbrem's novel *Between the Times.*[105] In the realm of epistolary satire Weisbrem's technique compares favorably with anything in the Hebrew novel of the period.

From what precedes, the dual role which letters play in these novels as motivating factors in the plot and as instruments for the propagation of ideas may be readily conceded. Indeed, the epistolary elements faithfully reflect the dual purpose of the hybrid novel of the movement of enlightenment, which attempts to combine an exciting tale of adventure and romance with serious social criticism and the propagation of ideas.[106] This uncomfortable juxtaposition of disparate elements was inevitably short-lived. With the gradual disappearance of the genre from the Hebrew literary scene toward the end of the nineteenth century, the epistolary element in the Hebrew novel undergoes a radical change, and evolves new forms and different relationships to the structure of the novel.

4

Sickness and Death[1]

THE TWENTY years following the death of Abraham Mapu, namely 1868–88, represent a period of transition and experimentation for the Hebrew novel. Mapu's historical novels, while comprising a notable contribution to the development of Hebrew literature, and constituting a remarkable attempt to utilize the elements of the Bible, especially its linguistic treasures, for the creation of a new genre in Hebrew fiction, had virtually exhausted the possibilities of such stringent criteria. Although far less satisfactory from an artistic point of view, and crudely naive in form and content, Mapu's long and rambling novel of contemporary life *The Hypocrite* served as a model—at least in terms of subject matter—for all the writers, both major and minor, of the succeeding period.

During the twenty years under review, apart from works by such major writers as Smolenskin, Braudes, and Abramowitz, Hebrew novels were composed by a number of minor writers, for example J. Leinwand, S. F. Meinkin, B. I. Zobeizensky, M. Manassewitz, N. M. Sheikewitz, A. S. Rabinowitz, I. J. Sirkis, and I. Weisbrem. Many of these writers have subsequently been forgotten so completely that their names are scarcely mentioned even in the various histories of modern Hebrew literature, while their works, in some cases, are now almost as rare as manuscripts. Fortunately, however, a number of the stories have been made available in recent years in microform. Nevertheless, in spite of the wide variation in both the length and quality of the stories, and the great difference in literary talent displayed by the authors, all the novels are characterized by two principal features, which endow them with certain common elements, thus enabling them to be treated as a whole.

In the first place, they are all concerned with the techniques of unfolding an imaginative story—sometimes in serial form—even though the author may, on occasion, attach only incidental importance to the plot.[2] Directed toward an audience of unsophisticated literary tastes, most of the stories[3] abound with crudely exciting and melodramatic episodes, as unconvincing as they are unexpected, but calculated to rivet the attention of a public only too willing to escape a drab and poverty-stricken life to a world of adventure and romance. Secondly, they are so passionately involved in the social, religious, and economic problems of contemporary Jewish life in Eastern Europe that a harsh didactic note is rarely lacking even in the most fanciful of the stories.

As a result the novel of the period bears a hybrid stamp, in which serious reflection, social criticism, and bitter satire nestle uncomfortably in what is frequently a wildly improbable framework. Such a fusion of realist and romantic elements stems, partly via Mapu, from the early nineteenth-century French and English novel. In the absence of an appropriate literary tradition as well as anything like an adequate linguistic medium, however, it remains very much inferior to its Western European counterparts. On the other hand, this fusion explains in some measure the ambivalent attitudes common to most of the novelists under review. The principal themes, which are highly repetitive, must frequently serve a dual purpose, at once exciting and instructive. The extreme difficulty of harmonizing blatant moralizing with subtlety of construction is largely responsible for the constant employment of thematic material of a somewhat crude and obvious nature.

Of the many themes which occur time and again within these novels, such as love and marriage, conspiracy and intrigue, theft, forgery, and imprisonment, persecution and violence, jealousy, revenge, and remorse—to mention only some of the more obvious—sickness and death in a variety of forms occupy a leading place, furnishing the novelists with two apparently inexhaustible sources of inspiration. As familiar and universal phenomena they may be introduced, wherever necessary, with a minimum of subtlety either to bolster a flagging plot or in the interests of crude melodrama. In this respect they frequently appear as highly exaggerated reactions to unexpected misfortune ranging from mere fainting to prolonged and incurable illness, insanity, or even sudden death.

Amid this weighty catalog of human suffering the heavy incidence of fainting is particularly noticeable. The malady affects a wide variety of characters, male as well as female, at every conceivable opportunity,[4] and affords a convenient method of concluding a dramatic episode, or preventing revelations or actions which might otherwise prematurely unravel the plot. Again, the device enables the novelist to emphasize or underline the enormity of misfortune or the stark horror of a situation, in the face of which the only saving reaction is loss of consciousness. The very prevalence of the device, however, seems to indicate that this propensity for fainting may well reflect a fairly familiar pattern of contemporary social behavior. In Victorian England ladies were equally prone to faint at the slightest provocation—and often with less reason than the characters in these novels.

The hero of Smolenskin's long novel *The Wanderer in the Paths of Life*, for example, faints on four occasions in the course of the story—on hearing that his friend Gideon has been press-ganged into military service,[5] on hearing that Dan, another friend, has been sentenced to life imprisonment[6] after shooting an opponent in a duel, and finally on realizing that the man he himself has killed was his own stepbrother, whose demise has hastened his father's death![7]

> —I am even worse than Cain, for my sin is greater than his! He murdered his brother, while I have murdered my brother and killed my father!—I cried aloud and my eyes went black, and I fell into a swoon.

In similar vein, many of the female characters may readily be conceded ample justification for fainting at the sight of their husbands or lovers about to be married to another woman,[8] or on learning that their betrothed is already a married man with children.[9] Again, the victims of such villainies as false arrest and imprisonment,[10] abduction,[11] or desertion[12] may well be forgiven for a temporary lapse of consciousness. At the other end of the scale, however, mothers will faint merely because a son dares to express his own views concerning the choice of a bride[13] or—in the case of one particularly tight-fisted woman in Weisbrem's *Eighteen Coins*—as a result of minor obstacles to her plan for arranging a suitable match for her daughter. The latter instance is outlined with slapstick humor:

> Zibiah went to the door and reached out for the handle. But at that moment the door burst open violently, and Malkah's two daughters together with the woman who had accompanied them, all tripped over the threshold, and the crockery they were carrying smashed into smithereens; for the one girl stumbled and fell on her sister, who in turn fell over the third woman, so that all three hurtled into the house with a tremendous clatter, while the elder daughter sprained her arm as well. Malkah was so frightened by the shock that she collapsed on the floor and fainted![14]

For all their frequency, however, the many instances of fainting are heavily outweighed by the examples of more prolonged and serious illness with which these novels abound.[15] In most cases sickness is introduced as a dramatic device, either as an integral element in the development of the plot, or to emphasize the impact exerted by a particular situation on the character concerned. Elsewhere it may serve to arouse the emotional sympathy of the reader or direct his attention toward some social abuse which the novelist is anxious to castigate. Again, resort is sometimes made to the device merely to introduce an element of action, no matter how peripheral, and thereby lend some slight momentum when the plot is manifestly wearing thin. Most of the above categories, however, lend themselves to a variety of treatment, and embrace a wide range of physical and mental ailments.

Of the numerous instances in which sickness is employed as an integral and motivating element in the plot, a number have far-reaching consequences. In the very first chapter of Smolenskin's *The Wanderer in the Paths of Life*, Josef's mother contracts an unspecified fatal illness which throws the young hero on the mercy of a hostile world and turns him into a penniless and homeless wanderer, in which role he dominates the entire novel. Similarly, the hero of a later novel by the same author breaks his foot in falling from a wagon, and is thereby fortuitously committed to the care of a family which subsequently occupies a central place in the story:[16]

> Zachariah had practically given up hope, so great was the pain, and his foot was so swollen that he could no longer remove his shoe. Suddenly he revived at the sound of turning wheels, and a moment later he saw a carriage harnessed to two powerful horses moving toward him. He let out a loud cry for help. The carriage stopped and a man of about fifty, of good appearance and dressed like an aristocrat, looked out and asked, "What has happened to you?" Zachariah quickly told him the story and the man, hearing his words, alighted from the carriage and said: "You are one of my brethren and I will gladly help you." He ordered the driver down, and together they lifted Zachariah into the spacious carriage. The man quickly took a knife from his pocket, cut the shoe off the throbbing foot, and bandaged it with a kerchief which he had dipped in water from a jug. In an instant it was as if he had breathed the breath of life into Zachariah.

Again, the epileptic tendencies and failing health[17] of the prospective bridegroom chosen by her parents for the heroine of Sheikewitz's *The Outcast*, in spite of all her protests, induce her to seek salvation in the elopement from which stems the long series of misfortunes that comprise the remainder of the novel. In similiar vein the heroine of Weisbrem's novel *Between the Times* contracts a nervous disorder[18] after being deserted by her fickle lover, and thereby makes the acquaintance of the other heroine, Miriam, their subsequent friendship becoming a decisive factor in the plot.[19] An interesting example of feigned illness occurs in Leinwand's novel where Gershom, an eminent lawyer, advises his old but foolish client, Abihail, whose villainous enemies have indicted him on a false charge, to write to the magistrate that he is unable to attend court because of a dangerous illness, and that he is protesting his innocence at death's door. It is indicative that even the heroes are allowed to indulge in such a dubious practice.[20] Elsewhere, sickness is used as an instrument of poetic justice in punishment for previous crimes.[21]

No less frequently, however, sickness is employed as a device to emphasize the role of other motivating forces in the plots. On a number of occasions frustrated love must bear responsibility for a sudden malady. Jacob Hetzron, the hero of Braudes' second novel, for example, although a married man with children, falls in love with Liza, and is so deeply affected that he begins to waste away, neither eating nor sleeping. His condition is described by his friend, Jorab, to Liza's brother as follows:

> I told you before that Hetzron is in love with your sister, Liza: but how can I give you any idea of what that love signifies? I simply cannot find words to describe it . . . I have seen plenty of lovers in my time and heard of many more; I've read of love and lovers in stories and novels, and seen many an example at the theater—but never in my life have I seen or heard of a love such as this.

> After all, Hetzron isn't a young lad; he wasn't born yesterday. Yet the love he bears Liza knows no parallel ... Ever since the scene that occurred when Barzillai brought the letter about his wife to your father's house, he has been going about bent double, all gloom and depression. But since I comforted him and encouraged him sufficiently to visit your father's house again, and Barzillai stirred up trouble a second time so that he has been forbidden to cross the threshold again until he has divorced his wife—since that day his depression has grown worse. It is quite impossible to console him. He weeps so bitterly that I'm afraid for his life ... I'm frightened he will go insane ...[22]

Liza, meanwhile, and another heroine, Shiphrah, who finds herself in similar straits, languish for love in a manner no less dramatic.[23] A similar stratagem is utilized by Smolenskin,[24] Manassewitz,[25] Sheikewitz,[26] and—as previously mentioned—Weisbrem.[27]

Sometimes the novelists resort to sickness in order to emphasize the tragic effects of villainy or crime. Smolenskin is particularly prone to the device, and many of his characters succumb to illness because of the machinations of the villains.[28] On one occasion a family is devastated on reading a newspaper report of their son's conviction for theft. When the young man makes his way home after escaping from prison, he is confronted with the tragic consequences of his crime:

> The newspaper had preceded him by three days. His intended bride, who looked after his sick old father like a daughter, had been reading the news to him. When she noticed the report, the paper slipped from her hand, and she fell off the chair in a faint. Terrified, the sick man shouted for help at the top of his voice, and his old wife hurried in fright to the rescue. After they had revived her and put her to bed, the patient asked his wife to see what had so upset her in the newspaper. Obediently the old woman sat down with the paper. But no sooner had she read a few lines than she too collapsed, but not merely in a faint, for she suffered a stroke and died. Nor did the old man long survive her, for on the very next day he was delivered from all earthly sorrow. Saul arrived home in time to see his father and mother being carried to thc cemetery, and his betrothed in a straitjacket—for she had gone insane.[29]

On the other hand, however, in Leinwand's novel, the illness of one of the heroes compels him to stay at home for three months, enabling him to learn of the villainies planned by his wicked stepmother against his aged father.[30]

On occasion the illness is contracted as a result of financial worry, bad news, or personal problems.[31] Of the latter the most interesting, perhaps, is the sickness of spirit experienced by Josef, the hero of *The Wanderer in the Paths of Life*, as a result of an incestuous passion for his stepsister, to which he readily confesses.[32] But no less frequently resort is made to sickness in order to arouse the emotional sympathies of the reader by presenting a harrowing scene of pain and sorrow.[33] In this latter respect, perhaps the most successful example occurs in Manassewitz's novel, where the fatal illness of a child is presented in moving terms, arousing a feeling of genuine pathos:[34]

> Words cannot describe my anguish at the sight of my child dying before my eyes, and my powerlessness to help him. He was trembling all over, his skin turned purplish, his eyes rolled in their sockets, and foam crept from his mouth. The wagon-driver and I did all we could to make his journey easier; the driver removed his coat and covered him with it; but nothing helped and before we reached the town, he expired in my bosom.

The great majority of instances of sickness, however, appear to have been introduced as incidental elements in the plot with the primary purpose of adding an element of action, in order to maintain the reader's interest.[35] This aim explains the many cases of raging fever, hallucinations, and insanity which the novels contain,[36] all of them calculated to arouse excitement, anguish, or violence in one or more of the characters, and thereby to exert upon the reader a certain fascination as self-contained episodes. It is significant that both Sheikewitz and Weisbrem (in *Eighteen Coins*) conclude their novels with an attack of insanity. It must be admitted that the ravings induced by high fever are often expressed in vivid and even gripping terms. But on one occasion Smolenskin introduces ingenious, if crude, psychological overtones into the ravings of one of his characters—a technique which represents a significant advance in modern Hebrew literature:[37]

> That evening, when the guard brought him supper in his cell, he was amazed to find for the first time in his experience a prisoner embracing him lovingly, calling him sweet names and addressing him as if he were female. He spoke at length of how glad he was to see her, and declared that sinful men would separate them no longer. The guard, used to being cursed by his prisoners, thought at first that this prisoner was trying to bribe him, so he replied with loving words hoping to catch him out. But when he heard himself being addressed as a woman, he shook his head in disbelief. After shaking his head once or twice, as though trying to recall if he had ever been female, he remembered that he never had been, and so decided that the man was either mad or that there was method in his madness. He lit a candle to examine the man more closely, and realized at once that he was not pretending. The face was all aflame, the eyes were bloodshot, and the hand, which gripped the guard's hand, was hot as a fiery coal. He hastened to inform the prison warden and the prisoner was immediately transferred to the prison hospital.

The various motives which determine the introduction of sickness by the novelists are closely paralleled in the frequent resort to death encountered in these stories. Here, again, the main purpose lies in the utilization of death as a convenient ingredient of the plot,[38] whether merely to introduce an element of action or remove unwanted characters on the one hand, or in order to portray an exciting, melodramatic episode or provide a significant development in the story on the other. Villainy, of course, remains the most lurid device for the promotion of sudden or untimely death,[39] but financial collapse,[40] grief,[41] shock,[42] or even a father's curse[43] all add their quota of fatalities. Death, too, constitutes a well-tried device for arousing the emotional sympathies of the reader, particularly in death-bed and graveyard scenes,[44] or in the lonely, unmourned passing of some righteous but misjudged and ostracized old man:[45]

> In silence and without a word they brought the dead man to burial. No one eulogized him or mourned his passing, and even Zachariah the preacher, who in his youth had been taught by him and eaten at his table, did not venture to mourn him publicly, lest the sins of his youth be remembered. Quietly the body was lowered into the grave, and no one reproved Caleb, the town jester, when he said the blessing (used when slaughtering fowls on the eve of the Day of Atonement) "This is my atonement ..." rather than from the burial service, "The Rock, his work is perfect ...," which everyone else was reading. The service was conducted without tears or sighs, and afterwards, when the participants left the burial grounds, they gladly drank a glass of wine ...

Again, death may serve as a most convenient instrument of poetic justice. In *The Wanderer in the Paths of Life*, for example, Josef's wicked aunt, who was responsible for all the misfortunes of his childhood, recognizes him during a violent storm at sea, and is dramatically washed overboard.[46] The effect is further heightened by the prior death of her own husband and eldest son.[47] In similar vein the wicked wife in Leinwand's novel dies of fright when her evil plans are finally discovered.[48] Zobeizensky, too, contrives the death of a murderer immediately after his confession of guilt.[49] Of greater significance, however, are the deaths of two of Smolenskin's heroes in a pogrom while courageously resisting the onslaught of a bloodthirsty mob.[50] In these instances, at least, death plays a deliberate and very serious role.

The melodramatic flavor of the great majority of the novels is emphasized by the many instances of violence, both real and threatened, which they contain. Although five of the six cases of actual suicide are confined to Smolenskin's novels,[51] there are many examples of threatened or attempted suicide.[52] In these latter cases, love plays an important if, perhaps, satirical role. A lovesick friend of the previously mentioned Josef, for example, declares that he is prepared to wait for one more year, but that if his love still remains unrequited he will then commit suicide as thousands do in London![53] It is of interest that when Josef is himself contemplating suicide, he also maintains that the number of suicides in London is enormous.[54] Similarly, *The Joy of the Godless* closes with a letter from the delinquent hero, David, protesting his love for the heroine and threatening to commit suicide.[55] In this example, at least, the influence of Goethe's *Werther* seems highly probable. The lovesick hero of Braudes' novel *The Two Extremes*[56] at one point also contemplates suicide—a solution he has read in many stories and seen many times at the theater.[57] The most facetious instance, however, occurs in Sheikewitz's *The Outcast*, which opens with a declaration by the heroine that she intends to commit suicide as soon as she has completed her story, while the final scene portrays her with a glass of water containing arsenic by her side fondly bidding farewell to the world, including her readers. Fortunately, however, she is enabled to change her mind at the last moment, and frankly admits her indifference to the reader's disappointment!

Even more numerous perhaps are the instances of murder[58] or attempted murder[59] which occur in many of these novels. The favored method would appear to be poison.[60] On occasion, such episodes are introduced with considerable dramatic skill, especially in Smolenskin's *A Donkey's Burial*, where the hero is murdered most unexpectedly by a peasant who bears him a grudge, and subsequently receives the "donkey's burial" from which the novel derives its name. Unaware that his enemy has bribed the peasant to kill him, the hero Jacob Chaim desperately attempts to convince the peasant of his identity. The dramatic irony of the situation may be readily appreciated:[61]

> How can I be sure that you are not deceiving me?
>
> I swear by the Lord that I'm speaking the truth.
>
> I don't trust an oath in the name of your God. Give me real proof. I know that Jacob Chaim wears a ring on his right hand given to him by the provincial governor.—Jacob Chaim showed him his hand, and the peasant took hold of it to look for the ring. Once having examined it, he shouted: That's all I wanted to know!—At the same moment Jacob Chaim pitched headlong, with only the words Oh! Esther! escaping his lips, and then silence! For on grasping his right hand, the peasant struck him on the head with his ax with such force that no second blow was necessary. A few moments later he was dead.

It is hardly surprising that in many of these novels the characters seem to die like flies!

Not infrequently, sickness and death are also employed for didactic purposes, to point out and castigate a wide range of abuses in society. Both devices are admirably suited for illustrating the consequences of the widespread, crushing poverty in terms of hunger, slum conditions, and malnutrition;[62] while the demoralizing effects of poverty are emphasized, for example, by Smolenskin's grotesque depiction of a band of traveling beggars deliberately disguising themselves so as to appear the victims of all sorts of physical deformities:[63]

> At dawn's light the old man, my so-called father, aroused me from sleep. On opening my eyes I saw the whole company sitting on the ground, each one intent upon his own activity. I looked about to see what they were doing, and one was simulating wounds on his leg, a second was putting a patch on his good eye, a third was binding his hand in a kerchief tied round his neck, while a fourth, who a moment ago had been running like a foal, was holding a crutch, and so on. Every one of them assumed some injury, and were I to relate all their afflictions, they would outnumber the plagues of Egypt according to Rabbi Akiba [namely 250] . . .

Sickness and death are equally effective for showing the evil results of forcing young girls into marriage against their will,[64] or the disastrous consequences of intermarriage and conversion,[65] while unpleasant personal characteristics such as snobbery[66] or miserliness[67] are equally liable to end in dire catastrophe. Rabinowitz, again, resorts to both devices in order to pour scorn on the irresponsibility of the new generation of so-called "enlightened" doctors,[68] while Braudes makes the death of a child the starting point of an attack on excessive rabbinical stringencies.[69] In similar vein both Manassewitz and Sirkis emphasize the tragedy of a child's death by depicting the harsh demands for payment of the burial fee in advance. As a result the poor heroine of the former tale is forced to leave her child unburied.[70] More powerful still is Smolenskin's treatment of the fatal illness of a young schoolboy as a result of seeing his brother press-ganged into military service.[71]

Most effective, however, is Abramowitz's humorous and bitingly satirical attack upon superstitious remedies for healing the sick. In his accounts the author supplies explanatory footnotes, showing himself to be thoroughly familiar with such practices.[72] After consulting her *Ṣaddiq* (holy man) Sarah in *Fathers and Sons* proffers the following remedy to her sick husband, insisting that she has been commanded to "stand a dove on your navel, and make you drink gruel made of *Hoša'noth* [willow branches used for ritual purposes] and recite this charm backwards and forwards seven times:

ינא ה׳ כאפור, אל הנאת כילא הער. הער כילא הנאת אל, כאפור ה׳ ינא.

And you must also change your name. No longer shall you call yourself Ephraim, but Isaiah Moses.[73] I have no doubt that by means of these excellent remedies you will soon be cured. Now listen to your wife's advice, Isaiah Moses, and drink plenty of *Hoša'noth* gruel."[74] Clearly, the treatment of the themes under review is by no means universally morbid.

One further point seems worthy of mention. The overall dissatisfaction of the novelists with their environment is perhaps unconsciously expressed by the inordinate incidence of death when viewed against the very small number of births which grace these novels. It is of interest that in violent contrast to the facts of the society which they describe, which witnessed a dramatic and, indeed, unparalleled increase in the Jewish population, the portrait which emerges from their novels is of a rapidly depopulating society!

5

Religion and Life

Modern Jewish history—as is well known—largely consists of a desperate attempt to catch up with Western European civilization, for in many respects the Jewish middle ages extend almost to the time of the French Revolution. From the end of the eighteenth century in Western Europe, and the middle of the nineteenth century in Eastern Europe, the Jewish people was faced with the formidable task of telescoping into a few decades a process of development which Western European countries had undergone slowly and painfully during two and a half centuries. The unity of Jewry in the middle ages, so largely self-contained and soberly integrated, was shattered by the impact of the modern world. A glittering panorama of fresh ideas and aspirations exerted a powerful attraction on successive generations of youth, so that many of the old ideals were all too rapidly abandoned in a search for the new and tantalizing values of the outside world. Enlightenment and emancipation gradually became the watchwords of large sections of the Jewish people, and if these concepts were not always compatible with traditional Judaism, then the latter had to be modified or reinterpreted to bridge the gap.

The struggle for civil rights and equality of opportunity found its first concrete expression in the writings of Moses Mendelssohn,[1] and particularly in his *Jerusalem* (1783).[2] In an attempt to harmonize his Judaism with the rationalist philosophy he had imbibed from the *Aufklärung* on the one hand, and with his patriotic aspirations on the other, Mendelssohn was compelled to define Judaism as a series of positive and negative injunctions untainted by any suspicion of dogma.[3] By arguing that Judaism leaves its adherents free to *believe* whatever reason and conscience dictate, provided only that the practical commandments be observed, and by adopting the maxim "Render unto Caesar that which is Caesar's," Mendelssohn prepared the ground for a series of interpretations which were to empty Judaism of its national and social content. Yet so powerful were his own reputation and personal influence that almost a century was to pass before his ideas were seriously challenged from within the ranks of the exponents of enlightenment, who had hitherto regarded Mendelssohn as their spiritual ancestor.

In Germany itself attention was focused upon the problem of integrating the Jew into German society. Within the movement for religious reform, strenuously propagated by such thinkers as Abraham Geiger and Samuel Holdheim,[4] the urgent desire to accommodate Judaism to the demands of loyal patriotism resulted in the abandonment of the messianic ideal and the hope of miraculous redemption. But the elimination of the eschatological aspects of Judaism gave rise to another problem, which has continued in large measure to the present time, namely: In what form was the continuation of Jewish life to be envisaged? This problem was by no means confined to the movement advocating radical religious reform. The counter-reformation of the Conservative movement advanced by, among others, Leopold Zunz, Zacharias Frankel, and Solomon Judah Rapoport, and the movement of Neo-orthodoxy as represented, for example, by Samuel David Luzzatto and Samson Raphael Hirsch,[5] are characterized by an equal awareness of the changed conditions facing Judaism, which demanded a rethinking of the traditional position. Each thinker in turn propounded his own solution to the problems facing Judaism, but the very variety of opinion only serves to emphasize the process of fragmentation to which Judaism was subjected in the course of the nineteenth century. One positive factor did, however, emerge. The continuous search for precedent in ancient practice to bolster the variety of opinions successively proposed fostered a growing awareness of the national past and strengthened the sense of historical continuity. Hence the paradox that a movement originally designed to limit Judaism solely to its religious aspects eventually helped to prepare the ground for a nationalist revival.

In Eastern Europe the drive toward emancipation and enlightenment began rather later and proceeded far more slowly. The great majority of the Jews of Europe were concentrated in the Russian Pale of Settlement, where very different conditions prevailed. There the density of settlement, the all-pervading intensity of Jewish life, and the hostility of the Russian government seriously impeded the propagation of such ideas in the first half of the nineteenth century. But in Eastern Europe, too, such writers as Nachman Krochmal and Isaac Baer Levinsohn[6] gave expression to their awareness of the new conditions facing Judaism. Through their penetrating studies in Jewish history they succeeded in focusing attention upon many aspects of Judaism, particularly its dynamic qualities, which they believed had been neglected or become fossilized in more recent times. No less than in the west, although in very different form, the exponents of enlightenment in Eastern Europe followed the dual tendencies of reform and increasing national consciousness.

The more liberal climate which prevailed in the first fifteen years following the accession of Czar Alexander II, and which allowed the Jews of Russia more economic freedom and wider educational opportunities, emboldened the advocates of enlightenment to press their views with greater vigor.

Following the lead set by the Russian literary critics of the "Positive" school during the sixties of the last century,[7] the younger Jewish *Maskilim* embarked upon a serious campaign for the amelioration of social conditions—but in this instance as applied to Jews. Their shafts were aimed primarily against the prevailing system of Jewish education and the economic pursuits favored by the Jews; at the same time they felt convinced that religious reform constituted a necessary step in the struggle for enlightenment and emancipation. Admittedly the reforms advocated seem negligible in the light of the radical changes introduced by the Reform movement in Germany. Nevertheless they aroused a wave of indignant opposition from the orthodox.

This opposition was neither new nor unexpected. Indeed, an intense antipathy on the part of the orthodox toward any attempt to spread enlightenment in any form had manifested itself in Russia for more than half a century previously, and the comparatively few exponents of enlightenment had frequently suffered ostracism and sometimes violent persecution. The orthodox regarded the new trends with the greatest suspicion, believing—and not without reason—that the spread of enlightenment without emancipation could lead only to conversion. Now, however, the situation was aggravated by the great increase in strength on the part of the enlighteners, both numerically in consequence of the new access to the high school and university and also—deriving from a conviction that the government was behind them—in morale. Their criticisms of the orthodox position became sharper and more outspoken and their demands for reform increasingly compelling. The orthodox, for their part, took up cudgels with avidity, hardening still further an attitude already rigid, and determined to defend their position to the last.

Although destined to continue in virulent form for at least another decade, the battle for religious reform reached its climax in Lithuania between the years 1869 and 1871. In great measure this proved to be a literary war, a veritable battle of the books, largely fought out in the pages of the Hebrew literary journals, the most influential media available to Hebrew writers for the propagation of their ideas at that time. Principally through the pages of *Ha-Meliṣ* and the less radical *Ha-Maggidh* the reformers, notably M. L. Lilienblum and Y. L. Gordon, hurled their broadsides against the orthodox citadels, while their opponents thundered back replies mainly via their own special journal, *Ha-Lebhanon*. The battle centering upon the question whether Judaism should be reformed to meet the demands of modern life was fought with virulence and passion, often degenerating into a series of scurrilous attacks, particularly on the part of the orthodox, against the writers of the opposing camp.[8]

The exponents of enlightenment did not, however, confine their attack to articles in the literary journals. They propagated their ideas in poems, in satirical dramas, and especially in the novel. For a period of some twenty years following the first skirmishes in this literary war, echoes of the struggle resound throughout the pages of the Hebrew novel. The issues had, indeed, already been raised in Abraham Mapu's *The Hypocrite*,[9] but Mapu's approach was cautious and restrained. During the period under review, 1868–88, the gloves are frequently removed enabling the novelists to hammer their opponents unmercifully. Almost all the major novels of this period are largely, if not primarily, social in content. Even the minor and very obscure novels, despite their frequently fantastic plots and unreal settings, scarcely ever lack a sense of social responsibility and lend their weight to the struggle against what their authors considered to be the abuses of their time.[10]

Most interesting, perhaps, of all these novels, insofar as it represents the most faithful portrayal of the battle at its height from the standpoint of the enlighteners, is R. A. Braudes' novel *Religion and Life*.[11] In an important preface to the second edition of this work Braudes is careful to point out that the first term in the title of his work, namely *Dath*, does not signify faith or religion in its ordinary sense, but in the special connotation of Judaism as codified in the *Šulḥan 'Arukh* (the last great codification of Jewish law to become generally accepted). The significance of thc title becomes immediately manifest. It was against what they considered to be the excessive stringencies of that code that the reformers had directed their stoutest shafts in the literary journals. Indeed, the author declares specifically that he has chosen the novel-form merely to make his chronicle of the events of 1869–71, when the struggle between "religion" and "life" engulfed the whole of Lithuanian Jewry, more palatable. Even more revealing is the author's preface to the third part of the novel, which was never completed. Here Braudes emphasizes that the purpose of literature is to increase the reader's awareness of life, and that he has couched his chronicle in novel-form so that the reader may be enabled to review the events the more dispassionately. He proceeds to the remark that whereas in the first two parts of the novel he has allowed the plot to take the lion's share of his work, in the third part he intends to lay the main emphasis on his depiction of the actual struggle, so that the reader is warned of the many diversions from the story to be expected. Braudes' own standpoint may be gauged from the fact that he modeled the hero of his story, Samuel, on M. L. Lilienblum, one of the principal protagonists in the struggle for reform.[12]

It is important to emphasize the fact that Braudes makes no criticism of religion as such. On the contrary, his hero Samuel is himself a strictly orthodox and observant Jew endowed, moreover, with a deep sense of loyalty to his people and an ardent wish to devote his entire energies to their cause. The attack is leveled solely against a too stringent and over rigid interpretation of rabbinical law, which the author believes does not accord with the dynamic principles of Judaism as they are reflected in the Talmud. For this reason the three issues which are selected to serve as examples in the course of the plot seem all the more peripheral to a religious controversy. But in each case the author is aiming at the alleviation of Jewish social misery, which stemmed primarily from the almost universal and crushing poverty of Jewish life in the Pale of Settlement, aggravated by the extraordinary increase in population throughout the course of the nineteenth century.

The first example[13] concerns the tendency of the local rabbi to take the negative view in cases where the ritual fitness of an animal slaughtered for consumption is subject to the slightest shadow of doubt. The story opens with a complaint that the rabbi has condemned three cows one after the other in a single day, even though the butcher argues that in his opinion, based on forty years of experience, the third is fit for consumption. As a result the whole village is left without food for the Sabbath, while the butcher sustains a ruinous loss. Next day in synagogue the butcher dramatically interrupts the service before the reading of the *Torah* to raise the point once again, and Samuel takes his side against the rabbi, denouncing the latter's tyranny. Samuel proves his point from the Talmud, while the rabbi supports his own case from the *Šulḥan ʿArukh.* Meanwhile the congregation is astounded to find that two such authoritative works can contradict each other! The rabbi, however, stands his ground, and accuses Samuel of heresy.[14]

The second example, too, is directed against the financial loss caused to the innocent victims of excessively rigid interpretation. A child dies in a house adjoining the courtyard of that occupied by Samuel's mother. As she and her neighbors have neglected to throw away all the water standing in their houses immediately after the death, all the food in their houses is pronounced unfit for consumption and, moreover, they are ordered to throw away all their cooking utensils and purchase new ones in their stead.[15] Once more Samuel attacks the decision on the basis of his own profound knowledge of the sources of Jewish law, and once more without success.

The third example is far more germane to the plot and revolves upon the question of the *Yabham.*[16] Rachel, one of the heroines of the story, has recently become a widow. Her father-in-law, Todros, had divorced his first wife under pressure from her relatives some thirty years previously, and left her pregnant. Since that time he has become so degenerate a drunkard that he cannot even remember the village in which his first wife lived. He is unaware whether she gave birth to a son or daughter, or whether the child is still alive. As the possibility exists, however, that the child is male and has survived, Rachel is refused permission to remarry until her late husband's hypothetical stepbrother has first waived his prior claim to her hand.[17] The unhappy plight of the unfortunate girl may well be imagined, and once more Samuel takes up the cause of the oppressed. It becomes obvious from these examples, however, that the type of reform envisaged in this novel constitutes anything but a radical attack on orthodox religion, but rather an attempt to purge it of what were considered excrescences quite out of line with its real spirit. In this respect it stands in marked contrast to the ideas propagated by the movement of Reform Judaism in Germany.

Braudes, indeed, devotes three chapters of his novel to an historical survey of the development of Judaism from the period of the Second Temple to his own times.[18] He is at pains to point out how the different factions of Jewry have constantly oppressed each other, with the object of demonstrating how such persecution only serves to strengthen the opposing party. After outlining first the struggles between the Pharisees and Sadducees and then the Rabbanites and Karaites, Braudes proceeds to trace the steady increase in the number of ritual laws formulated in the middle ages and the parallel growth of the Kabbalah, both of which developments, in his opinion, served to oppress the Jewish people. Admittedly only a certain proportion of the Jews had to bear the yoke of the Kabbalah, while rabbinic law weighed heavily upon the entire people. But whereas the latter embraced only the body, the Kabbalah dominated the mind, resulting in an even more rigorous servitude.

The real disaster for Israel, argues Braudes, occurred when rabbinic dialectic became united with Kabbalah to form the *Šulḥan ʿArukh*. The situation might well have been alleviated by the efforts of Manassah of Ilya on the one hand and Israel Baʿal Shem Tob on the other; but both were frustrated by the opposition of the Gaon Elijah of Vilna, who prevented Zalman of Ladi from uniting the two great divisions inside Jewry—the *Mithnaggedhim* and the *Ḥasidhim*. In Braudes' view the efforts of the Gaon of Vilna have been responsible for the increasing intransigence of the orthodox rabbis which he sees as leading to the total breakdown of Judaism. The rabbis, therefore, are the principal opponents of the men who desire to cleanse the religion of its accumulated dross.

The hero, Samuel, echoes Braudes' views. In the many serious discussions on Judaism, which form so important an element in this novel, Samuel argues—and the difference of approach from that of Mendelssohn is worthy of note—that Judaism in composed of both beliefs and ordinances. The Oral Law was primarily concerned with the latter, and much of it, in consequence, was dependent upon time, place, and circumstance. It was, therefore, in the nature of the Oral Law to modify the ordinances when the conditions of life so demanded. But with the destruction of the Second Temple the Oral Law came to an end. For the Mishnah and the Talmud represent not Oral Law but Written Law! The very act of writing it down deadened the spirit of the Oral Law. Hence the rabbis have sanctified the dead word and neglected the living inspiration of Judaism.[19] In answer to the objection that once any relaxations of rabbinic law are allowed the great majority of the Jews will proceed successively to abandon the law altogether, Samuel argues that such a view misjudges the character of the people. In Samuel's opinion the basis of reform must reside in a conformity between religion and life. The absence of that conformity is responsible for the fact that in the large cities religious transgression has become the rule.

After outlining the burdens accruing from the accumulated mass of ordinances relevant, for example, to the Passover, the Sabbath, and the

Dietary Laws, Samuel expressed the belief that the rabbis are empowered to alter even the rulings of the Talmud itself, let alone the later accretions, when the conditions of life demand it. His prime concern is that rabbinic severity is increasing the already dreadful poverty, and he cites the sufferings that followed the widespread famine in Lithuania in that very year as a typical example.[20] This latter scene, where the hero's feelings are expressed in almost lyric vein, represents in large measure the climax of the novel:[21]

> Do you know the land where poverty, hunger, want, and general distress prevail, which lies desolate because of the lack of initiative and depression of its inhabitants? ... Do you know the people who dwell there sunk in lethargy like a rotting corpse, weary of life, slumbering from birth to death in stupor and devoid of vision? People who never notice the sun even when it shines at its brightest, and shut their eyes to the moon and stars? Whose sons are savages, and whose daughters are like animals without proper education? Who tremble at the sound of a falling leaf, and are terrified of demons, spirits, ghosts, and anything else which cannot be seen or heard or comprehended? The only thing that does not frighten them is the burden of life itself, for they neither hesitate to take on the yoke of a wife and children, nor do they worry in the least about the problems of earning a livelihood or supporting a household—even though their ancestors were always homeless paupers, and they themselves are poverty-stricken, while their children will be equally oppressed and penniless. People upon whom the rabbis have placed an iron yoke, taking the last morsel of food from their mouths and hedging them about with laws and restrictions, prohibitions and regulations, decrees and customs beyond all bearing. The rabbis have so restricted every avenue of life, scarcely allowing the people to draw breath, that they have deadened their very spirit.

Nowhere in the Hebrew novels of this period is the case for religious reform argued with greater cogency and conviction.

A little over a decade following the publication of *Religion and Life* Braudes published a second novel, also concerned with religious attitudes, under the title *The Two Extremes*.[22] By 1888, however, the ferocity of the struggle between the exponents of orthodox and reform Judaism as depicted in the earlier novel had largely worn itself out. Both factions viewed with horror the wholesale desertions from Judaism and the cold indifference to tradition displayed by such large sections of the new generation which characterized much of Jewish life in Russia in the last quarter of the nineteenth century. *The Two Extremes*, which from the point of view of artistry is undoubtedly the most mature novel in Hebrew literature before the appearance of the works of Mendele, contains a very different message.

This novel,[23] which has something of the flavor of Goethe's *Die Wahlverwandtschaften*, depicts the strikingly different types of Jewish life obtaining in the great city of Odessa on the one hand, and a tiny Hasidic town symbolically named Sukkoth (Tabernacles) on the other. The plot revolves upon the remarkable effect which each of these two entirely different environments can bring to bear upon an individual who has grown up in the other. Jewish life in Odessa is portrayed as highly cultured and urbane, polished and sophisticated—but cold and empty.[24] Life in the small town, by contrast, is outwardly squalid and unprepossessing, with ignorance, bigotry, and blind fanaticism rampant; and yet it is so rooted in tradition and so faithful to its own standards, that once the ugly exterior is pierced a warm, loyal, and colorful society suddenly emerges.

Both environments furnish the novel with a hero, each of whom is accidentally brought into contact with the opposite milieu. In turn they succumb to the lure of a life which they have never known, and thereby provide the author with an opportunity to portray the virtues and vices of both worlds. Within the framework of his story Braudes castigates the emptiness of Jewish life in the large Russian metropolis, its rootlessness, indifference to tradition, and the frivolous habits of mind which it engenders. But while appreciating the warmth of Jewish family life in the small town, its piety, and the idyllic calm which pervades its sabbaths and festivals, Braudes is equally at pains to lay bare its darker undercurrents of fanatical obscurantism, debasing superstitions, and relentless persecution of all attempts in the direction of secular education. To Braudes the estranged exponent of enlightenment in the large city and the pious hypocrite in the small town are equally detestable. Indeed, the message unfolded in *The Two Extremes* is that religion and enlightenment must be combined in order to reach a middle way.[25] The best of both worlds must be carefully selected, and the unattractive and debased elements abandoned.

The *dénouement* of the plot is engineered by a *deus ex machina* in the shape of an old, long-lost grandfather from Vilna, who symbolizes in his own person a happy fusion of orthodox Judaism and secular enlightenment. This pleasing combination is presented to both heroes as a healthier subject for emulation than either of the two extremes which have captured their imagination hitherto. As the old man is, in addition, extraordinarily wealthy, not only is he able to solve the spiritual problems of his grandchildren—as both the heroes turn out to be—but he can also rescue them from their material dilemmas! But the issues are portrayed with far more conviction than the solution; and the reader is left with the impression that the remedy which Braudes offers may well succeed in individual cases, but is unlikely to meet with any widespread acceptance in the face of the forces of disintegration besetting Jewish life. The atmosphere even by that time was too heavily charged, while the pressures on the Jewish people, both external and internal, were too compelling for any counsel of moderation to win the day.

Braudes, of course, was neither the first nor the only novelist in this period to plead the middle way, although he does so with far greater skill than any of his contemporaries. Even such minor writers as J. I. Leinwand and B. I. Zobeizensky, whose very ephemeral novels are replete with all the worst forms of melodramatic device and cliché, and whose fate has been a complete and well-deserved oblivion, advocate this middle course in which traditional values are combined with enlightened views.[26] Zobeizensky, however, while opposed to any suggestion of irreligiosity, is also strongly in favor of reform. A young couple, for example, wishing to marry inside a synagogue, instead of in the courtyard as was customary in their town, encounter much malicious opposition to such "heresy." The author dismisses the gossipmongers as follows:[27]

> If someone of another religion, unaware of the customs and traditions of our people, had heard the remarks of these men, for whom it seemed an abomination for a marriage service to take place in a synagogue, he would surely think that the synagogue must be so holy to the Jews that even a wedding, a holy ceremony among all peoples, would be a sacrilege in the Jewish house of prayer. But we, who know how holy marriage is regarded by our people—ten times more so than in other faiths—and how secular our houses of prayer have become in the eyes of our fellow Jews, are well and truly astonished.

The prolific writer of popular Yiddish novels, N. M. Sheikewitz, one of whose very few Hebrew novels falls within the period under review, is no less careful to defend the more positive aspects of the traditional religious approach,[28] and is equally scathing with regard to religious bigotry and the infringements of religious practice.[29]

One striking exception to the general respect for enlightenment even at the expense of certain aspects of orthodoxy exhibited in these novels may be found in a work by A. S. Rabinowitz entitled *'Al ha-Pereq*.[30] Although in the course of time the negative results of the movement of enlightenment came to be more and more clearly recognized, and served as a target for the attack of many writers, especially P. Smolenskin, no other novel of this period adopts so constant and devastating an attitude in this respect.

'Al ha-Pereq is the story of a "Rake's Progress." But the rake, in this instance, is represented by a young man whose early traditional piety and naive sincerity are gradually corrupted by the forces of a pseudo-enlightenment, which lead him ultimately to ruin. The novel makes a powerful onslaught against the various evils accruing from the teachings of enlightenment, each of which the hero suffers in succession. At the same time his changing attitudes and behavior are constantly compared unfavorably with the orthodox traditional modes of thought he has abandoned. His rapid degeneration is emphasized by the steadfastness of the pious teacher, Judah, who answers the hero's argument that reform is necessary to bring religion into conformity with the demands of life by insisting that the real need is not for reform but rather for an increase in the knowledge of the *Torah*:[31]

> Just because the young seek leniency in small matters, should we grant it to them in large ones? Is that not what it amounts to? Just like when the Children of Israel asked of Rehoboam: Lighten our burden and we will serve you, but in

their hearts they really wished to remove the kingdom of the House of David. For Rehoboam had promised to make them golden calves whose worshipers can break the law and indulge in sin to their heart's content.

The climax of the story is represented by the views which Daniel, an idealist, utters from his sickbed. Daniel is aware of the excrescences which have attached themselves to Judaism, but he is even more conscious of the follies perpetrated in the name of enlightenment and argues that it is Judaism as an entity in which the real virtues are to be sought. A complete appreciation of the ethical values residing in *Torah*, however, can be acquired only from studying the sacred literature for its own sake and not with a view to earning a livelihood from it. Enlightenment, he admits, is important as a means of improving the economic conditions of the people and may even, perhaps, serve to purge the faith of certain tainted elements which have crept in. But it should never be regarded as a new ethical foundation for behavior and belief, for only an authority that stands above criticism can perform that function. Meanwhile he is convinced of the paramount importance of observing all the ordinances.[32] As for a solution to the steady deterioration of the Jewish material position, Daniel argues that neither religious nor esthetic theories can cope with a problem of such magnitude, and that he is in agreement with Peretz Smolenskin that only a return to the Land of Israel can provide a remedy.[33]

Prior to an examination of the view advanced by Smolenskin which, after reform, constitutes the second major attitude to Judaism presented in the novels of this period, one further position is worthy of note. Perhaps the most negative approach to traditional Judaism to be found in all these novels appears in S. J. Abramowitz's *Fathers and Sons*.[34] It is significant that this latter work ranks among the earliest of the novels chronologically. Although Abramowitz, too, on one occasion argues for the middle path as outlined above,[35] the main emphasis of his novel lies in a biting attack upon what he considered to be the darker sides of the traditional Jewish life of his time, namely its obscurantism, excessive stringency, hypocritical fanaticism, and harsh bigotry. Although a common feature in almost all these novels, Abramowitz's satire against Hasidism is particularly virulent.[36] This attitude is all the more surprising because his later writings, published under the pseudonym of Mendele Mokher Sepharim, are characterized by a depth of understanding of Jewish life and an intense sympathy toward its sorrows rarely equaled in Hebrew literature of that time. It was Mendele who first perceived in its fullest sense that the root of Israel's problems in the Pale of Settlement lay in the grinding poverty of the vast majority of the population. It was Mendele, too, who finally renounced all factionalism to demonstrate the inner light of Judaism lurking beneath the repellent exterior it had assumed.[37] In *Fathers and Sons*, however, there are few traces of this later understanding. Apart from a rather stereotyped appreciation of the national past,[38] the only passage of real interest in this respect is that in which the author discourses on the strange riddle of Israel's transformation from weekday shabbiness to a sudden splendor on sabbaths and festivals.[39]

The most important novelist of these years, however, is Peretz Smolenskin, whose six novels span sixteen[40] of the twenty years under consideration. One of the keenest thinkers of his time, Smolenskin kept his finger closely on the pulse of Jewish life, shrewdly basing his conclusions on the lessons of experience. It is not surprising, therefore, that his writings present a variety of views ranging over the whole field of Judaism. Smolenskin had himself passed through all the stages of Jewish intellectual development current in his time. Following the first naive adherence to the Berlin enlightenment as the panacea for all Jewish misfortunes, he experienced first a feeling of disillusionment and then a profound conviction of the utter bankruptcy of all such views before finally reaching the conclusion that only a revival of Jewish nationalism could ensure the continuance of Judaism. The reflections of these different attitudes are scattered throughout his novels and his essays. Both the major factions within orthodox Jewry—the *Mithnaggedhim* and the *Ḥasidhim*—are subjected to a searching scrutiny,[41] and while the latter are made to serve as the prime target for his biting satire, neither party escapes the lash of his invective. All the abuses of Jewish life already referred to are time and again subjected to a withering criticism. Indeed, so dark are the colors painted by Smolenskin that on more than one occasion even he, himself, seems shocked by his own virulence, and gives the reader to understand that the picture is after all not quite so black as it might appear from his descriptions:[42]

> When I considered all this [the sins and treachery of the world] I came to the conclusion that even the sinners among my people may be reckoned as righteous men and their wrongdoing as inconsequential as cobwebs and as foam on water in comparison with the sins of others—when I reviewed all this I came to understand that in my mind I had exaggerated the faults of my own people, for they are to be found among the individuals of every nation.

But at the same time he is no less aware of the positive values of traditional Judaism and its institutions, and frequently portrays its pious and even saintly aspects—the charm of its sabbaths, the significance of its festivals, its profound respect for traditional scholarship, and the importance of its spiritual and ethical truths.[43] If the novels contain numerous examples of wicked hypocrites masquerading beneath the guise of pious orthodoxy, they are no less replete with the renegade disciples of a false enlightenment, whom Smolenskin depicts with an even more withering contempt.

Acutely conscious of the negative results accruing from an uncritical abandonment of Judaism in favor of an only half-digested secularism, Smolenskin turns savagely on the movement whose ideals had formerly been his own. Particularly in the fourth part of his long autobiographical novel

The Wanderer in the Paths of Life, which contains some of the author's most serious views, Smolenskin launches a powerful attack upon the Berlin type of enlightenment and especially its founder Moses Mendelssohn.[44] From many passages in Smolenskin's writing it becomes clear that he held Mendelssohn responsible for having stripped Judaism of its national elements, hence paving the way for the Jews of Germany to regard themselves as "Germans of the Mosaic Persuasion"—and similarly in the other lands whither Mendelssohn's ideas had spread.[45]

To Smolenskin the national and social aspects of Judaism were inextricably bound up with the religious element. There could be no separation of Judaism from the Jews as a people. By focusing attention on the individual Jew the movement of enlightenment might well have succeeded in improving the conditions of certain individual Jews, but it had done nothing to help the Jewish people as a whole.[46] The latter could be aided only by a revival of the national consciousness, to foster a spirit of integration with self-preservation as the goal.[47] But it was useless, Smolenskin argued, to look to the enlightened Jews of Western Europe for help in this direction. They had become too cold and indifferent, closing their eyes to the fact that Jews are everywhere regarded as strangers. Moreover, conditions in Eastern Europe were entirely different, and made nonsense of the western ideas of enlightenment:[48]

> Alas, my heart is moved and fearful when I see the plight of my brethren, for whom there is no redeemer, no one to take pity on them or bring them succor. I know for certain that our brothers in other lands have the power to help them, if only they wanted to, if only they wished to save them and not fob them off with *Haskalah*. But why should I assail your ear and make you sad when there is naught you can avail? And should I entreat my brethren who have the power, I know from the start that no one will listen to me; for all they will do is hand out *Haskalah* in generous measure, *Haskalah* for those who are robbed and oppressed in broad daylight in this land, the land of Roumania.

Israel, Smolenskin insists, is primarily a people of the spirit,[49] and that single factor is the source of its eternity. That, too, is the reason why both the people and the language are holy. The real essence of Judaism lies in its conception of the unity and incorporeality of God. Hence religious reforms are conceivable in the practical sphere, and indeed there is a clear need to reform the power of the rabbis.[50] The beliefs, however, must remain immutable. In this way Smolenskin's attitude to Judaism embraces the concepts of both practical reform and ardent nationalism, thus forming a striking contrast to Moses Mendelssohn's approach.

One further aspect of these novels is worthy of note. Quite apart from the religious attitudes they reflect, they constitute a veritable treasure-house of information relative to the whole field of religious practice in the period under review.[51] On the one hand they provide much evidence concerning the three major divisions inside Jewry in the nineteenth century—the *Mithnaggedhim*, the *Ḥasidhim*, and the exponents of enlightenment, the *Maskilim*—and the mental climate of their respective milieus. Adequate allowance, however, must be made for the deliberate exaggeration and caricature natural to tendentious literature. On the other hand they furnish a wealth of illuminating detail about the physical and material channels of religious life.

The reader is provided with intimate glimpses into the lives of choirboys, beadles, cantors, and rabbis, their functions and conditions of work, their stratagems and devices, as well as their significance in the overall framework of society. Again, he is taken behind the scenes of the three main institutions of Jewish spiritual life, the Synagogue, the *Ḥedher*, and the *Yešibhah*, and presented with an intimate and penetrating account of their strengths and weaknesses. He is led through the labyrinths of religious communal life, and shown the intricacies of administration, the means of enforcing discipline, the pattern of intrigue, and the deep significance of the religious calendar. And finally he is introduced to a bewildering variety of superstition and folklore which throws much light upon the religious psychology of the time. These novels, in fact, for all their weaknesses, their literary inadequacies, and didactic pedantries, yield considerable information concerning one of the most storm-tossed and strife-ridden periods of Jewish life, and one which has proved decisive for subsequent Jewish history.

6

A Portrait of Hasidism

THE AIM of this chapter is to present a picture of Hasidism as it is portrayed in the Hebrew novel over a period of twenty years, from 1868 to 1888. In no sense does it purport to be a scientific study of Hasidism, but represents rather an attempt to describe the attitude adopted by Hebrew novelists toward that movement in the second half of the nineteenth century.[1] The significance of the approach—quite apart from the important light it sheds upon the intellectual and emotional formation of the novelists themselves—lies in the sobering effect of such a portrayal of Hasidism, especially when viewed against the highly idealized picture presented by later writers.[2] Indeed, in many respects it represents an extreme view in the opposite direction, and a markedly tendentious note is rarely lacking.

The Hebrew novel of this period is social in character, and largely written with the object of reform. In many of the novels this aim is primary, sometimes avowedly so;[3] in others it is incidental, but nowhere is it entirely absent. The objects of reform, the methods for their achievement, and the manner of propagating such ideas vary greatly from one author to the next, and sometimes even within different novels by the same author. But all the novels are written from the standpoint of the *Haskalah*, even though that term covers a wide range of varying points of view, some of which themselves become a target for the novelists' fire. In general, however, these works are characterized by a strong social conscience, a deep conviction that literature should play a specific role in society, and a serious awareness of the problems facing a disintegrating Jewish life. Opinions differ among the authors, however, as to the manner in which that disintegration should be combated, and it is doubtful whether the full magnitude of the complex of forces at work was properly understood.

Nevertheless in one respect all the *Maskilim* concur. Without exception, they were convinced of the necessity for an untrammeled approach to secular study in order to come to grips with the problems of modern life. The consequences of that conviction appeared in a bitter conflict, waged between the *Maskilim* on the one hand, and the two major divisions inside Jewry, the *Mithnaggedhim* and the *Ḥasidhim*, on the other. Both these latter factions, long at war with each other, viewed the movement of *Haskalah* with hostility and suspicion, rightly regarding the new doctrine as an inherent threat to their own position. The *Maskilim*, for their part, took up the cudgels with avidity, launching a powerful attack upon what they regarded as the narrowness, bigotry, and superstition of their opponents, denouncing obscurantism in all its forms, and losing no opportunity of pouring ridicule upon attempts to block the course of enlightenment.

The portrait of Hasidism in these novels, therefore, frequently assumes the proportions of a caricature, and must be reduced to a more correct perspective in order to perceive the element of truth which such caricatures may contain. This is particularly the case in the novels of P. Smolenskin, whose satire and ridicule against the *Ḥasidhim* is often of a most virulent kind, reinforced by his own intimate and personal knowledge of his victims.[4] Elsewhere, and particularly in the writings of R. A. Braudes, a much more sympathetic picture is painted, revealing the positive aspects of Hasidic life, whose values are frequently described as preferable to those resulting from the ideas of *Haskalah*. But even Braudes is at pains to denounce the darker sides of the Hasidic milieu.

More important, however, in this present context are those passages in which the novelists seriously outline their own conception of the philosophy and mental outlook of the *Ḥasidhim*. From such scattered references, it is possible to gauge the attitudes of some of the keenest observers of East European Jewry in the latter half of the nineteenth century toward the origins and development of Hasidism, stripped of all romantic idealization. Again the novelist can be relied upon to furnish many incidental details and characteristics of environment, sometimes overlooked even in serious studies of a period. In this respect they frequently provide enlightening glimpses into contemporary social history.

In the fourth part of his long novel *The Wanderer in the Paths of Life*, which contains some of the author's most serious views, Smolenskin gives the following account of Hasidism:[5]

> Ignorance of the Torah and the Talmud gave rise to the Hasidic faction among our people; many ignorant and unlettered men, incapable of studying the Torah, but desirous of acquiring honor, invented a single term to compensate for their shortcomings. This term is "the negation of reality,"[6] and the first step of the *Ḥasidh* is to negate all reality and deny its existence, and if all reality is nonexistent, he has no need of it, and therefore whatever he does not possess is no loss. When a *Ḥasidh* sees a rich, honorable, wise, and educated man, he stifles his feeling of awe by saying that he will negate him in his mind, and having once done so he no longer respects him, but rather disdains him and regards himself superior. In my youth I heard countless instances of this kind from lowly *Ḥasidhim*, and when I asked one of them: "Why do you act like that, seeing that the honorable Mr. So-and-so will not thank you for it?" he replied: "Mr. So-and-so? What value has he? I will negate him in my mind!" and this term has done away with many things such as knowledge, ethics, law, good

> manners, work, and any effort of which they are incapable, for what use are all such things to them, when they can destroy them with a single term? A man works hard, and tries to rise out of competition with his neighbor, but as a *Ḥasidh* can lower a man with a mere term, why bother to make the effort to rise?[7]

Earlier in the story, Smolenskin describes the rise of Hasidism as a reaction to excessive rabbinical stringency, representing its founder and adherents in the following terms:[8]

> ... And what did this redeemer demand of them? Only a merry heart, only happiness and mirth, only to remove the burden from their shoulders: to lower the dignity of the Torah and its scholars, so that in place of fasts there should be festivals, instead of mourning—gaiety, instead of learning—prayer; and even this prayer was no obstacle to a man wanting to work or go on a journey, for God did not demand prayer at fixed times, but only in exaltation of spirit and with joyful soul, when the heart was stirred with love for God—only then did they turn their thoughts to the Lord; but even when the spirit slumbered and forgot its Creator for days on end, even then the sinner had no need to fear the wrath of God, for the *Ṣaddiq* would save him, acting as an intermediary between him and God, and removing all guilt ... Moreover, he (the redeemer) gave them a new law, a hidden law, which not every man could understand or comprehend. Only the remnants of the chosen spirits could follow its holy paths. And it was obeyed by all who had previously been downtrodden by the community, and denied the name of scholar, but who now could raise their heads, denigrate the old law and its sages, and look down scornfully and contemptuously on all who hid themselves away like corpses in the houses of study listening to dead words, imagining that they themselves were following the living and not the dead. Their eyes were fixed upon their leader to whom alone the Law had been vouchsafed exclusively; and their ears were intent upon marvelous tales of wonder and innumerable miracles, for his word had power of life and death, it could make the womb fruitful or throw his enemies into confusion; and in their joy and exultation over the redemption and their change of fortune, they became a sect.[9]

In a further passage from the same story, Smolenskin expresses his views with equal forthrightness:

> The *Ḥasidhim* believe in their holy men and despise all wisdom and science, they even scorn the Holy Scriptures, and regard the Talmud as profane, for these works, they say, cannot elevate the soul to the realms of the Creator. They regard only the *Zohar* and the writings of the Kabbalists as holy; and those who study them, even if they do not understand them at all, will deserve to ascend to the uppermost heavens beneath the throne of glory. But even their study of these works is limited, for deeds are regarded as being more important than learning. And so they stuff themselves with food and rejoice the livelong day, making themselves drunk in the prayer-house, tippling at home, and even resorting to the bottle on fast-days, at the slightest excuse for a festivity. They possess only one good quality, namely the help they give each other.[10] If a man

> belongs to their circle, they will shield him and support him in bad times without inquiring too deeply into his behavior. Even if he sins against the law, transgresses against Israel's statutes, or breaks a contract, none of these things will be held against him, providing only that he maintains his faith in the holy man, and remains faithful to his fellow-*Ḥasidhim.* There are many among them who have committed all sorts of crimes both in secret and even openly, and yet occupy an honorable place because they are attached to the Hasidic sect. And how do they win respect in the eyes of their fellows? By violent persecution of all who hold different opinions to show that they are real *Ḥasidhim.*[11]

In another novel, Smolenskin sums up his opinion of the movement within a single, short sentence: "... and like the *Ḥasidhim* in our own land, they believe that by eating, drinking, and doing anything from which they derive enjoyment, they are giving pleasure to their Creator, and regard it as righteousness ..."[12]

A similar view is confirmed by Sirkis, who gives the following description of the sect:

> The new Kabbalah, or Hasidism, taught him to regard the *Ṣaddiq* as God. To know the *Ṣaddiq* ... was equivalent to possessing divine knowledge and seeing divine visions ... It was his practice to inform the *Ḥasidhim* of the great holiness of the *Ṣaddiq*, and the simple folk who had never seen the *Ṣaddiq*, nor understood what he, Kemuel, was saying, had only to lavish wine and spirits on the *Ḥasidhim*, that they might sit with him and listen to his teaching, in order themselves to ascend to the highest rungs of the ladder leading to heaven, and make sure of their portion in Paradise ...[13]

It is hardly surprising, therefore, that time and time again the novelists ridicule the superstitious framework, the conglomeration of base beliefs and semi-magical practices which they regarded as essential features of the sect, and which presented a blank wall to their own efforts to spread enlightenment. At the same time they portray a no less superstitious attitude prevalent among the *Mithnaggedhim*, and even pervading that sanctum of study, the *Yešibhah.*[14] The difference, however, lies in the fact that whereas among the *Mithnaggedhim* such beliefs are mere excrescences, for the *Ḥasidhim* they are represented as an integral and essential element of religious expression. The novels contain many examples of Hasidic tales of miracles and wonders, whose purpose Abramowitz satirizes delightfully by describing one of his characters as so skilled a story-teller that he would "lull his listeners into a pleasant mood of idleness."[15]

The portrait of the moral and ethical standards prevailing among the *Ḥasidhim* according to Smolenskin can only be described as ghastly. Lying, thieving, bribery, debauchery, and perjury are common features of their behavior. Sometimes he uses their unscrupulousness as a motivating factor in his plots, particularly when describing the evils which his *Ḥasidhim* are only too ready to perpetrate, in order to persecute innocent victims whose only crime consists of a refusal to subscribe to their beliefs.[16] A respectable proportion of his characters are consequently arrested on false charges of almost every conceivable crime at the instigation of villainous *Ḥasidhim*. Elsewhere, the author attacks their sense of values by direct description of their milieu, so that their behavior even toward one another is outlined in a most unfavorable light:

> The time for the afternoon prayer had already arrived, but it had not yet occurred to anyone to pray, even though crowds continued to stream inside until the house was packed to full capacity. As night fell the old man, who had been reading the book of the *Zohar*, approached the platform ... but he had barely uttered the word *'Ašrei* when a youth of about twenty came up to him saying: "Let me lead the prayers today." The old man refused, whereupon the youth gripped him by his coat-tails and dragged him away, simultaneously mocking him loudly with the words: "Get away you naughty boy!" I was astounded at such impertinence, that a youth should lay hands on an old man and call him "Naughty boy;" and I fully expected that all the congregation would fall on him and tear him to pieces, but I was mistaken. The old man struggled with him, refusing to yield his place, while the youth continued to drag him away, and the bystanders roared with laughter ...[17]

Subsequently, an impromptu auction is used to decide who shall lead the prayers, the honor falling to a bidder, symbolically named "Šikri,"[18] for three measures of wine and three roast ducks! Šikri, however, allows the old man to lead the prayers in his place, and the following scene ensues:

> After praying silently for a time, the old man raised his voice, but before he had managed to say "Blessed art Thou ..." Šikri hastened toward him and pulled him away, crying: "Get out of the way, vermin! I only let you take my place for the silent prayer, and now I shall lead the prayers because I paid for them." All the bystanders shouted with delight as though they had heard the wisdom of Solomon, only one of them venturing to suggest that it was unseemly to make sport at the time of prayer.
>
> "Punish him," they shouted in chorus, "give him ten strokes with a boot or let him give us a measure of wine, for he has spoken like a *Mithnaggedh* ..."

It is not strange, therefore, that Smolenskin later permits himself the remark: "But brazen insolence is one of the virtues in which the *Ḥasidhim* pride themselves ..."[19] More surprising, however, is the fact that Braudes, who by and large paints a very sympathetic picture of many of the aspects of Hasidic life in his novel *The Two Extremes*, stresses on several occasions the strange mixture of extreme piety and indifference characteristic of the *Ḥasidhim*.[20]

On numerous occasions the novels present glimpses into the general environment of Hasidic society, depicting the self-contained, inbred, heavily charged atmosphere of an *imperium in imperio*, bitterly hostile to the encroachment of all external influences, jealously watchful of a rigorous conformity to its own patterns of behavior, and subject to all kinds of peculiar characteristics. In the novel by Braudes mentioned above, much of the action takes place in a small town in Volhynia near the Galician border populated by *Ḥasidhim*, which symbolically bears the name Sukkoth (tabernacles) to signify a certain idyllic quality of peace and quiet which reigns there in contrast to the noise and bustle of life in Odessa. The author is at pains to describe the unprepossessing exterior of the town, which wallows in dirt, disorder, and filth, and is characterized by the complete disregard of its inhabitants for external appearances. The values of that society are thrown into relief by a description of the interests of Jacob Hetzron, which are apparently quite uncharacteristic and incur the suspicion of his fellow-*Ḥasidhim*. Jacob is portrayed as being unusual by virtue of the fact that even in his youth he preferred to keep himself clean and tidy, and to see that his clothes were neat, his boots polished, and his hair combed properly, as well as by his early interest in the beauties of nature. After his marriage, his deviations express themselves in the attention he pays to his garden, his love of flowers, and his efforts to decorate his house in accordance with his own esthetic tastes![21]

The extreme reluctance of the *Ḥasidhim* to run the risk of contamination by contact with environments other than their own is reflected in the author's observations when Jacob has to travel to Odessa for business purposes. "Do not, reader, regard such a journey lightly," Braudes remarks, "a journey undertaken by a *Ḥasidh* in the province of Volhynia to the town Odessa." Later he continues: "Formerly in Israel no *Ḥasidh* would have even dared contemplate such a journey,"[22] although he proceeds to temper his remark with the information that such visits have recently become more frequent. They are, however, still regarded with suspicion, and Jacob is careful to apply to his *Rebbe* for special permission to adopt "short clothes" for the journey, and to allow the hair between his *pe'oth* to grow, so as not to arouse undue comment in the great city.[23] The unworldliness of so many of the *Ḥasidhim* is exemplified by the use of the term *Ḥasidh Šoṭeh*,[24] implying a complete unfamiliarity with the practical affairs of day-to-day life.

This attitude of indifference to the practical world reaches a climax of sheer irresponsibility in the writings of Smolenskin, although it is partly explained as a consequence of the general practice of marriage at a very early age. Having decided to make a pilgrimage to see a *Ṣaddiq*'s court for himself, the hero, Josef, is joined by a young *Ḥasidh* who tells him that, although only eighteen, he has already been married for three years and has two children. When Josef replies that he is still single at seventeen, the young *Ḥasidh* refuses to believe him, arguing that Josef looks twenty, but that single men always pretend to be younger as an excuse for not being married. When Josef asks how he can leave his wife and children for so long a time without support, the *Ḥasidh* replies:

> "You must be joking! Does she depend on me? Was I born for work? I came forth from my mother's womb to serve the Lord."

Josef's innocent inquiry concerning the source of their livelihood is treated with derision:

> "Where from? Is my mother-in-law paralyzed that I should have to earn a living? Until the day the worms take up residence in her corpse, she will go on working and supplying our needs."

When Josef later asks what he will do if she dies, he replies blandly that he will divorce his wife, who is already making herself obnoxious by suggesting that he ought to look for some pupils to earn money!

Josef proceeds to compromise his position by asking how his companion will manage at the *Ṣaddiq*'s court, and is told that no real *Ḥasidh* would ever dream of asking such a question:

> "Everyone knows that all who seek shelter with the *Ṣaddiq* are provided for, so that they can serve God, devote their whole time to the *Ṣaddiq*'s teaching, and recount his wonders for the edification of their souls; for the commandment to relate the wonders of the *Ṣaddiqim* is greater than all the commandments specified in the Law, and is even greater than the commandment to read the *Zohar*."[25]

Even more telling, perhaps, is the scene which confronts Josef on arriving at a Hasidic house of prayer, which also serves to provide accommodation for the guests:

> I was, as yet, still unacquainted with the *Ḥasidhim* in their house of prayer ... and so this town afforded me the opportunity of witnessing a sight I had never imagined. The house of prayer was full of tobacco smoke ascending from the pipes which were never out of their mouths for a moment. The pipe is sacred to the *Ḥasidhim*, for as the smoke ascends, the soul soars upwards and induces the right frame of mind for divine contemplation.[26] Some of those present were lying on the benches, clutching their ankles and shouting happily, others sat leaning their heads on their palms, resting on the tables, chatting away complacently, while others walked up and down shouting and singing, so that the house of prayer resembled a peasants' inn or a public bath. No one was looking at a book except for two very old men who sat at different tables each with a book in front of him. One was reading psalms aloud, quite obviously without understanding what he was reciting, in spite of the constant interruption from the youths nearby, who would snatch his hat off, lift the bench he was sitting on, or remove his table, laughing and mocking at his curses. The other was reading the *Zohar* but silently, and the youths left him unmolested.

When Josef, who is used to the devotion to books of the *Mithnaggedhim*, examines the bookcase he is astounded:

> The bookcase in the house of prayer contained five or six copies of the Talmud, worn out with age and hard usage, for they served as ammunition in the battles waged there by the boys. After the supplies of handkerchiefs, caps, and clothes,

which they hurled at one another's heads, had been exhausted, they would resort to the books as weapons. Apart from that, there were three or four books of the *Zohar*, and all the rest were books of Kabbalah and Hasidism. Taking a Talmud, I sat down at a table, but immediately I heard a voice shouting behind me: "*Mithnaggedh*!"—I had not realized that by taking a book in my hand, I had let them know at once that I was unfamiliar with the *Ḥasidhim* . . ."[27]

Open hostility to learning and study—apart from their own esoteric works—but particularly in the case of all forms of secular study, is portrayed as a characteristic feature of the Hasidic milieu.[28] Not only are the *Ḥasidhim* constantly described as remaining deliberately ignorant of the language of the country in which they live—to such an extent that one of Smolenskin's characters is made to remark: "This is the first time I have ever seen a man dressed in Hasidic garb speaking the language of the country . . ."[29]—but such a knowledge is even regarded as shameful except in the case of men whose business necessarily brings them into contact with gentiles.[30] It is scarcely necessary to add that the mere mention of *Haskalah* is anathema, and anyone in the slightest suspected of enlightened views is dismissed with the one word *'Apiqores* (heretic), a term of abuse which occurs more than two hundred times within the novels.[31]

As a consequence, the novelists are at pains to satirize and castigate a system of education which they consider hopelessly inadequate, and one of the most powerful causes of Israel's sorry plight. Jacob Hetzron's friend Yurab, for example, attacks a concept of education which so studiously avoids the mention of such subjects as history, geography, science, and literature—considered fundamental by the exponents of *Haskalah*—that Jacob can ask the naive but revealing question: "What is literature?"[32] He is correspondingly surprised to find that his Hasidic friend displays so marked an esthetic appreciation of beauty.[33] Again, Benjamin confesses that his own education consisted almost entirely in hearing over and over again a succession of tales relating the marvels and wonders performed by the *Ṣaddiqim*.[34] One interesting sidelight is the revelation that in spite of the well-known devotion of the *Ḥasidhim* to singing, the only instrument known in Sukkoth is the violin, which, moreover, must in no circumstances be played from a written score, but solely by ear![35]

On the other hand, Braudes portrays one incident relating to the education of the very young with such sympathy that it deserves to be quoted in full. He describes the custom, on the Feast of Weeks, of allowing the youngest child in the family to demonstrate what he has learned. Before an assembly of guests a form of catechism is arranged with the young child of five standing on the table, and his questioner, another child, standing on a chair. The guests all take their watches and chains of gold and silver and pin them on the young examinee's clothes, presumably in encouragement. The procedure is as follows:

"Why have you been stood on the table?" asked the questioner.

"Because I have begun to learn *Ḥumaš*," the expositor replied.

"What is *Ḥumaš*?"

"*Ḥumaš* is the perfect Law of God which our God gave us at the hand of his servant Moses."

"And how does it concern you?"

"I am an Israelite commanded to do, to keep, and to perform everything written in it, and so I learn it to know what we have to do, and what commandments we have to keep and to perform."

"And what have you learned in this *Ḥumaš*?"

"The book *Wa-Yiqra'* [Leviticus]."

"What is *Wa-Yiqra'*, Jew or gentile?"

The audience smiled at the question.

"*Wa-Yiqra'* is not the name of a man," the young expositor answered reprovingly, "*Wa-Yiqra'* is a word."

"And what does it mean?"

The child translated the word into Judaeo-German.

"Who called?"

"The Lord God of Israel."

"To whom did he call?"

"To Moses."

"Who was Moses?"

"The greatest of all the Prophets."

"And what did God want with this Prophet?"

"To tell him his Law and his commandments."

"And what is the commandment written in the book *Wa-Yiqra'*?"

"In the book *Wa-Yiqra'* are written the laws of sacrifice."

"And why did you start by learning those laws?"

"To show that a Jew is commanded to sacrifice himself for his faith and his God."

"And what else can you tell me about *Wa-Yiqra'*?"

"The letter *'aleph* in the word *Wa-Yiqra'* is smaller than all the letters."

"And why?"

"To tell us that the Law can only be mastered by one who approaches it humbly; and whoever prides himself on his learning does not understand its message ... Moses, our teacher, was the greatest of the Prophets, yet the humblest of men, and from him everyone can learn not to boast of his learning over his friends."

"And why is the letter *'aleph* small, and no other letter?"

"Because *'aleph* has the meaning *lamadh*."[36]

"And why do you take such pride in this exposition?"

"God forbid that I should take pride in it."

"Then why are you standing on the table?"

"As you remind me of it, I shall get down."[37]

The mother's pride in her young son's achievement may well be imagined. But elsewhere, the female of the species is described in less flattering terms. On many occasions, the Hasidic women are portrayed as even more fanatical, bigoted, and superstitious than their male counterparts, and frequently they perform the task of preserving these characteristics from the slightest suspicion of contamination![38] The virulence of their opposition to any form of heretical enlightenment is emphasized by the frequently cited belief that such unforgivable crimes as the reading of profane literature are responsible for the deaths of innocent children![39] Conversely, their unbounded respect and reverence for the *Ṣaddiq* is even greater than that of their husbands, for they all aspire to bear a child who will himself turn out to be a holy man.[40] The men for their part entertain no doubts as to the place of woman in their society:

"Tamar," writes Braudes, "was born in Sukkoth, a town full of God-fearing *Ḥasidhim*, all of whom were quite decided that the daughters of the poor required no knowledge beyond that of household tasks, while the daughters of the rich should stay at home, and not let themselves be seen ..."[41] In this connection, it is interesting to learn that the Hasidic women are ashamed to read even such books as were considered fit for their perusal, for example *Ṣe'ena u-Re'ena*, in the presence of their menfolk.[42]

From time to time, the novels afford interesting examples of certain characteristics and peculiarities attributed by the writers to the sect. Unflatteringly, as usual, Smolenskin gives the following account of the typical *Ḥasidh*:

> A lively man, who banishes all the cares and worries of life from his head, and enjoys himself without a thought for the future leaving the morrow to look after itself; he will revel and sing, and wherever there is a celebration or a glass of wine, he is sure to be there, and you will see him intent on the present, on what exists now, on life! But you will not find him leading the life of a sensible man, but rather that of a madman, without rhyme or reason. His feelings will make him dance like a goat, and a glass of wine will start him singing as though man were never born to toil ...[43]

This addiction to the bottle is portrayed as one of the most characteristic features of the *Ḥasidh*, sometimes on an orgiastic scale,[44] but usually in such more modest terms as: "If you belonged to the *Ḥasidhim*, I would say you had been at the inn, and that wine had stirred up the evil spirit in you."[45] Or again: "We *Ḥasidhim* never do anything, and do not even discuss our affairs, unless there is first a bottle of wine on the table."[46] This feature is rivaled only by the repeated emphasis on the unbounded faith of the *Ḥasidhim* in the powers of their *Ṣaddiqim*. One illuminating example among many occurs in a passage from *Pride and Fall*, which represents a striking parallel with the scene mentioned above in *The Wanderer in the Paths of Life*, in which Josef makes a pilgrimage to the *Ṣaddiq*'s court accompanied by a young *Ḥasidh*. In an almost identical situation the hero, journeying to the court of the same *Ṣaddiq*, asks his Hasidic companion in all innocence: "According to what you say, does not the *Ṣaddiq* know everything that happens in the land, and can he not perform whatever he wishes?" The phrase "According to what you say" riles the *Ḥasidh* almost beyond endurance, and when the hero tries to expiate his crime by explaining that he has only asked the question because he has never actually seen such things with his own eyes, he receives the withering reply: "You have never seen them with your own eyes? And do you only believe what you have seen with your own eyes? That is a sign that your soul is not worthy to be a *Ḥasidh*, for you have no faith in the *Ṣaddiqim*, and you will never attain it . . ."[47]

This scene also supplies the information that it was considered a great merit to make the pilgrimage to a *Ṣaddiq* on foot, in spite of the long distances often involved in such journeys.[48] Elsewhere such miscellaneous details are provided as, for instance, that *Ḥasidhim* are averse to listening to itinerant preachers;[49] or that they do not thank a person for rendering them a service, lest the divine reward for that service be thereby reduced;[50] or that the title *Ba'al Hassaghah* bestowed upon a person with the power to penetrate the holy realms is very highly considered by the *Ḥasidhim*;[51] or that whenever a request is written to the *Ṣaddiq*, the writer signs himself as so-and-so, the son of such-and-such a *woman*.[52]

The novels also contain the following interesting items. It is maintained that Hasidic communities do not choose their rabbis, but accept uncritically whatever suggestion the *Ṣaddiq* makes for such an appointment.[53] Mention is made of a bereaved daughter reciting the memorial prayer over her dead parents.[54] Again, the phrase "a descendant of the *'Or Ḥadhaš*" bears a footnote that in Lithuania and Poland saintly authors are referred to by the names of their books.[55] The same source mentions a Hasidic prayer to make the suppliant attractive in the eyes of others.[56] Elsewhere, it is asserted, in a footnote, that the gentile peasants refer to the *Ḥasidhim* as "the Jews who roar in prayer,"[57] while the same novel describes a betrothal at which the guests divide, the men occupying one room, while the women congregate in another.[58] Most interesting, however, is the detailed description of the method of compiling the note of request (*Pithqah*) submitted by a *Ḥasidh* to his *Ṣaddiq* together with an offering (*Keseph ha-Pidhyon*).[59] The same source also explains the eagerness of a *Ṣaddiq* for German Jewish followers.[60] Of more significance, perhaps, are the remarks on the differences between the *Ḥasidhim* of Russia and Galicia,[61] and in particular the tendency of the latter to spoil their children,[62] while Braudes shrewdly analyzes the reasons why Hasidism had proved far less successful in Lithuania than in Volhynia, Bessarabia, and the Ukraine.[63]

A further point of constant emphasis is the bitter hostility raging between the *Ḥasidhim* and the *Mithnaggedhim*, which Smolenskin regards as one of the most tragic features in Jewish life.[64] His portrayal of the evils arising from both factions is equally unflattering, and he maintains an overall attitude of "a plague on both your houses." But on more than one occasion he gives the *Ḥasidhim* credit at any rate for their loyalty to each other, and for concerted action, which usually enables them to get the upper hand.[65] So bitter is their mutual antipathy that *Mithnaggedhim* will not eat together with *Ḥasidhim*, nor give them their daughters in marriage. Indeed, to desert to the opposing camp is considered the equivalent of leaving Judaism altogether.[66] The *Ḥasidhim*, in particular, are represented as very conscious of descent in this respect. Although willing to absorb *Mithnaggedhim* who sincerely desire to join their sect, there remains the telling proviso: "There is no comparison between a *Ḥasidh* the son of a *Ḥasidh*, and a *Ḥasidh* the son of a *Mithnaggedh*."[67] Only on one occasion are both factions represented as sinking their differences in the face of a common crisis, and even there, in a satirical context: "That day *Mithnaggedhim* and *Ḥasidhim* alike forgot their perpetual and bitter strife, whether to recite *Barukh še-'Amar* before *Hodhu* or *Hodhu* before *Barukh še-'Amar* . . ."[68]

Satire, indeed, comprises one of the most effective weapons wielded by the novelists to pour ridicule on the darker sides of Hasidic life, made all the more devastating by virtue of the element of fact lurking behind the caricature. The master of this medium is Abramowitz, who directs his lash against the charlatanism for which Hasidism provided such a vulnerable target, castigating the wiles of the typical impostor, posing as the *Nekhedh* or grandson of a *Ṣaddiq*, and turning the superstitious credulity of the *Ḥasidhim* to his own advantage.[69] In the same context, he ridicules the ecstatic nature of Hasidic prayer, which can be so easily imitated by the unscrupulous pretender to piety, while elsewhere there occurs a description of Hasidic methods of healing the sick, which scarcely differs from undisguised sorcery![70] Although less subtle, Smolenskin's satire is equally fierce. Perhaps his most sustained satirical passage is that in which two *Ḥasidhim*, who have resorted to physical violence following a quarrel concerning the relative greatness of their respective *Ṣaddiqim*, consult the same lawyer independently, each demanding that his opponent be convicted before a Russian court, and sentenced to a flogging as well as deportation to Siberia or its equivalent![71] Behind the humor of the scene, there is more than a suggestion of grotesque horror. On another occasion Smolenskin ridicules the reverence prevailing among the *Ḥasidhim* for hidden teachings:

> All of them thirst only after the hidden doctrines, and in that field any man whatsoever can make a name for himself. For what are hidden doctrines? They are whatever a man says which his audience finds incomprehensible; and if even the speaker himself cannot understand what he is saying, then his hidden knowledge will be regarded as belonging to the highest order . . .[72]

But such pleasantries pale before the terrible indictment which Smolenskin puts into the mouth of his hero, Josef, who decides to leave the Hasidic sect after a three years' sojourn, which he describes as follows:

> And after my eyes had been fully and painfully opened to the ways of the *Ḥasidhim*, their evil designs and villainies with which they daily pursue their

> prey on every side, destroying their enemies and swallowing up whoever refuses to aid them; and after I, too, had experienced the methods of these wicked men, who trample down without compunction all probity and righteousness, and stop at nothing to further the aims of their sect ... I decided to leave this city, which had become detestable to me, and this land where I had witnessed nothing but wickedness ...[73]

But the picture is by no means uniformly black. Smolenskin, it is true, gives little more than one rather grudging admission that there are indeed many righteous *Ḥasidhim*,[74] but Braudes portrays a very different situation. In his profoundly serious novel *Religion and Life*, he gives a sincere appreciation of Hasidism in its early stages as a genuine attempt to rescue Judaism from the terrible stringencies into which it had fallen, and to imbue it with new life and hope; although even he is careful to distinguish the original position from that of contemporary Hasidism.[75] A far more sympathetic portrait, however, is presented in another novel, *The Two Extremes*, where the peace and quiet of a small Hasidic town, especially on the Sabbath, are described in terms which sometimes savor of a panegyric.[76] The almost idyllic scene emphasizes the positive factors of Hasidic life, with its piety, charity, and family warmth,[77] where the visitor from Odessa finds a restful and comforting haven after the shallowness of life in a great bustling city. Despite the fact that Braudes is well aware of the evils—such as obscurantism, fanatical persecution, and superstition—which mar Hasidic society and attacks them with determination, he is equally conscious of the existence of traditional Jewish values, which serve as a fixative in life, and which compare favorably with the emptiness and rootlessness of many of the young "enlightened" generation of his day, who had abandoned the old, without successfully replacing it with something meaningful.

One final point is worthy of note in estimating the views on Hasidism presented in these novels. Without exception, the authors were staunch champions of the Jewish people and felt their Judaism very deeply. In attacking and pillorying many facets of Hasidic life, their object was not to weaken Judaism, but to strengthen it.[78] Their arrows were directed not against the principles of Judaism, but against such expressions of it as they regarded as excrescences and essentially unhealthy. When backed by their intimate knowledge of contemporary conditions, the portrait of Hasidism arising from their novels should not, perhaps, be too lightly disregarded.

7

A Portrait of the "Ṣaddiq"

THE REPRESENTATION of Hasidism in the Hebrew novel between the years 1868 and 1888 naturally includes numerous references to the pious leaders of that movement usually known as *Ṣaddiqim*.[1] Here again, the prevalent attitude varies from satire to open hostility;[2] but most of the authors[3] portray the *Ṣaddiq* with considerably greater restraint than in their treatment of Hasidism as a whole.[4] It must be remembered that in Eastern Europe the *Ṣaddiqim* were revered by hundreds of thousands of Jews, who regarded them as saints endowed with the power of interceding directly with the Divine. So widespread and absolute was their authority that even their opponents rarely dared to embark upon a full-scale, personal assault. Moreover, the genuine piety and commanding personality of many of the Hasidic leaders were recognized far beyond the ranks of their adherents. In consequence, many of the episodes relating to the *Ṣaddiqim* in these novels preserve the flavor of first-hand observation by actual, if skeptical, spectators. Although their presentation of the scene is obviously very different from that of fervent adherents, their descriptions frequently sound the note of truth. Their most biting satire is directed against the charlatanism which such unrestrained credulity was bound to occasion; and as exponents of the doctrine of enlightenment, the novelists lose no opportunity of pillorying the undesirable obscurantism of many of the Hasidic leaders toward any form of secular knowledge. Both these aspects are clearly recognizable in the following extract from Abramowitz's first novel,[5] in which the credulous Sarah consults an unscrupulous impostor masquerading as a *Ṣaddiq* about the movements of her errant son:

> "What has your son been up to?" the impostor[6] asked, raising his eyes on high and sighing piously.
>
> "He hasn't actually done anything wrong, God forbid," Sarah answered. "But my husband says he is going astray in wanting to study and in seeking enlightenment."
>
> "Enlightenment!" the impostor shouted angrily, like a man beside himself at the mention of his bitterest enemy's name. "What could be worse than that?"
>
> "What has your son been studying?" he asked further.
>
> "The Bible,"[7] Sarah answered in a faltering voice.

"My God! my God!" the impostor groaned.

"Can't you forgive him just this once?" Sarah cried with a sob.

"Are there any of the new-fangled enlighteners in Kissalon?"[8] the impostor asked again.

"There are indeed!" Sarah replied. "It's that tramp of a schoolmaster, who has led my son off the straight and narrow. The Devil take his grandfather! And what's worse, to add insult to injury, he's living in my house at this very moment."

"Oh, my goodness," the impostor shouted, growing pale. "What's the rascal doing in the house of one of my *Ḥasidhim*? Make haste and chase him out, lest his impure soul defile all your souls so badly that even I won't be able to repair the harm you have brought about."

The numerous passages devoted to the *Ṣaddiq* in the novels under review may be divided, therefore, into two broad categories, each illuminating in a different way. Wherever the polemic, didactic, or satirical note is dominant, such information as can be derived is more reliable as a means of gauging the standpoint and psychology of the authors themselves, and their own estimate of the ills accruing from the objects of their attack, than as a means of evaluating the phenomena of the Hasidic movement as such. On the other hand, wherever the descriptive element is dominant, and the details supplied may be classed as incidental rather than deliberate, far more reliance may be placed on the information obtainable, certainly as far as the external manifestations of Hasidism are concerned. From this second category, then, it is possible to elicit many interesting details relevant to the *Ṣaddiq*'s office, and the attitude of his adherents. With regard to certain features of the sect the novelists reflect a large measure of agreement. This is, of course, particularly the case in the various descriptions contained in these novels of the unbounded respect which the *Ḥasidhim* entertain for the person of the *Ṣaddiq*. The following depiction by Smolenskin is quite typical:[9]

> The room resounded with the noise and clamor of the assembled throng. Everyone was talking at once, shouting, calling, scolding, and asking questions without listening to replies. Everyone was pushing and pressing forward to find a place near the table, at which the *Ṣaddiq* would sit when he appeared, and from which he would listen to each of their pleas ... Suddenly the tumult died away and silence fell upon the assembly. No one uttered a sound, while those who had their mouths open were left gaping. Each one stood as though turned to stone, moving neither hand nor foot, while every eye was riveted on the door which the *Ṣaddiq* was about to enter ... Young and old they regarded him with awe, scarcely daring to look at him before he took his seat like the Lord in judgment—ready to pardon all the penitents who had come to confess their sins and lay their sorrows bare before him ...

The supreme joy to be derived from the *Ṣaddiq*'s mere presence, and the boundless confidence in his ability to absolve his adherents from all sin, are clearly evident from an encounter between Josef, the hero of Smolenskin's

The Wanderer in the Paths of Life, and a young *Ḥasidh* making a pilgrimage to his *Ṣaddiq*'s court.[10]

> "When were you last in Ṣebhu'a'el?"
> "Four years ago, before I married, I went in search of the *Ṣaddiq* to beg his forgiveness for the sins of my youth, and to ask his blessing for my wedding."
> It was quite clear from the youth's expression that he was absolutely sincere about begging forgiveness from the *Ṣaddiq*. Still, I was eager to know whether the *Ṣaddiq*'s blessing had been fulfilled, and so I remarked: "I imagine the *Ṣaddiq* did give you his blessing."
> "Why do you talk like a *Mithnaggedh*? Would the *Ṣaddiq* withhold his blessing from any of his *Ḥasidhim* who desired his favor?"
> "And what is your purpose now?"
> "Only for the fact that you, too, are bound for Ṣebhu'a'el, I really would have taken you for a *Mithnaggedh*"—he exclaimed in astonishment.
> "Why am I going now? Were I able to stand on the *Ṣaddiq*'s threshold all my life, I could imagine no greater joy. Yet you ask what is my purpose now, when I have not been privileged to look upon the *Ṣaddiq*'s face for about four years! But this time I can at least draw comfort from the fact that I shall spend many days in the *Ṣaddiq*'s house, gazing upon the light of his holiness."

Braudes, in his novel *The Two Extremes*, reflects a similar attitude of unbounded respect on the part of the *Ḥasidhim* for their holy men, a sincere belief in their efficacy, and a complete willingness to support them materially to the limit of their ability. The wealthy father of Jacob Hetzron, one of the heroes of the novel, places implicit trust in his *Ṣaddiq* and is only anxious to be of service to him:[11]

> With all his heart and with all his might he loved the Lord and his *Ṣaddiqim*, those emissaries of God here on earth below; for this Hetzron was a *Ḥasidh*, and believed implicitly in his wonder-working master, lavishing his wealth upon him, and readily acceding to his every request.

Similarly, when Jacob Hetzron's wife, Sarah, is worried because she has received no word from her husband, who has gone to Odessa on business, her mother reassures her in the following manner:[12]

> "Jacob won't be led astray"—Nehamah Leah comforted her daughter.—"You know how faithfully he believes in the holy men, and the *Rebbe*—may God prolong his days—gave him his blessing before he left, so why all the fuss?"

Vivid testimony to the force of the *Ṣaddiq*'s personality and his powers of persuasion may be inferred from another episode from the same novel. Nathaneel, a confirmed *Mithnaggedh* deeply skeptical of the Hasidic movement, visits the *Ṣaddiq* with the object of confounding him. The *Ṣaddiq*'s adherents, however, are quite convinced that a single meeting will suffice to convert the doubter to their own beliefs. The pious Jeroham explains the grounds for their assumption, which subsequently proves to have been well founded, as follows:[13]

> "No one on earth could see the holy one of Israel without believing in his holiness. He was like an angel of the Lord in our midst, and even the hardest heart would melt on seeing him and listening to his holy utterances, which soothe the soul like balm."
>
> "Is his holiness so very great?" Ahitub asked innocently.
>
> "It is impossible to describe even the half of it. I simply couldn't find words to express all the wonderful deeds he has performed during his life. But my daughter's late father-in-law, may he rest in peace, will serve as an example."
>
> "Do you mean he became a *Ḥasidh*?"
>
> "It turned out exactly as we had foreseen," Jeroham replied conclusively. "He left here a confirmed *Mithnaggedh*—you've never seen the like—with his mind made up to argue with the *Rebbe* and confute him, so that we all might see the error of our ways ... But when he returned from the *Rebbe*'s home—he was a changed man ..."

The exalted nature of the *Ṣaddiq*, and his special status in the order of creation, a status which divides him sharply from the realm of ordinary mortals, for whose salvation he is destined constantly to strive, are outlined by Sirkis in the words of the devout *Ḥasidh* Kemuel:[14]

> In every generation there are *Ṣaddiqim*, ordinary mortals, and wicked men. The *Ṣaddiq* in each generation is as exalted as was Moses in his, and it is he who always keeps his eyes fixed on the Lord. For God has sent him to sustain and grant merit to all such men as support him and shower their money upon him. And since they assist the *Ṣaddiq* with the fruits of their earthly labor, their humble toil is regarded as great righteousness.

In view of this concept of divine election, it is scarcely surprising that the office should have been regarded as hereditary, as is clearly indicated by a passage from the novel of Smolenskin, to which reference has already been made:[15]

> The *Ṣaddiq*'s eldest son, *Rebbe* Judah ... stood in a corner of the room facing the east and praying in a sing-song voice. He had already been chosen to succeed his father. The *Ṣaddiq* addressed him as *Rebbe*, and whenever he spoke to him or took counsel with him he called him *Rebbe* Judah, and his brothers all did likewise.

By extension, the same principle was applied to other members of the *Ṣaddiq*'s entourage, so that the mere fact of being one of the *Ṣaddiq*'s servants was sufficient for a man to be regarded as both righteous and pious.[16]

That the *Ṣaddiqim* wielded immense authority over their numerous adherents is freely admitted by all the novelists. Indeed, the *Ṣaddiq* who plays an important role in Smolenskin's *The Wanderer in the Paths of Life* is credited with no less than one hundred thousand followers.[17] Such human sovereignty, however, pales into insignificance in comparison with the terrestrial and cosmic powers attributed to them by the faithful. The belief in the *Ṣaddiq*'s ability to command supernatural forces is well illustrated by a scene in which two devout adherents of rival *Ṣaddiqim* passionately defend the powers of their respective leaders. The first one gives the following account of his master's abilities:[18]

> "Who can relate his wonders or tell of his miracles? He controls the rain and snow; he holds the key to the gates of mercy. He can command the upper and the lower worlds at will. We, ourselves, have witnessed his righteous deeds innumerable times. There has never been his like, nor will there be his like again. For he protects the entire earth, and were it not for him the world would have already reverted to chaos because of the wickedness of its inhabitants. Indeed, the *Ṣaddiq* is the earth's sole foundation, and it is he who guards it with his righteousness . . ."

Not to be outdone, his opponent rushes to the defence of his own *Ṣaddiq* in terms no less extravagant:[19]

> "You ask for marvels? You look for signs? I can tell you of wonders, the like of which you have never heard. Listen, all of you, and be amazed! I will tell you of things I have seen with my own eyes. I have seen men in hundreds, thousands, whom the *Ṣaddiq* has saved from the point of death; hundreds of women flock to him every year because the Lord has shut up their wombs—and they give birth. He controls the rain and snow; even the angel of death will not disobey him."

At this point, apparently recognizing the futility of further argument, the rival partisans resort to physical assault upon each other, while the bystanders, dividing into two groups, enthusiastically hurl themselves into the fray!

In view of claims of such magnitude it is hardly surprising that a young *Mithnaggedh*, seeking to learn something of the mysteries of the sect before deciding whether himself to become a *Ḥasidh*, should pose the following question in all sincerity and without desiring to score any mere debating point:[20]

> "And now let me ask the question I wanted to ask initially: if the *Ṣaddiq* is really aware of everything and can do anything he likes, why does he not rescue Israel from her sorrows at one fell swoop? Why does he leave her a prey to all her enemies? Even the peasant boys deride us with impunity. Surely he knows of Israel's plight. Why then does he not redeem her?"

Typically, the query is brushed aside with a single, jeering taunt—*Mithnaggedh*!

An even more impressive catalog of the *Ṣaddiq*'s powers may be found in Zobeizensky's novel, most of which comprises a grotesque and clumsy caricature of the Hasidic movement in general and of the *Ṣaddiqim* in particular. The plot revolves upon the naive credulity with which the pious Sarah places her entire faith in a charlatan posing as a *Ṣaddiq*, thereby plunging her whole household into ruin. Quite apart from her belief in the *Ṣaddiq*'s cosmic powers, which transcend even the feats outlined in the passages quoted above, Sarah's concept of his abilities includes a number of more mundane but nevertheless revealing items:[21]

> With remedies and charms, amulets and prayer he could remove any affliction, and revive the bruised of spirit. Anyone suffering from a broken arm or leg, from heart-disease, bowel trouble, consumption, bronchitis, or other malignant disease had only to come to the *Ṣaddiq*; a wave of his hand over the affected spot, and the patient would be cured. Whenever any quarrel, strife, or mishap occurred between man and wife or between friends, they had only to visit the *Ṣaddiq*, who would iron out their differences in a moment, restore peace, amity, and friendship between them, and so put an end to all jealousy and hatred that they would at once embrace and kiss each other. Whenever anything was stolen, whether gold or silver, clothes or shoes, and the thief had vanished without trace, the *Ṣaddiq* by his mere breath would kindle a sudden all-consuming fire in the thief's heart, until he returned the spoil to its rightful owner.[22]

It is of interest that, according to Weisbrem, the *Ṣaddiq* could even use his staff in order to work miracles by proxy:[23]

> And every year the *Gabbai* used to make the rounds of all the cities in the province holding the *Rebbe*'s staff in his hands; and with that staff he performed signs and wonders, the like of which have never been known in all the earth . . .

A further example of the *Ṣaddiq*'s powers, on this occasion in the realm of finance, occurs in the same story. In dire straits, the impoverished but pious Simon brings the last remnant of his fortune, eighteen gold coins, as an offering to the *Ṣaddiq*, who gives him eighteen[24] copper coins—from which the novel derives its title—in return, together with his blessing. With the aid of this humble gift Simon rapidly amasses a great fortune, which he attributes entirely to the *Ṣaddiq*'s good will. It is significant that later in the story, when the *Ṣaddiq* becomes displeased with Simon, he threatens him with a demand for the return of the eighteen coppers unless he mends his ways.[25] A parallel instance occurs in another novel:[26]

> Samuel the merchant was poverty-stricken until he went to the *Ṣaddiq* complaining of his bitter fate. The *Ṣaddiq* gave him a silver coin, with which he began to trade; and now he is a rich man, and brings the *Ṣaddiq* a thousand silver coins each year for the redemption of his soul.

On this occasion, however, the author attempts to explain the phenomenon by an interesting process of rationalization:[27]

> Once Samuel had received a gift from the *Ṣaddiq*'s own hand, and all his adherents learned of the *Ṣaddiq*'s prediction that Samuel would become rich, they decided that it was their common duty to support the man in order to enhance the *Ṣaddiq*'s reputation. So they provided him with sufficient money to engage in business, with the result that he grew very rich . . .

From the same passage, however, it is made clear that the prediction merely stated the final result without reference to the means to be adopted. That Samuel prospered by all kinds of deception and swindling was considered of little consequence, provided only that the prophecy be fulfilled and new adherents for the *Ṣaddiq* be won.

A convincing illustration of the *Ṣaddiq*'s economic significance is twice recorded in these novels. On each occasion the information is the more readily acceptable for being supplied incidentally in the course of episodes which are entirely satirical and critical of the Hasidic movement. Smolenskin explains the prosperity of the town in which the *Ṣaddiq* resides in a single telling sentence:[28] "For in the wake of the many pilgrims who came to seek the word of God from him, prosperity reached the town." Leinwand confirms this circumstance by describing how the townsfolk earn a living by selling food to the many followers who come to visit the *Ṣaddiq*.[29] He is careful to add, however, that this function devolves upon the women, who also have to shoulder the entire domestic burden,[30] while the men spend their whole time smoking and relating the wonders of the *Ṣaddiq*.[31] An additional economic function may be inferred from the fact that a *Ṣaddiq* supplies one of his adherents with an open letter authorizing him to collect money for his daughter's dowry.[32]

The functions of the *Ṣaddiq*, however, are described as extending far beyond the scope of mere finance. The selection by the *Ṣaddiq* of rabbis for the communities living within his jurisdiction is described by Smolenskin once more in bitterly satirical terms. His statement of the fact, however, is unequivocal:[33]

> But I gave no heed as to whether he was worthy of the name [of rabbi] or not, just as the *Ṣaddiq* of Ṣebhu'a'el, who had raised him to the rabbinical office, had paid no attention to his knowledge of Israel's laws and statutes, and just as the congregation made little effort to investigate whether the *Ṣaddiq* was right in appointing him to be their spiritual guide. For none of the Hasidic communities choose their own rabbi, but accept the one chosen by the *Ṣaddiq*. Nor will anyone make so bold as to speculate why the *Ṣaddiq* has chosen him, whether for his knowledge of the Law, or for his Hasidic fervor.

The *Ṣaddiq* is expected to exercise an equally telling authority in the arrangement of marriages,[34] and in the treatment of the sick. In this latter respect Abramowitz affords an amusing and very satirical illustration of Hasidic methods of healing by semi-magical practices. Abramowitz, who supplies explanatory footnotes, is clearly familiar with such remedies.[35] Equally superstitious remedies are attested in other sources.[36]

A more effective illustration of a *Ṣaddiq* in the role of general counselor to his followers occurs in Braudes' *The Two Extremes*, when Jeroham begs the *Ṣaddiq* to help him recover his son-in-law, Jacob Hetzron, who has abandoned his wife and family in favor of the attractions to be found in Odessa. The *Ṣaddiq* declares that he knew from the start that such would be the case, an admission which provokes Jeroham to complain, albeit timidly, that the *Ṣaddiq* himself had given Jacob permission to undertake the journey. The conversation proceeds as follows:[37]

> "I did give him permission to travel ... I wanted to use the journey to test him ... to bring him into temptation ... but what do you want me to do now ... do you expect *me* to go to Odessa and rescue him?! ..." The *Rebbe* looked at Jeroham very hard. "Yes! I, myself, shall rescue his soul," the *Rebbe* went on in a tone that contrived to be both awe-inspiring yet kindly, closing his eyes. "I, myself, shall save his soul from hell ... I shall not let the evil powers capture the soul of one of my followers ... But you must return home, and don't go near the gates of that accursed city ... I shall bring about a great redemption ..." The *Rebbe* raised his eyes to heaven, and with the frozen expression of a corpse, sat motionless for some moments, while Jeroham gazed at him in dismay, his flesh creeping and trembling in every limb.
>
> Suddenly, the *Rebbe* came to life, as though rousing himself from sleep.
>
> "Give me his redemption-price," he shouted loudly, fixing Jeroham with his eye. "I shall save him from the pit, I shall save him ..."
>
> Jeroham silently took some money from his pocket and laid it before the *Rebbe* as bidden.
>
> "The time has come! ... Yes, it has come!" the *Rebbe* cried again, his face shining with joy. "The time has come when they shall know from afar that *the Ṣaddiq rules with the fear of the Lord*![38] The father of Nathaneel, Jacob's dead father, is still alive ... a *Mithnaggedh* ... God-fearing and pious ... and rich, too, ... you must write to him explaining what has happened ... let him go to Odessa and bring Jacob his grandson here ... and he, too, will surely become a *Ḥasidh* ..."

In spite of the seeming impossibility of persuading Jacob's grandfather, who lives in distant Vilna, and who had disowned his son, Nathaneel, when the latter became a *Ḥasidh* before Jacob was born, the *Ṣaddiq* insists that there is no other way, and maintains his position in spite of all subsequent pleas.[39] In the meantime, the *Ṣaddiq* sends a short letter full of enigmatic fragments and kabbalistic terminology to the erring Jacob. The letter concludes:[40]

> Your soul has fallen into a trap prepared by the forces of evil. You are a prey to the dark powers that lie in ambush for every Israelite, to rob his soul of its purity so that it may fall into their hands.

Jacob is terrified by the thought of the perils to which he has exposed himself, and his grandfather's ultimate arrival in Odessa does, in fact, induce him to return to the bosom of his family. So in the event, the *Ṣaddiq*'s advice turns out to be singularly shrewd and effective, even though Jacob's grandfather remains a convinced *Mithnaggedh* as before.[41]

One further function of the *Ṣaddiq* which is portrayed in these novels is the Sabbath exposition of Scripture, replete with mystical interpretation, which is satirized ferociously by Smolenskin, presumably on the basis of the intimate experience of a Hasidic environment, which he had acquired as a youth.[42] When Josef, the hero of Smolenskin's novel, first hears the Sabbath exposition, he observes that it is the *Gabbai*'s task to repeat the *Ṣaddiq*'s words from memory. Endowed, himself, with an excellent memory, Josef later wins a considerable reputation by his ability to repeat the complete exposition by heart, even though he scarcely understands a single word of what he is saying![43]

The same episode furnishes an interesting description of a *Ṣaddiq*'s residence, and the comparative splendor of his living conditions against the background of the dire and almost universal poverty of the majority of his adherents. Josef's first impressions of the scene are described as follows:[44]

> The *Ṣaddiq*'s court resembled that of a prince surrounded by the dwellings of his servants. Some five strongly built wooden houses on stone foundations served as a residence for himself and his sons. The building in which he lived contained a synagogue, as well as living quarters for the guests, attracted from afar by his renown.

Josef is even more impressed, however, by his first glimpse of its master:[45]

> The door opened and the *Ṣaddiq* appeared. He was an old man of about seventy, tall and distinguished, with a white, woolly beard that covered his chest, and with clear eyes gleaming with youthful vigor. He was dressed from head to toe in a garment of reddish-white silk, while even his hat and stockings were of silk. His whole appearance bespoke dignity, as he slowly advanced, his glance sweeping the entire assembly of petitioners with the radiance of a kindly and benevolent deity.

The crowds of pilgrims were all anxious to approach the *Ṣaddiq* as closely as possible. Many of them, too, had individual requests for his assistance. Indeed, on first entering the crowded room where the *Ṣaddiq* was about to hold audience, Josef had witnessed numerous men, women, and youths writing petitions to be presented to the *Ṣaddiq*, while two scribes sat at a table writing for the illiterate in return for a fee.[46] A similar picture of urgent petition is drawn by Abramowitz when Sarah visits the charlatan masquerading as a *Ṣaddiq*, in whom she so fervently believes:[47]

> Sarah had already tried a number of times without success to force a way through the great throng to the man of God ... Nor will anyone, who has ever once been privileged to make the journey to visit a *Ṣaddiq*, be surprised, for such a one will remember how people hurry to reach the holy seat many days before

> the New Year festival to delight in the *Ṣaddiq*'s presence and unburden their hearts to him. And there they tarry even many days after the festival, without regard to the time, the trouble, and the great expense involved . . .

When Sarah finally manages to secure an interview after waiting for several hours—and even then only because she is known to be a wealthy woman—she at once becomes an object of universal envy:

> Everyone present looked at Sarah and envied her as though she had stumbled on a fortune. As she moved, a crowd closed in behind her intent on bursting into the room with her, like lost souls clutching at the *Ṣaddiq*'s wings as he passes over Hell and Gehenna in the hope that he may raise them to God's heaven. But as they reached the door, they were violently thrust back.

Mention has previously been made of the practice of offering a gift to the *Ṣaddiq* in return for his favor or advice.[48] But the novels also contain an interesting example of a handsome gift being sent to a *Ṣaddiq* by one of his adherents because the latter had reached a decision *without* any such consultation.[49] The passage in question bears a footnote added by the author to the effect that in Galicia nobody would undertake any business transaction without prior consultation with the *Ṣaddiq*. It may be readily imagined that the *Ṣaddiq* derived a considerable income from this practice. A further profitable source of income is described by Smolenskin in the following conversation:[50]

> "Are you not familiar with the activity of the emissaries?" he asked in astonishment.
>
> "I have never heard of them."
>
> "Surely everyone knows that the emissaries travel round the whole country twice a year collecting money for the *Ṣaddiq*."
>
> "Where do you find the money?"
>
> "Have you not seen a little iron box on the wall of every Hasidic household, in which each person puts a contribution every week? If anyone has given way to temptation, or if there is a sick person in the house, or if a man has made a vow and wants to pay it, he puts money in the box. The box is locked, and the keys are held by the emissaries who also put a seal on it. When they have collected the money, they bring it to the *Ṣaddiq*. The men chosen to be emissaries are always excellently-connected, and also good Kabbalists, so that they can preach to the people. And everyone adds a gift for the *Ṣaddiq* far in excess of what the box contains . . ."

The *Ṣaddiq*'s gift is portrayed as being of such significance that it overrides and atones for even the most unethical conduct. Josef's wicked aunt, for example, is able to console her conscience-stricken husband for the terrible evils he has brought upon his brother's household in the following words:[51]

> All pious folk will bear witness that you have grown rich by just and fair means. And even if you had committed evil, it would no longer be regarded as sinful, since you have atoned for it by the gift you gave the *Ṣaddiq* . . .

In view of such an attitude to Hasidic morality, it is not surprising that on occasion invective of the bitterest kind is leveled against the *Ṣaddiq*. An explanation of the villainies lurking in the passage just quoted appears in a letter written from prison by Josef's father, in which he protests that he has been falsely convicted by the machinations of his own brother:[52]

> The *Ṣaddiq* of the town of Ṣebhu'a'el, may his name be cursed on earth and in heaven, after lengthy plotting finally discovered a way to lure me into a trap, because I had turned my back on his teachings, his law of death, and refused to join his wicked and dastardly band of followers. He used my own kith and kin to destroy me, by advising the blackguard who sucked the breasts of my own mother to enter my home and change all my securities for forged documents ...

Criticism of a more general and less dramatic kind is directed against the irresponsible behavior of the Polish *Ḥasidhim* by a young *'Agunah*, or deserted wife, who has been searching for her husband for five years! She blames the cult of Saddiqism for the plight of many unfortunate women like herself:[53]

> They [the Polish Jews] despise the word of God and regard all law and justice as something foreign. And of what does their wisdom consist? Merely in boasting of the glory of the *Ṣaddiq*, adoring him, and idolizing him. Whereas young Lithuanian Jews leave home in search of knowledge, going from strength to strength until they become great scholars and crown their households and their families with glory, the Polish Jews abandon their wives merely to sport in the *Ṣaddiq*'s house, eating, drinking, and making merry on all the spoil which the *Ṣaddiq* collects during his travels ...

Reference has already been made to Zobeizensky's gross and melodramatic caricature of a charlatan *Ṣaddiq*, whose long list of infamies includes forgery, adultery, and murder.[54] But whereas Zobeizensky's tremendous onslaught dissolves into pure fantasy, more serious consideration must be given to two other points of criticism found elsewhere in these novels. All the more effective because of his general sympathy with the Hasidic movement is Rabinowitz's restrained censure of a *Ṣaddiq* who always welcomed a visit from a certain wealthy adherent because the latter never failed to leave a handsome gift: "For some of our *Ṣaddiqim* not only like to enjoy hospitality as Elisha did, but sometimes they also behave in the manner of Gehazi ..."[55] Of a different order, and far more biting, is Smolenskin's criticism of the Jews of Roumania for placing their trust in the power of the *Ṣaddiq* to save them from the oppressors instead of resorting to self-defence. With bitter sarcasm, Smolenskin outlines their reasoning as follows:[56]

> And if the *Ṣaddiq* has not yet risen with his companions to make an end of them [the oppressors], surely that is a sign that the time is not yet ripe, but when it is, the *Ṣaddiq* will bring about the redemption.

Not all the novels, however, indulge in unmitigated criticism. On the contrary, a number of them contain very significant passages, in which the positive virtues of at least some of the *Ṣaddiqim* are enumerated with considerable sympathy. When for example one faithful adherent, impoverished by drunkenness, goes to consult his *Ṣaddiq*, not only does the latter refuse to accept a gift from him, but even gives the poor man money, at the same time admonishing him against his drunkenness, and promising to pray for husbands for his seven daughters.[57] Rabinowitz is prepared to go much further. When the pious teacher Judah is asked whether he believes in *Ṣaddiqim*, his answer is discerning, moderate, and shrewd:[58]

> We Israelites are commanded to believe in God and his *Torah*, but we are not commanded to believe in *Ṣaddiqim*. In any case, my forefathers were *Ashkenazim* and I, too, prayed according to the Ashkenazy rite until I came to this town, all of whose inhabitants are *Ḥasidhim*. But as we are enjoined not to make separate factions,[59] I began to pray in accordance with the Sephardic rite,[60] for it really makes no difference whether one recites *Hodhu* before *Barukh še-'Amar* or *vice versa*,[61] provided only that one prays sincerely. Nevertheless, far be it from me to denigrate the *Ṣaddiqim*. Admittedly, there are a number who are reputed to be deceitful and corrupt, boasting that God will fulfill whatever they decree, and fixing the exact amount of tribute to be paid by each individual that recognizes their authority. But the *Rebbe* M. M. [Menahem Mendel] of Lubavitch has never boasted of his righteousness; but throughout his life he has meditated on God's *Torah*, and composed many excellent books. Nor has he ever demanded payment from anybody, like the *Ṣaddiqim* of Volhynia and Poland. And what if a rich man sometimes gives him a gift which he accepts—is that any reason to brand him as a scoundrel and a villain? He has led no one astray, nor has he ever taught his disciples to deceive, rob, or commit adultery. On the contrary, he has guided them along the paths of righteousness, to keep the *Torah* and its commandments. Moreover, let me say that even though I do not dabble in the hidden learning or the mysteries of the Kabbalah, that did not prevent me from going to celebrate the New Year festival in Lubavitch. And there I beheld a delightful and impressive spectacle—a kind of secret power attracting the scattered remnants of Israel from the far corners of the land to one center on terms of friendship and equality. For there the rich man does not boast of his wealth, nor does the poor man humbly bend his head. The merchant does not rush away to his business, nor does the pauper lament his poverty. But everyone helps his neighbor in true brotherly fashion.[62]

An equally sober, if more skeptical, appreciation of the *Ṣaddiq* may be found in a novel by N. M. Sheikewitz. When the heroine speaks of the *Ḥasidhim* and *Ṣaddiqim* in derogatory fashion, she is astounded by the indignant rebuke she receives from her lover, Jacob, whose great learning she deeply respects. Jacob claims that all her knowledge of the subject has been derived from "modern writers" who accuse the *Ṣaddiqim* of every conceivable crime, although neither she nor they have any first-hand experience of them. To her question whether the *Ṣaddiqim* are really divine, Jacob replies:[63]

> The *Ṣaddiq* whom the *Ḥasidhim* revere and adore as though divine is an ordinary mortal with no claim to superiority over his fellow-men. But his *Ḥasidhim* fervently believe him to be a friend of God, into whose hands the keys of heaven have been delivered. As a result, many of the *Ṣaddiqim* really do believe that they have been especially chosen and endowed with supernatural knowledge, which overshadows even that of the angels. We, then, who are aware of their folly may rightly regard them as deluded, but certainly not as charlatans. Admittedly, in recent times some *Ṣaddiqim* have appeared who extort money from their adherents and beguile them into parting with their wealth. But ought we to brand them all because of the occasional sinner? Indeed, if you examine the practices of the *Ḥasidhim* closely, you will be forced to conclude that from their faith in the *Ṣaddiqim* very many of them derive considerable advantage.

When the heroine asks what advantages can possibly be derived from such a faith, Jacob lists them as follows:

> (1) The *Ḥasidhim* stand in the same awe of the *Ṣaddiq* as they do of the government. As a result no one is prepared to commit a crime against his fellow lest word of it reach the *Ṣaddiq*. (2) No one will dare to cheat his neighbor or make bold to rob him of his livelihood for fear of the *Ṣaddiq*'s wrath. (3) If a *Ḥasidh* is in dire straits, his companions will not allow him to be ruined; the rich will support him generously, and see to it that he is set on his feet again. (4) When a *Ḥasidh* is in desperate plight and has suffered some dire misfortune such as the theft of his money, or the loss of beloved children, he will at once find refuge in the *Ṣaddiq*, who will so console him in his hour of sorrow, that far from despairing he will accept his ill-luck with resignation. (5) There is no joy or happiness in all the world to compare with that of a *Ḥasidh* sitting at his *Ṣaddiq*'s table, and eating and drinking of his food and wine. So tell me now, my darling, how can you decry the *Ṣaddiqim*, who bring such blessings to the tens of thousands of *Ḥasidhim* who believe in them?

While emphasizing once again that he is neither a *Ḥasidh* nor a believer in the *Ṣaddiqim*, Jacob proceeds to remark that as the *Ḥasidhim* are certainly not fools, would they continue to believe in the *Ṣaddiqim* if the latter were guilty of such crimes as adultery, blasphemy, cupidity, or murder? Moreover, the fact that they appear to be so rich is scarcely surprising, since their followers regard each of them as a veritable Sultan. Why, then, should they not accept gifts in return for their protection? But in fact, Jacob asserts, most *Ṣaddiqim* are poor, because their doors are always open to every afflicted *Ḥasidh*, and everything they possess they share among the poor *Ḥasidhim*.

It is as well to balance these more moderate and perceptive views of the role and function of the *Ṣaddiq* against the more extravagant and satirical descriptions which the other novels contain. It is not unreasonable to suppose, however, that much of the incidental detail, as portrayed by writers personally acquainted with the Hasidic *milieu*, is accurate, and that many of the external features described are genuinely representative of certain aspects of the movement as they appeared to the opposing side. Certainly the skeptical, critical, and bitingly satirical presentation of what was, after all, a contemporary and familiar environment should not be totally ignored.

8

Aspects of Language

THE PURPOSE of this chapter is to present certain aspects of language in the Hebrew novel over a period of twenty years, from 1868 to 1888. Although more in the nature of a preliminary survey than an exhaustive study, the attempt may serve to illustrate a number of the formidable obstacles lining the path of the Hebrew writer during an important transitional stage in the development of modern Hebrew literature.

For some eighty years prior to the death of the first Hebrew novelist, Abraham Mapu, in 1867, the great majority of Hebrew writers associated with *Haskalah* deliberately opted to imitate the style and language of the Hebrew Bible, in an attempt to refine and purify the language of such elements as they considered to be detrimental in the somewhat crude, crabbed, and ungrammatical forms of contemporary rabbinical composition. It is worthy of note that biblical Hebrew was treated as a single stratum of language, regardless of the fact that it spans not less than a millennium. The final consummation of this mock-biblical style may be observed in Mapu's historical novels, which demonstrate both the artistic possibilities and the practical limitations involved in utilizing biblical Hebrew as the sole medium for the modern novel.[1]

His immediate successors adhered in great measure, and in some cases almost exclusively, to the stylistic patterns laid down by the *Maskilim* in general and by Mapu in particular. But whereas Mapu's historical novels were concerned with events in ancient Israel at the time of Isaiah, for which setting the style and language of the Bible proved relatively suitable, his successors concentrated on the contemporary social scene of Jewish life in Eastern Europe. In this respect, too, they followed the example of Mapu's social novel *The Hypocrite*, at the same time largely ignoring Mapu's own warning, which appears in the preface to the extant fragment of a further novel *The Visionaries* (*Ḥozei Ḥezyonoth*), that he had exhausted the possibilities of composing novels in the restricted language of the Bible, and that his successors would be well advised to avail themselves of the rich linguistic strata of post-biblical Hebrew. The validity of Mapu's prediction was only fully substantiated in the subsequent period with the appearance of S. J.

Abramowitz's Hebrew versions of his Yiddish novels published under the pseudonym Mendele Mokher Sepharim.

The transitional nature of the novels of Mapu's immediate successors becomes manifest by comparison with Mapu's more faithful allegiance to biblical forms on the one hand, and Mendele's novels, in which all strata of Hebrew—together with substantial elements of Aramaic—are subtly fused into an adequate and pleasing medium of expression on the other. Artistically, they are inferior to both Mapu's historical novels and Mendele's tales of contemporary life, even though the more talented of the writers under consideration far outstripped Mapu in clarity, vividness, and the ability to formulate complex ideas. They reflect an important experimental stage from the point of view of language as well as form. Hebrew was still a literary medium, and the first attempts to revive it as a spoken idiom were as yet embryonic.[2] While the contribution of these novelists to the revival of the language remains considerable, their efforts to fashion Hebrew into a sufficiently flexible instrument for the expression of a wide range of ideas were only partially successful.

The overall adherence of the writers under review to the vocabulary and phraseology of the Bible while maintaining a sentence structure only biblical in part accounts for much of the incongruity which characterizes these novels.[3] The attempt to convey the concepts of the modern world and the problems of contemporary society while adhering almost exclusively to biblical vocabulary and idiom inevitably gave rise to violent stresses and strains.[4] The situation was further aggravated by the absence of both a suitable literary tradition and the generally accepted conventions necessary for the expression of a wide range of ideas in clear, precise, and economical terms. The introduction of concepts previously alien to Hebrew molds time and again compelled the novelists to stretch and distort the language in the attempt to adapt it to new purposes. Only too often the forcible injection of literary material into unsuitable linguistic patterns seriously distorts the harmony between the form and content of their stories, with the matter bulging and sagging pathetically through a patchwork covering of biblical phrases. The enforced resort to clumsy circumlocutions and crude approximations even for the expression of common objects and ideas frequently resulted, as will be seen, in a cumbersome terminology which sometimes borders on the grotesque.[5]

No less importantly, for want of a spoken, colloquial idiom the dialog is largely composed of stiff and stilted phrases in place of the terse, pithy, and colorful idioms of living speech. Here, again, the novelists were forced to resort to all sorts of circumlocutions and halting approximations in the attempt to create a sustained and comprehensible dialog. That they were able to compose full-length novels within so unlikely a linguistic framework constitutes a striking tribute to their tenacity, ingenuity, and devotion to Hebrew. But it is scarcely surprising that much of the conversation—

particularly in the short, rapid snatches of repartee where the idiomatic deficiencies proved most formidable—is labored, artificial, and unconvincing.[6]

A further consideration stems from the inadequate attention to the refinements of Hebrew grammar occasionally displayed by most of the authors under review—in spite of the great emphasis laid on a thorough grammatical training by the *Maskilim*, and the scorn which the novelists themselves pour upon their orthodox opponents, who are portrayed in their stories as religious bigots and obscurantists, fanatically opposed to the study of grammar.[7] The fact that Hebrew was not the mother tongue of these novelists, coupled with the furious speed with which they were often compelled to write,[8] may well account for the lapses in grammar which occur from time to time throughout the stories.

Of the linguistic usages distinguishing their writings from those of Mapu, one of the most striking is the change in attitude to the employment of the *waw consecutive*. Whereas Mapu adhered closely to the biblical usage, his successors indulge in a marked variety of treatments. Although Braudes, Zobeizensky, Sirkis, and Weisbrem frequently resort to the device, Smolenskin, Abramowitz, Manassewitz, Sheikewitz, and Rabinowitz are far less prone to use the construction. On a number of occasions, however, the *waw consecutive* is employed for deliberate effect. Smolenskin, for example, introduces it seven times in a single sentence in order to emphasize the restlessness of his hero, Josef.[9] In similar vein Braudes succeeds in conveying Samuel's tense anxiety in a paragraph beginning: ויהי ביום השני וישכם שמואל בבקר וירץ ביתה־המדרש להתפלל.[10] Weisbrem, again, makes an interesting if unsuccessful attempt to indicate the inferior speech of an ignorant laborer with the help of the *waw consecutive*.[11] The construction is particularly noticeable in conjunction with the root ישן (sleep), where it is frequently used with marked literary effect.[12]

The main purpose of this chapter is to illustrate some of the principal difficulties experienced by the novelists in expressing their ideas in Hebrew. These difficulties may be recognized most evidently from the very numerous explanations of their own terminology which the writers feel obliged to append, either in brackets or in the form of footnotes. But they are also apparent in the many transliterations—either in direct or adapted form—of foreign words, in the resort to clumsy circumlocutions, in the use of stilted conversational idioms, and in the repeated employment of particular phrases, largely for want of alternative expressions. Each of these items deserves more detailed consideration.

The most common method adopted for the explanation of terminology consists of adding in brackets a translation of the doubtful word or phrase usually in Yiddish or German, less commonly in Russian, and even, exceptionally, in Latin. Smolenskin, for example, who normally eschews all such practice, on one occasion appends "(Nihil)" to the expression לא־הוא.[13]

By such means the writers endeavored to foster generally accepted conventions in order to invest what were in many cases vaguely generalized terms with a specific significance. Braudes, who was particularly aware of the urgent necessity for widening the range of Hebrew,[14] resorts to such explanations on numerous occasions, as the following examples may serve to illustrate:[15] **זאב מים** (Hecht);[16] **בית־התחנות** (**באהנהאף**);[17] **מחלת־האבעבעות** (**פאקען**),[18] that is, "chicken pox;" **בעלת־מעשה** (**רעאליסטין**);[19] **בעל מחשבה** (**אידעאליסט**);[20] **המוסמכים** (**אוטוריטעטים**);[21] **תוכן־הלמודים** (**פראגראם**);[22] **הן רוח גבר חכם בעז** (**געניע**);[23] **מליצה** (**פראַזע**);[24] **הדוק** (Feder);[25] **הדרך הישר** (**דירעקט**);[26] **פרור** (**בולווארד**);[27] **ציוני־הנגון** (**נאטען**);[28] **שווי־הערך** (**הארמאניע**);[29] **היכל־ה׳** (**טעמפעל**);[30] **יודע דת ודין** (**אדוואקאט**);[31] **המנים** (Klavier);[32] **כתב־הנגינות** (**נאטען**);[33] **שער־השטרות** (**בארזע**);[34] **חמין** (**טשאלענט**),[35] that is, "the traditional Sabbath dish."

Many of the minor novelists are almost equally prone to adopt the practice. Leinwand, for example, explains a number of his terms as follows: **ציר הלוחות** (**שילדער מאלער**);[36] **השומרים הסובבים בעיר** (**פאטראואיללען**),[37] meaning "patrols;" **העוזר במשחק כדורים** (**מארקעער**),[38] apparently for a "billiard-marker;" **אגרת סתר** (**אנאנימעס שרייבען**),[39] for an "anonymous letter;" **שטרי פרזבל** (**פראנאלאנגאציאנסוועקסעל**),[40] for "long-term credit;" **פרזון** (**קאנקורז פערעפפענגטליכונג**),[41] for "public tender." Sarah Meinkin appends the following explanations in her novel *The Love of the Righteous*: **תמונות שונות** (**שטאטוען**)[42]—a rather feeble attempt; **בית משפט הנעלם** (**געהיימע פאליצייא**);[43] **בית נזירות** (**נאנען קלאסטער**);[44] **שר הפנים** (**לאנדעסמיניסטער**)[45]—a successful usage; **הקרדום** (**גווילאטינא**);[46] **לשחוק בלוחות** (**קארטין**);[47] **כלי קרב** (**שאכשפיעל**).[48]

Zobeizensky, who is even more prone to explain his terms, frequently resorts to Russian as well as German to convey the desired meaning: **משרת בחדרי המלמדים** (**בעהעלפער**);[49] **משנה שר מאה** (**אונטער אפיציר**);[50] **פקיד החיל** (**אפיצער**);[51] **חכמי הנפש** (психологи),[52] "psychologists;" **תכונת העצבים** (**נערוועען**);[53] **תנועת הגו והאברים** (гимнастики),[54] "gymnastics;" **תקופת השנה** (**יאהרצייט**);[55] **מי זדון** (**סאדע וועססער**);[56] **תחנות אנשי הצבא באהלים** (лагеры),[57] for "soldiers' camps;" **סמי רפואות** (**רעצעפטען**);[58] **מוכר נפשו** (охотникъ),[59] for "volunteer;" **מכתבי תעודות גבול** (паспорты),[60] "passports." Manassewitz, on the other hand, appends an explanation on only one occasion: **שחוק צעצועים** (**דאמינע**).[61]

Sheikewitz returns enthusiastically, if sometimes a little gratuitously, to the device, including among his numerous explanations one example in Russian: **גי החזיון** (**אמפפ׳יטהעאטאר**);[62] **אסתר המלמדת** (**אסתר דיא רעביצקע**);[63] **נשמע זמרת הנותן זמירות בלילה** (**נאכטיגאל**);[64] **הררי־אלף** (**אלפאנגעבירגע**);[65] **בעלי המכס** (**אקציזניקעס**);[66] **בית אוסף הילדים** (**פינדעלהויז**);[67] **בתי המשתה** (**בופֿעתען**);[68] **משלחי החפצים** (багажъ);[69]

המתינות (געדולד);[70] סמי־ארס (ארסעניק).[71] Rabinowitz, too, resorts to Russian for some of his explanations, while occasionally placing his Hebrew term in quotation-marks: „הזמן" (סעמעסטער);[72] „מחול הפרש" (козагокъ),[73] i.e. "cossack-dance;" נטיתם הטבעית (אינסטינקט);[74] מקנאים (פֿאנאטיקער);[75] המכונה המבקרת (контрольный снарядъ),[76] "an instrument for measuring spirits for taxation;" תורת המנהגים היפים (עטיקעט);[77] רוח „אד־קלון" (одеколонь),[78] for "eau-de-cologne;" מאשרי־השטרות (нотаріусъ),[79] for "notaries;" תבת־המחזה (גוקקאסטין),[80] that is, some primitive form of "magic-lantern;" הסופר המזכיר (סעקרעטער);[81] מטבעו ומדת מזגו (טעמפעראמענט).[82] Both Sirkis and Weisbrem, however, provide such explanations only on very rare occasions: החובש (פעלדשער);[83] החורים (גראפען).[84]

Although Abramowitz entirely refrains from explaining his terminology in brackets, he indulges in explanatory footnotes in a number of instances. These footnotes give the idiomatic equivalent of the phrase to be clarified in Yiddish,[85] followed by a short note in Hebrew defining the meaning. The phrases עשינו לו מנורה and לא אנחנו הלבשנוהו הכובע are translated respectively in a footnote געמאכט אַ לעמפעל and אן געטהון אַ שטריימל with the additional information that they are applied in a derogatory manner.[86] The phrase אשחר בחיי הבל is translated פערשווארצט ווערען and explained in the sense of suffering misfortunes.[87] The expression חברה לבנה is noted as ווייסע חברה—a term of reproach applied to mischievous boys.[88] The phrase נכד שכורי אפרים is explained as איין אייניקיל דעם שכורי אפרים׳ס, namely the grandson of the author of the book „שכורי אפרים".[89] The nicknames ברוך כבד־הפה and שבח־החרום are noted respectively as ברוך זאאיקעוואטע and שבח־בעז נאסע.[90] Finally, the phrase אכן קמת היום על צדך השמאלי is translated אויפגעשטאנען אוף דער לינקער זייט, and applied to a person wearing an angry expression in the morning—the equivalent of the English idiom of getting out of bed on the wrong side.[91]

Even Smolenskin, who normally eschews the use of footnotes in his novels, on one occasion translates the term שבלולים as שנעקען, and proceeds to explain that the latter word was used in Vienna to dismiss a matter as impossible.[92] Braudes, on the other hand, is at pains to provide detailed explanations of his specific usages. In a footnote to the word רומן, for example, he claims to be the first Hebrew writer to have used this word for "novel."[93] Similarly, he clarifies his own particular usage of נביא,[94] קליז,[95] שמות,[96] פשפש,[97] כלי־הקדש,[98] אבן־טוען,[99] for "Auskunfts Bureau," צמיד for "bracelet,"[100] שדרות,[101] "Alleen," מְזָוֶן,[102] "Speise-Schrank" (deduced from Ps. 144[13]), and צרו, "Nebenbuhler."[103] Of the minor novelists, only Rabinowitz and Weisbrem resort to the device. The former defines מצחה as козырокъ,[104] that is, "peak" (of a cap), while Weisbrem oddly justifies his use of ספה[105] for "sofa" from 2 Sam. 17[28], and somewhat gratuitously explains חדר הנשים[106] as בודואר.

The introduction of transliterated foreign words, either in direct or adapted form, without recourse to explanation provides a further illustration of the difficulties experienced by the novelists under review in their attempt to deal with the phenomena of the modern world. It is significant, for example, that Smolenskin follows his use of the word **בארזה**, "stock-exchange," with the confession that he has resorted to it in spite of his disinclination to introduce foreign words into Hebrew.[107] He is also compelled to adopt the form **עלעקטריציטאט**.[108] Braudes is less fastidious and his novels include numerous examples such as **אוטריטעטים**,[109] **פרזאי**,[110] **אוניווערזיטאט**,[111] **טיאתר**,[112] **אפער**,[113] for "opera," **מאדע**,[114] for "fashion," **מיססיאנער**,[115] **טלגרף**,[116] and **דוקטור**.[117]

Most of the minor writers use such transliterations only sparingly. Leinwand introduces two different forms of the word "coffee," namely **קאפפעע** and **קאפע**, on a single page.[118] Meinkin resorts to **עלעקטרי**,[119] **מאגנעט**,[120] **ציוויליזאטיאן**,[121] and **מעדאילאן**.[122] Manassewitz contents himself with **גימנאזיום**,[123] and Rabinowitz with **צערמאניאל**.[124] Sheikewitz, Sirkis, and Weisbrem, however, resort to transliterations more frequently. The former uses **מאדע**,[125] **אנטיסימיטיזמוס**,[126] **אבטוריטטים**,[127] **באנקרוטים**,[128] **ארטודוקתים**,[129] **אריסטוקרותים**,[130] **קאפיטעל**,[131] for "chapter," **ביליטיריסטיק**,[132] **לאקאמאטיף**.[133] Sirkis, who introduces an element of philosophic speculation into his novel, constantly resorts to foreign terminology: **רעאליסטים**,[134] **נאמינאליסטים**,[135] **עגאיזם**,[136] **ספיריטואליסטים**,[137] **טעאלאגים**,[138] **מאטעריאליזמוס**,[139] **פזיטיפיסט**,[140] **פאקטים**,[141] **מטאפרים**,[142] **סאציאלזיה**,[143] **טעאריות**,[144] and **פרדכס**.[145] Weisbrem's usages deal with more concrete items: **ציגארעטטא**,[146] **ציגרי האוואנא**,[147] **קאפעע**,[148] **אדרעסים**,[149] **פאסט**,[150] **תלגרמה**,[151] **פיאנא פארטא**,[152] **טעלעגראף**,[153] and **זאנדמים**.[154] Zobeizensky, perhaps appropriately, confines his transliteration to **מיזאנטראפ**![155]

The evidence provided by the necessity to explain terminology or introduce foreign words in transliteration is supplemented in a striking manner by the very numerous examples of clumsy and unwieldy phrases to which the novelists were compelled to resort time and time again in order to express their ideas via an inadequate linguistic medium. The following examples of some of the more flagrant instances may serve to illustrate the point: a "tuning fork" becomes **מזלג ברזל שתי השנים המשמיע קול**;[156] the word for a "file" is compounded of two biblical phrases **פצירה פים ומורג חרוץ**;[157] the expression used for a "sled" is **עגלת חורף אשר אין לה אופנים**;[158] a short irritable remark such as "the food's spoiling" becomes **והאש הקדיחה את התבשיל בסיר**;[159] "museums" are noted as **בתי האסף לדברים עתיקי ימים**;[160] "restaurants" and "dance halls" become **לבתי המאכל והמשתה, לבתי השחוק והמחולות**;[161] a "six-shooter" is described as **קנה רובה בעל ששת פיפיות**;[162] "thigh-boots" are **בתי רגלים אשר עד הירכים הגיעו**;[163] a "bath-chair" is expressed as **כסא ארוך אשר גלגלים לו**;[164] the "construction of railroad and telegraph" becomes **לבנות מסלות**

מרכבות ברזל ולמתוח חוטי ברזל לשלח בהם דברינו;[165] "a famous pianist will perform tomorrow" is rendered מחר וינצח בנגינות־המנים איש מפליא לנגן;[166] "fashion magazines" are described as מכתבי־עתי לחרשת־בגדים ולמדי־לבושים;[167] a "wig-maker" becomes אשה מגדלת־שער, עושה בפאה נכרית;[168] "to adorn a lady with a flowered straw-hat and parasol" is expressed as ויתנו על ראשה מגבעת־תבן מעשה ארג מפארה בפרחים ושושנים מעשה ידי אדם, ויתנו מחסה־שמש בידה.[169] The "sign in a building pointing upstairs" is described in equally clumsy terms—באולם הבית הכליל יראה פח מרקע על הקיר ועליו משוחה בשער אדם יד שלוחה אל מעלה המדרגות;[170] "to behave like an actor" becomes כי כמעשה המתחפשים בבמת ישחק יעשה;[171] and an attempt to describe a "man writing shorthand" is anything but brief—ישב איש על הגליון בחפזון נמרץ ובארח קצר מאד.[172] Even so simple an expression as "to make tea" is rendered להכין למכונה ולהזיד נזיד טהעע.[173]

An equally significant reflection of this struggle for terminology may be discerned in the numerous phrases and circumlocutions which are employed to represent the same concept. Smolenskin, for example, renders "insurance company" as החברה העורבת ערבה בעד תבערת אש,[174] while Weisbrem expands the phrase to החברה העורבת ערבה בעד כל פגע ואסון מאש וממים.[175] Zobeizensky, however, uses the much neater חברת בוטחי האש.[176] Similarly, the following different phrases are employed for "photograph:" צל צלם,[177] צלם דמות תבנית,[178] and התמונה הפאטגרפית.[179] The terminology connected with "locomotives" and "railroads" encompasses an astonishing variety including מרכבות אש,[180] עגלת הקטור,[181] מרכבת הקטור,[182] מרכבות הברזל,[183] מסילות הברזל,[184] המכונה[185] (locomotive), תחנת מסלת הברזל,[186] תחנת המסלה,[187] and מכונת הקטור.[188] The same applies to words denoting "mail" and "mailman:" בית הרצים,[189] בית משלוח המכתבים,[190] בית המכתבים,[191] רצי־המלך,[192] דואר,[193] בית הדואר,[194] נושא המכתבים,[195] תחנת הבי־דואר,[196] תחנת בית הרצים,[197] נושא האגרות,[198] ארגז המכתבים.[199]

Words and phrases connected with "smoking" display a similar state of fluidity: אבק עלי מרורים,[200] עשן עלי קטור,[201] עלי מרורים בתכריך ניר,[202] עלי טאבאק,[203] עלי מרורים[204]—together with בד גפרית[205] and עץ גפרית[206] for "match." "Newspapers," too, are rendered by a variety of terms: המכתב העתי,[207] מכתב החדשות,[208] מכתבי־העת,[209] עלים המשמיעים חדשות,[210] עלי העתים,[211] המכתב העתי,[212] עלה מכתבי העתים,[213] and מכתב עתי.[214] "Institutions of advanced learning" attract a number of renderings, such as: בית מדרש החכמות,[215] בית הלמודים לחכמת השיר,[216] בית תחכמוני,[217] and בית מדרש המדעים לחכמת הרפואה.[218] The phrases employed for "kitchen" are equally numerous: חדר המבשלות,[219] בית המבשלים,[220] בית המבשלות,[221] and חדר הבשול.[222] The terms for "office" are limited to תא־הסופרים[223] and לשכת הסופרים,[224] while the expressions for "chief-accountant" are restricted to ראש חושבי חשבונות,[225] מנהל ספרי החשבון,[226] and רואה

חשבון.[227] For "umbrella" only two phrases are employed: מחסה מגשם[228] and מחסה־ממטר,[229] although two more are used for parasol.[230] The single expression מורה השעות, with or without the definite article, is used to designate a "watch" or "clock."[231] In consequence, for such an idiomatic phrase as "what's the time?" recourse is made to the rather clumsy: וכמה מורה השעות כעת?.[232]

Such conversational idioms, as stated above, confronted the novelists with one of the most serious difficulties of all; and time and again they display their helplessness for want of the simple phrases which abound in any spoken language. Although the material is naturally far too voluminous for any comprehensive, detailed analysis, a selection of typical examples confined to a few narrow areas of conversation may serve to illustrate the formidable nature of the problem. It is significant that in modern colloquial Hebrew shorter and more pithy expressions have evolved in almost every case.[233]

Even such elementary turns of phrase as "quite right" or "you are right" produce stilted and artificial forms like: צדקת בדבריך,[234] כדבריך כן הוא,[235] טוב הדבר,[236] מישרים דברו שפתיך,[237] יהי כדבריך,[238] הלא דבר הוא.[239] Expressions such as "all right, I'll do it" or "we shall do what you want" are rendered by equally awkward phrases: טוב הדבר אני אעשה כדבריך,[240] כדבריך אדוננו נעשה,[241] דבר אדוני כי מחכה עבדך,[242] בכל לבבי אמלא אחרי דבריך,[243] דבר כי שומע עבדך.[244] A phrase like "make it brief" becomes דבר, אך מהר לכלות דבריך.[245] "Please do so" is rendered ויהי נא חסדך לעשות כזאת,[246] while "I don't understand" is expressed as דבריך נשגבים מבינתי.[247] Even so simple an idiom as "what happened?" receives such varied treatment as מה נהיתה,[248] איכה נהיתה כזאת,[249] and איככה היה כדבר הזה.[250] "I'm very grateful to you" is contorted into such stilted forms as נפשי ולבבי יביעו תודות לאדוני על חסדו זה[251] or רב תודה וברכה תביע לך נפשי.[252] Similarly, "at your service" becomes הנני כי קראת לי.[253] No further commentary is required on the ferocious problems of creating any sort of convincing dialog which confronted the Hebrew novelists under review.

One further indication of the extreme limitations of the linguistic resources at the disposal of these writers arises from the constant repetition of particular phrases, which occur so frequently that it is almost impossible to overlook them. It would appear that once having opted for a certain idiom—almost invariably biblical in accordance with their basic predilections—the novelists resorted to it almost without variation on every occasion when it seemed even remotely applicable. Some of these phrases are common to virtually all the novelists, while others are favored by individual authors. Many of them had previously been heavily employed by Mapu and, perhaps, gained greater currency for that reason. In attempting to assess the comparative frequency of these phrases, however, it must be remembered that Smolenskin's novels *The Wanderer in the Paths of Life* and *The Inheritance* are by far the largest of all the works under consideration. The same author's *The Reward of the Righteous*, the two novels by Braudes, Sheikewitz's *The Outcast*, and Weisbrem's *Eighteen Coins* are medium-length novels of considerably more than three hundred pages, while the remainder are comparatively short.[254]

Of all the recurring idioms to be encountered in these novels, some form of the phrase **מצא חן בעיני** is by far the most common.[255] Next in popularity are various forms of the idioms **[יש] לאל יד**[256] and **קצרה יד**.[257] As advocates of enlightenment, the novelists employ a number of phrases expressing the ideals of that movement, and in particular some form of the phrase **נפקחו עיני לראות**.[258] Other expressions which command fairly wide acceptance are **בכליון עינים**,[259] **[לשים] מחסום לפה**,[260] **בשאט נפש**,[261] and **הכרת פניו ענתה בו**.[262] The following idioms are favored chiefly by Smolenskin, but sometimes by other authors in addition: **לחפש חפש מחפש**,[263] **מפח נפש**,[264] **מחוז חפצו**,[265] **אלוף נעוריה**,[266] **ערש דוי**,[267] **מה עול [מצאת] בו**,[268] **עד ארגיע**,[269] **בכי תמרורים**,[270] **אזלת יד**,[271] **אחת דברתי ולא אשנה**,[272] **היו לא יהיה**,[273] **רוח עועים**,[274] **לעת מצוא**,[275] **ויעקם שפתיו**,[276] **אנחת שברון מתנים**,[277] **אבן מעמסה**,[278] and **כגבר עברו יין**.[279] Braudes also inclines to the phrases **במה כחך גדול**[280] and **אחת הנה ואחת הנה**,[281] while Weisbrem is attracted by **עוד חזון למועד**[282] and **כל ישעו וחפצו**[283]—both of them favorite expressions in Abraham Mapu's stories.

These examples clearly illustrate the formidable problems which confronted Hebrew writers during the second half of the nineteenth century in their search for viable and convincing modes of expression. It is all the more surprising that much of what they wrote remains interesting and even, at times, compelling. Far from being mere curiosities or museum pieces, these novels shed considerable light on an important stage in the development of modern Hebrew both in its literary and its linguistic aspects, as well as reflecting the social, economic, and cultural conditions of contemporary Jewish life in Eastern Europe. From the considerations outlined in this chapter, however, it follows that any attempt to estimate the achievements of these novelists and evaluate the esthetic qualities of their stories should properly take into account the linguistic disabilities besetting them on every side. A real understanding of their significance, therefore, demands the application of relative as well as absolute criteria. In that way, alone, is it possible to evaluate the literary merits of their novels in any valid measure, and arrive at a genuine appreciation of the extraordinary advances made by their more illustrious successors.

9

Israel Weisbrem[1]

In modern Hebrew literature, as in all literatures, the novel made a comparatively late appearance. Little more than a century and a quarter has passed since Abraham Mapu diffidently published the first Hebrew novel, *The Love of Zion*, in 1853. Although destined subsequently to play a major role in modern Hebrew literature, the novel made slow progress for several decades—certainly from a quantitative point of view. The thirty five years following the publication of *The Love of Zion* were graced by barely a score of Hebrew novels, an average of little more than one every two years; and although a number of them, such as Mapu's *The Hypocrite* or Smolenskin's *The Wanderer in the Paths of Life* or Braudes' *Religion and Life*, are admittedly very long, an equal number at least are very slight.

It may readily be conceded, then, that the total bulk of Hebrew literature in novel-form during the three and a half decades following the first appearance of this new genre is negligible when measured against the production of novels in all the major European literatures during those same years. Yet the impact which these Hebrew novels made on Jewish life and the influence which they exerted is out of all proportion to their extremely modest number—particularly in view of the fact that scarcely more than half that total were responsible for the achievement.

These novelists, in fact, may be clearly divided into major and minor writers. The former class comprises Abraham Mapu, Peretz Smolenskin, Reuben Asher Braudes, and Shalom Jacob Abramowitz, all of whom won renown within their own lifetimes, and whose place in the history of Hebrew literature rests upon firm foundations. The latter class includes such authors as A. S. Rabinowitz, I. J. Sirkis, S. F. Meinkin, J. Leinwand, M. Manassewitz, the prolific Yiddish writer N. M. Sheikewitz, B. I. Zobeizensky, and not least Israel Weisbrem, the author under review.[2] Most of these writers are now so obscure, and their writings have proved so ephemeral, that not even the various histories of literature so much as mention them. In many cases biographical information of even the most elementary kind is extremely difficult to locate. Moreover, actual copies of their novels are now so rare—in many cases as rare as manuscripts—that frequently recourse must be made to copies in microform in order to read them at all.

It would be absurd, therefore, to pretend that these minor novelists have any real significance either from the point of view of intrinsic merit or with respect to their influence on the course of Hebrew literature. In literary terms they offer little that is new, while their themes and methods of presentation for the most part merely constitute an inferior imitation of their more gifted contemporaries. Almost without exception these stories fall within the class of social novels, to which all the major novels of the period—apart from Mapu's historical romances—invariably belong. Again, for the most part, they partake of all the literary deficiencies and limitations of their peers with respect to plot, characterization, language, style, and form, without the saving graces of a certain rugged strength and purpose, which have preserved the latter from oblivion. And yet even these minor novels contain much that is of interest both for the historian of Hebrew literature and for the historian of the rich complex of Jewish life in Eastern Europe in the second half of the nineteenth century. For not only do these novels reflect the aspirations of Hebrew literature at that time and the bitter, often pathetic struggle to adapt the nascent Hebrew language to the demands of modern life, but they also represent a treasure-house of information relative to the social conditions in the Jewish Pale of Settlement.

From the novels alone it is possible to reconstruct a broad and fairly detailed picture of the patterns of life within that society. Clothes, manners, food, marriage customs, occupations, education, religious practice, communal organization, and a host of kindred subjects are all described with a wealth of detail. Moreover, if due allowance is made for the prejudices and tendentious opinions advanced inside these novels, it is equally possible to recapture something of the mental climate prevailing at that time—the splits and divisions in Jewish life, and the bitter discord between the old generation rooted in tradition, and the young generation, thirsting for a richer life and ready to cast aside its heritage in an all too uncritical acceptance of an alien culture. It is these aspects which lend the novels interest and reward the careful reader with some vivid glimpses into a vanished world.

Among the minor novelists Israel Weisbrem stands a little apart from the rest in several respects, and at times displays evidence of considerable literary ability. Of his three novels, the first, *Between the Times*,[3] appeared in 1888, the second, *Eighteen Coins*,[4] in the same year, and the third, *The Lottery and the Inheritance*,[5] in 1892—all of them in Warsaw. *Between the Times* bears the following explanatory note on its title page: "Between the time which has lost its vigor and the modern time which writers term enlightened." The hint of irony is subsequently developed. The title *Eighteen Coins* is followed by the alternative "Give me Money! Give me Money!" which again provides an inkling of the type of plot to be expected. The title of *The Lottery and the Inheritance* is qualified by the following illuminating phrase: "A story from the life of Jews and Christians in the villages and small towns of Western Russia." This latter statement contains the seed of one of the most interesting facets of

Weisbrem's novels, and one which distinguishes him from most of his colleagues, who are prone to confine their stories to Jewish life.

Between the Times is concerned with Gershon, the shiftless son of Peretz and Hannah Rekin, who own a shop in a little town in Lithuania.[6] Gershon irresponsibly takes their small store of capital and absconds with Tamar, the only surviving child of Nahum Tobiah, the local rabbi. But almost at once Gershon abandons her in order to woo the rich former mistress of a deceased Polish noble, to whom Gershon discovers he bears an extraordinary likeness. The lady in question, Miriam, for her part is anxious to marry into a respectable Jewish family in order to appease her parents, who have never been able to forgive her previous misconduct. Meanwhile the abandoned Tamar falls into a decline and is taken to hospital, where she is befriended by a rich Polish noblewoman, Elenora, a devout Catholic who takes her to her estate and nurses her back to health. One day Elenora introduces Tamar to her neighbor Miriam. The young women at once strike up a friendship, and Miriam invites Tamar to stay with her. Inevitably Miriam learns of Gershon's double dealings and reluctantly breaks off their betrothal. This misfortune has a sobering effect on Gershon, who decides to seek his fortune abroad.

Meanwhile, rabbi Nahum's adopted son Jonathan, who has always loved Tamar, finds life intolerable without her presence and seeks his fortune in America, where all trace of him is lost. Gershon, too, sails for America, where after some five years of hardship, including two years in a coalmine, he is befriended by a rich man called Conelly, who finds employment for him in Quebec. During all these years Tamar, who has returned to her parents' home, resists all proposals of marriage in the hope that Jonathan will one day return. Miriam, too, who has become reconciled to her parents, entertains similar aspirations with respect to Gershon.

Suddenly the little town is electrified by the news that Sir Conelly of Quebec is coming to open a factory nearby. Sir Conelly eventually calls on rabbi Nahum and turns out to be none other than Jonathan! After his engagement to the faithful Tamar, Jonathan journeys to Quebec to settle his affairs, returning five weeks later with his assistant—Gershon! A double wedding serves to round off the happy ending.

The improbabilities of *Between the Times* are closely rivaled by some of the more startling events woven into the plot of Weisbrem's second novel. But then *Eighteen Coins* is in any case a much longer novel consisting of more than four hundred pages and divided into two parts. This somewhat tortuous story is outlined against a background of the conflict which raged between the *Ḥasidhim* and the *Maskilim* in Eastern Europe during the nineteenth century.[7] In actual fact that contest was three-sided; but the third warring faction, comprising the *Mithnaggedhim*, is scarcely mentioned.

The plot centers upon the efforts of Gedaliah and Malka Skopitzki, a very rich, but miserly couple, to marry off their daughter Eve to Joseph, the son of the wealthy Simon Rebetzek. Both Gedaliah and Simon are pious *Ḥasidhim* and faithful supporters of the local *Ṣaddiq*—so much so that their belief in the latter's supernatural powers constitutes an important element in the plot. Indeed, when the fire insurance companies raise their premiums[8] the tight-fisted Gedaliah—most of whose wealth is in the form of merchandise—decides to send a gift to the *Ṣaddiq* in exchange for the latter's protection, even though he is told explicitly that the *Ṣaddiq*'s own property is insured! Simon's faith in the *Ṣaddiq*'s powers rests on firmer foundations. He attributes his success to eighteen copper coins which the *Ṣaddiq* once gave him—in return for eighteen gold coins—at a time of dire hardship. The coins have proved so efficacious that Simon, rising from strength to strength, has finally become the sole agent of a wealthy Polish nobleman, an absentee landlord, whose entire estates he supervises, even dwelling in the ancestral mansion. Simon treasures his eighteen coins, which he considers to be the source of his extraordinary good fortune,[9] and generously contributes to his *Ṣaddiq*'s funds. For his part the *Ṣaddiq* is anxious to foster an alliance between his two wealthy supporters, and details Shemaiah, a rather dubious character, to be Simon's secretary in order to expedite the proceedings. The only obstacle is that Joseph, Simon's son, who has enjoyed a liberal education and moves in a circle of young Polish nobles, refuses even to consider the match proposed for him.

Now Joseph has a young friend, Michael, whose father David Rosen is a wealthy *Maskil.* Joseph falls in love with Michael's sister Elisheba, while Michael himself is attracted to Rebecca, the second of seven poor sisters who earn a precarious living with the needle. As the prospect of such a double wedding is not likely to be to the *Ṣaddiq*'s advantage, Shemaiah determines to put a spoke in the wheel, and prevails upon Azriel Romberg, a pseudo-*Maskil,* to further his plans. With the help of an expert forger they send slanderous letters to the young lovers and their parents, as a result of which Joseph's mother pines away and dies.

In the course of time, however, the misunderstandings are resolved, and in Part Two of the novel Simon remarries, taking none other than Rebecca's older sister Sarah, who brings Rebecca along to live with them. Simon invites the Rosen family to spend a holiday on the estate, and goes so far as to write to the *Ṣaddiq* asking permission for Joseph to marry Elisheba. But this the *Ṣaddiq* indignantly refuses, demanding that Simon should either break off relations with the *Maskil* David Rosen or return his eighteen coins. Nor are Michael's marriage plans any more successful. His mother scornfully rejects his plan to marry a girl of such lowly origins, and to spare Rebecca further embarrassment Simon suggests she should spend some time at a lonely hunting lodge in the forest.

Meanwhile Azriel has been pressing Shemaiah for a reward for his herculean, though unsuccessful, attempts to divide the lovers. To be rid of him Shemaiah has him captured and imprisoned in a dungeon in that self-same hunting lodge. On hearing of this the *Ṣaddiq* decides that it would be best to induce Azriel to emigrate to America, and when the latter's wife Esther arrives to ask the *Ṣaddiq* of her husband's whereabouts, he tells her to make ready to join her husband in America. Esther, vastly impressed by the *Ṣaddiq*'s omniscience, sells up her possessions in preparation for the journey. In the hunting lodge, however, Rebecca is beginning to suspect that all is not well, and sends a message to Simon to that effect.

At this juncture the miserly Gedaliah reveals that he is about to pay off an old score against a minor Polish noble, Glupski. The latter has borrowed money from Gedaliah on the security of his estate, but Gedaliah is careful not to remind him of the expiry date. Instead he turns Glupski and his family out of their home with such callousness that the half-demented nobleman sets fire to the miser's entire property—which is not, of course, insured. At the risk of their lives, Joseph and Michael rescue Glupski from the flames, and almost at once courageously rescue Rebecca, who has been kidnaped by Shemaiah and his henchman with the object of holding her to ransom. The young lovers are reunited, and their parents consent at last to the double union. The *Ṣaddiq* dispatches the villains to the Holy Land to repent, while Azriel and Esther are reunited. But in her heart Esther always believes in the *Ṣaddiq*, and Simon, too, continues to send his contributions and maintains his faith in his eighteen coins. But Gedaliah goes mad with grief and spends the rest of his days running up and down his room in the asylum shouting "Give me money! Give me money!"

In contrast to the stirring events of the first two novels, the plot of the third, *The Lottery and the Inheritance*, is very slight and such interest as it arouses is largely incidental. The novel centers upon a small Lithuanian town and the efforts of two Jewish factors, David and Pesach, to make a precarious living as marriage brokers after their plans to serve the local Polish nobleman have come to grief. David adopts the cause of Rolashka, a minor government official, in the latter's efforts to woo Stephanie, the daughter of the rich Rebnitzki, one of the nobleman's chief administrators. On David's advice Rolashka borrows sufficient money to make the initial payment on an estate which is for sale, at the same time pretending that he has inherited it from his aunt. The ruse is successful, the hoodwinked Rebnitzki eagerly agreeing to what seems so favorable a match. The novelty lies in the fact that in this instance a Jewish marriage broker is used to bring about a gentile wedding. Meanwhile David's rival, Pesach, is desperately engaged upon the task of persuading the rich Zevulun, another of the nobleman's agents, to wed his daughter to Aaron Stein, a teacher in the local government school. Zevulun, however, is more interested in wealth than learning and Pesach makes little progress until he is able to inform Zevulun that Aaron Stein is the fortunate owner of a winning lottery ticket. The hard-headed Zevulun insists upon seeing the ticket, and not realizing that it bears the winning number of the previous year, joyfully gives his consent. Only after the wedding does he learn the bitter truth, but by then, of course, it is too late. Finding themselves in the same boat, the two duped fathers Rebnitzki and Zevulun decide to accept the inevitable and reconcile themselves to their impecunious sons-in-law. Zevulun, moreover, does derive some consolation from Aaron's learning, for the schoolmaster is able to prove by algebra to the extravagant wife of the nobleman just what the compound interest on a loan which she is urging her husband to make, to buy a new carriage, would amount to at the end of twenty years. The reader is not informed, however, whether that lady curbs her expensive habits. Presumably she is at least forced to agree with her husband's view that his Jewish employees are not without their usefulness. For all the frailty of its plot *The Lottery and the Inheritance* affords some very interesting insights on the social conditions prevailing at that time.

It becomes evident from these summaries that subtlety is scarcely a major feature of Weisbrem's plots. Recourse is made to a wide variety of dramatic devices quite apart from those already noted, namely such motifs as the eighteen lucky coins, the lack of fire insurance, the pretended inheritance,[10] or the spurious lottery ticket. The imprisonment of Azriel, for example, is effected by villains disguised as police, so that the victim does not even suspect foul play.[11] Much use is made of the confusion of names. When Gershon Rekin wishes to disguise his origins he refers to himself as Gregory, the son of Peter Rekin. Miriam's inquiries, however, can only locate a Peretz Rekin, a fact which allows the author to adapt the well-known quotation אל תקרא בניך אלא בוניך[12] "Do not say your children but your builders" to אל תקרא פרץ אלא פטר "Do not say Peretz but Peter."[13]

A different type of confusion is used in one of the most effective and original episodes to be found in all the Hebrew novels of this period. After reaching South America Jonathan writes to rabbi Nahum that any letters to him should be addressed to Mr Jonathan Cohn at Rio de Janeiro

Bresil [*sic*]

Post restant.[14] [*sic*]

Rabbi Nahum, who is not familiar with Latin script,[15] invokes the aid of Zevulun, the *Melammedh*, to address his reply.[16] Zevulun, who has frequently been enlisted by the local women to address letters to their husbands who have emigrated to England or France, claims to have learned French from addressing letters and from his study of Rashi! He informs the rabbi that Jonathan has clearly not yet mastered that language, for he has written *rio* instead of *rue*. Moreover, Zevulun labors under the impression that "Post restant" is the name of a city. In answer to the rabbi's query he explains that Bresil lies between India and Abyssinia, and that the country is so called because it was founded by the descendants of Barzillai of Gilead! Although it is clear from Jonathan's subsequent reproachful letters that the rabbi's missives, addressed by Zevulun, have failed to reach their destination, and in spite of Tamar's attempts to explain some elementary facts of geography, Zevulun obstinately clings to his misconceptions until finally all three letters are returned stamped with an official "address unknown."[17] Even allowing for the author's own uncertain spelling, it is difficult to imagine a more damning indictment of the prevailing educational system.[18]

The more violent type of melodrama is mainly limited to the novel *Eighteen Coins*. Apart from Azriel's capture and his melancholy and prolonged confinement in a loathsome dungeon,[19] excitement is added by the dramatic rescue of the demented arsonist Glupski, and of Eve the daughter of Gedaliah, his victim, from the flames. "Who is for God, after us!—cried Joseph Rebetzek and Michael Rosen simultaneously,"[20] plunging into the flames. Scarcely have the heroes had time to catch their breath when they must gallop away to the rescue of the kidnaped Rebecca. At midnight on a narrow road the heroes battle manfully against heavy odds,[21] Joseph with brute strength and Michael with skill, or "gymnastic devices," as the author puts it.[22] These episodes of physical prowess betray a trace of wistfulness felt by a people far removed from the stormy world of action.

Melodramatic elements of a less violent kind, however, may be found in all three stories. In the novel *Between the Times* that favorite device of popular fiction, coincidence, plays a major role—not only in the final *dénouement* when Sir Conelly and his assistant turn out to be Jonathan and Gershon, but equally in Gershon's amazing likeness to Miriam's dead lover and in the lucky circumstance that Elenora, Tamar's benefactress, happens to own the estate bordering on that of Miriam, which enables the two heroines to become acquainted. In *Eighteen Coins* an equally fortuitous development sends Rebecca to that same hunting lodge beneath which Azriel is held a prisoner. Another familiar device lurks in the glitter of large fortunes which form a background to all three novels. Great sums of money, varying between five thousand and a hundred thousand shekels—the normal equivalent of roubles in the Hebrew novel of the nineteenth century—bob in and out of the narrative on every conceivable occasion.[23] A more personal type of melodrama may be sought in the fainting fits to which the characters—both male and female—frequently succumb,[24] while such minor melodramatic crimes as forgery and theft are much in evidence.[25]

One further element of melodrama is worthy of note. The revenge motif occurs at least once in all three novels. When Shemaiah, for example, is threatened with exposure for having stolen Gershon's money, he revenges himself by writing an anonymous letter to Miriam, stating that Gershon has deceived Tamar.[26] Similarly in *The Lottery and the Inheritance* Pesach plots revenge on his rival David, who has jeopardized his livelihood.[27] The most effective examples, however, occur in *Eighteen Coins*. Not only is the miserly Gedaliah motivated by revenge to dispossess Glupski, but the latter in turn revenges himself on his oppressor by setting fire to his property. Before doing so, however, Glupski first vents his wrath on the Jews in general by destroying the "Sabbath limits"[28] in the little town where Gedaliah is staying overnight. As a result the town is virtually paralyzed. As the news of the atrocity reaches the congregation when they are returning from the synagogue on Sabbath morning, they send at once for the rabbi to solve the difficulty and the following scene ensues.

> Gedaliah Skopitzki was among those who stood awaiting the rabbi's reply so that they might know how to act in accordance with the correct ritual. Gedaliah waited rooted to the spot, as though his legs were bound in fetters; for not only was he holding a prayer shawl and some books, but in addition he was carrying banknotes, statements of accounts, letters of credit, and valuable documents sewn up in his breast pocket.

(A footnote gives the following explanation: "Gedaliah had heard from learned men that in this way it was permissible to carry things on the Sabbath in a place where there were Sabbath limits." The necessary rabbinical references are then quoted.)[29]

> After they had all been standing like marble statues for half an hour or more, a succession of messengers arrived one after the other from the rabbi with the news that everyone might proceed in this fashion: They might walk for less than four cubits and then stop to rest; while they were standing still any burden they were carrying must be put on the ground, and afterwards they might lift it, walk the same distance, and stop and rest again, and so on until they reached their destination. Gedaliah was informed that because he was carrying banknotes and equally valuable letters of credit, and might be afraid to put them on the ground in full public gaze, he should walk less than four cubits and then sit down to refresh himself . . . and so proceed until he arrived at his hotel.

(Again a footnote gives the rabbinical authority.)[30]

Before reaching his hotel, however, Gedaliah learns that his house is on fire. Without a moment's compunction he leaps into a carriage, Sabbath or no Sabbath, and hastens home. Quite apart from the considerable humor in this episode, the author effectively satirizes—as is frequently the case in the novels of the *Haskalah*[31]—the striking contrast presented by extreme ritual piety side by side with an utter ruthlessness and immorality in business.

Love, as might be expected, constitutes a major motif in all three stories, although in *The Lottery and the Inheritance* the young lovers themselves all play very minor roles—indeed, the young ladies scarcely appear. In the other novels, however, the heroes and heroines are all central figures in the action. Apart from the more obvious devices of Tamar's touching faithfulness to her long-lost lover,[32] or Rebecca's avowed intention of remaining true to Michael even after determining that she ought never to see him again,[33] or the emotional scenes in which Joseph pours out his love to Elisheba[34] in a manner so deservedly satirized by the contemporary Hebrew novelist A. S. Rabinowitz,[35] there is one episode of more specific interest. When the idea is first mooted to Gershon that he should abandon Tamar in order to woo the wealthy Miriam and her thirty thousand shekels, Gershon at first indignantly rejects the idea with the remark that such things are never done in the love stories of the *Haskalah*![36] Although contributing to that very genre, the author is not unaware of its weaknesses. A similar ambivalent attitude will appear again.

One further device, which is common to most Hebrew novels of the period, is the large number of letters which find their way into the stories and which frequently constitute important elements in the plot.[37] Although *The Lottery and the Inheritance* has only one,[38] *Eighteen Coins* contains nine,[39] and *Between the Times* no fewer than sixteen.[40] Letters are regularly left by such of the characters as leave home, or they may be used to convey information vital to the plot.[41] They may be anonymous,[42] or forged,[43] or opened by mistake.[44] Sometimes the contents may be given only in reported speech.[45] But the most interesting are those written by Joel, the *Ṣaddiq*'s right-hand man, in *Eighteen Coins*. These letters,[46] three in all, are deliberately written in barbaric style to satirize the type of Hebrew ascribed to *Ḥasidhim*. On each occasion the author includes them only as footnotes, prefacing each one with the satirical remark that he is presenting them for the benefit of readers who delight in polished Hebrew! Although the author's own command of Hebrew is not always above reproach, so that his remarks contain something of the pot calling the kettle black, the device is nevertheless an effective means of satire, although not original to Weisbrem.[47]

More original, however, as far as the contemporary Hebrew novel is concerned, is the use made of modern devices within the plots. Such elements as photographs,[48] telegrams,[49] advertisements in the press,[50] and fire insurance companies[51] indicate at least a willingness to exploit a wider range of dramatic expedients than is normally the case among his contemporaries. A further positive feature lies in the skillful resort to dramatic irony in *Eighteen Coins*. Simon and Joseph, for example, discuss methods of discovering who has sent the anonymous letters in the presence of Shemaiah, the man responsible for them, and even enlist his aid.[52] David Rosen, too, seeks Shemaiah's help for that very purpose.[53] Again, Azriel is delighted with Shemaiah for arranging his rescue, unaware that the latter was responsible for his imprisonment.[54] Esther's gratitude to the *Ṣaddiq* for revealing the whereabouts of her husband falls into a similar category.[55]

In spite of the many weaknesses of construction, the gross improbabilities, the loose technique, the wild extravagance, and the inability to handle such thorny problems as arise, for example, from the passage of time[56] or the integration of events,[57] the plots do exhibit a certain dramatic skill, while the stories are frequently enlivened with the excitement of rapid action.

But whereas his plots are occasionally relieved by flashes of artistry, most of Weisbrem's characterizations have little to recommend them. With few exceptions they are flat and lifeless, with little sign of individuality. It appears at times, moreover, that even the author is scarcely concerned with his characters. We learn, for instance, that Sarah and Rebecca are the eldest of seven sisters;[58] but nearly two hundred pages elapse before we are informed that the two youngest girls are called Rachel and Tamar,[59] while the other three remain anonymous. Similarly the names of Gedaliah's two eldest daughters, Eve and Braina, are not revealed until well into the second part of the novel—even though the attempt to get Eve married is one of the major themes of the plot—while the other three daughters are merely referred to as third, fourth, and fifth.[60] Yet in one respect Weisbrem does represent an advance over the classical characters of the *Haskalah.* His portraits are rarely drawn solely in absolute black or white. His heroes are not the irritating paragons of virtue, nor are his villains the very devils incarnate commonly found in the Hebrew novels of the period.

From time to time, moreover, there are touches of real literary skill. The novelists of the *Haskalah* never acquired any real ability in developed characterization, but they did in time learn something of the techniques of sketching character. Thus it is that many of the minor characters are much more convincing than the principal heroes and heroines in their novels. This phenomenon applies equally to Weisbrem. In *Eighteen Coins* only three figures can lay claim to any real spark of life—Jekutiel, the dauntless and irrepressible marriage broker, who wastes no opportunity in plying his trade; the miserly Gedaliah; and Malka his equally tight-fisted wife. Gedaliah, indeed, is portrayed in strong colors as a strange mixture of superstitious credulity and down-to-earth hard-headedness in which a scrupulous devotion to ritual piety is blended, as illustrated above, with an utter ruthlessness. He is, at least, a man who knows what he values in life and is prepared to go to any lengths to attain his ends.[61] His wife Malka is portrayed as a woman worthy of such a mate, and some of her exchanges with Zibiah, her neighbor, provide perhaps the liveliest elements in the story.[62] *Between the Times* is noteworthy for the characterization of rabbi Nahum Tobiah, of whom the author paints a most sympathetic portrait. The rabbi emerges as a simple, upright, pious, and understanding figure, with a great capacity for quiet courage in the face of misfortune.[63] One of the most attractive scenes in the book is that in which he convenes a meeting of the leading members of the community because the inclement weather has made it impossible to recite the blessing over the new moon. The assembly affords Weisbrem an opportunity for some amusing character sketches, not least that of the bigoted Zevulun, who attributes the divine punishment to the arrival in the town of a number of teachers of grammar![64]

The flatness of the characters is naturally reflected in their conversation; although perhaps the process should rather be considered in reverse. The very difficulty of writing any sort of convincing dialog in Hebrew was one of the most obstinate problems confronting the novelists of the nineteenth century. While their contribution to the revival of the spoken language must not be underestimated, it remains true that the limited linguistic materials at their disposal necessarily engendered a stilted type of conversation, which in turn affected the quality of characterization. In this respect Weisbrem labors beneath the same disabilities as the rest. The very fact that a serving lad is made to say "Your servant hears" in the absence of an idiomatic equivalent for "Yes, sir" provides sufficient indication of the type of problem involved.[65] Nevertheless on more than one occasion the author has succeeded in creating the impression of lively dialog, as when David and Pesach quarrel over who shall have the privilege of acting as factor to the Polish nobleman in *The Lottery and the Inheritance*;[66] or in the scene in which Malka abuses her neighbors for daring to suggest that she should contribute to charity.[67] But only too often the dialog has a sadly stilted and unnatural flavor.

In other respects, however, the general style of Weisbrem's novels presents a number of attractive features. His writing is clear and straightforward, light and lively, and has a certain swing unusual in the novels of this period. Moreover, the frequent interspersion of humorous and satirical episodes adds a refreshing touch of light-heartedness to his stories, especially when compared with the deadly seriousness of much of the work of his contemporaries. To label Weisbrem's writing "biblical" would be misleading, for no Hebrew novelist after Mapu deliberately essayed to imitate the Hebrew of the Bible. Nevertheless all the novelists of the *Haskalah* limited themselves almost entirely to the vocabulary of the Bible, and in this respect Weisbrem's stories form no exception. Phrases drawn directly from the Bible are used quite frequently, while many more sentences have a strong biblical flavor. The origin of such a construction as **ויהי היום ותבוא מרים העירה** ...[68] is clearly unmistakable. The author's marked fondness for the books of Ruth and Ecclesiastes appears in such reminiscent phrases as "May the Lord grant that your daughter shall find peace in her husband's house"[69] or "And this is not a thing of which it can be said 'behold this is new.'"[70]

Although the biblical *waw consecutive* appears not infrequently in all Weisbrem's novels, its use is comparatively restricted, thus marking a stage along the road to linguistic emancipation, at least in one respect. One unusual feature, as stated previously, lies in the fact that the speech of a poor woodcutter in *Eighteen Coins* is dominated by the *waw consecutive*.[71] This seems to be a deliberate device to indicate the inferior speech of an ignorant laborer. Although clearly unsuccessful, the attempt in itself is interesting as an indication of the author's awareness of the problem. Another positive feature is the comparative rarity of that high-flown euphuistic type of phrase called *meliṣah*, so beloved by the early *Maskilim*.[72]

The severe limitations of biblical vocabulary compel Weisbrem, again in common with all his contemporaries, to resort to a number of devices injurious to his style. A large number of modern terms, such as *post, address, police, gendarme, credit, telegraph, telephone, gymnasts*, and so on, are merely transliterated into Hebrew from European languages. Alternatively, a doubtful attempt to express a concept for which no adequate term exists sometimes requires an explanatory footnote, as the following examples illustrate. The phrase **בתי מקוה הסוחרים** is clarified as **בארזע** ("stock-exchange");[73] בתי האוצר לכסף is defined, perhaps gratuitously, as באנק ("bank");[74] שער הסוסים is explained as פפּערדע מארקט ("horse market");[75] while the interesting גוננה is adapted as an equivalent of זאננעשירם ("parasol").[76] Elsewhere equally cumbersome phrases such as ספר מפקד האורחים[77] for "hotel register," or תכריך המכתבים[78] for "envelope," or רב הסריסים[79] for "chief waiter," to quote a few of many, are apparently deemed self-evident. At times the author is so hard pressed in his search for terminology that the results are quite grotesque. His paraphrase of a "college of agriculture and forestry" for example becomes בית מדרש החכמה לעבודת האדמה ולגדול עצי יער;[80] "in the newspapers" is expressed by בכתבי העתים המודיעים חדשים לבקרים ילדי יום יום.[81] For the term "forger" Weisbrem rather surprisingly resorts to the following: איש אשר יכין לכתוב כתב איש איש כדמותו וכצלמו ואותותם לא ינכרו כי אשר זר כתבם;[82] but the delightful term קנה רובה קטן בעל ששת פיפיות for "six-shooter" is unfortunately not original.[83] No further commentary is required to illustrate both the pathos and the heroism which characterizes the Hebrew novelists of the period under review.

The same limitation of language is further responsible for a monotonous repetition of idiom which pervades all the novels of the *Haskalah*, those of Weisbrem not excepted. Some form of the idiom מצא חן בעיני occurs no less than fifty eight times in these three novels;[84] the idiom יד קצרה is found thirty seven times;[85] the phrase נפקחו עינים לראות appears thirty three times,[86] while some form of כל ישעם וכל חפצם is used on twenty five occasions[87]—to note only a few of the more common examples. Lack of vocabulary, too, is largely responsible for the poor quality of description, which is characterized by either a succession of stock phrases[88] or a woeful struggle for terminology.[89] The rare passages of natural description suffer a similar fate.[90]

Certain aspects of Weisbrem's style, however, show a marked advance over most of his contemporaries. Almost all the novels of this period are bedeviled by a literary device, which once exercised an hypnotic influence on novelists in general, and was imported wholesale into Hebrew literature, namely the ingenuous intrusion of the author in the first person and the exhortation to the reader. Some form of: "And now, dear reader, let us transport you ..." is as common in the novel of the *Haskalah* as in contemporary European literature.[91] Weisbrem's novels commendably resort to this device only on comparatively rare occasions. The author intrudes into each novel scarcely half a dozen times, while the reader is personally addressed on four occasions in *Eighteen Coins*,[92] only twice in *Between the Times*,[93] and in *The Lottery and the Inheritance* not at all!

Moreover, as mentioned previously, the humorous and satirical elements are introduced with considerable artistry. This is true not only in such examples as Zevulun's prowess in the realm of foreign correspondence or Glupski's violation of the Sabbath limits quoted above, but in the author's satirical attack on the prevailing heavy-handed methods of education[94] and on the more spurious forms of Hasidism and *Haskalah.*[95] The most attractive examples are those scenes in which Gershon tries to hide his Jewish identity by adopting the name Gregory, but experiences great difficulty in finding an equivalent for "Tamar," which he eventually changes to "Theofilia;"[96] and where Gershon, again, imagines he is increasing his prestige by speaking a blood-curdling mixture of broken Polish and Russian.[97] This satire on the degrading attempt to assume a foreign culture is strangely reminiscent of the device used so successfully by Lessing in his *Minna von Barnhelm* to pour scorn on the eighteenth-century German habit of speaking bad French.

The literary qualities of these novels, however, are perhaps of less significance than the social background which they portray. Much of the information which may be gleaned stems from the strong didactic tendencies of the author, which often contrast starkly with the romantic fantasies of his plots. But many interesting details of the social conditions prevailing are purely incidental—that is, not deliberately introduced by the author to point a specific lesson. Some light is shed on types of occupation, for example, by an examination of the activities of the many characters introduced into the stories. Apart from the merchants, petty traders, moneylenders, or such community professionals as the marriage brokers, the striking feature is the large proportion of the *Luftmensch* type, the people with no real occupation at all. Many of the characters engage in a wide variety of pursuits, still without being able to make a livelihood;[98] others wring a precarious living by performing minor services for the Polish nobility or Catholic clergy.[99] This circumstance only heightens the absurdity of a mental climate which despises craftsmen and manual workers.[100] Of particular interest are the references to smuggling goods across the frontier,[101] and the decline in the practice of innkeeping in consequence of the coming of the railroad.[102]

No less than his contemporaries Weisbrem is much concerned with the prevailing state of education and culture. Time and again his sallies are directed against the narrow traditional education, and more particularly its exponents, the frustrated bigoted *Melammedhim*, whose sole pedagogical principle appears to have been the infliction of savage beatings on their pupils.[103] No wonder, therefore, that Gershon so readily blames his harsh education for his later misdemeanors.[104] The obscurantist attitude which denied daughters any education also comes in for attack,[105] and one of Michael's first actions in his wooing of Rebecca is to promise that he will help her acquire an education.[106] Nevertheless it is of interest that the Polish *Ḥasidhim* are portrayed as permitting their daughters a smattering, however inadequate, of that secular education which was forbidden to their sons.[107]

Toward the whole question of *Haskalah*, which naturally looms large in all three novels, Weisbrem adopts the ambivalent attitude already noted. He firmly advocates the positive achievements of *Haskalah*, particularly on its practical side. His ideal hero, Michael, has studied agriculture,[108] employs

Jewish workers on his estates,[109] and draws an idealized picture of their prospects. Noteworthy, too, is the stand which Michael takes as an exponent of practical Zionism against the religious messianism of the *Ḥasidhim*, who claim that the *Ṣaddiq* will bring about the redemption.[110] Not only is Weisbrem careful to stress that the acquisition of secular knowledge is a lengthy and arduous process[111]—a rather optimistic period of two years is suggested—but he is equally at pains to differentiate the sort of knowledge which has a practical application, namely the earning of a livelihood, and that which has not.[112] In spite of the satirical treatment of Gershon's attempt to hide his Jewish origin by using a smattering of Polish and Russian, both Gershon and Jonathan are portrayed as benefiting greatly once they have acquired a mastery of foreign languages.[113] In *The Lottery and the Inheritance* there is a fierce discussion on whether or not science has brought benefit to the world,[114] and although the proofs are not altogether convincing, there can be no doubt where the author's sympathies lie. Aaron Stein's algebraic calculations provide a further illustration of the lesson.[115] Equally important, however, are the author's forthright attacks on the type of pseudo-*Haskalah* which was obviously prevalent. He scathingly satirizes the attitude of mind which preferred to assume the outward trappings of westernization, while eschewing the mental discipline required for the real acquisition of knowledge.[116] The young *Ḥasidh* Dov Shahor, for example, deciding that it will take him too long to acquire the knowledge necessary to become a real *Maskil*, determines merely to discard his long coat for the short one favored in *Haskalah* circles, in the belief that this in itself will make him more attractive to the fair sex![117] Weisbrem's condemnation of the changing attitude of the *Maskilim* to Hebrew, and their rapid abandonment of their former attachment to that language, is equally sincere.[118] Certainly his attitude represents an advance on the earlier naive beliefs of *Haskalah*, which tended to regard secular knowledge as a panacea for all the evils of Jewish life.

Comment on the information relative to the Hasidic movement which may be gleaned from *Eighteen Coins*[119]—such as the methods by which petitions were forwarded to the *Ṣaddiq* by his followers,[120] or the reasons for relating a man to his mother instead of his father,[121] or the custom of shaving the head between the temples[122]—must be confined in this instance to the author's mode of presentation. Although in the early part of the story the movement is portrayed in a favorable light, Weisbrem's attitude gradually changes to one of severe criticism. The *Ṣaddiq* himself, however, is spared most of the author's vituperation. While the evils perpetrated by his lieutenants are scathingly denounced, it remains equivocal whether the *Ṣaddiq* is aware of them—although the remarks of one or two of the villains ostensibly working in his cause would seem to indicate his acquiescence.[123] Admittedly in the scene in which he is personally introduced, the *Ṣaddiq* refuses to countenance villainy directly, but the reader is left wondering to what extent he is prepared to turn a blind eye to the actions of his subordinates.[124] Certainly his plan for shipping Azriel off to America smacks more of expediency than of integrity.[125]

All three novels devote considerable attention to the question of relationships between Jews and gentiles. The problem of anti-Semitism is treated on a number of occasions, with particular reference to its causes. Not only is mention made of the spurious grounds advanced by such Polish papers as *Rola* and *Wiek*,[126] or of the fashionability of anti-Semitism,[127] but also of Jewish practices and characteristics which genuinely arouse gentile hostility.[128] Of particular interest is the discussion in which the Polish nobleman explains to his young wife the difference between being anti-Semitic in theory and the practical running of his affairs without the aid of Jews.[129] This episode, incidentally, outlines the economic situation in Poland in a manner strikingly similar to that portrayed by Solomon Maimon in his well-known *Autobiography*, although the latter was describing conditions prevalent almost one hundred and thirty years previously.[130]

Weisbrem frequently adopts the air of *apologia*, so frequently encountered in the novels of the *Haskalah*, no matter how romantic the framework. In *Eighteen Coins* a discussion develops at the home of David Rosen concerning Jewish economic activities, in which the Jews are valiantly defended against calumny.[131] Earlier in the same story the young heroes argue the case for the civilizing influence of Judaism with a group of young Polish nobles. The Jewish attitude of compassion toward animals, for example, is contrasted with the delight in blood sports exhibited by the young Poles.[132] There is a pathetic note in this whole conception of young Jewish *Maskilim* expounding the virtues of Judaism to Polish noblemen. These Hebrew novels, after all, were written for Jewish readers, and could only conjure up a picture of what Jews might like to happen while remaining powerless to contribute toward the realization of such an end. The cause of good relations is similarly advocated by the help given to Tamar by Elenora, the rich Catholic lady. Subsequently Tamar is aided by a Catholic priest, and this enables the author to express his appreciation of the truly devout adherents of all religions,[133] although the force of his remarks is tempered by a reminder that such types are rare![134] In similar vein the nobleman in *The Lottery and the Inheritance*, in spite of his irritation at the antics of his Jewish factors, nevertheless expresses a deep sympathy with their unfortunate plight.[135]

Weisbrem's novels, therefore, constitute an odd mixture of serious grappling with social problems and light-hearted, melodramatic fantasy. The wildly improbable happy endings denote a wistfulness which represented, perhaps, the pipe dreams of whole multitudes of poverty-stricken Jews in Eastern Europe, while beside them the pettiness of so many of the themes, and the purposeless occupations of so many of the characters, only serve to emphasize the miserable half-life of Jewish reality at that time. Thus in spite of the many literary weaknesses, the linguistic inadequacies, and above all the ephemeral nature of these novels, which have condemned them to so utter an oblivion, they may still shed light on many interesting facets of Hebrew literature, and open a window on many aspects of Jewish social conditions in Eastern Europe in the second half of the nineteenth century.

10

Ancient Hebrew Law in Modern Hebrew Literature

THIS CHAPTER is concerned with two cases of "court-type" scenes in the modern Hebrew novel, one in R. A. Braudes' *Religion and Life*[1] and the other in M. Shamir's *The King of Flesh and Blood.*[2] In both instances the episode is governed by a point of law, and in both the dramatic element arises from a confrontation. Separated by more than three quarters of a century, the two novels differ radically in style, theme, period, and place. Whereas the former is concerned with a controversy over minor religious reform which raged among the Jews of Lithuania between the years 1869 and 1871,[3] the latter depicts the stormy events of the first five years of the reign of Alexander Jannaeus in the little kingdom of Judaea, in 103 to 98 B.C.E. Braudes describes a miniature, parochial, self-contained, and inward-looking world, while Shamir uses a wide canvas for an exciting tale of royal conquests and defeats, the struggle for power of Pharisee and Sadducee, the clash of Greek and Hebrew civilizations. Yet both authors have given expression to the role of law as a central force in Jewish life, and both have utilized the device of legal confrontation as a powerful and dramatic element in their respective plots.

The use of the court scene as a literary device enjoys a long and varied history, but one which seems to have attracted less critical attention than it perhaps deserves. The literatures of antiquity provide a number of pertinent examples which employ this setting for literary effect. Of these, some take the form of a heavenly confrontation, as for example in a council of the gods in the *Epic of Gilgamesh*,[4] or in the trial of strength between God and Satan in the book of Job.[5] Alternatively as in the fateful clash of goddesses in the judgment of Paris,[6] or in the trial of Orestes in *The Eumenides*[7] by Aeschylus, the court scene may embrace both divine and human characters. Elsewhere, as in the trial scene depicted in Homer on the shield of Achilles[8] or in the famous judgment of Solomon[9] or the intriguing story of Susanna,[10] with its emphasis on the isolation of witnesses, the setting is mundane. But whether staged in heaven or on earth the cut and thrust of argument, the interplay of character and personality, and the moments of excitement and suspense produce dramatic tension and arouse a sense of curiosity and anticipation, which exert considerable literary appeal.

Of the precedents formulated in ancient literature, two in particular seem to have caught the imagination in medieval times, namely betrayal in love and the struggle for man's soul. The amorous consequences of the judgment of Paris[11] foreshadow the medieval Court of Love as a widespread literary motif, in which a sin against love or an insult to Venus and Cupid is punished by a quasi-legal court made up of the pagan gods.[12] Chaucer describes a Court of Love in the proem to the *Legend of Good Women*, while the Scots poet Robert Henryson introduces the device in *The Testament of Cresseid*, a continuation of Chaucer's *Troilus and Criseyde*. The tradition was still sufficiently alive for Spenser to use it in the *Faerie Queene*[13] where he depicts the trial and punishment of Mirabella for arrogance toward her lovers. In more mundane and sober terms the trial theme is powerfully embodied in Shakespeare's *Measure for Measure*.[14]

Similarly, the celestial struggle for man's soul, depicted in the Prologue to the book of Job, may be discerned, for example, in the medieval *Processus Belial*, of which many versions exist in French, Latin, Catalan, and Dutch. In the *Processus Belial*, the Devil appears in the court of heaven to demand that mankind be delivered over to him, as his right in consequence of the Fall. Once the court has opened God, the judge, asks through the angel Gabriel for an advocate for mankind. The Virgin Mary consents to represent the defence, answering the Devil's demand for justice with the argument that mercy is as much an attribute of God as justice. The Devil then produces scales, and demands that his due portion of mankind be weighed and handed to him. But finally he is driven out of the court in disgrace. It is not difficult to discern the analogues in the trial scene in *The Merchant of Venice*, with Shylock substituted for the Devil, Portia for the Virgin Mary, and Antonio for mankind.[15] A similar usage of a celestial "court" is introduced by Milton into *Paradise Lost*, Book 3, in which the Father and the Son debate the case of Man and the possibility of his redemption. The later utilization of the court scene as a forum for the propagation of ideas is already foreshadowed.

Before proceeding to consider briefly some aspects of the device to be encountered in the novel, the case of Lessing's play *Nathan der Weise*[16] is worthy of mention. Nathan's parable of the three rings, with its well-known trial scene in which the wise judge exhorts each of the three sons claiming to own the true ring—the one which makes its possessor beloved of God and man—to emulate the virtues which that ring bestows upon its owner, represented a courageous attempt on Lessing's part to invest Judaism with the same dignity and authority assumed by Christianity and Islam. Lessing's play, with its outspoken appeal for mutual respect, proved to be a source of fascination for the *Maskilim*. It was translated into Hebrew both by Simon Bacher [Bacharach][17] and by Abraham Baer Gottlober.[18] In reviewing Gottlober's translation, R. A. Braudes was at pains to emphasize how much the Jews of Russia might learn from the play regarding religious tolerance![19] Within two years, in 1876, he had started publishing his important novel which is devoted to that very theme,[20] himself adopting a device which is closely allied to a trial scene.[21]

With the development of the European novel the dramatic possibilities of the court or quasi-court scene gained increasing recognition and found expression in a variety of forms. While examples may be discerned in the English novel of the eighteenth century,[22] the device was employed more frequently from the second decade of the nineteenth century by Walter Scott,[23] and then successively by Edward Bulwer Lytton[24] and Charles Dickens.[25] Similarly, the court scene was utilized in the French novel as an important ingredient by Victor Hugo,[26] Eugène Sue,[27] and Alexandre Dumas.[28] In German literature during this period, however, the use of trials and court scenes is less evident in the novel than in drama, where it was adopted with some enthusiasm.[29] In Russian literature prior to 1876 surprisingly little resort was made to a device which was later to be employed so powerfully by Dostoievsky.[30]

The trials and court scenes embodied in these novels serve a variety of purposes and fall into a number of categories. There are courts whose proceedings the reader is inclined to credit, where—apart from human fallibility—the administration of justice is fair and proper.[31] There are courts, on the other hand, whose authority the reader is loath to accept, either because of their illegal constitution[32] or because the reader's sympathies are on the side of the prisoner,[33] because the case happens to be unfairly weighted against him on personal grounds or due to the prevailing climate of opinion.[34] Indeed, the threat of a miscarriage of justice—a theme that may be traced back to Susanna—is a powerful device for arousing the reader's pity and even terror.[35] Again, there are cases in which the point at issue arises from a difference of belief or adherence between the court and the accused.[36]

The dramatic tension and entertainment value of such scenes can be considerable, a fact to which the extensive use of the courtroom in the film and television industries in recent times bears ample testimony.[37] But apart from the excitement, often sharpened by the fluctuating fortunes and alternating success and failure of the protagonists,[38] the court or quasi-court scene frequently serves a didactic purpose by providing a forum for the propagation of ideas. The author may be concerned with social or political wrongs, the rectification of legal abuse, or, as in Braudes' case, the advocacy of religious reform. Certainly, the court or its equivalent provides an effective platform for the dissemination of proposals while the reader's interest is firmly engaged. Moreover, the role of the spectators provides an additional means of emphasizing the author's message, and their reactions may serve to arouse the reader's sympathies for or against the arguments produced in court.

The case in Braudes' *Religion and Life* employs most of the literary techniques outlined in the preceding paragraph, but in addition contains a number of features which derive from its specifically Jewish background. The scene takes place not in a courtroom but in a synagogue where a confrontation is made possible by virtue of the traditional Jewish device known as *'Ikkubh ha-Qeri'ah.*[39] In accordance with ancient practice, the reading of the *Torah* may be interrupted to seek the redress of a wrong, thereby allowing an individual to protest publicly against what he considers to be an injustice perpetrated against him. As the service could not be resumed nor the congregation easily return home until the matter had been settled, or a deferment to the following Sabbath arranged, the procedure served as an effective method for settling disputes. Since rituals tend to allow for a certain amount of interruption—although not, of course, enough to destroy them—the sudden and unexpected interruption of a religious service, funeral procession, or a wedding ceremony[40] can produce high drama. The interrupted reading of the *Torah* coupled with the clash of ideas and personalities generate all the tension of a trial in court. The plot of *Religion and Life* is designed to illustrate what Braudes considered to be the over-stringent decisions emanating from the rabbis in Lithuania with respect to the interpretation of Jewish religious law.[41] The author portrays the readiness of the local rabbi to pronounce a slaughtered animal ritually unfit if there was even the slightest shadow of doubt. The novel opens with the rabbi condemning three cows in a single day, in spite of the protests of the butcher—a man with forty years' experience—who is convinced that the third was fit for consumption, since the suspicion of a defective lung is tenuous in the extreme. The whole community is left without meat for the Sabbath, while the butcher sustains a ruinous loss.

On the following day the butcher dramatically interrupts the service in synagogue before the reading of the *Torah* to remonstrate against the rabbi's decision. The hero of the novel, Samuel,[42] himself an accomplished Talmudic scholar, takes his side against the rabbi, arguing that because the animal has unlawfully been pronounced ritually unfit, the rabbi must himself compensate the butcher for his loss. Although at first nonplused, the rabbi vigorously defends his decision, and a fierce argument ensues. Finally, the rabbi calls for a *Šulḥan 'Arukh*[43] and triumphantly supports his ruling by reference to Isserles' commentary on the passage in question.[44] But Samuel asks why the rabbi has not called for a Talmud, the real fountain-head of Jewish law, and argues the merits of the early authorities while denouncing the ever-increasing stringencies of the later commentators. When a Talmud is produced, Samuel is able to prove his point by demonstrating chapter and verse.[45] The hushed congregation is astounded to find that two such authoritative works can contradict each other:

> The men looked on in astonishment. For Jews, and particularly in Lithuania, the sanctity of the *Šulḥan 'Arukh* is as firmly established as that of the Talmud itself. For the generality of Jews, the *Šulḥan 'Arukh* is a compendium of the Talmud which, while dispensing with excessive length and unnecessary subtlety, presents the reader with the best and clearest summary of Talmudic decisions and enactments. Such is the prevailing climate of opinion. But here they were faced with a glaring contradiction between *Šulḥan 'Arukh* and Talmud, the one allowing what the other forbids; the one declaring ritually unfit what the other declares ritually fit. And they are at a loss to know which should be given preference. They regard them both as being equal in value, sanctity, tradition, and authority, and who can determine which of them should carry greater weight? . . . Nonplused, they stood between the rabbi and Samuel, glancing from the *Šulḥan 'Arukh* to the Talmud in blank incomprehension.[46]

The rabbi is constrained to ask how he can possibly give a decision contrary to Isserles, but Samuel asks in turn how Isserles could have contradicted all the authorities preceding him. When the rabbi argues that Isserles merely made the laws more stringent, Samuel demonstrates that such a procedure is contrary to the spirit of the Talmud. He contends that the rabbis should be mindful of the people's welfare, and that the later commentators have led the people astray. The rabbi seizes the opportunity to break off the dispute by accusing Samuel of being an *'Apiqores*[47] (heretic), a cry which is at once taken up by the spectators:

> "*'Apiqores*!" the sound floated up to him from all the congregation.
>
> "*'Apiqores*!" Even the women were chanting it from behind the grills in the women's gallery—But the rabbi's voice rose even stronger:
>
> "What a sin I have committed in answering you . . . I always regarded you as a scholar who enjoyed arguing with me over fine points of law. But now that I see that you are simply an *'Apiqores*, I have no desire to answer the heresies you keep mouthing . . . Get out of here before you defile this holy place . . . and never cross my threshold again . . ."[48]

Samuel, who has fallen deeply in love with the rabbi's stepdaughter, is thrown into confusion by this last prohibition, and breaks off the dispute, allowing the congregation to infer that he has been defeated in argument. The rabbi orders the reading of the Law to be resumed, the remainder of the service is conducted in hushed tones, and the congregation leaves for home in silence.[49]

The chapter exerts a powerful impact, with all the suspense and dramatic tension usually associated with a court scene. The protagonists are both powerful representatives of a point of view. The rabbi, defending a rigid orthodoxy, is determined not to retreat one inch from what he considers to be the correct interpretation of the Law, however severe, while Samuel is clearly advocating the case for reform in order to reconcile the demands of religion with the changing needs of life. In this classic struggle for men's minds, the author's didactic purpose is thrown into sharp relief, and there cannot be any doubt where his own sympathies lie. But at the same time the reader is made aware of the woman in the background, and the weakening influence exerted upon the hero by the knowledge that his passionate antipathy to the rabbi's position is damaging his prospect of personal happiness—although in the event his love is not returned.[50] Again, the tension is heightened by the fluctuating course of the debate, and the alternating success and failure of the opponents. The rabbi's initial discomfiture turns to triumph as Samuel, after his earlier onslaught, finally relapses into silence, apparently admitting defeat. The congregation, moreover, fulfills the role of a chorus, reacting to the arguments, dismayed by the contradiction of hallowed authorities, and finally branding Samuel with the charge of heresy in spite of the fact that his main motivation has been the alleviation of their economic plight. This crowning irony helps to establish the scene as one of the most effective in Hebrew literature of the period.

The court scene in *The King of Flesh and Blood* is of a more conventional kind,[51] and concerns a ruling in the case of a false witness. The material is derived from a well-known incident in rabbinical literature,[52] whose origin the novelist attempts to explain with the help of imaginative insight. The passage reads as follows:

> Witnesses cannot be adjudged perjurers until the trial has been completed. They cannot be scourged, fined, or put to death, until the trial has been completed. One of the witnesses cannot be adjudged a perjurer without the other; and one cannot be scourged without the other, or put to death without the other, or fined without the other. Said R. Jehuda, the son of Ṭabbai: "May I not live to see the consolation, if I did not once put to death a perjured witness in order to root out the opinion of the Boethuseans,[53] who used to say that a perjured witness could not be put to death till after the accused had been put to death." Simeon, the son of Sheṭaḥ, said to him: "May I not live to see the consolation, if thou hast not shed innocent blood! For the Law says: *At the mouth of two witnesses or three witnesses shall he that is to die be put to death.* Just as there are two witnesses, so there must be two perjurers." At that time Jehuda, the son of Ṭabbai, agreed that he would never utter a legal decision except in agreement with Simeon, the son of Sheṭaḥ.

In utilizing the dramatic possibilities of this episode, Shamir has rightly recognized that Judah's verdict arose from the struggle for supremacy between Pharisees and Sadducees, and his own unquestioning adherence to the former. Hence, the trial again reflects a struggle for men's minds, while the emotional antipathy of the antagonists is sharpened by the knowledge that a man's life is at stake. In the case of false testimony, the Pharisees maintained that it is punishable only if unsuccessful, while the Sadducees argued that it is punishable only if it succeeded. The former base their decision on the biblical text:[54] *You shall treat him* [the false witness] *as he intended to treat his fellow*, while the latter follow the injunction: *Life for life, eye for eye, tooth for tooth, hand for hand, foot for foot.*[55] According to the Pharisaic interpretation, however, the false witness is punishable only after the accused has been condemned, so that the testimony would have to be proved false—as in the case of Susanna—between sentence and execution.

In Shamir's novel, Judah ben-Tabbai arrives at the trial in a highly emotional state, convinced that the Sadducees must be defeated as a necessary step in his plan to depose the wicked king Alexander Jannaeus. He finds that the defendant, Hananiah, an innkeeper and a supporter of the Pharisees, had been condemned on a trumped-up charge of murder by the rich and powerful family of Mar-Akba, who own a rival inn. But just in time it had come to light that one of the witnesses had given false evidence, so that the court of twenty three judges wished to condemn the false witness for his crime. But the Sadducees refused to allow it, and Mar-Akba's family was threatening to hinder the course of justice.[56] Ben-Tabbai is determined to see justice done:[57]

Rising to his feet he proclaimed:

> "The Law states that once a verdict has been given a false witness can expect no reprieve. He is condemned to death." The rowdies immediately started shouting louder and advanced menacingly on the elders. Ben-Tabbai saw that they were intimidating the court, and that several of its twenty-three members might easily revoke their opinion even though they had already given judgement against the false witness. In that case the citizens would infer that a judgement could be annulled by threats, and then what could the sages avail for all their Law and their reforms?
>
> At that moment one of the elders of the court arose and said:
>
> "False witnesses are put to death only if the man condemned by their evidence has already been executed. Then it is a case of a life for a life. As the condemned man was not put to death in this instance there is no question of a death penalty, and the false witness should not be executed."
>
> "Sadducee!" ben-Tabbai thought to himself as he heard a ripple of excitement sweeping through the bystanders. From now on he was consumed not only by a desire for justice but with rage. He was determined to thwart them, come what may. Nevertheless he spoke calmly as befitted a sage:
>
> "*And you shall do to him what he designed against his fellow.* That is the principle on which a false witness is condemned. If it were otherwise what would become of us? Whoever wanted to harm his neighbour could bear false witness against him. If his testimony were accepted—his evil design would succeed; if not—what would he have to lose? Therefore the Law states: *You shall do to him what he designed against his fellow*; not what he actually *did*, but what he *designed* to do."
>
> "A life for a life," ben-Tabbai was interrupted in the middle by the shout that rose from someone among the crowd. "Control yourself," ben-Tabbai thundered back in an even louder voice. "Listen to what I have to say. And so," his voice resumed its normal calm, "why does the Law specify a life for a life? Because one might argue: *and you shall do to him what he designed against his fellow* applies from the moment his evidence is accepted; for as soon as it is accepted, the false witness is already in the category of an evil-doer. But the Law warns us specifically: not from the moment his evidence is accepted, but only after the verdict has been given. Then it is a case of a life for a life—because the verdict is equivalent to the sentence, and that is the final step."

But his last words were drowned by the uproar from Mar-Akba's family and their supporters who began shouting and waving their arms in frenzy. But ben-Tabbai stood his ground: "That is the final step, and that is the essence of the matter. But then there arises the most important question of all: whose opinion shall prevail—that of the mob, or that of the court of law? There can be no doubt about that—the verdict of the court is binding. And indeed, what salvation can Israel expect if not from her Law? Where else can she bring her complaints? What else can put a stop to the wicked, be he king, or priest, or innkeeper?"

Judah turned to face the two janitors appointed to serve the court. At the same time he noticed the false witness with the guilt clearly visible on his face, which had already taken on the pallor of death. He saw the furious expressions of his opponents, the thronging crowds who were as eager for blood as for justice, regardless of whether the victim were innocent or guilty. He heard his conscience whispering: "tyrant, murderer!" But just as quickly he controlled himself, conjuring up a picture of the poor city ground down by the wicked, bled white by tax-farmers, a prey to the whim of tyrants, groaning beneath the weight of evil, oppression, poverty and affliction, with none to save. And side by side he saw a vision of all the towns of Israel, and all the villages and hamlets whose only hope resided in the Law, but for which justice and security would vanish, and men would be no better than wild beasts.

Summoning up all his reserves of strength ben-Tabbai drew himself erect, and pointing his finger at the false witness cried loudly:

"Take him away for execution."

The episode contains many of the classic elements of the court scene in literature.[58] The tension and excitement are enhanced by the fluctuating fortunes of the trial and by the clamor of the spectators, their sympathy for the victim, and the threat of physical intervention. The argument, with its underlying concerns and wider consequences, is passionate, and the reader's interest is quickened and sustained. And yet a lurking doubt remains that justice is not being exercised quite so completely as ben-Tabbai affirms, that reason is being clouded by emotion, and that the final irrevocable decision has been taken, perhaps, with too much haste.

The doubt resurfaces when ben-Tabbai later recalls the trial in urging the sages to take action against the wicked king by declaring him unfit to serve as High Priest, a course which ben-Shetah believes can lead only to violence and bloodshed:[59]

"I quote my own experience even though it is well known. Heaven is my witness that I have never tried to instruct my teachers, but in the present instance my example may serve to prove that a single individual acting in good faith can prevail against an evil multitude. You remember the case of the false witness, when the Sadducees were preventing the course of justice. Is there any need to recount what happened? Suffice it to say that by obstinately clinging to his belief, one man was able to give a judgement according to the Law and force the Sadducees to consent. Despite their physical superiority and the awe in which they were generally held, the villains were frightened into accepting the verdict, so that justice prevailed."

"What is that supposed to show?" someone asked.

"I am speaking of a court entirely composed of Sadducees," ben-Tabbai answered slowly and emphatically. "The verdict had been given but the condemned man had not been executed—nevertheless, so may I live to see the redemption, I had the false witness put to death!"

"So may I live to see the redemption," Simeon suddenly sprang to his feet and thundered in a strange, new voice, "you have shed innocent blood!" "... You have shed innocent blood, ben-Tabbai, for our sages have interpreted the Law as follows: False witnesses must not be put to death, nor flogged, nor fined, unless *two* of them have borne false witness, in accordance with the text: *On the evidence of two witnesses*,[60] and so on ..."

Ben-Shetah then solemnly warns ben-Tabbai to repent and resume the yoke of the Law.

In the devastating silence which follows, ben-Tabbai's mind is in turmoil, while his overpowering urge to declare the king unfit for the priesthood struggles against the horrifying realization of his heinous decision, which has led to wrongful execution. At that moment word is brought that one of ben-Tabbai's disciples has taken the law into his own hands and smashed the skull of his father's murderer, a servant of the king.[61] The news leads to ben-Tabbai's total capitulation:[62]

Judah stepped forward. This was a sign from heaven to teach them all. Slowly Simeon raised his arm, although it was not clear whether the gesture signified the fulfilment of his prophecy or whether he intended to embrace ben-Tabbai. The latter stepped forward again and bowed his head.

"I bind myself to pronounce no judgement except in the presence of Simeon ben-Shetah," he said, "so that when I err he may correct me."

This final confrontation of two great exponents of rabbinical teaching demonstrates the central role of law in Jewish tradition. It may also serve to illustrate the dramatic possibilities which modern Hebrew literature can derive from the great treasure-house of ancient Hebrew law.

II

From Mapu to Mendele: In Search of Artistry

In the light of the quantity, range, and sophistication of contemporary Hebrew literature, it is easy to lose sight of its meager and somewhat naive origins. It is important to recall that from the end of the eighteenth century, modern Hebrew literature was regarded as an instrument of change. Its small company of enthusiasts envisaged it as a means, however belated, of ushering the Jewish communities first of Western and later of Eastern Europe from the "darkness" of the middle ages to the "enlightenment" of European society. Emancipation was the goal, and self-improvement seemed the method.[1] All the centuries of persecution and humiliation must have been caused, it was felt, by some terrible mistake, some tragic lack of communication. Now that "reason" had become the all-powerful goddess, social disability would yield to "sweetness and light." In order to qualify for an agreeable and harmonious membership in European society, the Jews need only modify their educational curriculum to include the disciplines of Western culture.[2] In its early phases, a considerable proportion of modern Hebrew literature was composed with this immediate aim in view.

The encouragement of a wider range of intellectual interests, the cultivation of good taste, and the ability to express oneself grammatically in elegant and well-turned periods became primary goals for the Hebrew movement of enlightenment. Its advocates entertained high hopes but enjoyed few assets. Their ambitious plans and lofty sentiments could find expression only in the shape of poems, epigrams and fables, articles and textbooks, whether original or translated, composed in a contrived neo-biblical Hebrew style, which came to be regarded as more esthetic and elevating than the less elegant and polished rabbinic Hebrew which it sought to oust. In making Hebrew literature the vehicle of their aspirations, the exponents of enlightenment assigned it a mammoth task, which exceeded its capacities and made it appear grossly pretentious. Only gradually, throughout the nineteenth century, was literature able to establish contact with the realities of Jewish life, and work out more viable and convincing modes of expression. For that it required the reluctant abandoning of a myth.

As stated above, the sad but persistent self-delusion which affected so many Jews throughout much of the nineteenth century arose, in part, from the time lag governing the penetration into Jewish thought of formative ideas from the outside world.[3] The immense importance attached to reason and enlightenment, which exerted so powerful an appeal in Western Europe in the eighteenth century, made its full impact on many Jewish thinkers only in the nineteenth. By then, however, other ideologies such as nationalism and socialism were beginning to play a dominating role. But again, these new currents of European thought effectively penetrated Jewish life only in the last decades of the century.[4]

Hence, the constant appeals for enlightenment emanating from Jewish intellectual circles—first in Western Europe and later in the more numerous settlements in Eastern Europe—for almost a century following the French Revolution seem strangely unreal. The efficacy of reason as a remedy for their ills commended itself to many Jews almost as Europe was reluctantly beginning to recognize the limitations of reason as a guide for the understanding of human behavior. During most of the nineteenth century the Jewish exponents of enlightenment pinned their faith on an eighteenth-century panacea. In consequence, their hopes and aspirations often appear curiously tangential to reality.[5]

Insofar as it reflects the ideals and ambitions of many of the most passionately concerned Jewish thinkers and writers in the long and sometimes grotesque struggle for emancipation, modern Hebrew literature runs the whole gamut of mood from a lofty and optimistic self-delusion to a grim awareness of harsh reality. Its descent from Olympus is punctuated by a number of works of real merit, in which talent and sensitivity combined to sound a more convincing note. But it required a fusion of imagination, insight, and an intuitive sense of national reality bordering on the prophetic to enable vision to dispel illusion and artistry, pretence. These are the qualities that assure a place for Abraham Mapu in modern Hebrew literature.

Mapu's novels comprise a strange blend of vision and illusion, and they are satisfactory only to the extent that his instinct was able to put aside the blinkers of ideology. Although intellectually drawn to the theories of enlightenment, the extraordinary force of his vision contrasts sharply with his didactic advocacy of illusory paths toward the goal of emancipation—a fact which helps to explain the paradoxical element in his writings. His historical romances, *The Love of Zion* and *The Guilt of Samaria*, as well as his novel of contemporary Jewish life in Lithuania, *The Hypocrite*, are permeated with the aspirations of enlightenment.[6] Both in the ancient homeland and in the modern diaspora, Mapu's heroes and heroines combine a passionate loyalty to the national heritage with an equally sincere commitment to the pursuit of enlightenment and reason.[7]

But while the heroes of the historical novels are at least portrayed in a well-established tradition of historical romance with all the quick excitement of adventure, chivalry, and daring exploit, the heroes of Mapu's Lithuanian saga cut a somewhat sorry figure. They are cast as the harbingers of a new day, when young, well-educated, and practical-minded Jewish gentlemen and their gracious ladies, equally at home in Jewish or gentile circles, might lead a dignified and useful life in Eastern Europe in an atmosphere of liberty, equality, and mutual respect. Despite Mapu's valiant attempts to give substance to this ideal, his characters remain curiously unconvincing, pale shadows in an unreal world.[8]

It is instructive to contrast Mapu's idealized relationships with the gulf separating Jews and Russians portrayed in the following snatch of conversation from Peretz Smolenskin's *The Wanderer in the Paths of Life.* The novel contains marked autobiographical elements and the passage describes conditions in the early fifties of the last century. After walking for six days and losing himself in a snowstorm at night, the young hero, Josef, is finally offered the loan of a horse by a passing traveler. Only some time later, when they arrive at an inn, are they able to see one another, and the spectacle gives rise to mutual astonishment.

> When he saw me at the inn, he called out in amazement: "Are you the man who was traveling with me?"
>
> "Yes! Why are you so surprised?"
>
> "A man like you, dressed in Hasidic clothes, speaking the language of the country fluently. That's something I never expected to see."
>
> "I know many Jews who speak it just as well"—I replied.
>
> "I know that, too. I'm a Jew myself. But this is the first time I've seen a man dressed as a *Ḥasidh* speaking it."
>
> But I was even more surprised to hear that he was a Jew, for I had never expected to find a Jew dressed like a gentile in these parts. During the whole time I had spent with the *Mithnaggedhim*, I had never seen another instance of it.

Brief as it is, the conversation speaks volumes concerning the relations between Jews and their gentile neighbors in Russia in the middle of the nineteenth century.[9]

Mapu seems, himself, to have been aware of his characters' deficiencies. His gradual disenchantment with the movement of enlightenment is reflected in *The Hypocrite* in the unedifying portrait of Emil, who personifies its negative results, with his tendencies toward abject assimilation, a half-baked secularism, and an irritating self-importance.[10] But even his more favored characters do not escape unscathed. Elisheba, for example, praises Azriel's elegant correspondence as a model.[11]

> "Would that letters such as this might appear more often in our literature! For only such refinement of language will teach the youth of Israel good taste and fine understanding, and inspire their minds."

But her remark draws a stern rebuke from Shuval, who describes how he had once flirted with enlightenment before growing to despise it:

> "In my youth I toyed with their glowing coals, and so scorched my fingers that even today I feel the scars. All who look for righteousness in them are deluded; for their fine words are like deadly flies that hover boldly about the flowers of paradise, daring even to penetrate the sanctuary and pollute the fragrant oil. They are saturated with lies, they shoot out their lips against both God and man, and tear out holy ideas root and branch, leaving not a shred and rejecting them utterly."

When his friend Yair charges him with bigotry for deriding Azriel merely because of his fine command of language, Shuval vigorously defends his position:

> ". . . You know that I, too, once trumpeted in praise of fine words and elegant language. But once my eyes were opened by experience to see the world clearly, I so learned to disdain them and despise their honeyed sweetness, that they became anathema to me. For they are destroying Israel."

In spite of the lingering extravagance of style, there is considerable cogency in Shuval's argument. Nevertheless, it is in the very letter that is under fire that Mapu's prophetic vision attains its peak. The devotion to Zion, the emotional identification with the ancient homeland, the extraordinary ability to conjure up a convincing portrait of a land he had never seen, which lend the historical novels so powerful an appeal, become even more poignant in the novel of contemporary life. Writing back to his friends in Lithuania from the slopes of Mount Zion on the eve of Passover, "In the year five thousand six hundred and thirteen according to the Jewish calendar" (that is 1853), Azriel makes a sudden and compelling contact with one of the major forces in Jewish history, the dual vision which tries to make dream and reality coalesce.[12]

> "Yea, a new light shall shine on Zion, which now lies desolate and mourning. The sons, which she bore in bewilderment, shall flock to her sacred ruins. They shall come streaming in from all the lands of the dispersion, for they are all her children, who bear her name upon her lips with every outpouring of prayer. They shall come to her and say that through all their sorrows and afflictions they have remembered her, and the love of Zion shall never be erased from their hearts."

Then, after conjuring up a picture of the thronging crowds that came to celebrate the Passover in Jerusalem in ancient times, Azriel prophesies a splendid renaissance, a veritable rebirth of language and people. His enthusiastic affirmation of faith—written more than forty years before the first World Zionist Congress—is still impressive.

> "Hurrah! I thought—wake up, my soul, and awaken the love of the eternal people. Remember the days of old, that they may bring comfort at the present time. And you, too, O sacred tongue, don your holy garb and your spirit of noble grace, and sing to your lover, the youth of Israel, borne on the arms of God since the days of Egypt. Make your voice resound, that your words be heard to the very ends of the earth, wherever the sound shall reach. But sing your song only for him that loves

you, for the people that has chosen you, for they are all your delight. Hurrah! My spirit wanders proudly, walking the eternal paths of old. And with the power of imagination I hear a rustling from the grave, a cry from out the rock, the voice of the world's dead that sleep in the dust of the ground, rising rejuvenated from the ashes of death, and living before me in my sight. This is the great cry, which breaks forth from the Hebrew tongue to her people, resounding as in the days of her youth."

The extraordinary force of Mapu's vision forms a striking contrast to the situation of the Jews in Russia in the nineteenth century. The hostility of the Czarist administration to what was considered an alien and hence suspect people living so close to a strategic frontier was sharpened by the wave of nationalism which swept across Russia following the Napoleonic wars. The government embarked upon a policy aimed at the "russification" of its Jewish subjects and attempted throughout the nineteenth century to undermine their separateness. For the most part resort was made to naked and unashamed oppression. However, during the first period of the reign of Alexander II who ascended the throne in 1855, the road toward at least partial assimilation was smoothed by the alleviation of a number of Jewish disabilities, and by granting permission for Jews to enter high school and university.[13] The orthodox Jews preferred to keep contacts between Jews and gentiles to a minimum, regarding separateness as an effective safeguard for the preservation of traditional Judaism. They frowned upon the growing tendency for Jewish children to be taught Russian, while the teachers of Russian were viewed with contempt. Orthodox Jews were willing to go to considerable lengths to prevent what they considered to be the corruption of their children in government schools. In this, as well as so many other aspects of their lives, the Jews of Russia resorted to bribery in order to circumvent a legal system devised for their oppression.

In his early novel *Fathers and Sons* (1868), Shalom Jacob Abramowitz describes the virulent opposition of many Jews, particularly the Hasidic faction, to the governmental decree founding compulsory elementary schools for Jewish children, designed to supersede the traditional Jewish school or *ḥedher*. After describing how the Jewish community bribed the gentile headmaster to let them know the date on which the government inspector was due to appear—not unlike Gogol's *The Inspector General*—so that the school was packed with children on that day, much to the inspector's satisfaction, although otherwise it remained empty, Abramowitz presents the headmaster's rationale:[14]

The headmaster justified his action on two counts.

In the first place, even if he had taken issue with his fellow citizens, it would have been of no avail. He, himself, was an old hand in the evasion of the law, and the word of a single individual was never accepted. "If two people tell you that you are drunk," to quote the old proverb, "go and lie down." In the second place, he was

> not of their faith, nor were his ancestors of the faith of their ancestors. So why should he be interested in improving them, or sacrificing himself on the altar of enlightenment for the Jews? Why should he put himself out for people in whom he had not the slightest interest? It was all the same to him whether they had Jewish instructors, *Melammedhim*, or teachers, or whether they studied in *ḥedher* or an elementary school. He didn't hold with any of them! Was it for this that he had acquired wisdom and knowledge in the upper division of the theological college—to educate the Jews? ... Even without it, he told himself, the Jews are cunning, and can get the better of us by guile. Admittedly, they have bribed me with their own money, but won't they get it back from me again? Yesterday, Moses the peddler squeezed money out of me. Today Samuel got the better of the bargain, and tomorrow some other Jew will relieve me of whatever little money I have left ... The Jews have given, and the Jews have taken away, the Devil take them! In this way the headmaster constantly justified himself and granted himself a pardon. He would repeat the phrase "Go to the Devil! Go to the Devil!" a few times, and then stretch out his palm for a secret bribe.

The exponents of enlightenment, on the other hand, endeavored to foster such teaching by every means at their disposal and fully supported the Russian government in its attempt to enforce the teaching of Russian by decree. The *Maskilim* regarded themselves as the disciples of Moses Mendelssohn, and advocated a synthesis of traditional Judaism and European culture—much to the chagrin of *Mithnaggedhim* and *Ḥasidhim* alike.

Although the enlightenment movement in Germany which Mendelssohn had inspired was directed toward a very different social and cultural environment, the ideas themselves, often in half-baked or ill-digested form, were propagated in the entirely different conditions prevailing in the Russian Pale of Settlement with enthusiasm. Only a thoroughgoing change in Jewish social, cultural, and religious attitudes, or so it was believed, could lead to any real amelioration of the Jewish plight. But in spite of herculean efforts, the *Maskilim* achieved only limited success.

The ruthless oppression of the Jews in Russia throughout much of the nineteenth century and the successive waves of repressive legislation were rendered more painful still by a phenomenal growth in the Jewish population. At the end of the eighteenth century, the Jewish population in the Russian Empire numbered approximately one million. By 1897 there were five million Jews living in the Pale of Settlement, and the consequent deterioration of an economic situation already desperate occasioned a number of attempts on the part of the Jews to alleviate their condition. In the second half of the nineteenth century Hebrew fiction became increasingly concerned with the reformation of Jewish social, educational, and religious life.

> "Were a man to come from Western Europe," R. A. Braudes proclaims in his powerful novel *Religion and Life*,[15] "and with his own eyes see this backward people, their degradation, their level of culture, the education they give their sons and

daughters, and their manner of life, without any doubt he would pose the question: 'Can reforms be of any avail? Is it still possible to reform them? Could even the third generation enter the society of men who are aware of life and all its manifestations?' ... Yet Nahman, the teacher from Minsk, could say to Samuel, for all the latter's long harangue during the 'Great Sabbath:' 'We do not yet know whether our generation needs reform.'"

What kind of reform and how best to bring it about exercised the minds of Hebrew writers in different ways. Abraham Mapu attempted to advocate social change by projecting his ideas into a fictionalized past. It was as though he wished to use the past in order to instruct his own generation in the proper way to live, and to contrast the dignity of Jewish life in biblical times with its contemporary degradation. In *The Love of Zion*, the hero Amnon and the heroine Tamar, both of aristocratic families, are betrothed at birth, but the hero is wickedly exchanged in the cradle and brought up as a shepherd. They meet for the first time as adults, and the following scene ensues:[16]

But Tamar gave no heed to Maacah's words. Instead she approached Amnon and addressed him: "Give me, good youth, the garland of roses which is in your hand, if your heart be as generous as your looks are kind."

As Tamar spoke to him he paled and said: "Here it is, my mistress, if you but deign to take it from your servant's hand."

Then Tamar continued: "I heard you say, The roses of the valley are the shepherd's garland, to grace the head of his beloved. So tell me, then, who is your beloved? For I would fain see her, and give her some gift in exchange for this garland of roses which you meant for her, but which I have taken from you."

And Amnon lowered his eyes and said: "I swear, my mistress, that out of the thousands of maidens my eyes have seen I have not yet found my beloved."

And Tamar answered: "It would seem, proud youth, that if you seek your beloved among thousands, then she must indeed be rare and choice." Then Maacah, her handmaid, took her arm and said: "Enough, my mistress, let us arise and go. For someone is coming and it does not befit your honor to stay and bandy words."

It is, perhaps, difficult for a modern audience of sophisticated tastes to realize quite how daring such an encounter must have appeared in 1853. This mildly flirtatious, if somewhat quaint, conversation between a young man and woman came as a veritable bombshell at a time of arranged marriages, when bride and bridegroom frequently met for the first time under the wedding canopy. Abramowitz, through the eyes of his literary *persona*, Mendele the Bookseller, attacks the practice of such arrangements with mocking irony. Mendele's companion, Reb Alter, is in desperate financial straits, with his wife having just given birth and his eldest daughter in need of a dowry. He has just attempted to earn a few coppers at a fair by arranging a match between the children of two visiting dignitaries, and was on the point of success when it transpired that both the young people concerned were boys! Mendele attempts to comfort his friend as follows:[17]

> "Have no fear, Reb Alter! If you have just failed to make a match between two young men, you will make up for it, God willing, by arranging another match. Don't despair, Reb Alter, keep your spirits up. I can see that you have all the makings of an expert, and you have grasped the art of it at once, at the very first attempt, like a real master. Indeed I can assure you that you have made a good beginning in this new trade of yours as a district match-maker, a very good beginning indeed. What's that you say?—The boy? ... That's nothing ... Just wait till a girl falls into your hands—you won't let her go sour! Blind, lame, drunk—Come on, my girl, you will say, and away with you! Away with you to the canopy and the best of luck! The printer needs his money, and the horse needs fodder, my eldest daughter must be wed, and my wife, bless her, has given birth to a son. So come along, girl, and off with you to the canopy!"

Hebrew literature in the nineteenth century frequently pillories both the old orthodoxy and the Hasidic faction for their adherence to superstitious beliefs and old wives' tales, incidentally supplying many an interesting glimpse into current folklore and custom.[18] In a bitter attack on ignorance and superstition, Mendele resorts to biting satire in deploring the custom of marrying cripples in the graveyard as a device to get rid of a cholera epidemic:[19]

> At first the community decided upon Yontel, a renowned cripple, who used to crawl about on his thigh, supported by two wooden blocks in his palms. They matched him with an equally famous beggar-girl, with widely spaced teeth and minus her lower lip. The plague took fright in the face of this marriage, and after taking a heavy toll of the citizens finally took to her heels and fled; and then the choice fell on Nehumtzi, the local idiot. The latter spread his wings, or rather the wedding veil, in the presence of the community elders in the graveyard, over a young lady who had worn a wreath of leprosy all over her head and forehead since her youth, and about whom it was rumored that she was androgynous. They say that anyone who failed to see that wedding, romping merrily among the graves, missed the chance of a lifetime. The guests frolicked and drank, and danced before the bride shouting "What a lovely, charming bride," not, God forbid, as some said, to endear her to the cholera, but to endear her to her husband, the idiot. But that's another story.

The conflict between the old generation and the new, so frequently encountered in the novels of the period, is treated in a variety of ways. Sometimes it is the young generation that is blamed for rebelliousness, frivolity, and indifference, while elsewhere, and more frequently, the older generation is accused of obscurantism, intolerance, and obstinacy. A typical example of the latter occurs in a scene from Braudes' *Religion and Life*, where the young hero, Samuel, who has recently been introduced to *Haskalah*, is discovered reading a secular book by his father-in-law Issachar, and the latter's eldest son, Isaac:[20]

On entering the house they found Samuel sitting in his room reading a Russian book.

"That I should live to see this!" Issachar groaned bitterly. Samuel, who had been engrossed in his book and had not noticed them come in, was so startled at suddenly hearing his father-in-law's voice that the book fell out of his hand. But he pulled himself together at once and picked it up from the floor. "Why are you shouting at me?" he calmly asked his father-in-law. "How can you have the impertinence to ask, you heretic?" Issachar roared at the top of his voice. "Was it for this that I brought you here without a shirt to your back, so that you could spend the whole day reading heresies? Was it for this that I clothed your nakedness and married my daughter to you, so that you could turn out to be a sinner and a scoundrel?" "What's all this?" Leah and Deborah enquired simultaneously, brought to the room by Issachar's shouting.

"Just look what your son-in-law's up to. That will make you happy ..." Issachar replied angrily. "Here I am at the age of fifty, and just when I was getting old and expected to see some joy from my offspring, the Lord has brought this on my house ... I had to bring a *heretic* here ..."

"A heteric? ..." Leah faltered after her husband.

A smile, albeit tinged with both sadness and anger, flickered across Samuel's lips, but Leah didn't notice.

"I don't want a her-tic ... What did you call him?"

"Heretic," Issachar and his son quietly corrected her.

"I don't want such a scoundrel to be my son-in-law or my daughter's husband."

"And I don't want to be a heretic's wife"—Deborah chimed in loudly.

"All right then," Samuel replied fiercely, assuming a cold expression. "In that case let's go to the rabbi and get a divorce."

"Did you hear that?" Leah shouted—"it's a mere nothing for him to go to the rabbi and divorce my daughter, and they haven't been married a year ..."

"What do you want me to do, then?"

"Listen, Samuel," Isaac said in calmer tones. "You're not such a fool as to believe you can get away with that when you know very well how much money has been spent on you ... The best thing for you to do is to apologize, beg their pardon, and henceforward stop reading those filthy corrupting books. They will forgive you if you mend your ways."

"I will not mend my ways because I haven't done anything wrong," Samuel answered equally calmly. "We live down here on earth, not up in heaven, and so we ought to understand the people we live among, and their language. And so I have started to learn to understand the language of this country, and I have begun to read books which explain how people in this land live. I intend to pursue them, and I won't budge one inch ..."

"How dare you say such things in my presence," Issachar roared, beside himself with rage. "I can't believe my own ears. You won't give up your heresies? And do you think I shall allow you to carry out your evil designs in my house?"

The reader may easily imagine the insults and curses that followed.

The positive sides of traditional Jewish education, particularly in the *Yešibhah*, are also represented. Apart from the interest and companionship it afforded the growing boy, the social function it performed of keeping lads from roaming wild in the streets, and the continuity of Judaism which it safeguarded, the important formative influences which it exerted on the minds of the better students are described by Smolenskin in glowing terms. In outlining the source of the intellectual and spiritual integrity which so distinguishes Simon, the hero of his first novel *The Joy of the Godless*, the author makes the following almost lyrical and certainly unequivocal pronouncement.[21]

> Who implanted within him such knowledge, and justice, and sublimity of expression? Who kindled the divine spark in his soul to pursue truth with such devotion? Where else but in the *Yešibhah*? All praise and strength to you, O sacred institutions, the retreat and refuge of the remnant of Israel! It is from your gates that the chosen few still continue to emerge, who are destined to serve as a torch for their people and infuse the spirit of life into dry bones. Who knows but that the Spirit of Israel might not have vanished completely from the face of the earth like a cloud; who knows but that the springs of truth might have been stopped up with the silt of nonsense and deceit brought by false teachers in such abundance and presented as jewels to all who would behold; who knows but that such falsehoods might have been implanted in the minds of the younger generation in the name of the Lord and his prophets? Except that this small and humble people aroused itself, and for all its lowliness succeeded in rescuing God's law from the midst of chaos—at a time when all justice, truth, righteousness, and brotherly love had been rejected as the stumbling blocks of society by the philosophers of destruction with their perversions of God's word and their passionate desire to defile every avenue of faith.

Education was always made a central plank in the platform of the *Haskalah* movement, and the widening of mental horizons beyond the confines of the traditional institutions of learning, the *Ḥedher* and the *Yešibhah*, is advocated in a variety of situations. The heroes and heroines, as noted above, are almost always staunch champions of enlightenment, and represent in their cultural, intellectual and professional ambitions and achievements the ideals of *Haskalah*. Conversely, the villains personify blind obscurantism and passionately oppose the teachings of the *Maskilim*. Here again Mapu uses his hero Amnon to advocate the wisdom of turning to nature for inspiration—in the manner of Shakespeare's "Books in the running brooks, sermons in stones, and good in everything:"[22]

> And it came to pass one day that Uz visited the pastures and found Amnon sitting wrapped in thought, watching a lily withering beneath the scorching heat and speaking thus: "How lovely you are, my soft and tender lily, when dawn's first light steals upon you, when your cup is brimming with the dew of heaven, and even the great trees look enviously upon you! How beautiful you appear, my lovely one, in the light of the morning, when the clear drops of dew sparkle on your sweet petals, and you drink your fill and in good time blossom forth in joy. But now the scorching heat has smitten you, the dew of heaven has dried within you, and your face is wan, your bloom has withered, and you have become an object to be pitied. Thus even the plants of the field can teach us, and from whatever our eyes behold we can draw

a moral. The heavens stretch an open book in front of us, while the earth, and all its host, spreads out its lesson before our very eyes. The word of God is stamped upon it, telling us: Read in this great book all the days of your life, for only then shall you act wisely and with understanding!"

Braudes, as usual, is more direct. Convinced that literature should be a force in life with a definite role to play in the shaping of society, he describes how the heroine of *Religion and Life* deliberately engineers the hero's introduction to Russian positivist literature, fully aware of the conflict which the new ideas will arouse in his mind. The passage accurately reflects the manner in which the new concepts were actually propagated from the sixties onwards:[23]

Rachel had brought her books with her from Naharayim, the latest Russian books at that time, devoted to questions of *community life*, a word then in vogue, and of reform in social life in general; questions of bread and butter, work and money, the people and its rulers, men and women, and many similar matters. They also probed into the question of faith and religion in general, subjecting them to searching criticism in the light of natural science—matter and force, Darwin's theory of the Origin of Species, the ideas of materialist philosophy, and the theories of determinism in nature and history. All such ideas were brought together and treated at length in these books which aroused great interest among the youth. Rachel, too, had read and thought about them a lot, and had become a devotee of their ideas. She always kept a selection of them near at hand, and had brought them to Pelagut with her. Now she handed them over to Samuel to read, to learn his opinion of them . . .

Of Mapu's immediate successors the most illustrious were Peretz Smolenskin[24] and Reuben Asher Braudes. Both novelists inherited Mapu's social conscience, and gave expression to it in more telling and effective forms. Smolenskin's plot fantasies were sometimes more intriguing than his predecessor's,[25] while Braudes displayed a better sense of structure.[26] But while both writers, and particularly Smolenskin, are highly imaginative and inventive, their novels lack the element of vision—the most effective weapon in Mapu's armory. Smolenskin does, indeed, come close to the matter in an important passage in his last novel, *The Inheritance*, where one of his characters defends his wife's extreme thriftiness on the grounds that her aim is to collect sufficient money for the family to go to the Land of Israel:[27]

"—To the Land of Israel?!"—Zerahiah exclaimed in astonishment—"That's a fine ambition for you and your children! And what will your sons do there? Weep at the Western Wall and study the *Zohar*?—"

"—Even if such were the case, I still would not regard it as so stupid as you think. What sort of a future lies in store for them here? In school they are beaten by the children and persecuted by the teachers: and when they grow up there will be no place for them. I doubt if their position would be any worse crying at the Wall but unmolested than living in comfort here at the risk of having their faces slapped."

The importance of such a statement, uttered in the earliest days of the national revival, scarcely requires reiteration. But although in his later years Smolenskin vehemently argued the case for a national return in article form and in his story *Neqam Berith*, the view of Israel's destiny propounded in his novels is that of a leaven on the spirit of mankind:[28]

> "Like the spirit of life Israel moves from one country to the next, and wherever we pass we quicken the spirit. Thus our ancient heritage has consisted in wreaking a beneficent revenge, for we bring advantage to our foes and requite with good all those who harm us, by carrying light, righteousness, justice, and integrity to those very places where we have been robbed of them."

It is, however, in another direction that Smolenskin's novels mark a significant trend. For all their extravagance and fantasy, the intrigues, the melodrama, and the wild improbabilities of plot,[29] the novels are characterized by a gradual awakening, a sloughing off of self-delusion, a healthy recognition of the absurdity of any attempt to apply the refined theories of Moses Mendelssohn, as embodied in the so-called "Berlin enlightenment" of the second half of the eighteenth century, to the Jewish plight in Eastern Europe almost a hundred years later. "What connection can there be between European enlightenment and Roumania?" Smolenskin shrewdly enquires.[30] Hence the strange dichotomy apparent in the great majority of Hebrew novels in the period, between the lofty and, indeed, grandiose ideas upon which the theories of enlightenment are based and the pettiness of the practical forms in which enlightenment is expressed. There is little organic connection between aspiration and application, theory and practice.

Smolenskin bitterly attacks the same exponents of enlightenment for advocating that the Jews of Eastern Europe alleviate their miserable economic plight by forsaking petty trade and business, and training themselves instead to become craftsmen and farmers. He cleverly points out that far from too few Jews being employed as craftsmen, the root of the trouble lies in the large number of Jews so occupied in proportion to the amount of work available.[31] His penetrating analysis of the harsh realities of Jewish life in Eastern Europe adds a new and powerful dimension to the Hebrew novel. Smolenskin's descriptions can be naked and brutal, and on occasion chillingly prophetic.[32]

Elsewhere he resorts to cutting satire in order to lay bare what he considers to be the evils besetting Jewish life. Anything sham, pretentious, or hypocritical was fair game for the lash of his invective and his trenchant wit.[33] Yet side by side with the most serious social purpose and reforming zeal, there runs a persistent thread of melodramatic fantasy presented in the most naive and undisguised form. Melodrama is, indeed, a regular feature of Smolenskin's novels, with the incidents portrayed in lurid detail.[34]

This strange juxtaposition of bitter realism and escapist fantasy is largely responsible for the lack of balance in Smolenskin's novels. Aggressive social purpose and wildly improbable melodrama make strange bedfellows, with both partners pulling simultaneously in different directions. In general, the dichotomy exerts an adverse influence on plot construction, style, and characterization. But sometimes the effect is that of a pantomime horse. Although the rear portion may appear to function quite independently of the front, yet by sheer verve and skill the grotesque element takes on an entertaining and indeed hilarious quality. Smolenskin's talent was immense, if frequently undisciplined. Time and again it bursts through the bonds of a restricted vocabulary and contrived phraseology to fashion a powerful and effective prose.[35] His sincerity and moral earnestness carry great conviction, and compensate in some measure for the slapdash elements and artistic lapses due to the exigencies of an over-hasty mode of composition.[36]

Nevertheless, a far more rigorous concern with artistry and detail was required to raise the level of Hebrew fiction. The stories of R. A. Braudes represent an important transitional stage toward this end. An unfinished novel, *Religion and Life*, served as a harbinger of new developments. It is far less flamboyant both in language and style than Smolenskin's stories. There is a restraint and self-control which compare favorably with the extravagance and fantasy of contemporary Hebrew writing. But many weaknesses remain. Braudes composed his novel with very serious intent. Essentially, it is a plea for religious reform, with the argumentation presented in the form of a novel, only—as the author freely admits—in order to sugar the pill.[37] The writing is overtly didactic and carries a strong flavor of Russian positivism.

The refreshingly clear and straightforward style, largely unspoiled by unnecessary verbiage or deliberate striving after effect, was enhanced in Braudes' second novel by the growing ascendancy of the artist over the advocate of reform. *The Two Extremes* displays greater maturity and a much more skillful structure. Although the title of the novel indicates the author's social purpose, which is to illustrate the harmful effects of extremism at both ends of the religious spectrum, and to advocate a middle course combining orthodoxy and enlightenment, the didactic element is cleverly integrated into the main stream of the novel.[38] As the social purpose is treated as an organic element, the story achieves an inherent unity, so painfully lacking in the other novels of the period. The work is remarkable for the delicate balance of its plot construction, in which the impact of each of two contrasting environments upon a visitor from the other is portrayed with insight and imagination.[39]

While Braudes' merit resides in his stabilization of the Hebrew novel, it was Mendele who raised it to the realm of artistry. Prior to the appearance of his novels, modern Hebrew literature exerts a fascinating appeal largely because of the light it sheds on the development of language and literature, the sociology and history of European Jewry, and the ideological and religious upheavals in Jewish life in the nineteenth century. With Mendele's novels the literature becomes esthetically viable. The achievement is partly the result of their author's personal odyssey. *Fathers and Sons* consists of a mixture of blatant propaganda for *Haskalah* and crude melodrama within the framework of an improbable plot.[40] It displays many of the weaknesses of the *Haskalah* novel, and only the touches of humor, the odd stroke of characterization, and the cleverly integrated natural description[41] foreshadow the novelist's future achievements.[42]

Over the following twenty years Mendele composed a series of novels of an entirely different order in Yiddish. The rich and varied idiom of a living, spoken language provided him with a flexible and sensitive instrument for shaping his material. When his interest in Hebrew rekindled, he turned the best of his novels into that language, but the Hebrew versions are less translations than transmutations. The relationship of the two versions of each work is extremely complex, and a thorough investigation of the problem involved is in its barest infancy.[43] Suffice it to say that the appearance of *Sepher ha-Qabbṣanim* (The Book of the Beggars), *Mass'oth Binyamin Ha-Šeliši* (The Travels of Benjamin the Third), and *Susathi* (My Mare) represents a powerful stride forward in the art of Hebrew fiction.[44]

With Mendele the real nature of the Jewish situation in Russia is finally and devastatingly brought home, and then less by direct assault than by humor, irony, and consummate artistry. For Mendele, Czarist repression and the all-pervading, grinding poverty is compounded by a fecklessness and lack of worldliness which, in his view, pervaded many of the little towns and villages of the Pale of Settlement. Where Mapu points to the need to learn from nature, Mendele declares that Jewish life and nature are seriously out of joint. His masterpiece, *The Book of the Beggars*, opens thus:[45]

> Now that the wind blows warm and sunny days are on the way, and all God's world is full of light and joy—we Jews will soon be facing days of mourning, tears, and fasting, one after the other, from the spring sowing at Passover until the autumn rains. This is the busy season for me, Mendele the Bookseller, when I do the rounds of the little townlets in the Pale, providing all the necessary for a good cry, namely dirges, supplications, penitential prayers, rams' horns, solemn lectionaries, graveside elegies, pietistic tracts, and whatever else is happily conducive to tears. Our fellow Israelites lament and spend the summer weeping—and I make my living from it. But that's another story.

It is the seventeenth of Tammuz, the black day in the Jewish calendar, when the walls of the Temple were breached by Nebuchadnezzar's hordes. Driving his old horse and wagon along a country lane our hero attempts to recite the laments appropriate to the sadness of the occasion, while the beauties of a lovely summer's day beckon seductively on every side. Finally dozing off in the middle of his prayers, his wagon collides with another horse and cart, and the following scene ensues:[46]

> I must apparently have nodded off asleep, right in the middle of my prayers, may such a thing never befall you! I see my wagon sinking in a pond, with the axle of

another wagon stuck in one of its rear wheels. One of my horse's legs is standing outside the traces, and he is being pulled and pressed and squeezed, and is in a very bad way. From the far side a stream of piercing curses in Yiddish rises aloft punctuated by coughs and groans. So you're a Jew are you!—I say to myself—in that case, there's nothing to fear. So I get to my feet at once and go round the other side full of rage. There I see before me a Jewish fellow entangled in his prayer shawl and phylacteries squirming under a wagon. The straps and whips are all tied up, as he struggles to free himself with all his might. "What's going on?" I shout at him in astonishment. And he replies at the top of his voice: "You might well ask what's going on!" I vent my wrath on him, heaping all the insults on him I can conjure up; and he hurls them back at me, without either of us seeing the other's face. I say to him, "Are you not ashamed to be a Jew and fall asleep in the middle of your prayers?" And he replies, "How can a Jew be so little God-fearing as to doze off like that?" I curse him by his father, and he throws my mother into the bargain. I beat his horse, and he manages to free himself, and get up, and starts beating my horse. The horses take fright and rear up, while we angrily take each other's measure, preparing to grasp each other's sidelocks. For a little while we stand in silence gazing into each other's faces. What a spectacle we make! Two Israelite heroes in their prayer shawls and phylacteries under the open sky, furiously preparing to box each other's ears ... What a sight for sore eyes! A rain of blows is just about to descend—when suddenly we both draw back, each of us crying out in simultaneous surprise:

"Oi, Reb Alter!"

"Oi, oi, Reb Mendele!!"

For all the light-hearted and humorous style, the perceptive reader will be aware of sad and serious undertones. The portrait of these two unfortunate Jews, clad in prayer shawls and phylacteries, squabbling in the mud, is sketched in highly evocative language. The Hebrew original of "while we angrily take each other's measure" is *Ko'asim U-mišta'arim*. Both sound and rhythm are reminiscent of the phrase *Kor'im U-mištaḥabhim* (we bow and prostrate ourselves), sacred language from the well-known *'Aleinu* prayer. Again the Hebrew underlying the translation "What a sight for sore eyes" is *'Ašrei 'Ayin Ra'athah Ẓo'th* (Happy the eye that saw this), which evokes the famous description in the liturgy of the Day of Atonement of the High Priest in all his splendor entering the Holy of Holies in the Temple, a once-yearly happening, a description punctuated time and again with the phrase *'Ašrei 'Ayin Ra'athah 'Elleh* (Happy the eye that saw these). There is more to come.

During Reb Alter's recital of his bad luck at the fair at which, as mentioned above, he almost betrothed two boys, the friends are disturbed by the approach of a band of Russian peasants:[47]

But while Alter was cursing Yarmolinitz together with its fair, a number of farm-carts drew near, with the farmers clearly wondering why our wagons should be standing there blocking the road. No sooner were they close enough to see us wearing prayer shawls and ritual fringes, with phylacteries strapped to our heads and on our arms, than they started mocking us aloud and crying: "Look at those

> fancy boys! The Devil take their fathers and mothers. Hey! Make way there, you fringy Jews!" We at once bestirred ourselves and set about moving our wagons. As for the gentiles, in spite of their not belonging to the seed of Israel, I can testify to the fact that they observed the commandment *Thou shalt go to the help of thy neighbor*, and they stood by us in our hour of need. By dint of their mighty efforts our wagons emerged safely from the pond. Had it not been for them, who knows how long it would have taken us to get them out. Perhaps we might never have managed it. Our coats were all muddied and our prayer shawls torn. For indeed, what are we and what is our strength? But the strong hands of these sons of Esau made light work of it. They did all the pushing, and from the way they went about it, it was obvious that the hands were the hands of Esau. But as for us, all our strength is in the mouth—the voice is the voice of Jacob. So while they pushed, we shouted: "Together heave! Together heave!" because shouting goes well with pushing. We, ourselves, were groaning and twitching in every limb, and we looked just as though we were pushing—but that's another story. Once the road was clear, those sons of Ham went their way, turning back to look at us in mockery and scorn because we were tending our horses in priestly vestments and serving our creator with sticks and reins. Some of them screwed up the corners of their coats to look like pigs' ears, and pushed them under our noses to aggravate us. Alter paid no heed to them, dismissing them with the remark, "Who cares about hooligans like them?" But as for me—their mockery pierced me like a scorpion's sting. God in Heaven! Why all this mockery? Why? Why? . . .

The biblical references are, of course, too clear to require comment. But the Hebrew behind the translation "Together heave! Together heave!" is, for example, *Daḥaphu Heiṭeibh, Heiṭeibh Daḥaphu* (push well, push well), which is again clearly reminiscent of the Talmudic description of the priests preparing the incense for the offering and shouting *Hadheiq Heiṭeibh, Heiṭeibh Hadheiq* (pound well, pound well). The meaning of the passage is rendered unequivocal in the phrases, "Tending our horses in priestly vestments and serving our creator with sticks and reins." The irony of a God-intoxicated people wallowing in mire, with its head in the clouds and its feet in the mud, is inescapable. Just as elsewhere the irony of a people, whose genius has traditionally been expressed in the field of law, forced to live against a law aimed at its destruction, is equally made manifest.

The episode is an exercise in self-awareness. Unlike so many of his predecessors and contemporaries, however, Mendele does not resort to tub-thumping and blatant didacticism to convey his message, but rather demonstrates that art itself is the great teacher. His work was all the more effective for that reason. Mendele's ambivalent attitude to Jewish life in Czarist Russia, comprising a deep loyalty and sincere compassion on the one hand, with biting satire and reforming zeal on the other, exerted a profound impact on the Hebrew-reading public. "I laugh with one eye and cry with the other," he once remarked about himself. His readers laughed and cried with him.

It is pertinent, perhaps, to conclude with one last example in Hebrew fiction of exhortation to change the nature of Jewish society in the Russian Pale of Settlement. In 1899, M. Z. Feierberg published his novella *Whither?*, one of the finest Hebrew stories of its day. The "madness" contracted by its young hero is more social than psychological, insofar as he—like many of his contemporaries—is no longer able to accept the religious tradition which governed social life, nor live outside it. Finally he propounds a Zionist solution to the Jewish plight and delivers a remarkable peroration at a local meeting, concluding with the radical idea that the Jewish people must look for its salvation not to the West but to the East, and play a part in what he hopes will be a veritable Eastern Renaissance:[48]

> And so, my brothers, in journeying eastward, do not go as enemies of the East but as its admirers and loyal sons. Make sure you are bringing it life and not death. Millennia have elapsed from the days of the prophet Balaam until now, and still we feel that we are only in the middle of the way and that we must say about ourselves as he did: "I see him, but not now; I behold him, but not nigh." I was driven mad because I didn't know where to turn or how to escape, and now it's too late for me to change. There were days when I thought that I myself would stand in the vanguard of my people, but I now know that this cannot be. Let a new generation go before the people. And if the Jewish people has a destiny to fulfill, let it forge that destiny and that truth for itself and take them with it to the East. Not just to Palestine but to the entire East . . . only then can it know that it has taken the right and the natural path! And finally, my brothers, let none of you have the presumption to think that your generation can finish the task by itself. Let it be written on your banners: "I see him, but not now; I behold him, but not nigh." To the East! To the East!
>
> There was a sudden stirring among the audience. One of the young men loudly interrupted the speaker. The madman, however, did not seem to mind, nor did he wait to find out how his remarks had been received. Beads of perspiration fell on his flushed face, which was then remarkably handsome. Without another word, he walked out and went home.

An excellent example for any speaker!

Hence, the concern of Hebrew literature with the plight of Jewish society in Russia in the nineteenth century and the self-awareness which it fostered played no small part in the growth of attitudes which, following the cataclysmic events in 1881, gradually found expression in dramatic and far-reaching action. For all its apparent parochialism and limited horizons, nineteenth-century Hebrew literature helped to prepare the ground for developments of major importance in modern Jewish history and for events which still command a by no means negligible place upon the world stage.

Of the three great movements in Jewish life following the pogroms of 1881, Hebrew fiction exerted its main impact on the growth of Zionism and focused attention on Palestine as a solution to the Jewish plight. Its influence on Jewish migration to the United States of America and on Jewish participation in the revolutionary movements in Russia, although worthy of remark, was much smaller. The great migration westwards and the remarkable growth of Jewish socialism in Russia prior to World War I were affected more forcibly by a parallel development in Yiddish literature. But that—as Mendele might have said—is another story.

12

Epilog: The Transference of Hebrew Literature from Eastern Europe to 'Ereṣ Yisra'el[1]

In modern Hebrew literature the main center of gravity has shifted twice—from Western and Central Europe eastwards into Russia, and from Eastern Europe southwards into Palestine and Israel.[2] In the course of the nineteenth century the literary center moved from areas of comparatively small Jewish settlement in Germany[3] to the much more numerous and closely knit communities first of the Austro-Hungarian Empire and then, especially, the Russian Pale of Settlement.[4] The shift coincided with a demographic change of major importance. The century following the accession of Czar Alexander I in 1801 witnessed a veritable explosion of the Jewish population in Russia, whose consequences were to prove both dramatic and profound.[5]

The second shift—the one with which this chapter is concerned—began to gather momentum in the years following the abortive Russian revolution in 1905,[6] and reached its peak in the twenties and thirties of this century. In the space of some three decades Hebrew literature pulled its roots out of Europe and transplanted itself to a Palestine under the aegis first of the Ottoman administration and later the British Mandate. This second movement involved a transference of literature from a society comprising many millions of inhabitants to an extremely sparse Jewish population, which in 1914 numbered only eighty five thousand souls, a figure which was further reduced during the deprivations of the war years to some sixty five thousand in 1918.[7] Of this number, the greater part comprised the old *Yiššubh*, which was largely concentrated in the four "holy cities," Jerusalem, Tiberias, Safed, and Hebron. Not surprisingly, the transition was neither smooth nor easily accomplished.

Any attempt to understand the complex problems accompanying this extraordinary shift, which can have few if any parallels in world literature, must also take into account the remarkable improvement in quality, which characterized Hebrew literature in Eastern Europe in the quarter of a century prior to World War I. After a hundred years of quixotic experimentation during which, in deference to a deliberate but, in the event, unsatisfactory juxtaposition of literary and social theories, a neo-biblical style had been clumsily employed for propagating the ideas of the movement of enlightenment,[8] Hebrew literature came of age with startling suddenness. From 1890 onwards, the literature was graced with writings of high order, in poetry as well as prose, in fiction and publicistic works alike, which raised it from the level of mere didacticism to the realm of art.[9] Reforming zeal gave way to an artistic self-awareness, infusing a new subtlety into literary structure, style, and use of language. The earlier all too obvious striving after effect by means of frontal assault was replaced by a more sophisticated resort to irony and ambiguity, skillfully aimed at sharpening the reader's sensibilities instead of bludgeoning him into an outraged acquiescence. This growing maturity of form was matched, moreover, by a surer, more convincing range of themes. Crude melodrama was replaced by a subtle use of the grotesque. Stripped of unlikely contrivance, environment became increasingly a framework for the portrayal of the inner life, the starting point for a probing, questioning analysis of the national and individual predicament[10] Instead of lagging painfully behind other European literatures as had been the case throughout most of the nineteenth century,[11] Hebrew literature advanced so rapidly during the two decades before the outbreak of World War I that the time lag was largely eliminated if not actually reversed. Much of the writing, indeed, reflects considerable originality and depth—to a degree which has begun to receive due recognition only in comparatively recent times.[12]

This literature was the product of a deeply rooted society in transition. The patterns of Jewish life in Eastern Europe at the end of the last century were intricate, involved, and broadly based. Families were prolific, and relatives richly abundant. Apart from fathers, mothers, brothers, and sisters, there were grandparents and grandchildren, uncles, aunts, cousins, and the whole range of more distant relatives by blood or marriage in scores if not in hundreds. For marriage purposes, family trees were often scrutinized for no less than seven or eight generations,[13] so that the ubiquitous marriage broker was often a veritable encyclopedia of genealogy. A deep awareness of ancestry and a sense of continuity bolstered individual identity inside the community confines. Uncertainty and confusion arose mainly when the individual abandoned the areas of dense Jewish settlement in search of new experience in the outside, alien, and hostile world.[14]

For all the poverty, hardship, and oppression which formed a constant accompaniment to life, Jewish tradition still provided a warm and comforting spiritual environment for large sections of the community. The colorful ceremonies of Sabbaths and festivals, the daily all-pervasive rituals, the comforting rhythms of regular communal worship together induced a widespread feeling of spiritual satisfaction and a certain psychological stability. The weight of custom and habit with its rich symbolism reflected a legacy of generations, subtly indicating the right and proper way to live, and fortifying the spirit against the increasingly savage buffetings of the outside world. Protected by the close ties of a stable family structure and nourished almost exclusively on traditional Jewish texts, which fostered an identification with an intellectual universe so self-contained and timeless that the contemporary scene frequently appeared less real than the world of the Bible and the Talmud, the Jewish child lived in a harsh and cruel environment suffused with the glow of a romantic image. Indeed, the tendency to make dream and reality coalesce comprises an important element in this discussion.[15]

Simultaneously, however, disintegrating forces were rending the fabric of Jewish life. The waves of emigration from Russia, mainly to the United States, in the wake of the pogroms of 1881 and 1903, and the ruthless oppression by the Czarist administration that followed, led to profound changes in Jewish demography, and eroded the stability of Jewish social patterns. The emigration of almost two million Jews within a quarter of a century represented a violent sundering from the parent body which inevitably engendered social and psychological instability among those left behind. The process was exacerbated by a parallel erosion of the spiritual edifice of East European Jewry. The impact of ideas deriving from the movement of enlightenment and materialist philosophies played havoc with traditional beliefs. The seeds of uncertainty and doubt rapidly produced a crisis of faith, which in turn induced a wholesale flight from the time-honored institutions of Jewish learning.[16] The encroachment of the outside world was hastened by a crumbling of the central pillars of belief. The turmoil and ferment in Jewish society may be attributed to spiritual no less than physical pressures.

It is upon this background of a community in transition that Hebrew literature reached its peak in the twenty five years prior to World War I with a galaxy of talented writers in prose and poetry. It is sufficient merely to recall that the period includes such writers as Mendele, Ahad Ha-Am, Bialik, Tschernichowsky, Shneur, Berdichevsky, Feierberg, Ben-Zion, Brenner, Gnessin, and Shofman—to mention only the more illustrious—in order to appreciate its importance. The positive aspects of a long and rich tradition, rooted in social and religious patterns reflecting many generations of continuous adherence, were suffering erosion and loss with increasing rapidity, and the forces of disintegration may be discerned time and again in the writings of the period.[17] But the impact of the winds of change upon a deep and hitherto stable tradition seems to have uncovered a powerful source of creativity, and engendered a spate of literary works of real merit. It is curious, however, that the writers involved were highly skeptical of their own worth.[18] Whereas much of the literary criticism in the previous generations, when Hebrew literature was inferior, contained a large element of mutual admiration,[19] most writers during the period under discussion bitterly attacked the work of their contemporaries and were all too prone to dismiss each other's writings as worthless!

In retrospect, however, the originality and artistic merit of much of the prose and poetry of the time is indisputable. As the culmination of a long period of serious experimentation, Hebrew literature reflects the material poverty and spiritual wealth of East European Jewry, its sufferings and oppression, the bitterness of its plight, the heartache of a society in dissolution, the humor, irony, and self-deprecation of a people all too familiar with the cruel quirks of fate, and yet aware of its own distinctive qualities. It has a maturity and depth which command considerable respect. Esthetically as well as socially, the literature still remains valid.

The process of transferring the center of Hebrew creativity from Eastern Europe to *'Ereṣ Yisrael*[20] involved the removal of this weighty literary tradition from a solid base, in terms of the size and social stratification of a closely knit and long-established population, and its re-establishment on the much flimsier and more precarious structure of a numerically tiny population, much of it of comparatively recent vintage.[21] Admittedly, a modest literary productivity in Hebrew in its modern sense may be traced there as far back as the sixties of the last century when a Hebrew press began to appear.[22] In comparison to the East European center, however, it remained very restricted both in quantity and quality—in spite of the herculean efforts of such enthusiasts as Eliezer Ben-Yehuda and A. M. Luncz.[23] At best, a certain scaffolding existed which was able to give some support to the first attempts to establish a new literary center. More important was the struggle to make Hebrew the language of instruction in the schools, an effort which, as far as Hebrew literature is concerned, was ultimately to prove decisive.[24] Meanwhile, however, it was far from easy for the small *Yiššubh* to bear the accumulated weight of Hebrew culture, or, in the words of Uri Zvi Greenberg, "to carry the Hebrew globe with its weight of sorrow."[25]

A difficult process of adjustment is, of course, encountered in some degree by every writer, indeed by every person who emigrates from one country to another, and is forced to adjust to a radically different environment. Such a change involves a complex series of psychological, physical, and social factors. Apart from the individual capacity to accommodate to new surroundings, the stage in life at which such a transference is made usually proves decisive. The ability to acquire and speak a new language like a native, for example, appears to have a threshold usually about the age of ten.[26] Prior to that age an immigrant can learn a new vernacular without accent—an extremely rare accomplishment in the case of older immigrants. Age is equally decisive in determining the cultural formation of the immigrant. Indeed, the heritage which an immigrant carries with him may vary from very little to a very great deal. Again, a young immigrant is likely to absorb the social and cultural patterns of his land of adoption much more readily and thoroughly than the adult whose mind and attitudes have already been formed. For the former, the old country is merely a prelude to a new life, whereas for the latter the new country is largely a sequel to the really formative experiences already gained. Indeed, the older immigrant may come to regard himself as a cultural emissary, with an obligation to defend and propagate in the country of his adoption the cultural values acquired in his native land. Depending upon the individual, such ambitions may prove either beneficial or frustrating; they may bolster his sense of importance or cause him constant irritation. Certainly, a harking back to origins, whether with admiration or disdain, is almost inevitable.

Admittedly, in the case of Hebrew writers migrating from Europe to *'Ereṣ Yisra'el* there were mitigating factors. Although their first vernacular was usually Yiddish, most had studied Hebrew as their first literary language from a very tender age.[27] Immigration, in consequence, did not involve the acquisition of an entirely new language—as was the case with the vast majority of Jews migrating to the United States, for example, during the same period—but rather a different application of a largely familiar language.[28] Further mention will be made of the complex ramifications involved in this process of adaptation.[29] Again, the emotional ties and loyal devotion of a large section of diaspora Jewry to the Holy Land were deeply rooted and conducive to radical action—as witnessed by the extraordinary growth of national aspirations that fashioned the movement of Zionism. Far from imagining that they were migrating to a foreign land, Jewish immigrants to *'Ereṣ Yisra'el* were convinced that they were returning home, and that their title to the land was absolute.[30]

The importance of this factor can scarcely be overemphasized. For the Jewish child in Eastern Europe, education began with the Hebrew Bible at kindergarten age, and his familiarity with the patriarchal narratives was constantly strengthened by their annual recitation in the synagogue. To many Jewish boys the exploits of their ancestral heroes in the ancient land of Israel seemed far more intimate and real and certainly more appealing than the squalid misery of the hostile environment in which they lived.[31] However harsh and long drawn out, the exile was a temporary circumstance, and redemption might occur at any time. The daily prayers were redolent with hope for the restoration to Zion, and there was no question that sooner or later it would come to pass. The religious festivals were related topographically and climatically to Jerusalem. The complex regulations governing the agricultural cycle, so important in both synagogue service and classroom studies, were geared entirely to the geography of *'Ereṣ Yisra'el*, regardless of the conditions of Eastern Europe, or anywhere else.[32]

This yearning for *'Ereṣ Yisra'el*, so firmly enshrined in the tradition, was powerfully reinforced in the second half of the nineteenth century by the novels of Abraham Mapu,[33] whose vision of the return to Zion bordered on the prophetic. His description of the children of Zion streaming in from the lands of the dispersion, and reviving the sacred Hebrew tongue in all its grace and nobility of spirit, profoundly influenced at least one generation of writers and remains impressive to this day.[34] The appeal was more a product of his instinct than his intellect. Mapu's advocacy of enlightenment as a prelude to emancipation now seems somewhat naive,[35] whereas the national aspirations which he encouraged have been remarkably fulfilled. His success derived from his ability to harness the traditional hopes and longings of the Jewish people and give them concrete expression. After the pogroms of 1881 his vision received powerful support from Peretz Smolenskin, Moshe Leib Lilienblum, and the movement of *Ḥibbath Ṣiyyon*.[36]

Jewish entitlement to *'Ereṣ Yisra'el* seemed so natural and absolute that its exponents were long able to ignore almost entirely any unpalatable mention of other occupants, despite all evidence to the contrary.[37] During the forty years from the appearance of Mapu's *The Love of Zion* in 1853 to the publication of Ahad Ha-Am's searing articles "Truth from *'Ereṣ Yisra'el*" in the years 1891–3,[38] Hebrew literature contains scant reference to the real political and demographic facts of Palestine in the nineteenth century. Indeed, the following snatch of conversation from a novel by A. S. Rabinowitz is sufficiently uncommon to warrant special mention:

> "In my view Smolenskin is quite correct in saying that there is no way out of our impasse other than settling in *'Ereṣ Yisra'el*.
>
> Ha, ha, ha! Settling in *'Ereṣ Yisra'el*! You would be better advised to say settling in Palestine, the land of the Turks, for the land does not belong to us now, but to the sons of Ishmael, the wild Turks who are quite uncivilized."[39]

It is no wonder, then, that Ahad Ha-Am's contention that the amount of good land currently unoccupied was not large and that the Arabs were not "wild men of the desert" as was usually supposed, caused such consternation.

> The peasants are delighted when a Hebrew colony is founded in their midst, for they are well rewarded for their labor, and prosper from year to year, as experience has shown. And the big land-owners are also delighted when we come, for we pay a price for their wastelands such as they never dreamed about. But if in course of time the Jewish holding in the country develops to such an extent as to encroach in some degree on the native population, the latter will not easily give up its position.[40]

The clash of image and reality is a factor of central importance in the shift of Hebrew literature from Eastern Europe to *'Ereṣ Yisra'el*. The exponents of nationalism had viewed the land so consistently through a rose-colored monocle, which allowed little shift in perspective, that physical contact with the country would seem to imply only two possibilities. Either the vision would have to shatter against the harsh reality of Palestine, or an attempt would have to be made to make the land conform to the vision of *'Ereṣ Yisra'el*.[41] But frequent resort was also made to a third possibility which demanded the simultaneous acceptance of both attitudes, however contradictory—engendering the kind of paradox not infrequently encountered where strong emotional factors are at work.[42] The dilemma permeates much of the major writing of the period, as the stories of Brenner, Agnon, and Hazaz—to mention only three of the more important authors—amply demonstrate. Indeed, a detailed investigation of this phenomenon, as manifested in the work of each individual migrant author, is clearly a major prerequisite for a proper understanding of the development of modern Hebrew literature—certainly from the early years of this century until the outbreak of World War II. Writer after writer left the shores of Europe in search of *'Ereṣ Yisra'el*, only to find themselves in Palestine!

The psychological stress resulting from the clash of image and reality was frequently the more disturbing for other reasons. The situation was aggravated by the nature of the immigration which consisted largely of individuals rather than family units. This was particularly the case among the young pioneers, who all too frequently found themselves without a single relative in their new land. When Greenberg described his departure from his parents' home in the line, "Father raged, mother wept, and a white bed was orphaned," the poignancy is exacerbated by the knowledge that not only the bed but the poet himself has been orphaned by his action.[43] In great measure the collective settlement became a substitute for the lost family structure, and there can be little doubt that the rapid growth and success of the collective was due, at least in part, to its social function.[44]

Hebrew literature was conditioned, however, not only by the physical and psychological odysseys of the individual writers, but to some extent by the nature of the readership. It is important to recall that prior to World War I, and largely—although in ever-decreasing measure—in the period between the two world wars, the majority of readers of Hebrew literature lived in Eastern Europe, which also supported most of the Hebrew publishing houses and the leading Hebrew periodicals.[45] A sizable minority was, in addition, to be found in the Americas, particularly in the United States,[46] but environmental differences between the Jewish communities of the Old and New World were so great, that an investigation of the role of the Hebrew reader in America would require separate treatment, beyond the limits of this book.

In Eastern Europe the emotional expectations of Jewish readers living in conditions of extreme political and economic oppression must be regarded as a powerful force. Cherished illusions die hard, and the readers' susceptibilities tend to be taken seriously, particularly when the writer has shared their convictions to the arduous point of himself settling in *'Ereṣ Yisra'el*, and remains anxious to encourage Jewish immigration—or at the very least not discourage it. In such circumstances it requires courage of a high order to swim against the tide. Ahad Ha-Am's intellectual honesty earned him recognition as "the best-hated critic of the Zionist Organization;"[47] while

Brenner's temperamental inability to tolerate illusion or camouflage[48] accounts for the fact that the initial impact of the stories he wrote in Palestine was so much greater for the young Jewish immigrants than for the readers of Hebrew literature in Europe. Yet even Brenner, whose opposition to romantic preconceptions was so strong that it affected his choice of vocabulary,[49] was finally able to discern a gleam of hope in the pioneering settlements in Galilee, and came to the conclusion that perhaps all was not yet lost.[50]

This geographical separation of author and readers is again a most unusual if not unique circumstance, and certainly worthy of consideration. The writer in exile is, of course, a common enough phenomenon, and his work is often directed to a mass readership in his lost homeland. But in the case of Hebrew literature the situation was reversed. Here, the writers who left Europe to settle in Palestine regarded themselves as being in their real homeland, while their readers in Eastern Europe were regarded—and, indeed, looked upon themselves—as being in exile.[51] Whereas the writer in exile in other literatures is concerned with the task of changing the conditions of his homeland so that he may himself return to his readers, the Hebrew writer in Palestine was concerned with the task of bringing his readers to him, and of helping to shape conditions to make such a major demographic shift possible.[52] It was a case—if the metaphor may be pressed into service—of making the mountain go to Mohammed! The methods and degrees of subtlety employed toward this end vary greatly in the case of each individual writer, and the whole process again requires detailed investigation. But the inherent logic of the situation would seem to be compelling. The psychological pressures on any writer in such a situation, where ideology, emotional inclination, and self-interest coincide, are clearly very great—hence the need to cherish the vision even in the face of harsh reality.

It is pertinent, perhaps, to quote a passage from Amos Oz's novel *Touch the Water, Touch the Wind*, in which Kumin (the author's grandfather?) relates the following anecdote:

> "My father was a kind of Hebrew poet, a kind of madman, a Zionist, a stray lamb in the streets of Odessa. All his life he wrote poems about Mount Carmel and Mount Tabor and Mount Moriah, and the wailing wall in Jerusalem, about the desert and the holy tombs ... a few years ago I packed him off to Palestine before it was the death of him or he was the death of me. And do you know ... what became of him there in the land of his dreams in the twilight of his life? The old man settled down, no doubt on one of the hills to which he had always lifted up his eyes, among his holy tombs, and there, in his long-dreamed-of Palestine, among the hills and tombs, there the old man goes on to his dying day writing heart-rending poems of longing for some other Palestine, the real one. All with perfect faith. All in Hebrew. And in Biblical language."[53]

Geography is responsible, too, for a further problem with which the immigrant authors were compelled to grapple. A writer's imagery is heavily dependent on the impressions and associations gathered in his most formative years. The climate and landscape, the flora and fauna, the geography of town and country, as well as the civic and domestic architecture of the native land together form a basic environment from which the literary imagination draws its sustenance. The metaphors and similes, the coloring, the light and shade of description reflect the impressions of the outside world upon the tender mind of the growing child. They are what Bialik called "pictures of my world in those first days ... the soul's basic, elemental scenes."[54]

> How true the saying is that a man sees and perceives only once; in childhood! The first visions, in that same innocence as on the day when they left the Creator's hand, they are the real essence and the very stuff of life; and those impressions that follow are secondary and deficient, seemingly like the first, but weak reflections of them, and not genuine ... All the sights of heaven and earth which I have blessed throughout my life, have received no nourishment except from the power of that first vision.[55]

It is not difficult to imagine the shattering effect exerted on a writer when all the physical ties linking him to his native environment are abruptly and finally sundered. "I am here, totally here," Leah Goldberg wrote, "in a foreign city in the heart of the great alien motherland."[56] The point is forcefully portrayed in Shimoni's idyll *Yobhel ha-'Eghlonim* (The Wagoners' Jubilee), in which a young poet describes the extent to which the radical change of landscape which he experiences in moving from Eastern Europe to *'Ereṣ Yisra'el* inhibited his poetic creativity.

> From the moment I came to the land my spirit was utterly downcast.
> Nature opened her book before me, but I did not know how to read.
> The letters were new and strange, their combinations oddly unfamiliar.
> I was captivated by their hidden beauty; I experienced the secret magic.
> But my heart did not leap for them as yet, like a bird for its nest.
> The full redeeming echo still did not well from the depths of my soul.
> And even in moments sublime, when the Muse descended upon me,
> And a torrent of feeling raged and blazed into vision before me—
> They were not the sights of the land of Israel—No! but the distant
> Sights of another land which had cradled my childhood ...
>
> My young bones were filled with the sights and sounds of the Russian landscape,
> The shadows of its dark forests and the majesty of its great rivers,
> The freedom of the green steppes and the gold of its wide meadows ...
>
> I saw a majestic palm and longed for the sad poplar;
> The winter-blossom charmed me, but I dreamed of a wilderness of snow.
> I recognized the beauty of the landscape, and knew that it was mine—
> But it had not yet penetrated my innermost being, my very soul.[57]

It takes a long time for a new country to start looking hospitable, even where the landscape is cultivated and gentle. In the wild harshness of what seemed a ravaged and neglected land, the process could be painfully slow. An uncomfortable aura of this kind pervades, for example, the novel *Land Without Shade* by Yonat and Alexander Sened.[58] But even for the generation of writers born or brought up in the country, the impact of whose work was first felt in the years following World War II, the landscape can arouse a sense of alienation or convey a feeling of primitive hostility. The characters in S. Yizhar's lengthy novel *Yemei Ṣiqlagh* (*Days of Ziklag*) are dominated by the inhospitable wilderness in which they find themselves, and with which they can establish no emotional rapport.[59] Yet the magnificent descriptions which form so integral a part of Yizhar's novel bear witness to an exact and detailed knowledge of the environment. Nature is clearly the source of literary inspiration; but in this instance the inspiration derives not from emotional affinity or sympathetic intercourse, but from a clear awareness of antipathy.

But in respect to geography, as with so many aspects of this complex theme it is also possible to discern sharp tendencies of an opposite kind. For many immigrants the romantic image of *'Ereṣ Yisra'el*, which had become so integral a part of their thinking, responded favorably to the geographical realities, and blended in the landscape, vegetation, contours, and coloring of the adopted land. Such coalescence of image and reality is responsible, for example, for the appeal exerted by the poetry of Rachel, for whom the process of fusion was so complete that the dividing line simply faded out of consciousness:

> ... my Kinneret, O my Kinneret.
> Are you real, or have I dreamed a dream?[60]

A passionate desire to recreate the homeland and change the values of society served as a powerful source of inspiration for much of the Hebrew poetry of the twenties. Total rejection of the exile, with its alien culture, implacable hatred, and social and religious persecution, spurred many writers deliberately to reject even those aspects of their native environment with which they felt most in tune, and to foster a positive relationship, however hard at first, toward their adopted homeland. In this respect Greenberg represents, perhaps, the most determined example. Again, for many writers the creative energies unleashed by pioneering and revolutionary fervor drew nourishment from the magical beauty and breathtaking variety of landscape, whose very strangeness and unfamiliarity appeared so well suited to the new forms and unfamiliar images increasingly employed in Hebrew poetry after World War I.[61] Even Shimoni's young poet ultimately felt in tune with his surroundings, and was able to draw inspiration from the landscapes of his adopted country:

> I stopped thinking of nature and its beauty, and had already laid down my pen;
> When one night as I sat idling near the stable door, quite suddenly
> I felt the veil fall away from my eyes, and I saw the magic of the night, uncovered, exalted, and near.
> I seemed to recognize it again after a long estrangement.
> And now when I look at the heavens, they are near to me, yet sublime.

> I remember the pain of estrangement, and I recall the delight of recognition.
> My heart is full to the brim, and I am drunk with excitement.[62]

The positive effects upon imagery are discernible in the renewed application of biblical phraseology to the environment which nurtured it. This is particularly true where the image depends upon geographical or climatic conditions. Back in its land of origin the term "seawards" meaning "westwards" is readily comprehensible while the phrase "winter days" as an epithet of youth is far more convincing in a Mediterranean setting than in Northern Europe, where its connotation might well have been the reverse.[63] Indeed, the renewed contact of land and language provided a powerful stimulus to the development of Hebrew which has led to great changes both in range and usage, and which is still manifestly at work.

The shift from the diaspora to Palestine, however, subjected Hebrew to new and disconcerting strains. Although throughout the nineteenth century Hebrew literature in Europe had struggled bravely to come to grips with the problems arising from its attempts to find the vocabulary necessary to portray modern life,[64] and although there is considerable evidence to support the view that Hebrew was frequently used as a vernacular in Palestine during the nineteenth century,[65] the deliberate adoption of Hebrew as the language of the *Yiššubh* engendered serious problems. In addition to its traditional function, Hebrew was called upon to fulfill the roles previously assigned to Yiddish, Ladino, Arabic, and a number of European languages. It is paradoxical that the return to the "Holy Land" demanded the secularization of the "Holy Tongue."[66] After many centuries of use primarily for religious and legal purposes, in which such words as *holiness*, *righteousness*, *repentance*, and *redemption* had occupied the center of the stage, the language had now to cope with *screwdrivers*, *rifles*, *can-openers*, and *back-axles*. But words have overtones and histories which they drag along with them, and which can only be stripped away and discarded at the risk of severe impoverishment. For the Hebrew writer the process of adoption was initially painful and strewn with pitfalls.[67] At a later stage, however, the new shades of meaning imposed upon old roots were utilized by skillful writers to express ambiguity and irony with powerful effect. It may at least be readily imagined that the revival of a language from what was primarily a literary medium to a highly successful vernacular confronted the Hebrew writer with formidable problems.[68] In this, as in so many other respects, modern Hebrew literature is worthy of investigation.

In moving from Europe to *'Ereṣ Yisra'el*, Hebrew literature was affected by an additional linguistic factor of major importance. Largely on the insistence of Eliezer Ben-Yehuda,[69] the *Yiššubh* adopted a *Sephardi*-type pronunciation of Hebrew in contrast to the *'Aškenazi* pronunciation prevalent in Central and Eastern Europe. Whereas the latter favors a penultimate stress, the former prefers the stress on the ultimate syllable. Moreover, the vowel sounds and certain consonants enjoy a different pronunciation in each tradition. The impact of such change on Hebrew writers who had grown up with the *'Aškenazi* pronunciation, only to find themselves compelled to adopt the *Sephardi* accent, was devastating. Worst affected were the poets, for whom the magical effects of language patterns and rhythmic sequences are all-important.[70] Imagine, for example, an English writer, accustomed from childhood to rhyming *kiss* with *miss*, suddenly confronted with the latter word rendered *mitt.* Supposing the pronunciation of the word *temporary* were suddenly declared to be *temporarý*, and *embarrassment* changed to *embarrassmént*; for the poet, with his delicately adjusted ear, the shock sustained would surely result in more than a *temporarý embarrassmént*! It is no wonder that poetry suffered and that a number of poets fell silent for a time or altogether.[71] Again, the effect on literature requires examination.

One further difference is, perhaps, worthy of mention. In the latter part of the nineteenth century, Hebrew literature in Europe as well as Yiddish literature contains elements of humor which are both characteristic and effective. A product of the paradoxical Jewish situation of a God-intoxicated people wallowing in mire,[72] the humor is self-deprecating and wonderfully subtle. A deep respect for law, as expressed in religion, had engaged the intellectual energies of the Jewish people literally for millennia.[73] Yet in Russia the Jew was compelled to live against the law of the state which was aimed at his destruction. A recognition of the absurdity of such a situation informs diaspora humor. It served as a means of self-preservation, in that it helped to make the intolerable somehow bearable. But in the homeland this could not be.[74] The demands of Jewish dignity in search of self-realization and peoplehood could not be reconciled with the self-deprecating stance of a minority in exile, and humor largely disappears from Hebrew literature for some decades. Such traces as remained and its reappearance since the creation of the State of Israel again deserve investigation.

From what precedes, some inkling of the complex problems caused by the shift of Hebrew literature from Europe to *'Ereṣ Yisra'el* may, perhaps, be gleaned. The process constitutes an essential key for understanding the remarkable development of Hebrew literature in the twentieth century. Because the circumstances of that development are without parallel, a detailed examination of some of the factors briefly mentioned in this epilog might well prove highly instructive. Certainly, following its dramatic release from artificial fetters, the Phoenix of Hebrew literature has soared in less than a hundred years to heights which were previously unattainable and even unimagined.

Abbreviations

THE FOLLOWING abbreviated titles are used for the editions and Hebrew titles of the novels under review.

ABR. S.J. Abramowitz, *Fathers and Sons* (*Ha-'Abhoth we-ha-Banim*), Odessa, 1868.

BRA.1 R.A. Braudes, *Religion and Life* (*Ha-Dath we-ha-Ḥayyim*), Lemberg, 1885 (1876–7).

BRA.2 R.A. Braudes, *The Two Extremes* (*Šetei ha-Qeṣawoth*), Warsaw, 1888.

Klausner, *History.* J. Klausner, *Hisṭoriah šel ha-Siphruth ha-'Ibhrith ha-Ḥadhašah* (*A History of Modern Hebrew Literature*), 2nd ed., vols.3–6, Jerusalem, 1953–8.

LEIN. J. Leinwand, *The Artful Villain* (*'Oseh Mezimmoth*), Lemberg, pt.1, 1875, pt.2, 1876.

Mapu *Kol Kithbhei 'Abhraham Mapu* (*The Collected Writings of Abraham Mapu*), Tel-Aviv, 1950.

Mapu's novels referred to in the text and notes, and the details of their first publication, are as follows:

The Love of Zion (*'Ahabhath Ṣiyyon*), Vilna, 1853.

The Guilt of Samaria (*'Ašmath Šomron*), Vilna, 1865–6.

The Hypocrite (*'Ayiṭ Ṣabhua'*), Vilna, pt.1, 1858, pt.2, 1861, pt.3, 1864. A second edition containing all five parts appeared in Warsaw, 1869.

MAN. M. Manassewitz, *The Parents' Sin* (*Ḥaṭṭa'th Horim*), Warsaw, 1884.

MEIN. S.F. Meinkin, *The Love of the Righteous* (*'Ahabhath Yešarim*), pt.1, Vilna, 1881.

RAB. A.S. Rabinowitz, *At the Crossroads* (*'Al ha-Pereq*), Warsaw, 1887.

SHEIK. N.M. Sheikewitz, *The Outcast* (*Ha-Niddaḥath*), Vilna, 1886.

SIRK. I.J. Sirkis, *Esther* (*'Ester*), Warsaw, 1887.

SM.1 P. Smolenskin, *The Wanderer in the Paths of Life* (*Ha-To'eh be-Dharekhei ha-Ḥayyim*), Warsaw, 1905 (parts 1–3, Vienna, 1868–70; all 4 parts, Vienna, 1876).

SM.2 P. Smolenskin, *The Joy of the Godless* (*Simḥath Ḥaneph*), Warsaw, 1905 (Vienna, 1872).

SM.3 P. Smolenskin, *A Donkey's Burial* (*Qebhurath Ḥamor*), Warsaw, 1905 (Vienna, 1874).

SM.4 P. Smolenskin, *Pride and Fall* (*Ga'on we-Šebher*), Warsaw, 1905 (Vienna, 1874).

SM.5 P. Smolenskin, *The Reward of the Righteous* (*GemulYešarim*), Vilna, 1903 (Vienna, 1876).

SM.6 P. Smolenskin, *The Inheritance* (*Ha-Yerušah*), Peterburg, 1898 (Vienna, 1878–84).

WEIS.1 I. Weisbrem, *Between the Times* (*Bein ha-Zemannim*), Warsaw, 1888.

WEIS.2 I. Weisbrem, *Eighteen Coins* (*Ḥay 'Aghoroth*), Warsaw, 1888.

WEIS.3 I. Weisbrem, *The Lottery and the Inheritance* (*Ha-Goral we-ha-Yerušah*), Warsaw, 1892.

ZOB. B.I. Zobeizensky, *For Love of Ṣaddiqim* (*'Ahabhath Ṣaddiqim*), Warsaw, 1881.

Notes

Notes to Chapter One

1. The main currents of modern Hebrew literature have been charted in such standard histories as J. Klausner, *Historiah šel ha-Siphruth ha-'Ibhrith ha-Ḥadhašah* (A History of Modern Hebrew Literature), 2nd ed., Jerusalem, 1952–8, henceforward designated *History*; F. Lachower, *Toledoth ha-Siphruth ha-'Ibhrith ha-Ḥadhašah* (History of Modern Hebrew Literature), 7th ed., Tel-Aviv, 1951; A. Shaanan, *Ha-Siphruth ha-'Ibhrith ha-Ḥadhašah li-Zeramehah* (Trends in Modern Hebrew Literature), Tel-Aviv, 1962; E. Silberschlag, *From Renaissance to Renaissance*, 2 vols., New York, 1973, 1977; M. Waxman, *A History of Jewish Literature*, rev. ed., New York, 1960; I. Zinberg, *A History of Jewish Literature*, tr. and ed. B. Martin, 12 vols., Cincinnati and New York, 1972–8 (orig. 1929–37). For a critique of such histories of literature see A. Holtz, "Prolegomena to a Literary History of Modern Hebrew Literature," in *From Literature East and West*, vol.11, no.3, 1968. More recent accounts of the development of modern Hebrew literature include that of G. Shaked, *Ha-Sipporeth ha-'Ibhrith 1880–1980* (The Hebrew Story 1880–1980), 3 vols., Tel-Aviv, 1977, 1983, 1988; and of D. Miron, *Bein Ḥazon le-Emeth* (Between Vision and Truth), Jerusalem, 1979. For the most recent, comprehensive survey of research on *Haskalah* literature see S. Werses, "Current Research on Haskalah Literature" (Hebrew text), in *Yedhi'on ha-'Iggudh ha-'Olami le-Madda'ei ha-Yahadhuth*, pt.1, no.25, summer 1985; pt.2, no.26, winter 1985; pt.3, no.27, winter 1987.

2. See E. Spicehandler, "Modern Hebrew Literature," *Encyclopaedia Judaica*, vol.8, p.178. For a concise account of the development of Hebrew see C. Rabin, *A Short History of the Hebrew Language*, Jerusalem, 1973.

3. See *The Life of Glückel of Hameln*, tr. Beth-Zion Abrahams, London, 1962, pp.45f.

4. C. Roth, *History of the Jews of Italy*, Philadelphia, 1946, p.402.

5. See below, p.128.

6. See below, ch.8.

7. For detailed information on this period see M. Pelli, *The Age of Haskalah*, Leiden, 1979.

8. G. Mosse, *Germans and Jews*, New York, 1970.

9. Cf. D. Patterson, *The Hebrew Novel in Czarist Russia*, Edinburgh, 1964, pp.182f.

10. The history of the Jews in Russia in modern times has been treated in such standard works as L. Greenberg, *The Jews in Russia: The Struggle for Emancipation*, 2 vols., New Haven and London, 1965 (orig. 1944); S. Dubnow, *History of the Jews in Russia and Poland*, tr. I. Friedlaender, 3 vols., Philadelphia, 1916–20; S. Baron, *The Russian Jew under Tsars and Soviets*, London and New York, 1976; J. Frankel, *Prophecy and Politics: Socialism, Nationalism and the Russian Jews 1862–1917*, Cambridge, 1981; L. Kochan, ed., *The Jews in Soviet Russia since 1917*, 3rd ed., Oxford, 1978.

11. Though the recruitment quotas for Jews and for gentiles were the same, the Jews were subjected to greater harassment and discrimination, and were frequently put under pressure to convert to Christianity. On the quotas, see M. Stanislawski, *Tsar Nicholas I and the Jews*, Philadelphia, 1983, pp.18ff.

12. See Patterson, *op.cit.*, pp.148ff.

13. See *ibid.*, pp.114f, and cf. below, pp.131f.
14. Cf. *ibid.*, p.145.
15. See below, pp.140ff.
16. See below, chs.6 and 7.
17. See below, chs.2 and 3.
18. See D. Patterson, *Abraham Mapu*, London, 1964, p.26.
19. See *ibid.*, pp.96ff.
20. See *ibid.*, p.64, n.2. Cf. D. Patterson, "Conversational Uses of the Root *Dabhar* in Neo-Biblical Hebrew," in *Essays on the Occasion of the Seventieth Anniversary of the Dropsie University*, eds. A. I. Katsh and L. Nemoy, Philadelphia, 1979, pp.365–70. See below, ch.8, n.6.
21. For a detailed study of Smolenskin, see D. Weinfeld, *Peretz Smolenskin's Art of the Novel*, a thesis submitted for the degree of Doctor of Philosophy, Hebrew University, Jerusalem, 1975. See also M. Yahrblum, *The Works of Peretz Smolenskin*, New York University, doctoral dissertation, 1965. For a serious treatment of Braudes see B. Feingold, *Yeṣiratho šel R.A. Braudes* (The Work of R.A. Braudes), 2 vols., Hebrew University, doctoral dissertation, 1978.
22. See *The Hebrew Novel in Czarist Russia*, pp.138f.
23. See *ibid.*, pp.227ff; see also Y. Mazor, "Traces of the English Victorian Novel in the Enlightenment Hebrew Novel: Between Dickens and Smolenskin," in *Hebrew Studies*, vol.xxv, 1984.
24. See *The Hebrew Novel in Czarist Russia*, pp.40f.
25. Cf. below, pp.56ff and 137.
26. Mendele Mokher Sepharim (Mendele the Bookseller) was the pen-name of Shalom Jacob Abramowitz (1835–1917). See below, pp.139ff. For a detailed study of Abramowitz, see D. Miron, *A Traveler Disguised*, New York, 1973. See also I. Even-Zohar's penetrating remarks on Mendele's method in "Gnessin's Dialogue and its Russian Models," in *Slavica Hierosolymitana*, vol.7, Jerusalem, 1985. See below, ch.11, n.42.
27. See e.g. M. Perry, "Thematic and Structural Shifts in Autotranslations by Bilingual Hebrew-Yiddish Writers," in *Poetics Today*, vol.2:4, 1981, pp.181–92. Cf. below, ch.11, n.43.
28. From the novel *Sepher ha-Qabbṣanim* (The Book of the Beggars), in *Kol Kithbhei Mendele Mokher Sepharim* (The Collected Writings of Mendele Mokher Sepharim), Tel-Aviv, 1958, p.92.
29. See below, pp.139ff.
30. See T. Carmi, ed., *The Penguin Book of Hebrew Verse*, Harmondsworth, 1981, pp.39f. See also D. Patterson, *The Foundations of Modern Hebrew Literature*, London, 1961, pp.41ff.
31. See *ibid.*, pp.54ff. For the Hebrew original see C. N. Bialik, *Sippurim* (Stories), Tel-Aviv, 1950, pp.200f. The title of this autobiographical story is an agricultural term used to denote the remnant of a previous year's crop which has grown of its own accord without replanting. Cf. A. Even-Shoshan, *Ha-Millon he-Ḥadhaš* (The New Dictionary), vol.4, Jerusalem, 1967, p.1829, s.v. *saphiaḥ*.
32. See *The Penguin Book of Hebrew Verse*, pp.40f. See also D. Aberbach, "Chaim Nachman Bialik: Paradoxes of a 'National Poet,'" *Encounter*, June, 1981, pp.41–8.
33. See E. Silberschlag, *Saul Tschernichowsky*, London and Ithaca, N.Y., 1968, and D. Patterson, "Saul Tschernichowsky," in *The Jewish Quarterly*, Autumn, 1973.
34. They had, of course, been sounded elsewhere in European literature. See C. Raphael, "The Two Traditions: The Hebraic and the Hellenic," in D. Daiches and A. Thorlby, eds., *Literature and Western Civilisation*, vol.1, *The Classical World*, London, 1972. For the revival of the question in nineteenth-century literature by Nietzsche, see *ibid.*, vol.5, *The Modern World ii: Realities*, I. Eörsi, "Poetry and Ideology," and A. Thorlby, "Irrationalism."
35. From a sonnet-cycle, *'Al ha-Dam* (On the Blood), tr. by L. Bernard in Silberschlag, *Saul Tschernichowsky*, p.168.
36. Cf. *ibid.*, pp.58–69.
37. See e.g. A.A. Rivlin, *Pulmos be-Širah* (Controversy in Poetry), Tel-Aviv, 1966, pp.17ff. See below, ch.12, n.18.
38. See L. Simon, *Ahad Ha-Am*, London, 1960. See also *idem*, *Selected Essays by Ahad Ha-'Am*, Philadelphia, 1948.
39. See below, ch.12.

Notes to Chapter Two

1. All references to Mapu's novels are drawn from *Kol Kithbhei 'Abhraham Mapu* (The Collected Writings of Abraham Mapu), Tel-Aviv, 1950, subsequently referred to as *Mapu*. Mapu's own letters, *Mikhtebhei 'Abhraham Mapu*, have been edited by Ben-Zion Dinur, Jerusalem, 1970. Many corrections, however, may be found in G. Elkoshi, "Abraham Mapu's Letters" (Hebrew text), in *Hasifrut*, vol.4, no.2, Tel-Aviv, 1973.
2. Parts I, 1858; II, 1861; III, 1864 were first published in Vilna. A second edition containing all five parts appeared posthumously in Warsaw in 1869.
3. *Mapu*, pp.217, 218, 220f, 221f, 224f, 225f, 229f, 233f, 235, 239f, 241, 242, 243, 247f, 250, 252f, 254f, 259f, 262, 264f, 270f, 273f, 275f, 276, 280, 284, 285f, 286f, 289, 294f, 297f, 306f, 313, 317f, 319, 325, 330, 339, 345, 347, 357f, 359f, 362f, 376, 376f, 382, 385f, 386, 389, 397, 417f, 430f, 431.
4. Reference to unquoted letters, although they may be important for the plot, may be found *ibid.*, pp. 217, 241, 242, 250, 325, 339, 347, 376, 389, 431.
5. *Ibid.*, pp.225f, 286f, 362f.
6. Cf. D. Patterson, *Abraham Mapu*, p.36.
7. See G. L. van Roosbroek, *Persian Letters before Montesquieu*, New York, 1932, p.82.
8. Cf. *ibid.*, p.12.
9. F.G. Black, *The Epistolary Novel in the Late Eighteenth Century*, Eugene, 1940, p.108.
10. See below, pp.32f.
11. See e.g. B. W. Downs, *Richardson*, London, 1928, pp.160f.
12. See Black, *op. cit.*, p.1.
13. See *ibid.*, p.63.
14. Footnotes are also to be found in non-satirical epistolary novels, see *ibid.*, pp.9, 64.
15. See above, ch.1, p.10.
16. S. Werses, "'Iyyunim ba-Mibhneh šel *Megalleh Ṭemirin* u- *Bhoḥan Ṣaddiq*" (Studies in the Structure of *Megalleh Ṭemirin* and *Boḥan Ṣaddiq*), in *Tarbiz*, vol.31, no.4, 1962.
17. J.L. Landau, *Short Lectures on Modern Hebrew Literature*, London, 1938, p.213.
18. Werses, *op. cit.*, p.389.
19. *Ibid.*, pp.384f. See also S. Werses, "Current Research on Haskalah Literature" (Hebrew text), *op. cit.*, pt.2, pp.21ff, and the literature mentioned there.
20. A.D. McKillop, "Epistolary Technique in Richardson's Novels," *Rice Institute Pamphlet*, vol.38, April, 1951, p.36. Nevertheless, the didactic element in Richardson's *Pamela* may well have influenced the vogue for short didactic epistolary stories to be found in *Haskalah* circles as exemplified in M.A. Günzburg's popular *Debhir*, I, Vilna, 1844. See S. Halkin, *Mabho' la-Siphruth ha-'Ibhrith* (Introduction to Hebrew Literature), Jerusalem, 1958, pp.242f.
21. Cf. Black, *op.cit.*, p.58.
22. Cf. Werses, "'Iyyunim . . .," *op. cit.*, p.389.
23. See above, pp.2ff and 15f.
24. Cf. Werses, "'Iyyunim . . .," *op. cit.*, p.387; and K.R. Mandelkow, "Der deutsche Briefroman. Zum Problem der Polyperspektive im Epischen," in *Neophilologus*, vol.44, 1960.
25. *Mapu*, pp.7, 8, 35f, 51, 54f, 64, 142f, 145, 151, 159, 163.
26. See Patterson, *op. cit.*, p.36.
27. Cf. Black, *op. cit.*, p.47.
28. *Mapu*, pp.7f; cf. Patterson, *op. cit.*, pp.111f.
29. *Mapu*, p.51.
30. *Ibid.*, p.55.
31. Cf. Patterson, *op. cit.*, pp.93ff; and *The Hebrew Novel in Czarist Russia*, pp.154f; cf. below, ch.11.
32. *Mapu*, p.64; cf. p.254. See also Patterson, "The Use of Songs in the Novels of Abraham Mapu," in *Journal of Semitic Studies*, 1, no.4, October, 1956.
33. *Mapu*, p.36.
34. *Ibid.*, pp.39f.
35. *Ibid.*, pp.145, 151, 159, 163. On p.145 Manoah gives Miriam a letter from her husband

confirming that he will arrive in the following week. The contents of the letter, p.151, which Eliphelet gives Manoah together with a gift to bring to Miriam are not revealed. The letter on p.159 is brought by Nathan from Hephzibah to Miriam describing Eliphelet's kindness.

36. *Ibid.*, pp.142f.

37. Cf. Patterson, *Abraham Mapu*, pp.61 and 130f.

38. See e.g. J. Fichman, *'Anšei Bhesorah* (Men of Good Tidings), Tel-Aviv, 1938, p.127, and J. Klausner, *History*, vol.3, p.349. See below, n.64.

39. See above, ch.1, p.11. Cf. Patterson, *Abraham Mapu*, pp.26f.

40. See *ibid.*, pp.36, 55f.

41. *Mapu*, pp.242, 262 (although the reader learns that the letter is a forgery only on p.268), 289, 319.

42. *Ibid.*, pp.243, 319.

43. *Ibid.*, pp.325, 330.

44. *Ibid.*, pp.242, 270f, 297f, 339.

45. *Ibid.*, pp.221f, 273f, 330, 359, 430.

46. The name is symbolic, connoting both "mouse" and "miser." The use of symbolic names is a common device in the Hebrew novel of the period.

47. *Ibid.*, pp.273f.

48. *Ibid.*, pp.317f, 376f.

49. *Ibid.*, p.318.

50. For other examples of letters used for dramatic effect, see *ibid.*, pp.294f, 376f.

51. *Ibid.*, pp.262, 264f. The barbaric practice of burning books is frequently satirized in the novels of the period, cf. *ibid.*, p.266.

52. *Ibid.*, pp.243, 276.

53. *Ibid.*, pp.294f. For the heavy incidence of fainting in the Hebrew novel of the period, see below, ch.4.

54. See *ibid.*, p.50. The influence of Goethe's *Werther* seems highly probable.

55. *Mapu*, p.382.

56. *Ibid.*, part I, ch.3.

57. *Ibid.*, pp.224f, 225f. Cf. also p.235.

58. *Ibid.*, pp.317f, and cf. above, n.49.

59. *Ibid.*, p.345.

60. *Ibid.*, pp.357f. For a translation of the letter, see Patterson, *Abraham Mapu*, pp.151f.

61. *Mapu*, pp.417f.

62. *Ibid.*, pp.259f.

63. *Ibid.*, pp.285f, 286f, 359f, 362f, 385f; and cf. Patterson, *Abraham Mapu*, pp.36, 52, 87f, and 160f. See also S. Werses, "Zeman u-Merḥabh be-Roman *'Ayiṭ Ṣabhua'* šel Mapu" (Time and Space in Mapu's Novel *The Hypocrite*), in *Meḥqarim be-Siphruth 'Ibrith* (Studies in Hebrew Literature), ed. R. Tsur and U. Shavit, Tel-Aviv, 1986.

64. See above, n.38. See especially T. Cohen, *From Dream to Reality, Descriptions of Eretz Yisrael in Haskalah Literature* (Hebrew text), Jerusalem, 1982, ch.2.

65. For the literary techniques of the frame-story, see e.g. H. Bracher, *Rahmenerzählung und Verwandtes bei G. Keller, C. F. Meyer und Th. Storm*, Leipzig, 1909; and E. K. Bennett, *A History of the German Novelle from Goethe to Thomas Mann*, 2nd ed. revised and continued by H. M. Waidson, Cambridge, 1961. For the use of the frame-story in the Hebrew novel of the period, see Patterson, *The Hebrew Novel in Czarist Russia*, pp.47f.

66. *Mapu*, p.286.

67. *Ibid.*, p.289. See above, n.41.

68. *Ibid.*, p.313.

69. For a translation of the letter, see Patterson, *Abraham Mapu*, pp.151f.

70. *Mapu*, pp.241, 376f.

71. *Ibid.*, p.252.

72. *Ibid.*, pp.221f, 225f. Cf. pp.233f, 273f.

73. See Patterson, *Abraham Mapu*, pp.53f.

74. See above, n.24.

75. See Werses, "'Iyyunim . . .," p.401.
76. See *Mapu*, p.313.
77. Cf. S. L. Ṣitron, *Yoṣerei ha-Siphruth ha-'Ibhrith ha-Ḥadhašah* (The Creators of Modern Hebrew Literature), Vilna, 1922, p.75.
78. *Mapu*, pp.270f; cf. pp.247f.
79. See Patterson, *Abraham Mapu*, pp.86f.
80. Cf. *Mapu*, pp.220f, 221, 221f, 225f, 233f, 252f, 264f, 397.
81. *Ibid.*, pp.247f. Cf. Patterson, *The Hebrew Novel in Czarist Russia*, pp.151f.
82. *Mapu*, p.347.
83. Cf. pp.220f, 221f, 252, 252f, 254f.
84. Cf. above, p.26 and n.31.
85. *Mapu*, pp.252, 252f, 254f, 430f.
86. *Ibid.*, p.286. Cf. Patterson, *Abraham Mapu*, pp.89f. Cf. below, ch.11.
87. Cf. above, p.22.
88. See below, chs.3 and 9.

Notes to Chapter Three

1. A Hebrew version of this chapter was read at the Fourth Congress of Jewish Studies, Jerusalem, 1965.
2. At least from chapter 2 onwards. For a list of the novels consulted in this and subsequent chapters and the abbreviations used for them, see below p.157f.
3. See above, ch.2, n.3.
4. See *ibid.*
5. See above, pp.23f and n.16.
6. See above, pp.23f.
7. See below.
8. Pt.1, pp.16, 47ff, 208ff; pt.3, pp.217ff.
9. Pt.2, pp.286ff.
10. Pp.21ff, 81, 146ff, 158f. For an analysis of Abramowitz's use of letters in *Fathers and Sons*, see S. Werses, "Ha-Roman ha-'Ibhri ha-Ri'šon šel Mendele we-Ghilgulaw" (Mendele's First Hebrew Novel and its Versions), in *Molad*, 20, 1962, pp.647f. Cf. below ch.11, n.40.
11. Pt.2, pp.18, 80ff.
12. *BRA.2*, pt.1, pp.73f; cf. pt.3, pp.306f.
13. See below, ch.4.
14. *LEIN.*, pt.2, pp.3ff; *MEIN.*, pt.1, pp.28, 30; *MAN.*, pp.34ff; *SHEIK.*, pt.2, p.13; *WEIS.1*, pp.76ff, 96ff; *WEIS.2*, pt.2, pp.157ff.
15. *SM.1*, pt.1, p.208; pt.2, pp.189ff, 242ff; pt.3, p.224; *BRA.1*, pt.2, p.42; *BRA.2*, pt.1, pp.73ff; *MEIN.*, pt.1, p.28.
16. See above, p.29.
17. *SM.1*, pt.2, pp.189ff, 242ff; *SM.5*, pt.3, pp.66ff.
18. *BRA.2*, pt.1, p.32.
19. *BRA.1*, pt.1, p.124; pt.2, p.61; pt.3, pp.74ff; *BRA.2*, pt.3, p.291; *LEIN.*, pt.2, pp.72ff; *SHEIK.*, pt.2, pp.70ff; *WEIS.2*, pt.1, p.170.
20. Pt.3, p.291. See below, pp.86f.
21. Pt.1, p.148.
22. See D. Patterson, *The Hebrew Novel in Czarist Russia*, p.234. Cf. *MEIN.*, pt.1, pp.28, 54ff. Even as sophisticated a writer as Braudes fluctuates widely in the use of inverted commas for his letters. Cf. *BRA.2*, pt.1, pp.73ff; pt.2, pp.139f, 193ff; pt.3, pp.289ff, 306; pt.4, pp.332ff. See also *ZOB.*, pt.1, p.48.
23. See above, pp.27f.
24. *SM.1*, pt.1, pp.211, 236, 246, 248.

25. See e.g. *SM.1*, pt.1, pp.209ff, 235ff; pt.2, pp.193, 206, 245, 257; *SM.2*, pp.239ff; *SM.5*, pt.3, pp.93ff; *LEIN.*, pt.2, pp.3ff, 10ff; *MEIN.*, pt.1, pp.28, 54ff, 114, 121, 140; *ZOB.*, pt.2, pp.62ff; *MAN.*, pp.34ff; *SHEIK.*, pt.3, p.76.

26. *SM.1*, pt.1, pp.209ff, 245; *SM.6*, pt.1, p.238; pt.3, p.281; *MEIN.*, pt.1, pp.113, 141; *WEIS.2*, pt.1, p.161.

27. *SM.1*, pt.3, pp.108, 116ff; *SM.5*, pt.3, pp.93ff; *MEIN.*, pt.1, p.113; *ZOB.*, pt.1, pp.57ff, 62ff; *SHEIK.*, pt.2, p.89.

28. *WEIS.2*, pt.1, p.119.

29. *ABR.*, pp.154ff. Cf. *The Hebrew Novel in Czarist Russia*, p.78; *ZOB.*, pt.2, pp.62ff.

30. *BRA.1*, pt.3, p.127; *BRA.2*, pt.2, p.197; *WEIS.1*, pp.91ff; *WEIS.2*, pt.1, p.119.

31. *LEIN.*, pt.1, p.119.

32. *SM.1*, pt.3, p.75; *SM.3*, p.275; *SM.6*, pt.3, pp.324ff; *ABR.*, pp.137ff; *ZOB.*, pt.1, pp.48, 60.

33. Pt.1, p.48.

34. *Ibid.*, p.60.

35. *Ibid.*, pp.57ff, 60, 62ff.

36. See above, n.13, and cf. *BRA.2*, pt.2, p.198; *MEIN.*, pt.1, pp.113, 114; *MAN.*, pp.34ff; *SHEIK.*, pt.3, p.76.

37. *SM.1*, pt.1, pp.234, 248; *SM.4*, pp.291ff; *ABR.*, p.72; *BRA.1*, pt.2, p.34; pt.3, p.127; *BRA.2*, pt.3, p.291; *MAN.*, pp.55ff; *WEIS.1*, pp.76ff.

38. *SM.1*, pt.1, pp.234, 248; pt.3, pp.116ff; *ZOB.*, pt.2, pp.62ff.

39. *SM.1*, pt.2, pp.167ff, 189ff; pt.3, pp.217ff; pt.4, pp.111ff; *ABR.*, pp.158ff.

40. *SM.1*, pt.1, pp.236f; see also pp.209ff; pt.3, p.233; *SM.2*, pp.239ff; *SM.4*, p.291.

41. *SM.4*, p.69; *SM.5*, pt.2, p.117; *ABR.*, pp.36ff, 96ff; *MAN.*, p.102; *WEIS.1*, pp.36, 39 (for an English translation see *The Hebrew Novel in Czarist Russia*, pp.108ff); *WEIS.2*, pt.2, p.125.

42. *SM.5*, pt.2, p.148; pt.3, p.52.

43. See above, p.30.

44. See *The Hebrew Novel in Czarist Russia*, pp.47ff.

45. E.g. *SM.1*, pt.2, pp.189ff, 242ff; *SM.5*, pt.2, pp.126ff; pt.3, pp.66ff; *ABR.*, pp.81ff; *LEIN.*, pp.10ff; *MAN.*, pp.80ff.

46. E.g. *ABR.*, pp.21ff; *MAN.*, pp.34ff.

47. *SM.1*, pt.4, pp.36ff; *MEIN.*, pt.1, pp.110ff.

48. *SM.6*, pt.1, pp.131ff.

49. Pt.3, p.196. Cf. below, pp.55ff.

50. Pt.2, pp.120ff. Cf. above, p.30.

51. Pt.2, pp.4ff.

52. Pt.3, pp.94ff. Cf. *The Hebrew Novel in Czarist Russia*, pp.215ff.

53. See above, pp.35 and 37.

54. Cf. above, pp.30f. See e.g. *SM.1*, pt.1, pp.209ff, 248; pt.2, p.193; pt.3, p.216; pt.4, pp.31ff; *ABR.*, pp.82ff; *BRA.1*, pt.2, p.61; *BRA.2*, pt.3, pp.306ff; *LEIN.*, pt.2, pp.9ff (very reminiscent of both Mapu and Smolenskin); *MEIN.*, pt.1, p.30; *SHEIK.*, pt.3, pp.76, 109; *WEIS.2*, pt.1, p.170.

55. *SM.1*, pt.1, pp.209ff; pt.2, pp.167ff; pt.3, p.233; pt.4, pp.7ff, 25ff, 50ff, 70ff, 113; *SM.2*, pp.239ff; *SM.4*, p.69; *SM.5*, pt.2, pp.117, 126ff; pt.3, pp.61ff, 66ff, 93ff; *SM.6*, pt.1, pp.118ff; *ABR.*, pp.21ff, 36ff; *BRA.1*, pt.3, pp.75ff; *BRA.2*, pt.3, p.289; *MEIN.*, pt.1, pp.54ff; *WEIS.1*, pp.98ff, 100ff.

56. Pt.2, pp.126ff.

57. Pt.3, p.62.

58. Pt.3, pp.289ff.

59. See S. Werses, "'Iyyunim . . .," p.387, and K. R. Mandelkow, "Der deutsche Briefroman. Zum Problem der Polyperspektive im Epischen." Cf. above, ch.2, n.24.

60. Cf. Patterson, "Hebrew Drama," *Bulletin of the John Rylands Library*, vol.43, no.1, 1960, pp.91ff, and *Abraham Mapu*, pp.78ff.

61. See S. Werses, "'Iyyunim . . .," p.401.

62. Cf. above, pp.30f.

63. *ABR.*, pp.4ff, 146ff; *WEIS.2*, pt.1, p.173; pt.2, pp.22, 152ff, and see below, p.95. Cf. S.

Werses, "Ha-Roman ha-'Ibhri . . .," p.647, and see below, ch.9.

64. Pt.3, pp.81ff.

65. Pt.3, p.291. Cf. above, n.20.

66. *SM.4*, p.69.

67. See e.g. G.L. van Roosbroek, *Persian Letters before Montesquieu*; F.G. Black, *The Epistolary Novel in the Late Eighteenth Century*. Cf. above, pp.21f.

68. For a brief treatment of this sadly neglected topic, see the synopsis of a paper by S. Werses, "The Letter-Writers of the Haskalah and their Literary Significance," delivered at the Second World Congress of Jewish Studies in Jerusalem in July–August, 1957, in the *Summaries of Papers* for the Hebrew Literature Section.

69. See above, pp.31f.

70. *BRA.1*, pt.3, pp.59ff. Cf. pt.2, pp.16, 33; pt.3, pp.32, 74ff, 193ff, 195ff.

71. *SM.1*, pt.4, pp.51ff, 57ff, 74ff, 96ff, 118. Cf. *SM.5*, pt.2, pp.126ff, and *SHEIK.*, pt.3, pp.74ff.

72. *SM.1*, pt.4, pp.7ff, 11ff, 14ff, 17ff, 19ff.

73. *Ibid.*, p.69; see also pp.72ff, 103ff, 111ff.

74. *Ibid.*, pp.77ff, 87ff, 121ff. Cf. *WEIS.1*, pp.98ff.

75. pp.36ff. Cf. pp.158ff. See also S. Werses, "Ha-Roman ha-'Ibhri . . .," p.648.

76. *WEIS.1*, pp. 110ff. For a full account of the episode, see below, pp.107f.

77. *BRA.1*, pt.3, p.109; *MAN.*, pp.55ff, 80ff. Cf. *The Hebrew Novel in Czarist Russia*, pp.152ff.

78. *BRA.1*, pt.2, p.33; *WEIS.1*, pp.85, 110ff.

79. Pt.2, p.89.

80. E.g. *SM.2*, pp.239ff; *SM.5*, pt.3, pp.66ff; *SM.6*, pt.1, pp.118ff; *BRA.1*, pt.3, p.127; *BRA.2*, pt.3, p.257; *MEIN.*, pt.1, pp.110ff; *SHEIK.*, pt.2, pp.13ff.

81. E.g. *SM.1*, pt.1, pp.235ff; pt.2, pp.189ff; *SM.2*, pp.239ff; *SM.6*, pt.1, pp.118ff; *ABR.*, pp.21ff; *BRA.2*, pt.3, pp.219ff; *LEIN.*, pt.1, pp.31ff; pt.2, pp.11ff; *MEIN.*, pt.1, pp.28, 54ff, 104ff, 110ff, 117, 138; *MAN.*, pp.34ff; *WEIS.1*, pp.88ff. For an example in English translation, see *The Hebrew Novel in Czarist Russia*, pp.108ff.

82. *SM.2*, pp.239ff; see also *BRA.2*, pt.3, p.257.

83. Pt.4, pp.7, 25ff, 28ff, 50ff, 70ff. Cf. below, ch.4, n.32.

84. pp.80ff. Cf. *The Hebrew Novel in Czarist Russia*, pp.25ff.

85. *SM.1*, pt.1, pp.235ff; *BRA.2*, pt.3, pp.289ff. Cf. the tearful emotionalism of a dying man's letter to his brother, *SM.1*, pt.2, pp.167ff.

86. *MEIN.*, pt.1, pp.117, 121, 140.

87. For examples of the mere mention of letters, although they may be of importance to the plot, see *SM.1*, pt.1, pp.16, 47ff; pt.2, p.151; pt.3, p.224; *SM.5*, pt.2, p.148; *SM.6*, pt.1, pp.23, 155; *BRA.1*, pt.3, pp.193ff, 195ff; *BRA.2*, pt.3, pp.257, 265; pt.4, p.316; *MEIN.*, pt.1, p.106; *WEIS.1*, pp.115, 121. For examples of letters where the contents are indicated without quotation, see *SM.1*, pt.1, p.248; pt.3, pp.75, 233; *SM.3*, pp.132ff; *SM.6*, pt.1, pp.120, 133; *ABR.*, pp.116, 137ff, 140; *BRA.1*, pt.1, pp.28, 45, 124; pt.2, pp.16, 33, 72; pt.3, p.136; *BRA.2*, pt.2, pp.147, 153; pt.3, p.257; pt.4, p.317; *MEIN.*, pt.1, p.30; *MAN.*, pp.90, 102; *SHEIK.*, pt.2, p.89; pt.3, p.109; *RAB.*, p.78; *WEIS.1*, pp.89, 112, 118, 122.

88. *BRA.1*, pt.3, p.32; see also pp.127, 195; *BRA.2*, pt.2, pp.194, 195; pt.3, pp.289ff (3 examples), 291; pt.4, pp.332ff.

89. See pp.11, 28, 57, 65, 72ff, 87, 94.

90. *BRA.2*, pt.2, p.153.

91. See above, n.49, and cf. *BRA.1*, pt.2, p.80. For an analysis of such techniques, see Wayne Booth, *The Rhetoric of Fiction*, Chicago and London, 1961, p.205.

92. Pt.2, p.72.

93. *BRA.1*, pt.2, pp.34, 83; *BRA.2*, pt.3, pp.219ff.

94. *WEIS.1*, p.111.

95. *SM.5*, pt.2, pp.120ff.

96. *LEIN.*, pt.1, p.6; *SHEIK.*, pp.70ff.

97. Cf. *SM.1*, pt.1, pp.16, 47ff and pt.2, p.151, with pt.1, p.208, pt.3, pp.217ff and pt.2, pp.189ff respectively; *ABR.*, pp.30ff, with pp.135 and 137ff, and p.145 with p.155; *BRA.1*, pt.1,

p.124, with pt.2, pp.32ff; and pt.2, pp.80ff, with pt.3, p.32.

98. See above, p.35.

99. Pt.1, pp.32, 73ff. Cf. above, p.35.

100. Pt.2, pp.139ff, 146.

101. Pt.2, pp.193ff; pt.3, pp.289ff.

102. Cf. *The Hebrew Novel in Czarist Russia*, p.233.

103. *ABR.*, pp.4ff, 36ff, 86; *MEIN.*, pt.1, pp.104ff; *ZOB.*, pt.2, pp.62ff; *WEIS.1*, p.111; *WEIS.2*, pt.1, p.173; pt.2, pp.22, 152ff. Cf. Werses, "'Iyyunim ...," pp.380, 389, and "Ha-Roman ha-'Ibhri ...," p.648. Cf. above, pp.23 and 25.

104. See above, p.39 and nn.61, 63, 64, 65, 66.

105. See above p.41, and n.76.

106. See *The Hebrew Novel in Czarist Russia*, p.220.

Notes to Chapter Four

1. A Hebrew version of this paper was presented at the Third International Congress of Jewish Studies, Jerusalem, 1961.

2. See e.g. Braudes' remarks in the preface to the third part of *BRA.1*, where he confesses that he has resorted to novel-form only in order to sugar a rather distasteful pill. Cf. below, p.139.

3. With the possible exceptions of *BRA.1* and *SIRK.*, although even the latter contains an example of attempted kidnaping! (ch.8).

4. See e.g. *SM.1*, pt.1, chs.18, 25, pt.2, chs.17, 22, 24, 29, pt.3, ch.38; *SM.2*, chs.13, 23; *SM.3*, chs.11, 14, 20, 21; *SM.4*, chs.5, 8, 10; *SM.5*, pt.1, ch.11, pt.2, chs.11, 12, 14, pt.3, chs.2, 13, 21; *SM.6*, pt.1, chs.3, 20, pt.2, ch.7, pt.3, chs.3, 7; *ABR.*, ch.32; *BRA.2*, pt.1, ch.20, pt.2, ch.25; *LEIN.*, pt.1, ch.18; *MEIN.*, chs.18, 19, 24; *ZOB.*, pt.1, chs.3, 13; *MAN.*, ch.2; *SHEIK.*, pt.2, ch.15, pt.3, chs.15, 19, 21; *SIRK.*, chs.5, 7, 8; *WEIS.1*, chs.6, 11; *WEIS.2*, pt.1, chs.2, 3, pt.2, ch.18.

5. Pt.2, ch.17.

6. *Ibid.*, ch.29.

7. Pt.3, p.264.

8. Cf. *SM.2*, ch.23 (the husband, a would-be bigamist, also faints!); *SM.5*, pt.3, ch.21; *BRA.2*, pt.2, ch.25; *ZOB.*, pt.1, ch.13.

9. *BRA.2*, pt.1, ch.20.

10. *SM.1*, pt.1, ch.18, pt.2, ch.24 (twice in a single chapter); *SM.6*, pt.3, ch.3 (twice); *LEIN.*, pt.1, ch.18; *MAN.*, ch.2.

11. *SM.5*, pt.2, chs.11, 12; *SM.6*, pt.2, ch.7; *MEIN.*, pt.1, ch.18; *SIRK.*, ch.8 (twice).

12. *WEIS.1*, ch.6.

13. *SM.6*, pt.1, ch.3; *WEIS.2*, pt.2, ch.18.

14. *Ibid.*, pt.1, p.15. For a comparable example, cf. *ibid.*, p.22.

15. Cf. *SM.1*, pt.1, chs.1, 2, 25, pt.2, chs.14, 24, pt.3, chs.21, 22, 25, 37, pt.4, chs.7, 8; *SM.3*, ch.10; *SM.5*, pt.1, chs.9, 11, pt.2, ch.7; *SM.6*, pt.1, chs.7, 8, 16, pt.2, chs.1, 2, 10, 15, 17, 24, pt.3, chs.6, 9; *ABR.*, chs.31, 33; *BRA.2*, pt.3, chs.1, 2, 33; *LEIN.*, pt.1, chs.7, 10, 16; *ZOB.*, pt.1, chs.8, 13, pt.2, ch.1; *MAN.*, chs.2, 3, 4, 8; *SHEIK.*, pt.1, ch.11, pt.2, ch.8, pt.3, chs.1, 3, 20; *RAB.*, chs.4, 8; *SIRK.*, ch.7; *WEIS.1*, chs.6, 9, 10; *WEIS.2*, pt.1, chs.2, 6, 7, 12, pt.2, chs.14, 18, 19, 22, 24. Also see below, nn.23, 24, 36.

16. *SM.6*, pt.2, p.219.

17. *SHEIK.*, pt.1, ch.11, pt.2, ch.8, pt.3, ch.3.

18. Described as *maḥalath ḍalleqeth ha-'aṣabbim* (illness of inflammation of the nerves).

19. See below, ch.9, p.104.

20. *LEIN.*, pt.1, ch.7.

21. *SM.1*, pt.3, ch.21. Cf. pt.2, ch.20.

22. *BRA.2*, pt.3, p.260. Cf. *ibid.*, pp.212, 215.

23. *Ibid.*, pt.3, ch.26, pt.4, ch.43.
24. *SM.4*, ch.5.
25. *MAN.*, ch.2.
26. *SHEIK.*, pt.3, ch.1.
27. See above, n.19.
28. Cf. *SM.1*, pt.1, ch.25, pt.2, ch.24; *SM.6*, pt.1, chs.8, 16, pt.3, ch.9.
29. *SM.4*, p.186.
30. *LEIN.*, pt.1, ch.16.
31. Cf. *SM.4*, ch.10; *SM.5*, pt.1, ch.9, pt.2, ch.7; *ABR.*, ch.31.
32. *SM.1*, pt.4, chs.7, 8. See above, ch.3, n.83.
33. Cf. *SM.6*, pt.3, ch.6; *MAN.*, ch.8; *WEIS.2*, pt.1, ch.7.
34. *MAN.*, p.64; see also *SIRK.*, ch.7.
35. Cf. *SM.5*, pt.1, ch.11; *SM.6*, pt.2, chs.2, 15, 17, 24; *LEIN.*, pt.1, ch.10; *ZOB.*, pt.1, chs.8, 13, pt.2, ch.1; *SHEIK.*, pt.3, ch.20; *RAB.*, ch.4 (in this case as elsewhere—e.g. *MAN.*, ch. 8—the illness is consumption or *maḥalath ha-šaḥepheth* (wasting disease)); *WEIS.1*, chs.9, 10; *WEIS.2*, pt.1, chs.2, 6, pt.2, ch.14, pt.3, chs.22, 23, 24.
36. Cf. *SM.1*, pt.2, ch.20, pt.3, chs.24, 25; *SM.4*, chs.5, 6, 8; *SM.5*, pt.2, ch.15; *SM.6*, pt.2, chs.8, 15, 24, pt.3, ch.9; *ABR.*, chs.9, 13; *MAN.*, ch.2; *SHEIK.*, pt.3, ch.22; *WEIS.2*, pt.2, ch.24.
37. *SM.6*, pt.3, p.282.
38. *SM.1*, pt.1, chs.1, 11, pt.2, chs.21, 24, 29, pt.3, chs.25, 32, 38; *SM.3*, ch.17; *SM.4*, ch.11; *SM.5*, pt.3, ch.12; *SM.6*, pt.2, ch.21; *ABR.*, chs.33, 34; *BRA.1*, pt.1, chs.2, 4, pt.2, ch.2; *BRA.2*, pt.1, ch.1; *LEIN.*, pt.1, ch.10, pt.2, chs.1, 2, 7, 14; *MEIN.*, chs.7, 13, 22; *ZOB.*, pt.1, chs.2, 3, 13, pt.2, chs.16, 18, 23, 24; *SHEIK.*, pt.1, ch.15, pt.2, ch.12, pt.3, ch.20; *RAB.*, chs.11, 13; *WEIS.2*, pt.1, ch.8, pt.2, ch.16.
39. *SM.1*, pt.2, ch.24, pt.3, ch.32; *SM.3*, ch.17; *SM.4*, ch.6; *SM.5*, pt.3, ch.12; *LEIN.*, pt.2, chs.1, 2, 7, 14; *MAN.*, pt.1, ch.13, pt.2, chs.16, 18, 23; *RAB.*, ch.13.
40. *SM.4*, chs.5, 6.
41. *SM.1*, pt.1, ch.23, pt.2, ch.14; *SM.5*, pt.3, ch.1; *MEIN.*, ch.4; *ZOB.*, pt.1, ch.1.
42. See above, n.29.
43. *SM.5*, pt.2, ch.12.
44. *ABR.*, ch.34; *MAN.*, ch.8; *WEIS.2*, pt.1, ch.12, pt.2, ch.15. Cf. above, n.34.
45. *SM.1*, pt.2, p.171.
46. Pt.3, ch.24. Cf. A. Mapu, *The Hypocrite*, pt.4, ch.17.
47. *SM.1*, pt.3, ch.22. Cf. above, n.21.
48. *LEIN.*, pt.2, ch.12.
49. *ZOB.*, pt.2, ch.23.
50. *SM.1*, pt.4, ch.24; *SM.6*, pt.1, ch.1.
51. *SM.1*, pt.2, ch.29, pt.3, ch.32; *SM.4*, ch.11 (three instances); *LEIN.*, pt.2, ch.4.
52. *SM.1*, pt.1, chs.23, 25, pt.3, chs.19, 24; *SM.2*, ch.24; *BRA.2*, pt.4, ch.41; *MEIN.*, chs.20, 21, 22; *SHEIK.*, pt.1, ch.1, pt.2, ch.10, pt.3, chs.21, 22.
53. *SM.1*, pt.3, ch.19.
54. *Ibid.*, ch.24.
55. Ch.24. See above, ch.3, p.37.
56. See above, n.22.
57. Pt.4, ch.41.
58. *SM.1*, pt.3, ch.32; *SM.2*, ch.13 (see below, n.61); *SM.3*, ch.17; *SM.4*, ch.6; *SM.5*, pt.3, ch.12; *LEIN.*, pt.2, chs.1, 2, 7, 14; *ZOB.*, pt.1, ch.13, pt.2, chs.16, 18, 23; *RAB.*, ch.13.
59. *SM.1*, pt.3, ch.32; *SM.6*, pt.3, ch.1; *MEIN.*, ch.10; *ZOB.*, pt.1, ch.13.
60. *SM.4*, ch.6; *SM.5*, ch.12; *SM.6*, pt.3, ch.1; *ZOB.*, pt.1, ch.13 (2), pt.2, chs.18, 23.
61. *SM.3*, p.159.
62. *SM.1*, pt.3, ch.37; *SM.6*, pt.1, ch.7; *MAN.*, chs.3, 4; *SIRK.*, ch.10.
63. *SM.1*, pt.1, p.43.
64. *MEIN.*, ch.22.
65. *SM.2*, ch.13; *SM.5*, pt.2, ch.15; *WEIS.2*, pt.1, ch.12.
66. *Ibid.*, pt.2. chs.18, 19.

67. *Ibid.*, pt.2, ch.24.
68. *RAB.*, chs.8, 9.
69. *BRA.1*, pt.2, ch.6. Cf. below, ch.5, p.57.
70. *MAN.*, ch.4; *SIRK.*, ch.11.
71. *SM.1*, pt.2, ch.14; the illness is described as מחלת הַיֵּרָקון מכאב לב (the illness of greenness from heartache), and the victim depicted as quite green with blood streaming from his nostrils. Smolenskin had himself witnessed the press-ganging of his older brother, a lad of about ten. The family never saw the child again. Smolenskin described the episode in a harrowing account in *The Wanderer in the Paths of Life*. See D. Patterson, *The Hebrew Novel in Czarist Russia*, pp.149f.
72. *ABR.*, pp.144f. See below, ch.7, pp.85f.
73. A footnote explains this charm to be a back-to-front version of the following line compounded of phrases from Ex.15^{26} and Ps.91^{10}: אני ה׳ רופאך. לא תאנה אליך רעה (I the Lord am your healer. No harm shall befall you). A second footnote states that the sect הראסקאלים (Schismatics) also has the custom of changing the name of a sick man, for example from Ivan to Stevan, to deceive the heavenly powers who have condemned him to die because of his sins.
74. For an account of superstitious remedies, see N. Marsden, ed., *A Jewish Life under the Tsars, The Autobiography of Chaim Aronson, 1825–1888*, New Jersey, 1983, pp.13f.

Notes to Chapter Five

1. For a definitive study of Moses Mendelssohn, see A. Altmann, *Moses Mendelssohn, A Biographical Study*, London, 1973. See also E. Jospe, ed., *Moses Mendelssohn, Selections from His Writings*, New York, 1975.
2. For a translation of *Jerusalem*, see A. Jospe, *Moses Mendelssohn, Jerusalem and other Jewish Writings*, New York, 1969.
3. See D. Patterson, "Moses Mendelssohn's Concept of Tolerance," *Between East and West*, London, 1958, and "Philosophers of Emancipation," in *Jewish Philosophy and Philosophers*, London, 1962.
4. See e.g. H.M. Graupe, *The Rise of Modern Judaism*, New York, 1978.
5. See *ibid.*
6. For a succinct outline of the attitude toward Judaism adopted by these thinkers and their younger contemporaries, see Y. Halevi-Zwick, *Mussagh ha-Yahadhuth bi-Thequphath ha-Haskalah* (The Concept of Judaism in the Period of Haskalah), Tel-Aviv, 1955. See also J. Guttmann, *Philosophies of Judaism*, New York, 1964.
7. Cf. above, p.19.
8. For a detailed study of this literary war, see G. Katznelson, *Ha-Milḥamah ha-Siphruthith bein ha-Ḥaredhim we-ha-Maskilim* (The Literary War between the Orthodox and the Enlighteners), Tel-Aviv, 1954.
9. See D. Patterson, *Abraham Mapu*, pp.163ff.
10. For a brief survey of the relative importance of the novels of this period, see D. Patterson, *The Hebrew Novel in Czarist Russia*, pp.228ff.
11. *Ha-Dath we-ha-Ḥayyim*, 2nd ed., Lemberg, 1885, designated in the notes to this volume *BRA.1*.
12. See below, ch.10, n.42.
13. For a more detailed summary of the plot, see *The Hebrew Novel in Czarist Russia*, pp.17ff.
14. *BRA.1*, pt.1, ch.7. See below, ch.10, pp.121f.
15. *BRA.1*, pt.2, ch.6.
16. See *Mishnah Yebhamoth*.
17. *BRA.1*, pt.2, ch.2; pt.3, ch.11.
18. *Ibid.*, pt.3, chs.1–3.
19. *Ibid.*, pt.2, ch.8.
20. Cf. G. Katznelson, *op.cit.*, pp.69f.
21. *BRA.1*, pt.2, pp.108f.; see also *The Hebrew Novel in Czarist Russia*, pp.202f.

22. *Šetei ha-Qeṣawoth*, Warsaw, 1888, designated in the notes to this volume *BRA.2*.
23. For a more detailed summary of the plot, see *The Hebrew Novel in Czarist Russia*, pp.19f.
24. For an account of Jewish life in Odessa, see especially S. Zipperstein, *The Jews of Odessa: A Cultural History, 1794–1881*, Stanford University, 1985.
25. *BRA.2*, pt.4, chs.44–6.
26. See *LEIN.*, pt.1, chs.5 and 12; and *ZOB.*, pt.1, ch.4.
27. *Ibid.*, pt.2, p.36.
28. *SHEIK.*, pt.1, pp.72f.
29. *Ibid.*, pp.52f, and pt.2, pp.30f.
30. For a detailed study of his life and works, see C. Bates, *A Study of the Life and Works of A. S. Rabinowitz*, D.Phil. thesis, Oxford University, 1972.
31. *RAB.*, pp.57f.
32. *Ibid.*, pp.146ff, and N.B. footnote in which the author states that after writing this section he has come across the same idea in an article by H. Oppenheim in *Ha-'Asiph*, 1887, p.260.
33. *Ibid.*, and see below, p.150.
34. The novel is satirized by Rabinowitz in *RAB*, pp.51f.
35. *ABR*, p.25.
36. It is surpassed only in the novels of P. Smolenskin and B. I. Zobeizensky. See below, chs.6 and 7.
37. See e.g. his story *Bi-Yešibhah šel Ma'lah u-bhi-Yešibhah šel Maṭṭah* (In the *Yešibhah* on high and in the *Yešibhah* down below).
38. *ABR.*, pp.120f.
39. *Ibid.*, pp.123f. This idea was later developed in his splendid allegory entitled *Susathi* (My Mare).
40. 1868–84. The novels were first published in Smolenskin's journal *Ha-Šaḥar* (The Dawn).
41. See below, chs.6 and 7.
42. *SM.1*, pt.2, p.64; see also p.266.
43. Cf. *The Hebrew Novel in Czarist Russia*, pp.194f.
44. *SM.1*, pt.4, chs.11 and 12.
45. Cf. especially Smolenskin's long essay *'Eth la-Ṭa'ath* (Time to Plant) (first published in *Ha-Šaḥar*, years 6, 8, and 9) in *Ma'amarim* (Articles), vol.2, Jerusalem, 1925.
46. Cf. *SM.6*, pt.2, ch.19.
47. *Ibid.*, ch.14. Apart from Smolenskin and Rabinowitz, I. Weisbrem expresses strong national sentiments in his novel *Eighteen Coins*, *WEIS.2*, pt.1, pp.124f, where he advocates the practical colonization of Palestine in preference to the messianism of the *Ṣaddiqim*.
48. *SM.1*, pt.4, p.62.
49. See his essay *'Am 'Olam* (The Eternal People) in *Ma'amarim* (Articles), vol.1.
50. *SM.2*, pp.144ff.
51. Cf. *The Hebrew Novel in Czarist Russia*, ch.7.

Notes to Chapter Six

1. An attitude of fierce criticism toward the movement of Hasidism formed, as is well known, a marked feature of modern Hebrew literature from the beginning of the nineteenth century and even before, and may be found in both the fiction and non-fiction of the period. The hostility of such writers as J. L. Mieses, N. Krochmal, J. Perl, I. Erter, and, less directly, A. Mapu—to name a few of many—was not effectively challenged until the sixties by M. Hess and more importantly E. Z. Zweifel. Both attitudes, but primarily the former, are naturally reflected in the novels under review. See above, ch.2, n.19.
2. Such as J. L. Peretz and S. J. Agnon.
3. See R. A. Braudes' preface to the second edition of *Religion and Life*, and particularly his introduction to pt.3. Cf. the preface to M. Manassewitz's *The Parents' Sin*.

4. Smolenskin spent the years 1858–60/1 among the *Ḥasidhim*, for the first few months at the court of the *Ṣaddiq*, Menahem Mendel, at Lubavitch and then at Vitebsk. See J. Klausner, *History*, vol.5, pp.27f. Klausner relates (*ibid.*, p.27, n.3) that Mordechai ben-Hillel ha-Cohen told him that 29 pages relative to the *Ḥasidhim* and Ṣebhu'a'el were erased by the censor from the third edition of *The Wanderer in the Paths of Life*. Klausner asserts, however, that there are not, in fact, so many erasures. I have not been able to trace any serious differences in this respect between the original version published in *Ha-Šaḥar*, vols.1 and 2, Vienna, 1868–71, and the edition quoted in this chapter. In any case, many of Smolenskin's remarks about the *Ḥasidhim* and *Ṣaddiqim* are so virulent that it seems unlikely that they could have passed a censor intent on erasing such references.

5. Pt.4, p.99.

6. *Biṭṭul ha-Yeš.*

7. Smolenskin proceeds to argue that the *Maskilim* have taken over this doctrine from the *Ḥasidhim*! A less biased account of the same doctrine appears in *SIRK.*, p.29: "A fundamental concept in the teachings of the *Ḥasidhim* is that one must try to foster the qualities of modesty and humility of spirit, and so ardently do they seek to attain this state that by virtue of constant habit, they imagine they have already achieved it, that they have humbled their souls to the dust, and any passer-by may tread on them. And this was also the case with Kemuel, so that when he raised himself in prayer and before his blood, excited by his shakings and rapid movements, had calmed down, he imagined that all his thoughts and ideas had been negated. This he regarded as a very lofty state for 'he clearly had the power to negate himself to this dread degree.'"

8. *SM.1*, pt.3, pp.49ff.

9. Smolenskin continues with a no less devastating attack upon the *Mithnaggedhim*. For the five principles to be adopted before becoming a *Ḥasidh*, see *WEIS.2*, pt.1, pp.89f.

10. The mutual aid practiced by the *Ḥasidhim* is frequently cited in the novels. For a striking example, see *SM.1*, pt.1, p.194. Cf. *WEIS.2*, pt.1, pp.86f and 91; *SHEIK.*, pt.2, p.90. It would appear, however, that such mutual aid is limited to the supporters of the same *Ṣaddiq*. See *ZOB.*, pp.61f, and see below, p.83.

11. *SM.1*, pt.2, pp.243ff. The persecution of their enemies is constantly portrayed as a characteristic of the *Ḥasidhim*. Cf. *ibid.*, pt.3, p.119. But persecution of erring members of their own sect is equally virulent. Cf. *BRA.2*, pp.297ff.

12. *SM.6*, pt.2, p.133.

13. *SIRK.*, pp.27ff.

14. Cf. *SM.1*, pt.2, pp.43 and 51ff.

15. *ABR.*, p.84.

16. Cf. *SM.1*, pt.2, pp.247ff.

17. *Ibid.*, pt.3, pp.29ff.

18. The word implies a drunkard.

19. *SM.1*, pt.3, p.90.

20. See *BRA.2*, pp.109ff.

21. *Ibid.*, pp.10ff and 152ff.

22. *Ibid.*, p.11.

23. See *ibid.*, p.10, for a reference to the Hasidic practice of shaving the head between the sidelocks. Cf. *WEIS.2*, pt.1, p.51. Cf. also *ABR.*, p.58. See below, p.115. Some *Ḥasidhim*, however, are alleged to wear short clothes, *ibid.*, pt.1, p.88.

24. Literally "Foolish *Ḥasidh*." See *BRA.2*, p.124.

25. *SM.1*, pt.3, pp.22ff. Josef, however, does not find such provision so readily forthcoming. *Ibid.*, p.57. Cf. also *ABR.*, pp.107 and 109.

26. For the practice described as prevalent among the *Ḥasidhim* of taking tobacco from each other without the formality of the owner's consent, see *SIRK.*, p.32. For the tendency for *Ḥasidhim* to spend their time smoking while the women act as breadwinners, see *LEIN.*, pp.77f. Cf. also *SM.4*, p.219.

27. *SM.1*, pt.3, pp.28ff.

28. Cf. *ibid.*, pt.3, p.119; *SM.3*, p.7; *BRA.2*, pp.51ff; *ABR.*, p.4.

29. *SM.1*, pt.3, p.95. Cf. below, ch.11.
30. *Ibid.*, p.98.
31. See D. Patterson, *The Hebrew Novel in Czarist Russia*, pp.214f. Cf. below, p.122.
32. *BRA.2*, pp.51ff.
33. *Ibid.*, p.9.
34. *Ibid.*, p.118.
35. *Ibid.*, p.10.
36. Both roots have the meaning "learn."
37. *Ibid.*, pp.185ff. A similar type of catechism at a *Bar-Miṣwah* ceremony as practiced by the Jews of Anatolia at the end of the nineteenth century is described in J. Burla's novel *'Aliloth 'Aqabhyah* (The Deeds of 'Aqabhyah), Tel-Aviv, 1948, pp.24f. See also M. G. Langer, *Neun Tore*, Munich, 1959, p.70. I am grateful to Prof. R. J. Z. Werblowsky for drawing my attention to this latter reference.
38. *BRA.2*, p.119.
39. *Ibid.*, pp.109 and 198; cf. *SM.1*, pt.1, p.126, and *SM.2*, p.6.
40. *SM.1*, pt.2, p.279.
41. *BRA.2*, p.179.
42. Nevertheless, reference is made on more than one occasion to the practice of *Ḥasidhim* allowing their daughters a smattering of the secular education, no matter how inadequate, forbidden their sons. See *WEIS.2*, pt.2, pp.7f, and *ZOB.*, p.31. See also *ABR.*, p.9. See below p.114, n.107.
43. *SM.1*, pt.3, p.53.
44. Cf. *ibid.*, pt.3, pp.31ff.
45. *Ibid.*, pt.2, p.81.
46. *BRA.2*, p.99.
47. *SM.4*, p.211.
48. *Ibid.*, p.210; see also *MEIN.*, p.134.
49. *SM.1*, pt.2, p.280; also *BRA.2*, p.168.
50. *Ibid.*, p.157.
51. *SIRK.*, p.23.
52. *SM.1*, pt.3, p.63. See *ABR.*, p.63. See also *WEIS.2*, pt.1, p.5, although on the same page occurs an example of the more familiar practice of relating a son to the father. On p.106 the Hasidic practice of relating a son to the mother is explained by the statement that the mother is always known for certain. Also cf. below, p.115.
53. *SM.1*, pt.2, p.280.
54. *RAB.*, pp.105 and 116.
55. *SHEIK.*, p.83. See also *ABR*, p. 86, although this custom long antedates the rise of the Hasidic movement.
56. *SHEIK.*, p.83.
57. *WEIS.2*, pt.1, p.164.
58. *Ibid.*, pt.2, p.83.
59. *Ibid.*, pt.1, pp.98f, 101, 105, and especially pp.106f. See also *ABR.*, p.63.
60. *WEIS.2*, p.108.
61. *MEIN.*, p.25. See e.g. S. Dubnow, *Toledhoth ha-Ḥasidhuth* (The History of Hasidism), Tel-Aviv, 1930/1, and R. Mahler, *Ha-Ḥasidhuth we-ha-Haskalah* (Hasidism and Haskalah), Merhavia, 1961.
62. *MEIN.*, p.133.
63. *BRA.2*, pp.312ff.
64. *SM.1*, pt.2, pp.243ff, and pt.3, pp.48ff, and see above, p.9.
65. *Ibid.*, pt.2, p.244, and pt.3, p.130. Cf. above, n.10.
66. *Ibid.*, pt.1, p.195. Cf. *WEIS.2*, pt.1, p.4.
67. *SM.1*, pt.3, p.26.
68. *SM.3*, p.86.
69. *ABR.*, pp.86ff. Cf. the wonder-worker in *SM.1*, pt.1, pp.53ff, and see *SM.5*, pt.1, pp.93f. Cf. also J. Klausner, *History*, vol.6, pp.473f.

70. *ABR.*, pp.145f, and see above, p.52, and below, pp.85f.

71. *SM.6*, pt.1, pp.211ff.

72. *SM.1*, pt.2, p.280. See also pt.3, pp.78ff. Although harsh invective against real or imagined opponents is commonly found in the literature of *Maskilim, Mithnaggedhim*, and *Ḥasidhim* alike.

73. *Ibid.*, pt.3, p.122.

74. *Ibid.*, pt.3, p.130. See also p.92.

75. Pt.3, pp.20ff. In this context the author makes a violent attack on the Gaon of Vilna as being responsible for the real breach in Israel. See above, p.58.

76. See p.77. Although even this novel contains some very serious criticism of Hasidism, see pp.353ff. Very sensible and moderate views on both Hasidism and *Ṣaddiqim* may be found in *RAB.*, p.79.

77. See p.114.

78. See *SM.1*, pt.1, ch.28.

Notes to Chapter Seven

1. The most frequent alternative term is *Rebbe*, but occasionally the *Ṣaddiq* is referred to as *Ha-Yašiš*. Cf. *ABR.*, p.36, where it is stated in a footnote that many of the *Ḥasidhim* in Galicia refer to the *Ṣaddiq* as *Ṭobh.*

2. Although R. A. Braudes, N. M. Sheikewitz, and A. S. Rabinowitz display considerable sympathy for the more positive aspects of the sect. See below.

3. With the notable exceptions of Abramowitz, B. I. Zobeizensky, whose caricatures are quite fantastic, and on occasion P. Smolenskin. See below.

4. Braudes, for example, is careful to omit the name of the town in which the *Ṣaddiq* whose influence in *The Two Extremes* is considerable resides. Cf. *ibid.*, pt.3, p.242. He does not even refer to it by a pseudonym, a device frequently adopted by other novelists. Cf. also below, p.81.

5. *ABR.*, pp.66f.

6. The Hebrew *Ha-Kazibhi* signifies the equivalent of "The Deceiver" or, more strictly, "the man from Deceitville."

7. Cf. *ibid.*, p.5: "For apart from the well-known fact that a father is forbidden to teach his son Bible, he is guilty of an even greater sin, by studying it with [Mendelssohn's] commentary." A footnote reads: "See *Ha-Karmel*, second year, no.7, a letter from four *Ḥasidhim.*"

8. Literally, "Foolstown."

9. *SM.1*, pt.3, pp.63f. Cf. *The Autobiography of Solomon Maimon*, tr. J. Clark Murray, London, 1954, pp.175f.

10. *SM.1*, pt.3, pp.23ff, and note the remarkable parallel passage in *SM.4*, pp.210ff. Cf. above, pp.75f.

11. *BRA.2*, pt.1, p.9.

12. *Ibid.*, pt.2, p.136.

13. *Ibid.*, pt.2, pp.150ff.

14. *SIRK.*, p.27f. Cf. *WEIS.2*, pt.1, p.8: "I feel sad for the *Ṣaddiqim* ... who spend most of their days in prayer and in the performance of holy deeds for our redemption and the salvation of our souls, while we obstruct their task with the multitude of our sins ..."

15. *SM.1*, pt.3, p.71.

16. Cf. *ibid.*, pt.2, p.212.

17. Pt.3, p.200. The same *Ṣaddiq* is also referred to in *SM.4*, pp.210ff, and in *SM.6*, pt.1, p.51.

18. *SM.1*, pt.1, p.69.

19. *Ibid.*, p.70.

20. *SM.4*, p.215.

21. *ZOB.*, p.5. It is indicative of the character of this novel that the charlatan later impresses Sarah immensely by his complete familiarity with her circumstances, on the basis of prior

information, and then informs her that by divine decree he is bidden to marry her daughter, *ibid.*, pp.65f. For a similar catalog of the *Ṣaddiq*'s powers, cf. *SHEIK.*, pt.1, p.42.

22. For another example of the *Ṣaddiq* being consulted in the case of a theft, see *SM.1*, pt.1, pp.23ff. Here, too, the *Ṣaddiq* is able to appear omniscient on the basis of prior information. In this respect cf. *WEIS.2*, pt.2, pp.120f.

23. *Ibid.*, pt.1, p.102.

24. The number is significant, being the numerical equivalent of the Hebrew word for "life."

25. *Ibid.*, pt.2, p.118.

26. *MEIN.*, p.24.

27. *Ibid.*, p.25.

28. *SM.1*, pt.2, pp.216f.

29. *LEIN.*, pt.2, pp.77f.

30. Cf. above, pp.71f.

31. Cf. above, p.72, n.26.

32. *SIRK.*, p.6. A similar letter is responsible for the lengthy wanderings of the hero of S. J. Agnon's novel, *Hakhnasath Kallah* (The Bridal Canopy).

33. *SM.1*, pt.2, p.280.

34. Cf. *WEIS.2*, pt.1, p.5, and frequently throughout the novel.

35. *ABR.*, pp. 144f. Cf. above, p.52, nn.73 and 74.

36. See N. Marsden, ed., *A Jewish Life under the Tsars*, ch.4, n.74.

37. *BRA.2*, pt.3, p.255.

38. A play on 2 Sam. 23^3.

39. Cf. *BRA.2*, pt.4, p.304.

40. *Ibid.*, pt.3, p.291. See above, ch.3, n.20.

41. For an example of the *Ṣaddiq*'s advice leading to unfortunate results, see *SM.4*, pp.77ff.

42. *SM.1*, pt.3, pp.78f, and cf. above, p.67, n.4.

43. *SM.1*, pt.3, pp.78 and 80f. For the practice of repeating the *Ṣaddiq*'s words, see also *RAB.*, pp.36 and 41.

44. *SM.1*, pt.3, pp.55f.

45. *Ibid.*, p.63.

46. *Ibid.*, p.62, and cf. above, p.76, nn.52 and 59.

47. *ABR.*, pp.64f.

48. See above, p.84, n.26, and cf., for example, *ABR.*, pp.74f.

49. *MEIN.*, p.39.

50. *SM.1*, pt.3, p.76.

51. *Ibid.*, pt.1, p.27.

52. *Ibid.*, pt.1, p.211, and cf. pt.2, pp.216f, where a different *Ṣaddiq* is represented as an adulterer!

53. *SM.2*, p.103, and cf. above, pp.71f.

54. See above, n.21; and see *ZOB.*, pt.1, pp.69 and 71f, pt.2, pp.13ff.

55. *RAB.*, p.41, and cf. 2 Kings 4^{10}, 5^{22}, and *Berakhoth* 10b.

56. *SM.6*, pt.1, p.8, and cf. *WEIS.2*, p.156, where a pious *Ḥasidh* prefers to send a gift to the *Ṣaddiq* for the protection of his property, rather than insure it. See below, pp.105f.

57. *WEIS.2*, pt.1, p.63.

58. *RAB.*, p.79. Cf. above, p.78.

59. Cf. *Yebhamoth* 13b with reference to Deut. 14^1.

60. The term Sephardi for *Ḥasidh* and Ashkenazi for *Mithnaggedh* is also applied by Braudes in *BRA.2*, pt.2, p.149.

61. Cf. above, p.77, n.68.

62. Cf. above, p.68, n.10.

63. *SHEIK.*, pt.1, pp.72f. See also pp.76f.

Notes to Chapter Eight

1. See D. Patterson, *Abraham Mapu*, pp.63ff. Cf. above, ch.1, n.20.
2. See e.g. E. Silberschlag, ed., *Eliezer Ben-Yehuda*, Oxford, 1981.
3. Of the novelists under review, the urgent need to widen the range of expression then available to Hebrew writers was perhaps most clearly recognized by R. A. Braudes. Cf. J. Klausner, *History*, vol.5, pp.399ff.
4. Even Mapu sometimes introduces post-biblical language. See Patterson, *op.cit.*, pp.64 and 74.
5. Cf. Patterson, *The Hebrew Novel in Czarist Russia*, ch.4.
6. Cf. *Abraham Mapu*, pp.78ff. See D. Patterson, "Conversational Uses of the Root *Dabhar* in Neo-Biblical Hebrew," in *Essays on the Occasion of the Seventieth Anniversary of the Dropsie University.* Cf. above, ch.1, n.20.
7. Cf. *SM.1*, pt.2, p.99; *ABR.*, pp.40f; *WEIS.1*, p.28; *WEIS.2*, pt.1, p.173, pt.2, pp.22, 152. Cf. below, p.111. A number of grammatical errors, such as lack of congruence, incorrect usage of the construct state, and the transitive application of intransitive verbs, were noted by contemporary critics. Cf. A. Zederbaum's review of *ZOB.* in *Ha-Meliṣ*, 1882, pp.425f, and an unsigned review of *SHEIK.*, *ibid.*, 1886, pp.366f, 1887, pp.861f. See also D. Frishman, *Kol Kithbhei Dawid Frišman*, Warsaw–New York, 1930, vol.5, p.36.
8. Smolenskin, for example, confesses that the installments to his novels were often written during the night before the printing date. See the preface to the 2nd ed. of *SM.1*, and see *The Hebrew Novel in Czarist Russia*, pp.40f.
9. *SM.1*, pt.3, p.166. For the *waw consecutive* see e.g. J. Weingreen, *A Practical Grammar for Classical Hebrew*, 2nd ed., Oxford, 1959, pp.90ff, 252f.
10. And it came to pass on the second day that Samuel rose early in the morning and ran to the house of study to pray. *BRA.1*, pt.2, p.95. Cf. *ABR.*, p.76.
11. *WEIS.2*, pt.1, p.97. Cf. below, p.112.
12. Cf. *SM.1*, pt.1, p.21, pt.2, pp.46, 55, 110, 130, 132, 157, 233, pt.3, p.166; *SM.4*, pp.68, 135, 218, 222; *SM.6*, pt.1, pp.31, 32, 159, pt.2, p.41, pt.3, p.220; *ABR.*, pp.99, 145; *BRA.1*, pt.1, p.88, pt.3, pp.44, 96; *BRA.2*, pt.2, pp.90, 175, pt.3, p.289; *MEIN.*, pp.21, 83, 124, 126, 128, 148, 149; *SHEIK.*, pt.2, p.96, pt.3, pp.30, 43; *MAN.*, p.112; *RAB.*, p.34; *WEIS.1*, pp.66, 76; *WEIS.2*, pt.1, pp.73, 177, pt.2, pp.135, 142.
13. *SM.1*, pt.4, p.100.
14. See above, n.3.
15. The following translations in round brackets appear in the respective texts after the Hebrew terms. Cf. *The Hebrew Novel in Czarist Russia*, p.104.
16. Water-wolf. *BRA.1*, pt.1, p.11. Cf. I. Erter, *The Watchman of the House of Israel*, 1st ed., 1858; the story in which the phrase appears (*Gilgul Nepheš*, i.e. Transmigration of Souls) first appeared in Leipzig, 1845; the phrase is on p.7, n.2.
17. House of stops (Bahnhof). *BRA.1*, pt.2, p.12.
18. Illness of spots (Pocken). *Ibid.*, p.15.
19. Mistress of deed (realist). *Ibid.*, p.66.
20. Master of thought (idealist). *Ibid.*
21. *Ibid.*, p.54. In the following line, however, **אוטוריטעט** (authority) is used alone.
22. Content of studies (program). *Ibid.*, p.69.
23. Behold the spirit of a mightily wise man (genius). *Ibid.*, p.77.
24. Euphuism (phrase). *Ibid.*, p.129.
25. Squeezing (Feder, i.e. a spring). *Ibid.*, pt.3, p.9.
26. The straight road (direct). *Ibid.*, p.90.
27. Suburb (Boulevard). *BRA.2*, pt.1, p.7.
28. Signs of the tune (notes). *Ibid.*, p.10. Although a little later (p.14) he changes the term to **אותות־הנגון** (letters of the tune).
29. Equilibrium (harmony). *Ibid.*, p.11.
30. Temple of God (Tempel). *Ibid.*, p.12.
31. Knowing law and judgement (advocate). *Ibid.*, p.13.

32. String instruments. *Ibid.* Braudes appends a footnote explaining the usage. For the keys of the piano he uses המנענעים (the movers), p.15.
33. Writing of the tunes (notes) *Ibid.*, p.37. Cf. above, n.28. This threefold terminology for musical notation provides a significant example of fluidity of terminology. Braudes is content to employ ספר (book) for "score."
34. Market of deeds (Börse) *Ibid.*, p.38.
35. Hot food or drink (cholent). *Ibid.*, pt.3, p.249.
36. Painter of boards (sign painter). *LEIN.*, pt.1, p.48.
37. Guards who go around the town. *Ibid.*, p.53.
38. The helper in a game of balls (marker). *Ibid.*, p.77.
39. A secret letter (anonymous writing). *Ibid.*, p.99.
40. *Prosbol* bonds (Prolongationswechsel). *Ibid.*, pt.2, p.108.
41. The Hebrew term is glossed as "making public," "competition." *Ibid.* For examples of valiant struggles with terminology, see N. Marsden, ed., *A Jewish Life under the Tsars*, pp.327ff.
42. Various pictures (statues). *MEIN.*, p.7.
43. The hidden court (secret police). *Ibid.*, p.63.
44. House of nuns (nunnery). *Ibid.*, p.55.
45. Interior minister (Landesminister). *Ibid.*, p.79.
46. The ax (guillotine). *Ibid.*, p.80.
47. To play with tablets (cards). *Ibid.*, p.95.
48. Weapons of battle (chess). *Ibid.*
49. Assistant in the teachers' rooms (Behelfer). *ZOB.*, pt.1, p.9.
50. Deputy officer of a hundred (Unteroffizier). *Ibid.*, pt.2, p.8.
51. Official of the army (officer). *Ibid.*, p.10. N.B. the fluidity of spelling.
52. Wise ones of the soul. *Ibid.*, p.29.
53. Abode of the pains (nerves). *Ibid.*
54. Movement of the back and limbs. *Ibid.*
55. Season of the year (Jahrzeit). *Ibid.*, p.37.
56. Turbulent water (soda water). *Ibid.*, p.38. An interesting example of the contemporary tendency to find Hebrew expressions reminiscent in sound of their European equivalents, such as the well-known חלירע (literally, a bad illness) for cholera.
57. Stations for soldiers in tents. *Ibid.*, p.44.
58. Elixirs of remedies (prescriptions). *Ibid.*, p.30.
59. Selling himself. *Ibid.*, p.45.
60. Letters of border documents. *Ibid.*, p.62.
61. Game of toys (dominoes). *MAN.*, p.39.
62. Valley of vision (amphitheater). *SHEIK.*, pt.1, p.7. The term appears on a number of occasions in Mapu's *The Hypocrite.*
63. Esther the teacher (Esther the female teacher). *Ibid.*, p.8.
64. The singing of that which gives its songs in the night was heard (nightingale). *Ibid.*, p.13.
65. A thousand hills (after Psalm 50[10], harerei-aleph) (the Alps). *Ibid.*, p.35. Cf. above, n.56.
66. Masters of tax (excise collectors). *Ibid.*, pt.2, p.24.
67. House of collection of children (orphanage). *Ibid.*, p.59.
68. Houses of feasting (buffets). *Ibid.*, pt.3, p.57.
69. Consignments of possessions (baggage). *Ibid.*, p.87.
70. Restraint (patience). *Ibid.*, p.97.
71. Elixirs of poison (arsenic). *Ibid.*, p.107.
72. "The term" (semester). *RAB.*, p.6.
73. "Horseman's dance." *Ibid.*, p.13.
74. Natural inclination (instinct). *Ibid.*, p.63.
75. Zealots (fanatics). *Ibid.*, p.85.
76. Checking machine. *Ibid.*, p.106.
77. The law of good conduct (etiquette). *Ibid.*, p.111.
78. The scent of "mists of shame" (sounding as *eid-qalon*). *Ibid.*, p.114. Cf. above, n.56.
79. Confirmer of deeds. *Ibid.*, p.126.

80. View-box (Guckkasten). *Ibid.*, p.128.
81. The scribe who reminds (secretary). *Ibid.*, p.134.
82. From his nature and composition (temperament). *Ibid.*, p.144.
83. The binder (Feldscher). *SIRK.*, p.80.
84. The nobles (Grafen). *WEIS.1*, p.39.
85. An interesting reflection on the author's positive approach to Yiddish.
86. We made a lamp for him, and it was not we who put the hat on him, explained respectively as we laid a trap for him, and it was not by our wiles that he fell into the trap. *ABR.*, p.27.
87. I expect a life of vanity (to suffer). *Ibid.*, p.34.
88. White company (roguish gang). *Ibid.*, p.48. Abramowitz appends the following reference, קנאת האמת צד בהערה (Qinath ha-'Emeth, 94 footnote).
89. A grandson of the drunkards of Ephraim. *Ibid.*, p.86. The reference is, of course, satirical.
90. Baruch heavy of mouth and Shevach the flat-nosed (Baruch the stammerer and Shevach without a nose.) *Ibid.*, pp.102, 103.
91. Surely you got up today on your left side. *Ibid.*, p.112.
92. Snails (Schnecken). *SM.6*, pt.3, p.277.
93. The Hebrew word is *roman*. *BRA.1*, pt.1, p.8.
94. Literally prophet. The term is used by thieves to denote their leader. *Ibid.*, pt.2, p.7.
95. *Klause*. The term is used to denote a house of study or *yešibhah*. *Ibid.*, pt.3, p.69.
96. *Šemoth*. The term is used for the pages of a torn book to indicate they are holy and cannot be used for profane purposes. *Ibid.*
97. *Pišpaš*. The term is used for a little door in the gate. *Ibid.*, p.84.
98. *Kelei ha-Qodheš*. The term is used to denote anyone holding a communal appointment. *Ibid.*, p.113.
99. Information bureau. *Ibid.*, p.136.
100. *BRA.2*, pt.1, p.67.
101. *Ibid.*, pt.3, p.214.
102. *Ibid.*, p.259.
103. Rival. *Ibid.*, p.302.
104. *RAB.*, p.26.
105. *WEIS.1*, p.64. The reference is incorrectly given as 1 Sam. 17^{28}.
106. Ladies' room. Boudoir. *WEIS.2*, pt.1, p.68.
107. Bo'rzah (bourse). *SM.4*, p.1. See below pp.112f, n.73.
108. 'Ele'qṭriṣiṭe'ṭ (electricity). *SM.1*, pt.4, p.64.
109. 'Oṭoriṭa'ṭim (authorities). *BRA.1*, pt.1, p.18.
110. Proza'iy (prosaic). *Ibid.*, p.96.
111. 'Uniwwe'rziṭe'ṭ (university). *BRA.2*, pt.1, p.16.
112. Ṭi'ather (theater). *Ibid.*, p.22.
113. 'Ophe'r. *Ibid.*, p.26.
114. Mo'dha'. *Ibid.*, p.67.
115. Missi'one'r (missionary). *Ibid.*, pt.2, p.189.
116. Ṭeleghraph (telegraph). *Ibid.*, pt.4, p.355.
117. Doqṭor (doctor). *Ibid.*, p.360.
118. Qa'phphe'' and Qa'phe'. *LEIN.*, pt.2, p.8. Such fluidity in spelling is not uncommon. See below n.148.
119. 'Ele'qṭriy (electric). *MEIN.*, p.7.
120. Ma'ghne'ṭ (magnet). *Ibid.*, p.33.
121. Ṣiwwiliza'ṭi'on (civilization). *Ibid.*, p.56.
122. Me'dha'ylo'n (medallion). *Ibid.*, p.88.
123. Gimna'ziyyum (gymnasium). *MAN.*, p.13.
124. Ṣe'rimo'nia'l (ceremonial). *RAB.*, p.116.
125. Mo'dh'a (mode, fashion). *SHEIK.*, pt.1, p.7. Cf. above, n.114.
126. 'Anṭisimiṭizmus (anti-semitism). *Ibid.*, p.11.
127. 'Abhṭoriṭeṭim (authorities). *Ibid.*

128. Ba'nqroṭim (bankrupts). *Ibid.*, p.13.
129. 'Orṭodhoqtim (orthodox). *Ibid.*, p.52.
130. 'Arisṭoqrothim (aristocrats). *Ibid.*
131. Qa'piṭa'l (capital). *Ibid.*, p.55.
132. Biliṭrisṭiq (bellettristic). *Ibid.*, p.74.
133. Lo'qo'moṭiph (locomotive). *Ibid.*, pt.3, p.57.
134. Re'a'lisṭim (realists). *SIRK.*, p.28.
135. No'mina'lisṭim (nominalists). *Ibid.*
136. 'Egho'izm (egoism). *Ibid.*, p.82.
137. Spiriṭu'alisṭim (spiritualists). *Ibid.*, p.118.
138. Ṭe'o'lo'ghim (theologians). *Ibid.*
139. Maṭe'ri'alizmus (materialism). *Ibid.*
140. Poziṭiphisṭ (positivist). *Ibid.*
141. Pha'qṭim (facts). *Ibid.*
142. Meṭa'phorim (metaphors). *Ibid.*, p.122.
143. So'ṣi'aliziyyah (socialisation). *Ibid.*, p.119.
144. Ṭe'o'riyyoth (theories). *Ibid.*
145. Paradhokhs (paradox). *Ibid.*
146. Ṣigha're'ṭṭe' (cigarette). *WEIS.1*, p.45.
147. Ṣigharei Ha'wwa'na' (Havanna cigars). *Ibid*; on p.46 spelt **האוואנע**. Cf. above, n.118.
148. Qa'phe'' (coffee). *Ibid.*, p.73. Cf. above, n.118.
149. 'Adhre'sim (addresses). *Ibid.*, p.112.
150. Po'sṭ (post). *Ibid.*, p.121.
151. Teleghramah (telegram). *Ibid.*, p.61.
152. Pi'ano'pho'rṭe' (pianoforte) *WEIS.2*, pt.1, p.74.
153. Ṭe'l'eghra'ph (telegraph). *Ibid.*, p.183, pt.2, p.31, spelled **תלגרף**. Cf. above, n.118.
154. Zandamim (gendarmes), *Ibid.*, p.131. On p.133 twice spelled **זשאנדרמים**. Cf. above, n.118.
155. Miza'nṭroph (misanthropist). *ZOB.*, pt.1, p.32.
156. An iron fork of two teeth which emits a sound. *SM.1*, pt.1, p.160.
157. A file and threshing instrument. *Ibid.*, p.204. Cf. 1 Sam. 13[21] (the passage is obscure) and Isa. 41[15].
158. A winter cart without wheels. *Ibid.*, pt.3, p.95.
159. And the fire spoiled the food in the pot. *SM.2*, p.5.
160. Houses of collection for things ancient of days. *Ibid.*, p.98.
161. Houses of eating and drinking, houses of laughter and dancing. *SM.4*, p.4. Rabinowitz prefers **בית אספת העליזים אשר ישחקו שם עד אור הבקר** (A meeting house for the merry who sport there until the light of morning). *RAB.*, p.30.
162. A shooting stick with six little mouths. *SM.5*, pt.3, p.13. Cf. below, p.113, for this and similar phrases, such as "twelve-shooter."
163. Leg-houses which reached the thighs. *SM.1*, pt.2, p.28.
164. A long chair which has wheels. *Ibid.*, pt.3, p.140.
165. To build paths for chariots of iron and to stretch out threads of iron on which to send our words. *SM.6*, pt.2, p.79.
166. Tomorrow there will play on the notes of the piano a man who plays wonderfully. *BRA.2*, pt.1, p.22.
167. Timely writing (in the sense of, periodical) for manufacture of clothes and fashions. *Ibid.*, pt.2, p.81. Although Sheikewitz prefers **מכתב עתי המשמיע את כל המאדות החדשות** (a periodical which makes known the new fashions). *SHEIK.*, pt.2, p.31.
168. A hair-dressing woman, making a false wig. *BRA.2*, pt.4, p.321.
169. And they put on her head a straw bonnet of woven work adorned with flowers and roses made by hand, and they put a parasol in her hand. *Ibid.*
170. In the general hall of the house there was to be seen a metal plate on the wall in which was painted in red paint a hand pointing up the stairs. *LEIN.*, pt.1, p.17.
171. For he did as the deeds of those who dress up on the play stage. *Ibid.*, p.106. Smolenskin employs the much simpler **משחקים בבמה** (players on stage). *SM.4*, p.58.

172. A man sat over a page with great speed and in a very short manner. *LEIN.*, pt.1, p.90.
173. To prepare the machine and brew a broth of tea. *WEIS.2*, pt.1, p.144.
174. The company which goes surety for conflagration. *SM.6*, pt.3, p.198.
175. The company which goes surety for every mishap and disaster from fire and water. *WEIS.2*, pt.1, p.144.
176. Company of assurers of fire. *ZOB.*, pt.2, p.16.
177. Shadow of semblance. *SM.4*, p.280. Cf. also צל-צלמי אנשים (image of images of people). *SM.6*, pt.3, pp.275, 278.
178. Semblance of likeness of image. *LEIN.*, pt.2, p.9.
179. The photographic picture. *WEIS.1*, p.60.
180. Chariots of fire. *SM.2*, p.98; *WEIS.1*, p.10, in the singular.
181. Steam cart. *SM.1*, pt.4, p.43; *MEIN.*, p.149; *SHEIK.*, pt.3, p.57.
182. Steam chariot. *SM.4*, p.170; *ZOB.*, pt.1, p.55.
183. Chariots of iron. *SM.6*, pt.1, p.39.
184. Paths of iron. *BRA.2*, pt.1, pp.7, 8, and pt.3, p.304, in the singular; *LEIN.*, pt.2, p.13, in the singular; *MEIN.*, p.149; *WEIS.1*, pp.10 (singular), 63 (singular).
185. The machine. *MEIN.*, p.149.
186. Station of the path of iron. *SIRK.*, p.116.
187. Station of the path. *Ibid.*, p.122.
188. Steam machine. *WEIS.1*, p.12.
189. House of the runners. *SM.1*, pt.2, p.39.
190. House of sending of the letters. *Ibid.*, pt.3, pp.105, 108.
191. House of letters. *SM.6*, pt.2, p.171.
192. The king's runners. *BRA.1*, pt.3, p.32.
193. Mail. *Ibid.*, pp.42, 59.
194. House of the mail. *BRA.2*, pt.3, p.220.
195. Carrier of the letters. *Ibid.*, pt.2, p.193.
196. Station of the mail-house. *RAB.*, p.83.
197. Station of the house of the runners. *WEIS.1*, p.91.
198. Carrier of missives. *Ibid.*
199. Box of letters. *SHEIK.*, pt.3, p.95.
200. Powder of bitter leaves. *SM.1*, pt.2, p.53; *SM.3*, p.38.
201. Smoke of leaves of burning. *SM.5*, pt.3, p.129.
202. Bitter leaves in a paper shroud. *SM.6*, pt.1, p.181.
203. Leaves of tobacco. *Ibid.*, pt.2, p.108.
204. Bitter leaves. *SIRK.*, p.96.
205. Sulphur material. *Ibid.*
206. Sulphur wood. *WEIS.2*, pt.1, p.32, pt.2, p.141.
207. The timely writing (in the sense of, periodical). *SM.1*, pt.2, p.253.
208. The writing of new things. *Ibid.*, p.254.
209. The writings of the time. *Ibid.*, pt.4, p.20.
210. Leaves which make new things known. *Ibid.*, p.111.
211. Leaves of the times. *SM.4*, p.185.
212. The timely writing. *ABR.*, p.160.
213. Leaf of writings of the times. *LEIN.*, pt.2, p.30.
214. Timely writing. *SIRK.*, p.49.
215. Seminary of wisdoms. *SM.1*, pt.2, p.150.
216. House of studies for the wisdom of song (in the sense of, music academy). *Ibid.*, pt.3, p.232.
217. House of wisdom. *ABR.*, p.160.
218. Science seminary for the wisdom of healing (in the sense of, medical school). *SHEIK.*, pt.1, p.20. Cf. below, p.113, n.80.
219. Room of the female cooks. *SM.1*, pt.3, p.42; *SM.2*, p.81; *MEIN.*, p.15; *RAB.*, pp.12, 17; *SIRK.*, p.3.
220. House of the male cooks. *ABR.*, pp.13, 112.

221. House of the female cooks. *SM.1*, pt.1, p.21; *SM.2*, pp.4, 86; *BRA.1*, pt.1, p.47; *BRA.2*, pt.1, p.73; *SIRK.*, p.46; *SHEIK.*, pt.1, p.23; *ZOB.*, pt.2, p.39.

222. Room of cooking. *SIRK.*, p.42.

223. Compartment of the scribes. *BRA.2*, pt.1, p.35; *LEIN.*, p.17; *WEIS.2*, pt.1, pp.40, 132; *ZOB.*, pt.1, p.59.

224. Chamber of the scribes. *WEIS.2*, pt.1, p.40.

225. The head of the reckoners of the accounts. *SM.4*, pp.34, 36.

226. The manager of the account books. *SIRK.*, p.34.

227. Overseer of the account. *SM.4*, p.150.

228. Cover from rain. *SM.6*, pt.3, p.235; *RAB.*, p.74; *ZOB.*, pt.1, p.34.

229. Cover from shower. *BRA.2*, pt.2, p.116.

230. See above, n.169, and see below, p.113, n.76.

231. Indicator of the hours. e.g. *SM.1*, pt.1, p.39; *SM.2*, p.25; *ABR.*, p.17; *BRA.1*, pt.1, pp.46, 116, pt.2, p.18; *LEIN.*, p.17; *WEIS.2*, pt.2, p.84; *SHEIK.*, pt.1, p.31.

232. And how much is the indicator of hours at this time? *MEIN.*, p.31.

233. See above, n.6.

234. You are right in your words. e.g. *SM.1*, pt.2, p.90.

235. As your words so it is. *Ibid.*, p.119.

236. The thing is good. *Ibid.*, p.152.

237. Your lips have spoken straight things. *Ibid.*, p.98.

238. May it be according to your words. *Ibid.*, p.125.

239. Is it not a thing? *Ibid.*, p.263.

240. The thing is good, I shall do according to your words. *Ibid.*, p.80; *BRA.2*, pt.1, p.32.

241. According to your words, our master, we shall do. *SM.1*, pt.3, p.209.

242. Speak, sir, for your servant is waiting. *BRA.1*, pt.2, p.58.

243. With all my heart I shall fulfil according to your words. *BRA.2*, pt.1, p.38.

244. Speak, for your servant is listening. *Ibid.*, pt.3, p.301. Cf. *WEIS.2*, p.161

245. Speak, but hurry to conclude your words. *SM.4*, p.99.

246. May it be your kindness to do like this. *SM.6*, pt.2, p.42.

247. Your words are higher than my understanding. *Ibid.*, p.113.

248. What did it become? *Ibid.*, pt.1, p.80.

249. How did it become like this? *BRA.1*, pt.2, p.37.

250. How was it like this thing? *Ibid.*, p.35.

251. My soul and my heart express thanks to you, sir, for this kindness. *Ibid.*, p.63.

252. My soul expresses to you great thanks and blessing. *Ibid.*, p.64.

253. Here I am, for you called me. *BRA.1*, pt.2, p.49; *LEIN.*, pt.1, p.45.

254. In the following notes, the frequency with which individual phrases occur is given in parentheses after the cited work. All these figures must be regarded as minimal. Frequencies are recorded only for those novels where the number makes the phrase significant. The absence of a figure for any author or novel, therefore, does not mean that the phrase is not found, but only that it does not occur sufficiently frequently to warrant special notice. See also below, p.113.

255. He found favour in my eyes. *SM.1* (85); *SM.2* (14); *SM.4* (26); *SM.5* (22); *SM.6* (33); *BRA.1* (58); *BRA.2* (55); *LEIN.* (29); *MEIN.* (12); *SHEIK.* (77); *RAB.* (12); *WEIS.1* (17); *WEIS.2* (33). See below, ch.9, n.84.

256. The hand has power (in the sense of, ability to do something). *SM.1* (78); *SM.2* (11); *BRA.1* (31); *BRA.2* (17); *LEIN.* (14); *ZOB.* (14); *SHEIK.* (33).

257. The hand was too short (in the sense of, inability to do something). *SM.1* (71); *SM.2* (19); *SM.3* (12); *SM.4* (19); *SM.5* (34); *SM.6* (36); *ZOB.* (10); *SHEIK.* (12); *WEIS.2* (24). See below, ch.9, n.85.

258. My eyes were opened to see (in the sense of, I became aware). *SM.1* (34); *SM.5* (23); *SM.6* (15); *BRA.1* (11); *SHEIK.* (30); *WEIS.2* (19). See below, ch.9, n.86. Other phrases falling into a similar category are **טוב טעם ודעת** (good taste and opinion) and **דעת לנבון נקל** (the wise man easily grasps).

259. With wasting away of eyes (in the sense of, impatiently). *SM.1* (18); *SM.4* (12); *SM.6* (13); *ABR.* (8); *LEIN.* (10); *SHEIK.* (15).

260. [To put] a curb to the mouth (in the sense of, to fall silent). *SM.1* (23); *SM.5* (16); *BRA.2* (8); *SHEIK.* (11).
261. With revulsion. *SM.1* (35); *SM.5* (16); *LEIN.* (10); *RAB.* (12).
262. His facial expression gave him away. *ABR.* (7); *BRA.1* (13); *SHEIK.* (27); *SIRK.* (7); *WEIS.2* (10).
263. To search diligently. *SM.1* (10).
264. Disappointment. *SM.1* (35); *SM.3* (8); *SM.6* (9); *ZOB.* (6).
265. His aim or goal. *SM.5* (11); *SM.6* (10); *SHEIK.* (6).
266. Intimate friend of her youth (in sense of, husband). *SM.1* (9); *SM.5* (11).
267. Sick bed. *SM.1* (8); *SM.6* (11); *ABR.* (8).
268. What evil [have you found] in him? *SM.1* (9); *SM.6* (6); *WEIS.2* (9).
269. Instantly. *SM.1* (39); *SM.5* (9); *SM.6* (14); *SIRK.* (7).
270. Bitter weeping. *SM.1* (24); *BRA.2* (6).
271. Powerlessness of hand (in sense of, helplessness). *SM.1* (35); *SM.4* (8); *SM.5* (8).
272. I have spoken once and I will not change. *SM.1* (11).
273. It shall not be. *SM.1* (14); *SM.5* (8).
274. A spirit of confusion. *SM.1* (16); *WEIS.2* (7).
275. For the occasion. *SM.1* (8); *BRA.1* (13).
276. And he twisted his lips. *SM.6* (13).
277. A loin-breaking sigh. *SM.1* (14); *BRA.1* (23); *BRA.2* (16).
278. A heavy stone (in the sense of, burden). *SM.1* (9); *SHEIK.* (7).
279. Like a man overcome by wine. *SM.2* (6); *SM.6* (6); *BRA.1* (6); *BRA.2* (6).
280. In what is your strength great? *BRA.1* (10).
281. One here one there (in the sense of, sporadically). *BRA.1* (10); *BRA.2* (5).
282. A further vision for the occasion (in the sense of, time will tell). *WEIS.2* (10).
283. All his salvation and desire (in the sense of, his deepest wish). *WEIS.1* (9); *WEIS.2* (12). See below, ch.9, n.87.

Notes to Chapter Nine

1. Israel Weisbrem was born in Grodno in 1840 and died in Warsaw in 1915 or 1917. He was one of eleven children of a wealthy merchant, Benjamin Zarah Weisbrem. As a result of the first publication of this chapter in the *Journal of Semitic Studies*, 4, no.1, 1959, Mr Leon Weisbrem of Melbourne, the grandson of Israel Weisbrem, compiled a family tree and commissioned Dr A. D. Crown of the University of Sydney to translate the fiction and poetry of Israel Weisbrem. The introduction to these translations, *Israel Weissbrem and His Work, Novels and Poems*, translated and introduced by Alan David Crown, Tel-Aviv, 1983, contains considerable biographical information. Dr Crown transliterates his name Weissbrem.
2. For information relative to these writers, see D. Patterson, *The Hebrew Novel in Czarist Russia*, ch.1.
3. בין הזמנים, 136 pages.
4. ח״י אגורות, pt.1, 184 pages; pt.2, 213 pages.
5. הגורל והירושה, 118 pages. A second edition appeared in Warsaw in 1895. Apart from these three novels Weisbrem also published a work called חזיון (vision) (Warsaw, 1902), which bears the subtitle על הציונים ומתנגדים (on Zionists and Opponents). A review of *The Lottery and the Inheritance* by J. L. Peretz was published in the daily הצפירה on the 27 Sivan 1892, no.127, p.519. In this review Peretz bitterly attacks the novel, criticizing it for the improbabilities of the plot, which he compares to that of a French operetta, for the author's strange neglect of his young heroines (see below), and for the moral turpitude of the characters. The latter criticism is quite unjustified. Weisbrem published a spirited reply in the same journal on the 19 Tammuz 1892, no.146, p.575, in which he stoutly defends his intimate knowledge of the conditions he has described, maintaining that all the events of the story are based on fact, and offering to name the places and persons involved (although unfortunately he does not do so). After successfully

defending his characters against the charges leveled by Peretz, he admits his neglect of the young ladies in the story, but excuses himself on the grounds that the love element is suitable to French but not to Hebrew tales! (but see below). Four days later the same journal, no.149, p.588 (misprinted 288), published the final paragraph of Weisbrem's reply, deleted from no.146, which represents an attack on Peretz's own writings. The same page contains a picture of a table of winning tickets in the state lottery for the year 1864.

6. A summary of the plots of Weisbrem's first two novels was included in *The Hebrew Novel in Czarist Russia*, pp.31ff. They are repeated here for the reader's convenience.

7. See above, chs.6 and 7.

8. From 7 to 10 per cent, pt.1, p.156. From *WEIS.3* we learn that the normal rate of interest on loans in Lithuania was 12 per cent, p.144.

9. Cf. the hero of Bialik's story *'Aryeh Ba'al-Guph*, who attributes his good fortune to a handshake given him by his *Rebbe, Kol Kithbhei Ḥ. N. Bialik* (The Collected Writings of C. N. Bialik), Tel-Aviv, 1947, p.100.

10. An advance on many contemporary novels, where fortuitous inheritances are quite common. Both Mapu and Smolenskin are fond of the device.

11. *WEIS.2*, pt.2, p.136. Cf. *LEIN.*, pt.1, pp.105ff, where a similar device is employed.

12. For which the reference ברכות ס"ד is given in the text. *WEIS.1*, p.62.

13. *Ibid.* The phrase is used as the heading for ch.5, p.52.

14. It is indicative of the prevailing cultural climate that the author appends the following information in two footnotes: (*a*) that Rio de Janeiro is the capital of Brazil; (*b*) that *poste restante* is written on the addresses of letters which are to remain in the post office until the addressee comes to claim them, *ibid.*, p.111.

15. Cf. the abortive efforts of rabbi Elijah Ragoler, Mapu's friend, to compose a letter of welcome in Latin, described by J. Klausner in *History*, vol.3, pp.277f.

16. *WEIS.1*, pp.112ff.

17. *Ibid.*, p.124.

18. Cf. below, p.114, n.100.

19. *WEIS.2*, pt.2, pp.142f.

20. *Ibid.*, p.190.

21. *Ibid.*, p.205. There is a similar incident in A. Mapu's *The Hypocrite*, pt.3, pp.163f. Indeed, the influence of Mapu may be traced time and time again in these novels. See below, p.113, n.90, pp.114f, nn.108 and 109.

22. ובתחבלות גימנסתיק עשה מלחמה (he made war with gymnastic devices), *WEIS.2*, pt.2, p.205.

23. Cf. *WEIS.1*, p.50; *WEIS.2*, pt.1, p.156; pt.2, pp.70, 162; *WEIS.3*, pp.84, 117.

24. Cf. *WEIS.2*, pt.1, pp.15, 22, 129; pt.2, pp.83, 103; *WEIS.3*, p.84. See above, pp.45f.

25. Cf. *WEIS.1*, pp.7f, 70f, 91; *WEIS.2*, pt.1, pp.72, 113; *WEIS.3*, pp.4, 29, 46f.

26. *WEIS.1*, pp.91f.

27. *WEIS.3*, p.60.

28. Cf. *Mishnah 'Erubhin*.

29. Pt.2, pp.178f. ש"ע א"ח סימן ש"א ס"ק ל"ג חיי אדם כלל נ"ד סימן ה', תפארת ישראל כלכלת שבת ז.

30. *Ibid.*, p.179. א"ח רס"ו וחיי אדם כלל נ"ד.

31. Cf. the parents of the heroine, Hannah, in *SHEIK.*, pt.1, pp.12f. Cf. above, ch.2, n.19.

32. *WEIS.1*, p.130.

33. *WEIS.2*, pt.2, pp.109f.

34. *Ibid.*, pt.1, pp.93f; pt.2, p.109.

35. See *RAB.*, pp.112f.

36. *WEIS.1*, p.50.

37. See above, chs.2 and 3.

38. pp.109f.

39. Pt.1, pp.119, 161, 170, 173; pt.2, pp.22, 26, 125, 152, 157.

40. pp.36, 39, 76, 85, 88, 89, 91, 96, 98, 100, 110, 114, 115, 118, 121, 122.

41. Cf. *WEIS.1*, p.110; *WEIS.2*, pt.2, p.157.

42. Cf. *WEIS.1*, p.91.
43. Cf. *WEIS.2*, pt.1, p.161.
44. *Ibid.*, p.119.
45. *WEIS.1*, p.118.
46. *WEIS.2*, pt.1, p.173; pt.2, pp.22, 152.
47. See above, ch.3, n.63.
48. *WEIS.1*, pp.60, 121.
49. *Ibid.*, pp.87, 100.
50. *Ibid.*, p.120.
51. *WEIS.2*, pt.1, p.156. The idea was also used by P. Smolenskin; see *SM.6*, pt.2, p.198. Cf. also *ZOB.*, pt.2, p.22.
52. *WEIS.2*, pt.1, pp.137ff.
53. *Ibid.*, pt.2, p.29.
54. *Ibid.*, p.147.
55. *Ibid.*, pp.120f.
56. Cf. *ibid.*, p.80.
57. Cf. *WEIS.1*, ch.5.
58. *WEIS.2*, pt.1, pp.60ff.
59. *Ibid.*, pt.2, p.31.
60. *Ibid.*, pp.62f.
61. Cf. *ibid.*, pp.73f.
62. *Ibid.*, pt.1, chs.2 and 3.
63. *WEIS.1*, pp.12, 37, and nn. 109, 124.
64. p.28. The study of grammar, vigorously pursued by the *Maskilim*, was regarded by the obscurantists as anathema. Cf. above, p.95.
65. *WEIS.2*, pt.1, p.161, and see above, p.100.
66. p.26.
67. *WEIS.2*, pt.1, pp.18ff.
68. *WEIS.1*, p.89 ... And the day came when Miriam went to town.
69. [sic] **יתן לך ה׳ ותמצא בתך מנוחה בבית אשה**, *WEIS.3*, p.102. Cf. also *WEIS.2*, pt.1, p.91.
70. **ואין זה דבר אשר יאמר ראה זה חדש הוא**, *WEIS.3*, p.47. Cf. *WEIS.2*, pt.1, p.168; pt.2, p.204.
71. Pt.1, p.97. See above, p.95.
72. But see Jonathan's letter in *WEIS.1*, p.39.
73. *WEIS.3*, p.41, gathering houses of merchants, and see above, p.98, n.107.
74. *Ibid.* Treasure houses for money.
75. *Ibid.*, p.29. Gate of horses.
76. *Ibid.*, p.49. Canopy.
77. *WEIS.1*, p.40. Book of muster of guests.
78. *Ibid.*, p.124, *WEIS.2*, pt.1, p.133. Shroud of the letters.
79. *WEIS.1*, pp.40, 126. Head of the eunuchs (in the sense of, chief officer).
80. *WEIS.2*, pt.1, p.68. Seminary of wisdom for working the land and growing trees of the forest.
81. *Ibid.*, p.75. In writings of the times which make known new every morning the events of each day.
82. *Ibid.*, p.113. A man who is able to write the script of every man according to its form and appearance, and the letters are not recognisable as being written by a stranger.
83. *Ibid.*, pt.2, pp.174, 193. A small shooting stick with six little mouths. Cf. *SM.5*, pt.3, p.13. In *SM.6* Smolenskin introduced an even more ambitious "twelve-shooter," **בעל שנים עשר פיפיות קנה רובים** (a shooting stick with twelve little mouths), *op.cit.*, pt.1, p.171. See above, ch.8, n.162.
84. He found favor in my eyes. Thirty three times in *WEIS.2*, seventeen in *WEIS.1*, and eight in *WEIS.3*. See above, p.101.
85. The hand was too short (in the sense of, inability to do something). Twenty four, nine, and four times respectively.
86. Eyes were opened to see (in the sense of, to become aware). Nineteen, nine, and five times respectively.

87. All their salvation and desire (in the sense of, their deepest wish). Twelve, nine, and four times respectively.

88. Cf. the description of Rebecca in *WEIS.2*, pt.1, p.68.

89. Cf. the attempt to describe a wealthy man's room, *ibid.*, p.160.

90. Cf. the description of the coming of spring, *ibid.*, pp.117f. Here again the influence of Mapu is very marked.

91. Cf. Wayne Booth, *The Rhetoric of Fiction*, pt.2.

92. Pt.1, pp.38, 47, 105, 149.

93. pp.11, 79.

94. Cf. *WEIS.1*, p.27.

95. Cf. *ibid.*, pp.24ff, and *WEIS.2*, pt.2, pp.82f. Cf. above, p.61.

96. *WEIS.1*, pp.25f.

97. *Ibid.*, pp.41ff.

98. Cf. *ibid.*, pp.28. 45.

99. Such as David and Pesach in *WEIS.3*; the Jewish factors possessively refer to the Polish noblemen and clergy whom they serve as "my nobleman" or "my priest," p.12.

100. Cf. *ibid.*, p.10, „הטרם תדע אדוני כי עושי מלאכה נבזים המה בעיני כל יושבי עירנו, נמאסים מאד" (Do you not know, sir, that manual workers are despised by all our townsfolk, very despised).

101. *WEIS.2*, pt.1, pp.84f.

102. *Ibid.*, p.87.

103. Cf. *ibid.*, pp.52f, 85; *WEIS.1*, pp.8, 28.

104. *Ibid.*, pp.98ff.

105. *Ibid.*, pp.15ff.

106. *WEIS.2*, pt.1, p.70.

107. *Ibid.*, pp.7f, and see above, p.75, n.42.

108. *Ibid.*, p.66. Mapu similarly endows Naaman, the young hero of *The Hypocrite*, with the profession of an agricultural scientist.

109. *Ibid.*, pp.124f. Mapu similarly champions a "back to the land campaign," *Mapu*, pp.233, 253, 440. A part of the practical work undertaken by the *Maskilim* consisted of attempts to found societies for the promotion of agriculture among the Jews. See J.S. Raisin, *The Haskalah Movement in Russia*, Philadelphia, 1913, pp.140–4.

110. *WEIS.2*, pt.1, pp.124f.

111. *Ibid.*, pt.2, pp.53f.

112. *WEIS.3*, p.62.

113. *WEIS.1*, pp.96, 110.

114. pp.76f. In a footnote on p.79 the author states that the conversation is based on one that actually took place.

115. *Ibid.*, p.116.

116. *WEIS.1*, p.65; *WEIS.2*, pt.1, pp.79ff; pt.2, pp.53ff.

117. *Ibid.*, pt.2, p.57.

118. *Ibid.*, pt.1, pp.115f.

119. See above, chs.6 and 7.

120. *WEIS.2*, pt.1, pp.106f.

121. *Ibid.* Cf. above, p.76.

122. *Ibid.*, p.51. Cf. above, p.71.

123. *Ibid.*, pt.2, pp.211f.

124. *Ibid.*, pp.116ff.

125. *Ibid.*

126. *WEIS.3*, p.18.

127. *Ibid.*, p.23.

128. *Ibid.* and p.30.

129. *Ibid.*, pp.18ff.

130. Cf. *The Autobiography of Solomon Maimon*, London, 1954, pp. 11ff.

131. Pt.2, pp.186ff.

132. *Ibid.*, pp.87ff.
133. *WEIS.1*, pp.79, 83.
134. *Ibid.*, p.84.
135. p.28.

Notes to Chapter Ten

1. First published in Lemberg in 1876–7. An enlarged, although still unfinished, version appeared in Lemberg, 1885. All references are to the second edition. Braudes explains in his preface that the word *Dath* (religion) in the title is used in the connotation applied by the Jews of Lithuania, namely the *Šulḥan ʿArukh*, the code of Jewish law compiled by Joseph Caro, first published in Venice, 1565. See *Encyclopaedia Judaica*, Jerusalem, 1971, vol.14, pp.1475ff. See above, p.56.

2. *Melekh Basar wa-Dham*, Merhavia, 1954. An English translation by D. Patterson appeared in London in 1958, from which all references and quotations are taken.

3. See D. Patterson. *The Hebrew Novel in Czarist Russia, passim*, and cf. above, ch.5, n.8. The controversy is well described in G. Katznelson, *Ha-Milḥamah ha-Siphruthith bein ha-Ḥaredhim we-ha-Maskilim* (The Literary War between the Orthodox and the Enlighteners), Tel-Aviv, 1954.

4. *The Epic of Gilgamesh*, tr. N. K. Sanders, Penguin, 1960, ch.3.

5. Ch.1 and 2.

6. The *Iliad*, book 24, lines 25ff.

7. Act 3.

8. The *Iliad*, book 18, lines 497ff.

9. 1 Kings 3:16-28. See D. Daube, "Dividing a Child in Antiquity," *California Law Review* 54 (1966), pp.1630–7.

10. *The New English Bible, The Apocrypha*, 1970, pp.267ff. See B. S. Jackson, "Susanna and the Singular History of Singular Witnesses," in *Acta Juridica*, Cape Town, 1977.

11. The theme was also very popular with painters in the Renaissance, and it features in English literature in a play by George Peele entitled *Arraignment of Paris* (1584). I am grateful to Mrs J. Speake for drawing my attention to this and other aspects of the theme.

12. See W.A. Neilson, *The Origins and Sources of the Court of Love*, Boston, 1899.

13. Book 6, vii, 28–39.

14. Act 5. The trial of Hermione in *The Winter's Tale* is more in the tradition of Susanna.

15. See J. D. Rea, "Shylock and the Processus Belial," in *Philological Quarterly*, 8 (1929), pp.313ff. See also G. Friedlander, *Shakespeare and the Jew*, London, 1921, ch.3, and J. Dunlop, *History of Fiction*, 2nd ed., Edinburgh, 1816, vol.2, p.375. E. Rosenberg, "The Jew in Western Drama," *Bulletin of the New York Public Library*, 72, no.7, September, 1968. See also G. W. Keeton, *Shakespeare's Legal and Political Background*, London, 1967, ch.9. *The Merchant of Venice* was translated into German in 1763, into French in 1768, and into Russian in 1833.

16. Act 3, Scene 7.

17. Vienna, 1866. See I. Shapiro, *Bibliography of Hebrew Translations of German Works*, New York, 1934. In the *Encyclopaedia Judaica*, vol.4, p.51, the date of publication is given as 1865.

18. Vienna, 1874. See I. Shapiro, *op.cit.*, and J. Klausner, *History*, vol.5, pp.300f.

19. See *ibid.*, p.355.

20. See above, n.1.

21. See below.

22. For example in Henry Fielding's *The History of Jonathan Wild the Great* (1743) and *Tom Jones* (1749). As Braudes was familiar with both German and Russian (see J. Klausner, *op.cit.*, p.352) the following notes make mention of German and Russian translations of a number of English and French novels containing court scenes. Only translations which appeared prior to 1876, the year in which the first edition of *BRA.1* began to appear, have been included. The fact that such translations were available implies no more than the possibility that Braudes may have read them. Their popularity, however, increases the likelihood of such a possibility.

23. *Waverley* (1814), *Old Mortality* (1816), *The Heart of Midlothian* (1818), *Ivanhoe* (1820), *Peveril of the Peak* (1823). Scott's complete works in 60 volumes were translated into French (1822–30), and into German in 174 volumes (1826–33). For Scott's impact on German literature, see L.M. Price, *English Literature in Germany*, Berkeley and Los Angeles, 1953, ch.23. *Ivanhoe* appeared in Russian in 1845, *Waverley* in 1874, and *Peveril of the Peak* in 1874. For information concerning translations into Russian in the nineteenth century, see Dikson, Me'zer, and Braginskij, *Bibliografičeskie ukazateli perevodnoj belletristiki* (bibliographical indices of translated *belles lettres*), with a prefatory note by J. S. G. Simmons, London, 1971.

24. *Pelham* (1828), *Paul Clifford* (1830), *Eugene Aram* (1832). All three appeared in French in the same year as the original English version. For Lytton's influence in Germany, see L. M. Price, *op.cit.*, pp.346f. A Russian translation of *Eugene Aram* appeared in 1860.

25. *Sketches by Boz* (1836), *The Pickwick Papers* (1836–7), *Oliver Twist* (1838), *Barnaby Rudge* (1841), *Bleak House* (1851), *A Tale of Two Cities* (1859). Dickens was very popular in French translation. La Bédollière's translation of *Oliver Twist* (*Les Voleurs de Londres*, Paris, 1850) had six subsequent impressions. *Bleak House* was translated in 1857 with nine subsequent impressions, while *The Pickwick Papers* appeared in French in 1859 with seventeen subsequent impressions. For Dickens in German see E. N. Gummer, *Dickens' Works in Germany 1837–1937*, Oxford, 1940. In Russia *Sketches by Boz* appeared in part in 1852, *The Pickwick Papers* in 1857, *Bleak House* in 1859, *A Tale of Two Cities* in 1859, and *Oliver Twist* in 1874.

26. *Les derniers jours d'un condamné* (1829). The novel was translated into German in 1829 and into Russian in 1865.

27. *Le Juif errant* (1844–5), translated into German in 1844–5 and into Russian in 1844–5. *Les Mystères de Paris* (1842–3) was translated into Hebrew by K. Schulman during the years 1857–60. For the influence of Sue and Dumas *père* on the Hebrew novel, see D. Patterson, *Abraham Mapu*, pp.102ff.

28. e.g. in *Le Comte de Monte Cristo*, which first appeared in Russian in 1845, *Le Collier de la Reine* (1850), in Russian in 1874, and *La Tulipe Noire* (1850), in Russian in 1852. The collected works appeared in German in 1844–59.

29. Particularly by Heinrich von Kleist. See H. Fehr, *Das Recht in der Dichtung*, Bern, 1931.

30. See I. T. Golyakov, *Sud i zakonnost v russkoy khudozhestvennoy literature XIX veka* (court and legality in Russian artistic literature of the nineteenth century), Moscow, 1956.

31. As, for example, in *Tom Jones, The Heart of Midlothian*, or *Oliver Twist*.

32. As, for example, in *Old Mortality* or *A Tale of Two Cities*.

33. e.g. *Ivanhoe, Paul Clifford*, or *The Pickwick Papers*.

34. As in *Peveril of the Peak*.

35. e.g. *Tom Jones, The History of Jonathan Wild the Great, The Heart of Midlothian, Ivanhoe, Peveril of the Peak, A Tale of Two Cities*.

36. As in Scott's Jacobite novels.

37. See e.g. R. D. MacCann, "The Problem Film in America," in *Film and Society*, ed. R. D. MacCann, New York, 1964. See also *The Film Index, vol. i: The Film as Art* (reprint), New York, 1966. Films such as *Twelve Angry Men* (1957) or *Judgement at Nuremberg* (1960) or television series such as "Perry Mason" and "People's Court" are obvious examples.

38. Cf. Earle David, *The Flint and the Flame*, London, 1964, p.251.

39. For this custom of interrupting the service, see *Encyclopaedia Judaica*, vol.4, p.1061, under entry *Biṭṭul ha-Tamid*, and the bibliography cited. Cf. also A. S. Sachs, *Worlds That Passed*, J.P.S., Philadelphia, 1928. See *BRA.1*, p.74.

40. The example in *Jane Eyre* may serve as illustration.

41. See above, p.56, and *The Hebrew Novel in Czarist Russia*, pp.17ff.

42. Samuel was modeled on the champion of religious reform M. L. Lilienblum. See Klausner, *History*, vol.5, p.352, and N. Marsden, *M. L. Lilienblum: His Life and Work*, Master of Letters thesis, Oxford University, 1971, p.24, n.42.

43. See above, n.1. The *Šulḥan 'Arukh* was widely accepted as the most authoritative codification of Jewish law. Braudes gives the relevant references to the authorities quoted in a series of footnotes. See *BRA.1*, pp.79ff.

44. His gloss to the *Šulḥan 'Arukh, Yoreh De'ah*, section 36, paragraph 8. It is of interest that the

well-known controversy between Moses Israel Isserles and Solomon Luria arose from a dispute concerning the defective lung of an animal. See *Encyclopaedia Judaica*, vol.9, p.1082.

45. Tractate *Ḥullin* 48b.

46. *BRA.1*, p.80.

47. See *Encyclopaedia Judaica*, vol.3, p.177, and vol.8, p.359.

48. *BRA.1*, p.83. For a translation of the whole passage, see *The Hebrew Novel in Czarist Russia*, pp.214f.

49. *BRA.1*, p.84.

50. *Ibid.*, pt.2, pp.95f.

51. There is, in fact, another court scene in the same novel, pp.327ff, which describes how the members of the Great Sanhedrin were frightened into silence by Alexander Jannaeus when trying his servant for murder. The episode is based on the Babylonian Talmud, *Sanhedrin* 19 a–b.

52. *Tosefta Sanhedrin* 6:6. The translation used here is by H. Danby in *Tractate Sanhedrin, Mishnah and Tosefta*, London, 1919, pp.66f.

53. Like the Sadducees, whose views resembled their own, the Boethuseans were in conflict with the Pharisees. The two protagonists, Jehuda, the son of Ṭabbai, and Shimeon, the son of Sheṭaḥ (coupled in *Mishnah Abhoth* 1:8), are, of course, the same as the characters referred to below as ben-Tabbai or Judah, and Simeon ben-Sheṭah or Simeon. On the versions and development of this tradition, see J. Neusner, *The Rabbinic Traditions About the Pharisees Before 70*, Leiden, 1971, vol.1, ch.5.

54. Deut. 19^{19}.

55. Deut. 19^{21}. cf. *Mishnah Makkoth* 1:6 and Babylonian Talmud, *Makkoth* 5b ff. For a discussion on witnesses, see B. S. Jackson, *Theft in Early Jewish Law*, Oxford, 1972, pp.226ff, and *Essays in Jewish and Comparative Legal History*, Leiden, 1975, pp.37–54. See especially D. Daube in *Witnesses in Bible and Talmud*, Oxford Centre for Postgraduate Hebrew Studies, 1986, pp.11f. Professor Daube argues that the Pharisees interpret the law correctly. See also J. Neusner, "'By the Testimony of Two Witnesses,' in the Damascus Document IX, 17–22 and in 'Pharisaic-Rabbinic Law,'" *Revue de Qumran* 8 (1973), pp.197–217.

56. *The King of Flesh and Blood*, pp.216f.

57. *Ibid.*, pp.218f.

58. See above, p.120.

59. *The King of Flesh and Blood*, pp.338f.

60. Deut. 17^{6}. Cf. Num. 35^{30}.

61. See above, n.51.

62. *The King of Flesh and Blood*, p.340.

Notes to Chapter Eleven

1. See above, pp.3ff, and cf. e.g. S. Halkin, *Modern Hebrew Literature, Trends and Values*, New York, 1950, pp.25ff.

2. Cf. e.g. M. A. Meyer, *The Origins of the Modern Jew*, Detroit, 1967, pp.42f, 115ff.

3. Cf. *ibid.*, pp.56, 86, 137ff. Cf. G. Scholem, "Jews and Germans," *Commentary*, 42, no.5, November, 1966.

4. For a striking illustration of such tardiness, see *ibid.*, p.37.

5. Cf. D. Patterson, "The Preservation of Enlightenment," *Jewish Heritage*, 10, no.2, 1967. Cf. above, p.4.

6. See D. Patterson, *Abraham Mapu*, pp.86ff.

7. See B. Dinur, **דמותו ההיסטורית של היהדות הרוסית ובעיות החקר בה** (The Historical Facies [*sic*] of Russian Jewry and Problems Connected with its Study), *Zion*, 22, nos.2–3, 1957, p.111, n.55. Cf. below, ch.12, n.5.

8. See *Abraham Mapu*, pp.62, 95.

9. *SM.1*, pt.3, pp.95f. Cf. *The Hebrew Novel in Czarist Russia*, pp.167f. Cf. above, ch.6, n.29.

10. See J. Klausner, **יוצרים ובונים** (Creators and Builders), vol.1, Tel-Aviv, 1925, p.188.

11. *Mapu*, p.360.
12. *Ibid.*, pp.359f. For an English translation of the chapter, see *Abraham Mapu*, pp.150ff. Cf. the shrewd comment of Charles Péguy quoted by G. Scholem, *op.cit.*, p.35. See also D. Patterson, "Revival of Literature and Revival of Language," in E. Silberschlag, ed., *Eliezer Ben-Yehuda*, A Symposium in Oxford, Oxford, 1981, pp.20ff. Cf. below, ch.12. The year 1853 is the year of publication of *The Love of Zion*. The Hebrew equivalent (5)613 is reminiscent of the 613 commandments. See e.g. *Encyclopaedia Judaica*, vol.5, pp.760ff.
13. Cf. above, p.9.
14. *ABR.*, pp.75f. Cf. *The Hebrew Novel in Czarist Russia*, pp.111f.
15. *BRA.1*, pt.2, p.110. Cf. *The Hebrew Novel in Czarist Russia*, p.203.
16. Ch.4. Cf. *Abraham Mapu*, pp.116f.
17. *Kol Kithbhei Mendele Mokher Sepharim* (The Collected Writings of Mendele Mokher Sepharim), Tel-Aviv, 1958, p.100; extract from the novel *Sepher ha-Qabbṣanim* (The Book of the Beggars), first version, in Yiddish, 1869. The Hebrew version appeared in 1909.
18. See *The Hebrew Novel in Czarist Russia*, pp.209ff. Cf. N. Marsden, ed., *A Jewish Life under the Tsars*, New Jersey, 1983, pp.29f.
19. *Kol Kithbhei Mendele Mokher Sepharim*, pp.97f.
20. *BRA.1*, pt.1, pp.42f. Cf. *The Hebrew Novel in Czarist Russia*, pp.161f.
21. *SM.2*, pp.202f. Cf. *The Hebrew Novel in Czarist Russia*, p.179.
22. *The Love of Zion*, ch.4. Cf. *Abraham Mapu*, p.122.
23. *BRA.1*, pt.3, pp.155f. Cf. *The Hebrew Novel in Czarist Russia*, pp.117f.
24. Cf. B. Dinur, *op.cit.*, p.110, n.53.
25. See *The Hebrew Novel in Czarist Russia*, pp.8ff and 228ff.
26. *Ibid.*, pp.232f; and cf. above, pp.13 and 42f.
27. *SM.6*, pt.2, p.158; cf. *The Hebrew Novel in Czarist Russia*, p.199.
28. *SM.6*, pt.2, pp.49ff. Cf. J. Heller, **משנתו של סמולנסקין ביהדות** (Smolenskin's Teaching in Judaism), in **מצודה** (Metsudah), December, 1943, pp.153–8.
29. See *The Hebrew Novel in Czarist Russia*, ch.2.
30. *SM.6*, pt.2, p.55.
31. *SM.1*, pt.4, pp.58ff and 74f; *SM.2*, p.94; *SM.6*, pt.2, p.55.
32. See e.g. *ibid.*, pp.265f. Cf. above, p.12.
33. See *The Hebrew Novel in Czarist Russia*, p.122, and see above, chs.6 and 7.
34. See *The Hebrew Novel in Czarist Russia*, pp.51ff.
35. See *ibid.*, pp.84ff, 112f.
36. See *SM.1*, pp.ix f, and *The Hebrew Novel in Czarist Russia*, pp.40f.
37. *Ibid.*, pp.131, 225; and cf. H. Ehrenzeller, *Studien zur Romanvorrede*, Bern, 1955, pp.132f. Cf. above, p.56.
38. See *The Hebrew Novel in Czarist Russia*, p.233.
39. See *ibid.*, pp.19f.
40. See *ibid.*, pp.5ff, 232; cf. S. Werses, **הרומאן העברי הראשון של מנדלי וגלגוליו** (Mendele's First Hebrew Novels and its Versions), in **מולד** (Molad), vol.20, 1962. Cf. above ch.3 n.10.
41. See D. Miron, **ארבע הערות לתיאורי־הטבע ב״האבות והבנים״ לאברמוביץ** (Four Notes on Nature Descriptions in Abramowitz's "Fathers and Sons"), in **מאזנים** (Moznayim), vol.28, no.4, March, 1969. Cf. *The Hebrew Novel in Czarist Russia*, pp.121, 232.
42. On Mendele's craftsmanship, see e.g. G. Shaked, **בין שחוק לדמע** (Between Laughter and Tears), 1965, pp.108ff. See also M. Perry, "Analogy and its Role as a Structural Principle in the Novels of Mendele Moykher Sforim," in *Hasifrut*, 1, no.1, Tel-Aviv, spring 1968; and "The Imaginary Equation," *ibid.*, 1, nos.3–4, fall–winter 1968–9. See above, ch.1, n.26.
43. See M. Perry, "Analogy . . .", *op.cit.*, and Y. Shentukh, "The Versions of Mendele's Short Stories in Hebrew and Yiddish," in *Hasifrut*, 1, no.2, summer 1968, pp.391–409, and C. Shmeruk, "The Yiddish Translations of the Book of Psalms by Mendele Mokher Sfarim," *ibid.*, pp.337–42. See also M. Perry, "Thematic and Structural Shifts in Autotranslations by Bilingual Hebrew-Yiddish Writers," in *Poetics Today*, vol.2:4, 1981, pp.181–92. Cf. above, ch.1, n.27.
44. Cf. e.g. J. Fichman, **אמת הבנין** (Building Plumbline), Jerusalem, 1951, pp.144ff.
45. *Kol Kithbhei Mendele Mokher Sepharim*, p.91.

46. *Ibid.*, p.92.
47. *Ibid.*, pp.92f. For Alter's dismissive attitude, cf. above, ch.6, n.7.
48. M. Z. Feierberg, *Le'an?* (*Whither?*) (1899). The passage is quoted from a translation by H. Halkin in *Whither? and Other Stories*, Philadelphia, 1973, pp.214f.

Notes to Chapter Twelve

1. The term *'Ereṣ Yisra'el* (Land of Israel) reflects the image in the minds of the Hebrew writers far more accurately than the name Palestine. See below, p.148.
2. See D. Patterson, "Moving Centers in Modern Hebrew Literature," in *The Great Transition*, eds. G. Abramson and T. Parfitt, New Jersey, 1985. The considerable Hebrew literature in the United States reflects another sizable shift in the center of gravity of Hebrew literature in the wake of the mass migration of Jews from Eastern Europe across the Atlantic during the last quarter of the nineteenth century and the first quarter of the twentieth. See e.g. E. Silberschlag, "Hebrew Literature in America at the Tercentenary," in *Jewish Book Annual*, 12, 1953–5, "Two Progenitors of Hebrew Literature in America," *J.B.A.*, 18, 1960–1, and "American Classics in Hebrew Translation," *J.B.A.*, 24, 1966–7. Cf. J. Kabakoff, לדמותה של הספרות העברית באמריקה (An Appraisal of American Hebrew Literature), *J.B.A.*, 13, 1955–6. See also M. Waxman, *A History of Jewish Literature*, vol.4, book 9, ch.15. A comprehensive survey is to be found in J. K. Mikliszanski, *A History of Hebrew Literature in America* (Hebrew text), New York, 1967. See also E. Silberschlag, *From Renaissance to Renaissance*, vol.I, ch.15.
3. Cf. R. Mahler, *A History of Modern Jewry, 1780–1815*, London, 1971, p.130.
4. The main currents of Hebrew literature in the nineteenth century have been charted in the standard histories of Hebrew literature. See above, ch.1, n.1. For material relevant to this chapter, see e.g. Klausner, *History*, vol.5, pp.143–68, and vol.6, pp.84–111; Lachower, vol.3, sec.1, ch.28, sec.2, ch.29, vol.4, ch.38; Shaanan, vol.3, pp.134ff; Waxman, vol.4, book 6, chs.2 and 3.
5. See e.g. B. Dinur, דמותה ההיסטורית של היהדות הרוסית ובעיות החקר בה (The Historical Facies [*sic*] of Russian Jewry and Problems Connected with its Study), in *Zion*, 22, nos.2–3, 1957. Cf. above, ch.11, n.7.
6. Although the process may be traced back for some decades earlier. See G. Yardeni, העיתונות העברית בארץ ישראל בשנים 1863–1904 (The Hebrew Press in *'Ereṣ Yisra'el* in the Years 1863–1904), Tel-Aviv, 1969.
7. See e.g. A.Ruppin, *The Jews in the Modern World*, London, 1934, p.374, and *Encyclopaedia Judaica*, vol.9, pp.472ff, where a figure of 57,000 is given for 1918.
8. See D.Patterson, *Abraham Mapu*, pp.5f, 63ff; cf. above, ch.1.
9. Cf. above, ch.11.
10. See e.g. S. Halkin, *Modern Hebrew Literature, passim.*
11. Cf. above pp.15f.
12. See e.g. M. Perry, "Analogy and its Role as a Structural Principle in the Novels of Mendele Moykher Sforim," *op.cit.*; D. Miron, "The Story 'Grandfather's Home'—its Role in U. N. Gnessin's Literary Work," in *Hasifrut*, 1, no.2, summer 1968. Cf. above, ch.11, n.42.
13. See e.g. M. Zborowski and E. Herzog, *Life is with People*, New York, 1952, pp.76ff.
14. The uprooted person (Hebrew: *Taluš*) occupies a prominent place in Hebrew fiction from the end of the last century, as many of the stories of writers such as I. D. Berkowitz, I. Bershadsky, M. J. Berdichewsky, and J. H. Brenner amply demonstrate. See e.g. A. Holtz, *Isaac Dov Berkowitz, Voice of the Uprooted*, London and Ithaca, 1973.
15. See above, ch.11. Cf. below, pp.149f. The outstanding example of this tendency is, of course, Benjamin, the hero of Mendele's satirical מסעות בנימין השלישי (The Travels of Benjamin the Third) in כל כתבי מנדלי מוכר ספרים (The Collected Writings of Mendele Mokher Sepharim), Tel-Aviv, 1958. See below, n.31.

16. The mood is, perhaps, best captured in such poems of C. N. Bialik as על סף בית המדרש (On the Threshold of the House of Study), המתמיד (The Assiduous Student), etc. See כל שירי ח. נ. ביאליק (The Collected Poems of C. N. Bialik), Tel-Aviv, 1962, pp.36ff, 319ff.

17. See e.g. the early novels of J. H. Brenner, בחורף (In Winter) and מסביב לנקודה (Around the Point), in כל כתבי י. ח. ברנר (The Collected Writings of J. H. Brenner), vol.1 (2nd printing), Tel-Aviv, 1964.

18. See A. A. Rivlin, פלמוס בשירה (Controversy in Poetry), pp.17ff. Cf. above, ch.1, n.37.

19. With such notable exceptions as S. J. Abramowitz, A. U. Kovner, and A. J. Papirna. See e.g. S. Breiman, א. א. קובנר ומקומו בתולדות הבקרת העברית (A. U. Kovner and his Place in the History of Hebrew Criticism), in מצודה (Metsudah), vol.7, London, 1954. Cf. above pp.19f.

20. See above, n.1. See Z. Shavit, "The Decline of the Hebrew Literary Centers in Europe and the Rise of the Center in Ereẓ Israel," in *Hasifrut*, 32, 1983.

21. Cf. S. Yizhar, "Writing in a Renascent Language," in *Ariel*, 4, winter 1963, p.24. "An entire culture, ancient and intact, having achieved a peak of transcendental expression, descended to build new foundations."

22. See above, n.6.

23. For the activities of Ben-Yehuda and Luncz, see e.g. G. Yardeni, *op.cit.*, *passim*. See also Eliezer Ben-Yehuda, החלום ושברו (The Dream and its Realization), in כל כתבי אליעזר בן יהודה (The Collected Writings of Eliezer Ben-Yehuda), vol.1, Jerusalem, 1941. See also E. Silberschlag, ed., *Eliezer Ben-Yehuda*, A Symposium in Oxford, Oxford, 1981.

24. See A. Arnon, תולדות החנוך העברי החדש (The History of Modern Hebrew Education), in האנצקלופדיה העברית (The Hebrew Encyclopaedia), vol.6, pp.983–96, and ששים שנה של בית הספר העברי בארץ (Sixty Years of Hebrew School in the Land), in הד החנוך (Hed ha-Ḥinnukh), vol.9, 1947, pp.8–40.

25. U. Z. Greenberg, למרגלותיך, ירושלים (At Your Feet, Jerusalem), in A. Barash, ed., מבחר השירה העברית החדשה (An Anthology of Modern Hebrew Poetry), Jerusalem, 1938, p.400. For an English version, see U. Z. Greenberg, *Jerusalem*, tr. by C. A. Cowen, New York, 1939, p.39.

26. See T. Andersson, *Foreign Languages in the Elementary School*, Austin and London, 1969, p.9. "Evidence supports the assumption that unless a child is exposed to another language under favourable conditions before the age of ten he is not likely to learn to speak it without accent. It can be done by some, but it takes time and a grim determination." See also pp.44f.

27. See e.g. M. Zborowski and E. Herzog, *op.cit.*, pp.88ff, and cf. S. Greenberg, "Jewish Educational Institutions," in *The Jews: Their History, Culture and Religion*, ed. L. Finkelstein, vol.3, Philadelphia, 1949, pp.924ff. See also Z. Scharfstein, תולדות החנוך בישראל בדורות האחרונים (History of Jewish Education in Modern Times), 2nd rev. ed., vol.1, Jerusalem, 1960.

28. It is important to recall that Hebrew was a prestigious language (if not the sole one) for the Jewish immigrant to *'Ereṣ Yisra'el*, just as English was the language of prestige for the immigrant to the United States.

29. See below, p.155.

30. See e.g. A. Holtz, *The Holy City*, New York, 1971, pp.143ff; A. Hertzberg, *The Zionist Idea*, New York, 1966, *passim*. See below, n.39.

31. For the importance of this world of fantasy, see e.g. M. Samuel, *The World of Sholom Aleichem*, New York, 1965, pp.289ff.

32. As a child in Liverpool, the author of this book was constantly surprised to find that prayers for rain were offered in synagogue in spite of the pelting rain outside. Only gradually did it dawn upon him that the prayers were concerned not with Liverpool but with Jerusalem!

33. See D. Patterson, *Abraham Mapu*, pp.86f.

34. *Ibid.*, pp.160ff. See also D. Patterson, *The Hebrew Novel in Czarist Russia*, pp.221f. Cf. above, ch.11.

35. Although the view was widely held among the Jews of Europe in the nineteenth century. See e.g. S. Bernfeld, תולדות הריפורמציון הדתית בישראל (The History of Reform Judaism), Krakau, 1900.

36. Cf. A. Hertzberg, *The Zionist Idea*, pt.2.

37. See Y. Ro'i, "The Zionist Attitude to the Arabs, 1908–1914," in *Middle Eastern Studies*, 4, 1968.

38. See L. Simon, *Ahad Ha-Am*, London, 1960, pp.60ff.
39. על הפרק (At the Crossroads), Warsaw, 1887, p.150.
40. כל כתבי אחד העם (The Collected Writings of Ahad Ha-Am), 2nd ed., Tel-Aviv and Jerusalem, 1950, p.24. Cf. L. Simon, *op.cit.*, p.62.
41. Cf. e.g. A. Elon, *The Israelis, Founders and Sons*, London, 1971, p.107.
42. The process is well illustrated in Ahad Ha-Am's essay שתי רשויות (Two Masters), in על פרשת דרכים (At the Crossroads), pt.1, Berlin, 1921, p.161.
43. U. Z. Greenberg, "At Your Feet, Jerusalem," *op.cit.*
44. See e.g. S. N. Eisenstadt, *The Absorption of Immigrants*, London, 1954, pp.36, 40.
45. For a list of Hebrew periodicals, see *Encyclopaedia Judaica*, vol.1, p.193. The role of the editors of these journals also constitutes a factor of importance which deserves detailed study.
46. Cf. above, n.2.
47. Cf. L. Simon, *op.cit.*, pp.174f.
48. Cf. D. Patterson, "Brenner," in *Work*, 10, no.29, January, 1960.
49. I am grateful to Mr. Amos Oz of Kibbutz Huldah, Israel, for drawing my attention to this aspect of Brenner's style.
50. See מכאן ומכאן (From Here and There), in כל כתבי י .ח. ברנר (The Collected Writings of J. H. Brenner), Tel-Aviv, 1964, p.374.
51. The concept of exile is rooted in Jewish tradition, and it was widely held by Jews in the diaspora; but not, of course, by those adhering to socialist revolutionary principles.
52. This emotional bond between writer and reader is well illustrated in Shalom Asch's *Three Cities*, tr. by W. and E. Muir, New York, 1933, p.355.
53. Translated by N. de Lange, Fontana ed., 1976, pp.91f.
54. C. N. Bialik, ספיח (Saphiaḥ), in ח .נ. ביאליק, ספורים (C. N. Bialik, Stories), Tel-Aviv, 1965, p.119. For an English translation of the passage, see D. Patterson, *The Foundations of Modern Hebrew Literature*, London, 1961, p.55.
55. *Ibid.*, p.57. Cf. Wordsworth's Ode, "Intimations of Immortality from Recollections of Early Childhood."
56. Leah Goldberg, מסע ללא שם (Nameless Journey), in ילקוט שירים (A Bag of Songs), Tel-Aviv, 1970, pp.104f, and see also p.60. Cf. T. Carmi, גלוי עינים ותפוס לילה (Caught Open-eyed in the Night), in משא (Massa'), 9, no.6, 1972.
57. D. Shimoni, ספר האידיליות (The Book of Idylls), Israel, 1962, pp.96f. (My translation.)
58. אדמה ללא צל (A Land without Shade), 3rd ed., Tel-Aviv, 1953. See also G. Shaked, "Wherefrom and Whereto: Introductory Remarks on the History of Hebrew Fiction Between the Two World Wars," in *Hasifrut*, 32, 1983.
59. S. Yizhar, ימי צקלג (Days of Ziklag), Tel-Aviv, 1958.
60. See שירת רחל (The Poetry of Rachel [Blaustein, 1890–1931]), 23rd ed., Tel-Aviv, 1972.
61. See L. I. Yudkin, *Isaac Lamdan*, London, 1971, pp.169ff.
62. D. Shimoni, *op.cit.*, pp.97f.
63. For examples of both usages, see E. Ben-Yehuda, *A Complete Dictionary of Ancient and Modern Hebrew*, vol.4, Berlin, 1910, p.1774.
64. Cf. above, ch.8.
65. See T. V. Parfitt, "The Use of Hebrew in Palestine, 1800–1882," in the *Journal of Semitic Studies*, 17, no.2, autumn 1972.
66. Just as the growth of political Zionism led to the secularization of religious "Zionism." Cf. e.g. S. Talmon, "The Bible in Contemporary Israeli Humanism," in *Judaism*, 21, no.1, winter 1972, pp.79f. See also M. Ben-Horin, "Judaeo-Zionism: Meaning Old and New," *ibid.*, 20, no.3, summer 1971, p.295 and n.1.
67. See above, ch.8, and cf. W. Chomsky, "The Growth and Progress of Modern Hebrew," in *Studies and Essays in Honour of Abraham A. Neuman*, eds. M. Ben-Horin, B. D. Weinryb, and S. Zeitlin, Leiden, 1962.
68. See M. Shamir, "Colloquial Language and Literary Language," in *Sifrut*, 3, London, 1957.
69. See E. Ben-Yehuda, המבטא בלשון העברית (The Pronunciation of Hebrew), New York, 1917.

70. See e.g. S. Burnshaw, T. Carmi, and E. Spicehandler, *The Modern Hebrew Poem Itself*, New York, Chicago, San Francisco, 1965, pp.194, 202f, 211f.

71. On the problems arising from the change in stress, see e.g. D. Pagis, "From Ashkenazi to Sephardi: A Crisis Reflected in a Holograph of David Vogel," in *Hasifrut*, 3, no.1, June, 1971. See also E. Kagan, "From Vessel to Vessel" (Hebrew text), in *Lĕšonénu*, 36, nos.2–3 and 4, 1972. It is instructive to compare the change of stress in English literature in the period between Chaucer and Shakespeare. See M. Halle and S. J. Keyser, *English Stress*, New York etc., 1971, p.109. "The language … differed from that of Chaucer's language in that uniformity was imposed where two centuries before there had been much diversity." It is tempting to suggest that the changing patterns of stress may account in part for the comparative dearth of good poetry in this period.

72. Cf. above, ch.11.

73. See above, ch.10.

74. The reaction against self-deprecation is strikingly evident in the poetry of U. Z. Greenberg:

"Hebrew was not my mother tongue, but the language of my blood,
And I was suffocated, there, in the foreign iambs."

Kelebh Bayith (House-dog), Tel-Aviv, 1929, p.30.

Selected Bibliography

For bibliographical information on the fiction examined in these studies see above, Abbreviations, pp.157f.

D. Aberbach, 'On Re-reading Bialik: Paradoxes of a "National Poet",' *Encounter*, June, 1981.

Ahad Ha-Am, *'Al Parašath Derakhim* (At the Crossroads), pt.1, Berlin, 1921.

Kol Kithbhei 'Aḥadh Ha-'Am (The Collected Writings of Ahad Ha-Am), 2nd ed., Tel-Aviv and Jerusalem, 1950.

A. Altmann, *Moses Mendelssohn, A Biographical Study*, London, 1973.

T. Anderson, *Foreign Languages in the Elementary School*, Austin and London, 1969.

A. Arnon, 'Šišim Šanah šel Beth-ha-Sepher ha-'Ibhri ba-'Areṣ' (Sixty Years of Hebrew School in the Land), in *Hed ha-Ḥinnukh*, vol.9, 1947.

A. Arnon, 'Toledhoth ha-Ḥinnukh ha-'Ibhri he-Ḥadhaš' (The History of Modern Hebrew Education), in *The Hebrew Encyclopaedia*, vol.6.

Shalom Asch, *Three Cities*, tr. by W. and E. Muir, New York, 1933.

S. Baron, *The Russian Jews under Tsars and Soviets*, London and New York, 1976.

C. Bates, *A Study of the Life and Works of A.S. Rabinowitz*, doctoral dissertation, Oxford University, 1972.

E. Ben-Yehuda, *A Complete Dictionary of Ancient and Modern Hebrew*, vol.4, Berlin, 1910.

E.K. Bennett, *A History of the German Novelle from Goethe to Thomas Mann*, 2nd ed. revised and continued by H.M. Waidson, Cambridge, 1961.

S. Bernfeld, *Toledhoth ha-Riphormaṣiyyon ha-Dathith be-Yisrae'el* (The History of Reform Judaism), Krakau, 1900.

C.N. Bialik, *Sippurim* (Stories), Tel-Aviv, 1965.

C.N. Bialik, *Kol Kithbhei Ḥ.N. Bialik* (The Collected Writings of C.N. Bialik), Tel-Aviv, 1947.

C.N. Bialik, *Kol Širei Ḥ.N. Bialik* (The Collected Poems of C.N. Bialik), Tel-Aviv, 1962.

C.N. Bialik, *Sippurim* (Stories), Tel-Aviv, 1950.

F.G. Black, *The Epistolary Novel in the Late Eighteenth Century*, Eugene, 1940.

Rachel Blaustein, *Širath Raḥel* (The poetry of Rachel [Blaustein, 1890–1931]), 23rd ed., Tel-Aviv, 1972.

Wayne Booth, *The Rhetoric of Fiction*, Chicago and London, 1961.

H. Bracker, *Rahmenerzählung und Verwandtes bei G. Keller, C.F. Meyer und Th. Storm*, Leipzig, 1909.

S. Breiman, 'A.H. Kovner u-Meqomo be-Tholdhoth ha-Biqqoreth ha-ʿIbrith' (A.U. Kovner and his Place in the History of Hebrew Criticism), in *Metsudah*, vol.7, London, 1954.

J.H. Brenner, *Kol Kithbhei Y.Ḥ. Brenner* (The Collected Writings of J.H. Brenner), 2nd printing, Tel-Aviv, 1964.

J. Burla, *ʿAliloth ʿAqabhyah* (The Deeds of ʿAqabhyah), Tel-Aviv, 1948.

S. Burnshaw, T. Carmi, and E. Spicehandler, *The Modern Hebrew Poem Itself*, New York, Chicago, and San Francisco, 1965.

T. Carmi, 'Galuy ʿEinayim we-Taphus Lailah' (Caught Open-eyed in the Night), in *Massa'*, 9, no.6, 1972.

T. Carmi, ed., *The Penguin Book of Hebrew Verse*, Harmondsworth, 1981.

W. Chomsky, 'The Growth and Progress of Modern Hebrew,' in *Studies and Essays in Honour of Abraham A. Neuman*, eds. M. Ben-Horin, B.W. Weinryb, and S. Zeitlin, Leiden, 1962.

T. Cohen, *From Dream to Reality, Descriptions of Eretz Yisrael in Haskalah Literature* (Hebrew text), Jerusalem, 1982.

A.D. Crown, *Israel Weissbrem and His Work, Novels and Poems*, translated and introduced by A.D. Crown, Tel-Aviv, 1983.

H. Danby, *Tractate Sanhedrin, Mishnah and Tosefta*, London, 1919.

D. Daube, 'Dividing a Child in Antiquity,' *California Law Review* 54, 1966.

D. Daube, *Witnesses in Bible and Talmud*, Oxford Centre for Postgraduate Hebrew Studies, Oxford, 1986.

E. David, *The Flint and the Flame*, London, 1964.

Dikson, Me'zer and Braginskij, *Bibliografičeskie ukazeteli perevodnoj belletristiki* (bibliographical indices of translated *belles lettres*), with a prefatory note by J.S.G. Simmons, London, 1971.

B. Dinur, 'Demuthah ha-Hisṭorith šel ha-Yahadhuth ha-Rusith u-Bhaʿayoth ha-Ḥeqer Bah' (The Historical Facies [*sic*] of Russian Jewry and Problems Connected with its Study), in *Zion*, 22, nos.2–3, 1957.

B. Dinur, ed., *Mikhtebhei 'Abhraham Mapu* (The Letters of Abraham Mapu), Jerusalem, 1970.

B.W. Downs, *Richardson*, London, 1928.

S. Dubnow, *History of the Jews in Russia and Poland*, tr. I. Friedlaender, 3 vols., Philadelphia, 1916–20.

S. Dubnow, *Toledoth ha-Ḥasidhuth* (The History of Hasidism), Tel-Aviv, 1930/1.

J. Dunlop, *History of Fiction*, 2nd. ed., Edinburgh, 1816, vol.2.

A. Even-Shoshan, *Ha-Millon he-Ḥadhaš* (The New Dictionary), vol.4, Jerusalem, 1967.
H. Ehrenzeller, *Studien zur Romanvorrede*, Bern, 1955.
S.N. Eisenstadt, *The Absorption of Immigrants*, London, 1954.
G. Elkoshi, 'Abraham Mapu's Letters' (Hebrew text), in *Hasifrut*, vol.4 no.2, Tel-Aviv, 1973.
A. Elon, *The Israelis, Founders and Sons*, London, 1971.
I. Eörsi, 'Poetry and Ideology,' in D. Daiches and A. Thorlby, eds., *Literature and Western Civilisation*, vol.5, *The Modern World ii: Realities*, London, 1972.
I. Erter, *Ha-Ṣopheh le-Bheith Yisrael* (The Watchman of the House of Israel), Vienna, 1858.

H. Fehr, *Das Recht in der Dichtung*, Bern, 1931.
M.Z. Feierberg, *Whither? and other Stories*, tr. H. Halkin, Philadelphia, 1973.
B. Feingold, *Yeṣiratho šel R.A. Braudes* (The Work of R.A. Braudes), 2 vols., doctoral dissertation, Hebrew University, Jerusalem, 1978.
J. Fichman, *'Amath ha-Binyan* (Building Plumbline), Jerusalem, 1951.
J. Fichman, *'Anšai Bhesorah* (Men of Good Tidings), Tel-Aviv, 1938.
The Film Index, vol.i: The Film as Art (reprint), New York, 1966.
J. Frankel, *Prophecy and Politics: Socialism, Nationalism and the Russian Jews 1862–1917*, Cambridge, 1981.
G. Friedlander, *Shakespeare and the Jew*, London, 1921.
D. Frishman, *Kol Kithbhei Dawid Frišman* (The Collected Writings of David Frishman), Warsaw and New York, 1930.

The Life of Glückel of Hameln, tr. Beth-Zion Abrahams, London, 1962.
Leah Goldberg, 'Masa' Lelo' Šem' (Nameless Journey), in *Yalquṭ Širim* (A Bag of Songs), Tel-Aviv, 1970.
I.T. Golyakov, *Sud i zakonnost v russkoy khudozhestvennoy literature XIX veka* (court and legality in Russian artistic literature of the nineteenth century), Moscow, 1956.
H.M. Graupe, *The Rise of Modern Judaism*, New York, 1978.
L. Greenberg, *The Jews in Russia: The Struggle for Emancipation*, 2 vols., New Haven and London, 1965 (orig. 1944).
S. Greenberg, 'Jewish Educational Institutions,' in *The Jews: Their History, Culture and Religion*, ed. L. Finkelstein, vol.3, Philadelphia, 1949.
U.Z. Greenberg, *Jerusalem*, tr. by C.A. Cowen, New York, 1939.
U.Z. Greenberg, 'Le-Margelothayikh, Yerušalayim' (At Your Feet, Jerusalem), in A. Barash, ed., *Mibhar ha-Širah ha-'Ibrith ha-Ḥadhašah* (An Anthology of Modern Hebrew Poetry), Jerusalem, 1938.
U.Z. Greenberg, *Kelebh Bayith* (House-dog), Tel-Aviv, 1929.
E.N. Gummer, *Dickens' Works in Germany 1837–1937*, Oxford, 1940.

M.A. Günzburg, *Debhir*, 1, Vilna, 1844.
J. Guttman, *Philosophies of Judaism*, New York, 1964.

S. Halkin, *Modern Hebrew Literature, Trends and Values*, New York, 1950.
S. Halkin, *Mabho' la-Siphruth ha-'Ibrith* (Introduction to Hebrew Literature), Jerusalem, 1958.
M. Halle and S.J. Keyser, *English Stress*, New York etc., 1971.
J. Heller, 'Mishnatho šel Smolenskin be-Yahadhuth' (Smolenskin's Teaching in Judaism), in *Metsudah*, London, December, 1943.
A. Hertzberg, *The Zionist Idea*, New York, 1966.
A. Holtz, *The Holy City*, New York, 1971.
A. Holtz, *Isaac Dov Berkowitz, Voice of the Uprooted*, London and Ithaca, 1973.
A. Holtz, 'Prolegomena to a Literary History of Modern Hebrew Literature,' in *From Literature East and West*, vol.11, no.3, 1968.
M. Ben-Horin, 'Judaeo-Zionism: Meaning Old and New,' in *Judaism*, 20, no.3, summer, 1971.

B.S. Jackson, *Theft in Early Jewish Law*, Oxford, 1972.
B.S. Jackson, *Essays in Jewish and Comparative Legal History*, Leiden, 1975.
B.S. Jackson, 'Susanna and the Singular History of Singular Witnesses,' in *Acta Judaica*, Cape Town, 1977.
A. Jospe, *Moses Mendelssohn, Jerusalem and other Jewish Writings*, New York, 1969.
E. Jospe, ed., *Moses Mendelssohn. Selections from His Writings*, New York, 1975.

J. Kabakoff, 'Li-Demuthah šel ha-Siphruth ha-'Ibrith be-Ameriqah' (An Appraisal of American Hebrew Literature), in *Jewish Book Annual*, 13, 1955–6.
E. Kagan, 'From Vessel to Vessel' (Hebrew text), in *Lešonenu*, 36, nos.2–3 and 4, 1972.
G. Katznelson, *Ha-Milḥamah ha-Siphruthith bein ha-Ḥaredhim we-ha-Maskilim* (The Literary War between the Orthodox and the Enlightened), Tel-Aviv, 1954.
G.W. Keeton, *Shakespeare's Legal and Political Background*, London, 1967.
J. Klausner, *Historiah šel ha-Siphruth ha-'Ibrith ha-Ḥadhašah* (A History of Modern Hebrew Literature), 2nd ed., Jerusalem, 1952–8.
J. Klausner, *Yoṣerim u-Bhonim* (Creators and Builders), vol.1, Tel-Aviv, 1925.
L. Kochan, ed., *The Jews in Soviet Russia since 1917*, 3rd ed., Oxford, 1978.

F. Lachower, *Toledoth ha-Siphruth ha-'Ibhrith ha-Ḥadhašah* (History of Modern Hebrew Literature), 7th ed., Tel-Aviv, 1951.
J.L. Landau, *Short Lectures on Modern Hebrew Literature*, London, 1938.
M.G. Langer, *Neun Tore*, Munich, 1959.

R.D. MacCann, 'The Problem Film in America,' in *Film and Society*, ed. R.D. MacCann, New York, 1964.

A.D. McKillop, 'Epistolary Technique in Richardson's Novels,' *Rice Institute Pamphlet*, vol.38, April, 1951.

R. Mahler, *A History of Modern Jewry, 1780–1815*, London, 1971.

R. Mahler, *Ha-Ḥasidhuth we-ha-Haskalah* (Hasidism and Haskalah), Merhavia, 1961.

K.R. Mandelkow, 'Der deutsche Briefroman. Zum Problem der Polyperspektive im Epischen,' in *Neophilologus*, vol.44, 1960.

N. Marsden, *M.L. Lilienblum: His Life and Work*, Master of Letters dissertation, Oxford University, 1971.

N. Marsden, ed., *A Jewish Life under the Tsars, The Autobiography of Chaim Aronson, 1825–1888*, New Jersey, 1983.

Y. Mazor, 'Traces of the English Victorian Novel in the Enlightenment Hebrew Novel: Between Dickens and Smolenskin,' in *Hebrew Studies*, vol.xxv, 1984.

M.A. Meyer, *The Origins of the Modern Jew*, Detroit, 1967.

Kol Kithbhei Mendele Mokher Sepharim (The Collected Writings of Mendele Mokher Sepharim), Tel-Aviv, 1958.

J.L. Mikliszanski, *A History of Hebrew Literature in America* (Hebrew text), New York, 1967.

D. Miron, ''Arba' He'aroth le-The'urei ha-Ṭebh'a be "Ha-'Abhoth we-ha-Banim" le-Abhramobhiṣ' (Four Notes on Nature Descriptions in Abramowitz's 'Fathers and Sons'), in *Moznayim*, vol.28, no.4, March, 1969.

D. Miron, 'The Story "Grandfather's Home"—its Role in U.N. Gnessin's Literary Work' (Hebrew text), in *Hasifrut*, 1, no.2, summer 1968.

D. Miron, *A Traveler Disguised*, New York, 1973.

D. Miron, *Bein Ḥazon le-Emeth* (Between Vision and Truth), Jerusalem, 1979.

G. Mosse, *Germans and Jews*, New York, 1970.

J. Clark Murray, tr., *The Autobiography of Solomon Maimon*, London, 1954.

W.A. Neilson, *The Origins and Sources of the Court of Love*, Boston, 1899.

J. Neusner, '"By the Testimony of Two Witnesses," in the Damascus Document IX, 17–22 and in "Pharisaic–Rabbinic Law,"' *Revue de Qumran* 8, 1973.

J. Neusner, *The Rabbinic Traditions About the Pharisees Before 70*, Leiden, 1971.

A. Oz, *Touch the Water, Touch the Wind*, tr. by N. de Lange, Fontana ed., 1976.

D. Pagis, 'From Ashkenazi to Sephardi: A Crisis Reflected in a Holograph of David Vogel' (Hebrew text), in *Hasifrut*, 3, no.1, June, 1971.

T.V. Parfitt, 'The Use of Hebrew in Palestine, 1800–1882,' in *Journal of Semitic Studies*, 17, no.2, autumn, 1972.

D. Patterson, *Abraham Mapu*, London, 1964, Ithaca, 1968.

D. Patterson, 'Brenner,' in *Work*, 10, no.29, January, 1960.

D. Patterson, 'Moving Centers in Modern Hebrew Literature,' in *The Great Transition*, eds. G. Abramson and T. Parfitt, New Jersey, 1985.

D. Patterson, 'The Use of Songs in the Novels of Abraham Mapu,' in *Journal of Semitic Studies*, 1, no.4, October, 1956.

D. Patterson, 'Conversational Uses of the Root *Dabhar* in Neo-Biblical Hebrew,' in *Essays on the Occasion of the Seventieth Anniversary of the Dropsie University*, eds. A.I. Katsh and L. Nemoy, Philadelphia, 1979.

D. Patterson, *The Foundations of Modern Hebrew Literature*, London, 1961.

D. Patterson, 'Hebrew Drama,' in *Bulletin of the John Rylands Library*, vol.43, no.1, 1960.

D. Patterson, *The Hebrew Novel in Czarist Russia*, Edinburgh, 1964.

D. Patterson, 'Moses Mendelssohn's Concept of Tolerance,' in *Between East and West*, London, 1958.

D. Patterson, 'Philosophers of Emancipation,' in *Jewish Philosophy and Philosophers*, London, 1962.

D. Patterson, 'The Preservation of Enlightenment,' in *Jewish Heritage*, 10, no.2, 1967.

D. Patterson, 'Revival of Literature and Revival of Language,' in E. Silberschlag, ed., *Eliezer Ben-Yehuda*, A Symposium in Oxford, Oxford, 1981.

D. Patterson, 'Saul Tschernichowsky,' in *The Jewish Quarterly*, Autumn, 1973.

M. Pelli, *The Age of Haskalah*, Leiden, 1979.

J. Perl, *Boḥan Ṣaddiq* (The Test of the Righteous), Prague, 1888.

J. Perl, *Megalleh Ṭemirin* (The Revealer of Secrets), Vienna, 1819.

M. Perry, 'Analogy and its Role as a Structural Principle in the Novels of Mendele Moykher Sforim' (Hebrew text), in *Hasifrut*, 1, no.1, Tel-Aviv, spring 1968.

M. Perry, 'The Imaginary Equation' (Hebrew text), in *Hasifrut*, 1, nos.3–4, fall–winter 1968.

M. Perry, 'Thematic and Structural Shifts in Autotranslations in Bilingual Hebrew–Yiddish Writers,' in *Poetics Today*, vol.2:4, 1981.

L.M. Price, *English Literature in Germany*, Berkeley and Los Angeles, 1953.

C. Rabin, *A Short History of the Hebrew Language*, Jerusalem, 1973.

J.S. Raisin, *The Haskalah Movement in Russia*, Philadelphia, 1913.

C. Raphael, 'The Two Traditions: The Hebraic and the Hellenic,' in D. Daiches and A. Thorlby, eds., *Literature and Western Civilisation*, vol.1, *The Classical World*, 1972.

J.D. Rea, 'Shylock and the Processus Belial,' in *Philological Quarterly*, 8, 1929.

A.A. Rivlin, *Pulmos be-Širah* (Controversy in Poetry), Tel-Aviv, 1966.

Y. Ro'i, 'The Zionist Attitude to the Arabs, 1908–1914,' in *Middle Eastern Studies*, 4, 1968.

G.L. van Roosbroek, *Persian Letters before Montesquieu*, New York, 1932.

E. Rosenberg, 'The Jew in Western Drama,' in *Bulletin of the New York Public Library*, 72, no.7, September, 1968.

C. Roth, *History of the Jews of Italy*, Philadelphia, 1946.

A. Ruppin, *The Jews in the Modern World*, London, 1934.

A.S. Sachs, *Worlds That Passed*, Philadelphia, 1928.

M. Samuel, *The World of Sholom Alaichem*, New York, 1965.

N.K. Sanders, tr., *The Epic of Gilgamesh*, Harmondsworth, 1960.

G. Scholem, 'Jews and Germans,' in *Commentary*, 42, no.5, November, 1966.

Z. Scharfstein, *Toldehoth ha-Ḥinnukh be-Yisra'el ba-Doroth ha-'Aḥaronim* (History of Jewish Education in Modern Times), 2nd rev. ed., vol.1, Jerusalem, 1960.

A. and Y. Sened, *'Adhamah lelo' Ṣel* (A Land without Shade), Tel-Aviv, 1953.

A. Shaanan, *Ha-Siphruth ha-'Ibhrith ha-Ḥadhaŝah li-Zeramehah* (Trends in Modern Hebrew Literature), Tel-Aviv, 1962.

G. Shaked, *Bein Seḥoq le-Dema'* (Between Laughter and Tears), Givatayim–Ramat-Gan, 1965.

G. Shaked, 'Wherefrom and Whereto: Introductory Remarks on the History of Hebrew Fiction Between the Two World Wars' (Hebrew text), in *Hasifrut*, 32, 1983.

G. Shaked, *Ha-Sipporeth ha-'Ibhrith 1880–1980* (The Hebrew Story 1880–1980), 3 vols., Tel-Aviv, 1977, 1983, 1988.

M. Shamir, 'Colloquial Language and Literary Language,' in *Sifrut*, 3, London, 1957.

M. Shamir, *Melekh Basar wa-Dham*, tr. D. Patterson, entitled *The King of Flesh and Blood*, London, 1958.

Y. Shentukh, 'The Versions of Mendele's Short Stories in Hebrew and Yiddish' (Hebrew text), in *Hasifrut*, 1, no.2, summer 1968.

I. Shapiro, *Bibliography of Hebrew Translations of German Works*, New York, 1934.

Z. Shavit, 'The Decline of the Hebrew Literary Centers in Europe and the Rise of the Center in Ereẓ Israel' (Hebrew text), in *Hasifrut*, 32, 1983.

D. Shimoni, *Sepher ha-'Idiliyyoth* (The Book of Idylls), Israel, 1962.

C. Shmeruk, 'The Yiddish Translations of the Book of Psalms by Mendele Mokher Sfarim' (Hebrew text), in *Hasifrut*, 1, no.2, summer 1968.

E. Silberschlag, ed., *Eliezer Ben-Yehuda*, Oxford, 1981.

E. Silberschlag, 'Two Progenitors of Hebrew Literature in America,' in *Jewish Book Annual*, 18, 1960–1.

E. Silberschlag, 'American Classics in Hebrew Translation,' in *Jewish Book Annual*, 24, 1966–7.

E. Silberschlag, 'Hebrew Literature in America at the Tercentenary,' in *Jewish Book Annual*, 12, 1953–5.

E. Silberschlag, *From Renaissance to Renaissance*, 2 vols., New York, 1973, 1977.

E. Silberschlag, *Saul Tschernichowsky*, London and Ithaca, 1968.

L. Simon, *Ahad Ha-Am*, London, 1960.

L. Simon, *Selected Essays by Ahad Ha-'Am*, Philadelphia, 1948.

S.L. Ṣitron, *Yoṣerai ha-Siphruth ha-'Ibhrith ha-Ḥadhašah* (The Creators of Modern Hebrew Literature), Vilna, 1922.

P. Smolenskin, ''Am 'Olam' (The Eternal People), in *Ma'amarim* (Articles), vol.1, Jerusalem, 1925.

P. Smolenskin, ''Eth la-Ta'ath' (Time to Plant), in *Ma'amarim* (Articles), vol.2, Jerusalem, 1925.

E. Spicehandler, 'Modern Hebrew Literature,' in *Encyclopaedia Judaica*, vol.8, Jerusalem, 1971, p.178.

M. Stanislawski, *Tsar Nicholas I and the Jews*, Philadelphia, 1983.

S. Talmon, 'The Bible in Contemporary Israeli Humanism,' in *Judaism*, 21, no.1, winter, 1972.

A. Thorlby, 'Irrationalism,' in D. Daiches and A. Thorlby, eds., *Literature and Western Civilisation*, vol.5, *The Modern World ii: Realities*, London, 1972.

S. Tschernichowsky, *'Al ha-Dam* (On the Blood), tr. by L. Bernard in E. Silberschlag, *Saul Tschernichowsky*, London and Ithaca, 1968.

M. Waxman, *A History of Jewish Literature*, rev. ed., New York, 1960.

D. Weinfeld, *Peretz Smolenskin's Art of the Novel*, doctoral dissertation, Hebrew University, Jerusalem, 1975.

J. Weingreen, *A Practical Grammar for Classical Hebrew*, 2nd ed., Oxford, 1959.

S. Werses, 'Current Research on Haskalah Literature' (Hebrew text), in *Yedhi'on ha-'Iggudh ha-'Olami le-Madda'ei ha-Yahadhuth*, pt.1, no.25, summer 1985; pt.2, no.26, winter 1985; pt.3, no.27, winter 1987.

S. Werses, 'Ha-Roman ha-'Ibhri ha-Ri'šon šel Mendele we-Ghilgulaw' (The First Hebrew Novel by Mendele and its Versions), in *Molad*, 20, 1962.

S. Werses, ''Iyyunim ba-Mibhneh šel *Megalleh Ṭemirin* u-*Bhoḥan Ṣaddiq*' (Studies in the Structure of *Megalleh Ṭemirin* and *Boḥan Ṣaddiq*), in *Tarbiz*, vol.31, no.4, 1962.

S. Werses, 'Zeman u-Merḥabh be-Roman *'Ayiṭ Ṣabhua'* šel Mapu' (Time and Space in the Novel *'Ayiṭ Ṣabhua' by Mapu), in R. Tsur and U. Shavit, eds., Meḥqarim be-Siphruth 'Ibrith* (Studies in Hebrew Literature), Tel-Aviv, 1986.

M. Yahrblum, *The Works of Peretz Smolenskin*, doctoral dissertation, New York University, 1965.

G. Yardeni, *Ha-'Ittonuth ha-'Ibhrith be-'Ereṣ Yisra'el be-Šanim 1904–1863* (The Hebrew Press in *'Ereṣ Yisra'el* in the Years 1863–1904), Tel-Aviv, 1969.

E. Ben-Yehudah, *Ha-Ḥalom we-Šibhro* (The Dream and its Realization), in *Kol Kithbhei Eliʿezer Ben Yehudah* (The Collected Writings of Eliezer Ben-Yehudah), vol. 1, Jerusalem, 1941.

E. Ben-Yehudah, *Ha-Mibhṭa' be-Lašon ha-ʿIbhrith* (The Pronunciation of Hebrew), New York, 1917.

E. Ben-Yehudah, *A Complete Dictionary of Ancient and Modern Hebrew*, vol.4, Berlin, 1910.

S. Yizhar, 'Writing in a Renascent Language,' in *Ariel*, 4, winter 1963.

S. Yizhar, *Yemei Ṣiqlagh* (Days of Ziklag), Tel-Aviv, 1958.

L.I. Yudkin, *Isaac Lamdan*, London, 1971.

M. Zborowski and E. Herzog, *Life is with People*, New York, 1952.

I. Zinberg, *A History of Jewish Literature*, tr. and ed. B. Martin, 12 vols., Cincinnati and New York, 1972–8.

S. Zipperstein, *The Jews of Odessa: A Cultural History, 1794–1881*, Stanford University, 1985.

I. Even-Zohar, 'Gnessin's Dialogue and its Russian Models,' in *Slavica Hierosolymitana*, vol.7, Jerusalem, 1985.

Y. Halevi-Zwick, *Mussagh ha-Yahadhuth bi-Thequphath ha-Haskalah* (The Concept of Judaism in the Period of Haskalah), Tel-Aviv, 1955.

Index

Aberbach, D., 160 n. 32
Abramowitz, Shalom Jacob (Mendele), 19, 35, 39–40, 43–44, 52, 62, 69, 77, 79, 85, 87, 94–95, 97, 102, 131, 133, 160 n. 26, 163 n. 10, 172 n. 3, 176 n. 88, 189 n. 19
abuse, social and legal, 46, 51, 56, 120
action, dramatic, 46, 49, 110
adultery, as charge against Sadducees, 89, 91
advertisements, 110
Aeschylus, 118
Agnon, S. Y., 151, 169 n. 2, 173 n. 32
'Ahabhath Ṣiyyon, 11. See also *Love of Zion, The*
Ahad Ha-Am, 20, 147, 150–151, 190 n. 42
Akiba, 51
Alcoforado, Mariana, 22
'Aleinu (prayer), 141
Alexander I, Czar, 145
Alexander II, Czar, 9–10, 54, 131
Alexander Jannaeus, 118, 124
'Al ha-Pereq, 61. See also *At the Crossroads*
'Aliloth 'Aqabhyah, 171 n. 37
Altmann, A., 168 n. 1
ambiguity, as a literary device, 146, 155
America, 104, 106–107, 116, 143, 151
Anatolia, 171 n. 37
Andersson, T., 189 n. 26
anonymous letters, 29, 36, 108, 110, 175 n. 39
anti-Semitism, 1, 116
apostasy, 9
Arabic language, 155
Arabs, 150
Aramaic language, 14, 94
d'Argens, 23
Arnon, A., 189 n. 24
Around the Point, 189 n. 17
Arraignment of Paris, The, 184 n. 11
Aryeh Ba'al-Guph, 181 n. 9
Asch, Shalom, 190 n. 52
Ha-'Asiph, 169 n. 32
'Ašmath Šomron, 11. See also *Guilt of Samaria, The*
Assiduous Student, The, 189 n. 16.
assimilation, 129, 131
Atonement, Day of, 50, 141
At the Crossroads, 190 n. 39
At Your Feet, Jerusalem, 168 n. 2, 189 n. 25, 190 n. 43
Aufklärung, 53
author-intervention, 42
'Ayiṭ Ṣabhua', 11. See also *Hypocrite, The*

Ba'al Shem Tob, Israel, 58
Bacher [Bacharach], Simon, 119
Bag of Songs, 190 n. 56
Barnaby Rudge, 185 n. 25
Baron, Salo, 159 n. 10
Bates, C., 169 n. 30
Ben-Horin, M., 190 n. 66
Bennett, E. K., 162 n. 65
Ben-Yehuda, Eliezer, 148, 155, 189 n. 23, 190 n. 69
Ben-Zeev, Judah Lev, 6
Ben-Zion, S., 147
Berdichevsky, M. J., 15, 147, 188 n. 14
Berkowitz, Isaac Dov, 188 n. 14
Berlin, 6–7, 12
  enlightenment, 63–64, 138
Bernard, L., 160 n. 35
Bernfeld, S., 189 n. 35
Bershadsky, I., 188 n. 14
Bessarabia, 76
Between the Times, 43, 47, 103–104, 108, 110–111, 113
Bialik, Chaim Nachman, 17–18, 147, 153, 160 n. 31, 181 n. 9, 189 n. 16, 190 n. 54
biblical langage and style, 5, 6, 12, 13, 16, 44, 93–95, 98, 100, 112, 127, 152, 155
bigotry, 12, 43, 60–62, 67, 75, 95, 111, 114, 130
Black, F. G., 22, 161 nn. 9, 12, 21, 27, 165 n. 67

Bleak House, 185 n. 25
Boḥan Ṣaddiq, 10. See also *Test of the Righteous, The*
Book of Idylls, 190 n. 57
Book of the Beggars, 140, 160 n. 28, 187 n. 17
Booth, Wayne, 165 n. 91, 183 n. 91
Bracher, H., 162 n. 65
Braginskij, 185 n. 23
Braudes, Reuben Asher, 12–13, 35, 37, 39, 41–44, 47, 50, 52, 56, 58–60, 67, 70–71, 73, 75–76, 78, 81, 86, 95–98, 101–102, 118–121, 132, 134, 137, 139, 160 n. 21, 163 n. 22, 166 n. 2, 169 n. 3, 172 nn. 2, 4, 173 n. 60, 174 n. 3, 175 nn. 32, 33, 184 n. 1, 22, 185 n. 43
Breiman, S., 189 n. 19
Brenner, J. H., 15, 16, 42, 147, 151–152, 188 n. 14, 189 n. 17, 190 n. 49
bribery, as theme of novels, 38, 49, 51, 69, 132
in Russia, 8, 131
Bridal Canopy, The, 173 n. 32
Brill, Joel, 6
Burla, J., 171 n. 37
Burnshaw, S., 191 n. 70

caricature, 65, 67, 67, 77, 83, 89, 172 n. 3
Carmi, T., 160 n. 30, 190 n. 56, 191 n. 70
Caro, Joseph, 184 n. 1
Catalan, 119
Caught Open-eyed in the Night, 190 n. 56
centers, literary, 20, 145, 148, 188 n. 2
character, 24, 30–31, 38–39, 111, 118
characterizations, 15, 11, 27, 31–34, 39, 103, 110–111, 139
Chaucer, Geoffrey, 119, 191 n. 71
child marriage, 41
children, illness or death of, 48–49, 52, 57, 75
childhood experience, 17–18, 153
Chomsky, W., 190 n. 67
circumlocution, 5, 94–95, 99
Citizen of the World, 22
Clarissa, 22
Cohen, T., 162 n. 64
coincidence, as a literary device, 108
Collier de la Reine, Le, 185 n. 28
Comte de Monte Cristo, Le, 185 n. 28
conscription, military, 8, 38. *See also* military service
conversion to Christianity, 38, 52, 55, 159 n. 11
court scene, as a literary device, 118–126, 184 n. 22, 186 n. 51
Crimea, 18
criticism, literary, 6, 19–20, 55, 147, 174 n. 7, 180 n. 5
Crown, Alan David, 180 n. 1
Czarist administration, 8–9, 131, 147

Darwin, Charles, 137
Ha-Dath we-ha-Ḥayyim, 13, 168 n. 11. See also *Religion and Life*
Daube, David, 184 n. 9, 186 n. 55
David, Earle, 185 n. 38
Dawn, The, 169 n. 40
Days of Ziklag, 154, 190 n. 59
Debhir, 161 n. 20
Deeds of ʿAqabhyah, 171 n. 37
derniers jours d'un condamné, Les, 185 n. 26
description, as a literary device, 8, 14, 24, 31, 38, 69–70, 76–77, 79–80, 87, 91, 113, 138, 150, 153–154, n. 88
description, natural, 26, 113, 140
dialog, 11, 14, 41, 94, 100, 111–112
Dickens, C., 13, 120, 185 n. 25
didacticism, 11, 13, 24, 32, 40, 45, 51, 65, 80, 114, 120, 122, 128, 139, 142, 146, 161 n. 20
Dikson, 185 n. 23
Dinur, Ben-Zion, 161 n. 1, 186 n. 7, 187 n. 24, 188 n. 5
Dostoievsky, F. M., 120
Downs, B. W., 161 n. 11
Dream and its Realization, The, 189 n. 23
Dubnow, S., 159 n. 10, 171 n. 61
Dumas, Alexandre, 11, 120, 185 n. 27
Dunlop, J., 184 n. 15
Dutch language, 119

education, 4–6, 8–10, 14, 32, 40, 42, 54–55, 59–60, 73, 103, 105, 108, 114, 127, 131–132, 135–136, 149, 171 n. 42
Ehrenzeller, H., 187 n. 37
Eighteen Coins, 46, 49, 101, 103–104, 108, 110–113, 115, 116, 169 n. 47
Eisenstadt, S. N., 190 n. 44
Elijah, Gaon of Vilna, 58, 172 n. 75
emancipation, 3, 4, 9–10, 12, 18, 32, 53–55, 112, 127, 128, 150
emigration, 10, 18, 106–107, 147–148
England, 21, 45, 107
English literature, 1, 13, 16, 22, 25, 45, 120, 184 nn. 11, 22, 191 n. 71
enlightenment, 4–5, 7, 9–10, 12, 15, 17, 23–24, 26, 31–32, 34, 39–41, 43, 52–56, 60–65, 67, 69, 73, 75, 78–80, 101, 103, 127–129, 132, 136, 138–139, 146–147, 150
Eörsi, I., 160 n. 34
Epistolae Obscurorum Virororum, 10

epistolary devices and literature, 10, 21–43, 161 nn. 14, 20
'Ereṣ Yisra'el, 148–156, 188 n. 1, 189 n. 28. *See also* Israel
Erter, Isaac, 10–11, 169 n. 1, 174 n. 16
Eternal People, The, 169 n. 49
Euchel, Isaac, 6
Eumenides, The, 118
European literature and civilization, 1, 3–5, 11–12, 15–17, 21–25, 33–34, 39, 43, 45, 53, 102, 112–113, 120, 127–128, 132, 138–139, 146, 155, 160 n. 34
exaggeration, 13, 65

factionalism, 9, 58–59, 62–63, 66–67, 76–77, 90, 104, 131, 134
Faerie Queene, 119
fainting, 29, 37, 45–46, 108, 162 n. 53
fanaticism, 8, 60, 62, 75, 78, 98, 175 n. 75
Fathers and Sons, 35, 40, 43, 52, 62, 131, 140, 163 n. 10
Fehr, H., 185 n. 29
Feierberg, M. Z., 15, 143, 147, 188 n. 48
Feingold, B., 160 n. 21
festivals, religious, 14, 60, 63, 68, 88, 90, 146, 149
Fichman, J., 162 n. 38, 187 n. 44
Fielding, Henry, 184 n. 22
footnotes, as explanatory device in Hebrew novels, 23, 43, 52, 76, 86, 88, 95, 97, 109, 110 112, 168 n. 73, 169 n. 32, 172 nn. 1, 7, 175 n. 32, 176 n. 88, 181 n. 14, 183 n. 114, 185 n. 43
For Love of Ṣaddiqim, 36
foreign languages and vocabulary, 32, 41, 95, 98, 115
forgery, as theme of novels, 28, 30, 45, 89, 108, 162 n. 41
frame-story (= *Rahmengeschichte*), 30, 37, 162 n. 65
France, 107
Frankel, J., 159 n. 10
Frankel, Zacharias, 54
French language, 32, 107, 114, 119, 184 n. 15, 185 nn. 23, 24, 25
French literature, 1, 11, 45, 120, 180 n. 5, 181, n. 5, 184 n. 22,
French Revolution, 1–4, 16, 53, 128,
Friedlander, G., 184 n. 15
Frishman, D., 174 n. 7
From Here and There, 190 n. 50

Galicia, 7, 10–11, 23, 71, 76, 88, 172 n. 1
Galilee, 152
Geiger, Abraham, 54
German language, 4, 7, 95–96, 184 nn. 15, 22–23, 25–28
German literature, 1, 6, 11, 15, 120, 185 n. 23
Germany, 1, 4, 6–9, 54–55, 57, 64, 132, 145, 185 n. 24
Gilgamesh, Epic of, 118, 184 n. 4
Gilgul Nepheš, 174 n. 16
Ginzberg, Asher, 20. *See also* Ahad Ha-Am
Glückel of Hameln, 2
Gnessin, U. N., 15, 147
Goethe, J. W., 22, 50, 59, 162 n. 54
Gogol, N., 131
Goldberg, Leah, 153, 190 n. 56
Goldsmith, O., 22
Golyakov, I. T., 185 n. 30
Gordon, Yehudah Leib, 16–17, 55
Gottlober, Abraham Baer, 119
grammar, as educational subject, 5–7, 95, 111, 127, 182 n. 64
grammatical errors, 95, 174 n. 7
Graupe, H. M., 168 n. 4
Greek literature and civilization, 19, 118
Greenberg, Uri Zvi, 148, 151, 154, 159 n. 10, 189 n. 25, 27, 190 n. 43, 191 n. 74
Grodno, 180 n. 1
Guilt of Samaria, The, 11, 24, 26, 128
Gummer, E. N., 185 n. 25
Günzburg, M. A., 161 n. 20
Guttmann, J., 168 n. 6

Halevi-Zwick, Y., 168 n. 6
Halkin, S., 161 n. 20, 186 n. 1, 188 n. 10
Halkin, H., 188 n. 48
Halle, M., 191 n. 71
Ḥasidh Ṣoṭeh, 71
Hasidism, 9–10, 23, 31, 58–59, 62–63, 65–73, 75–83, 84–91, 104–106, 110, 114–115, 129, 131–132, 134, 169 n. 1, 170 nn. 4, 7, 9, 10, 11, 23, 26, 42, 72, 171 nn. 52, 55, 172 nn. 1, 7, 14, 17, 21, 72, 76, 173 nn. 22, 41, 43, 52, 56, 60
Haskalah, 4, 7, 10, 12–13, 16, 19, 31–32, 64, 66–67, 73, 93, 109–116, 134, 136, 140, 159 n. 1, 161 n. 20
Hazaz, 151
Heart of Midlothian, The, 185 nn. 23, 31, 35
Hebrew language, 1, 3, 5–8, 12–13, 15–17, 93–98, 101, 103, 110, 112, 115, 127, 148, 150, 155, 159 n. 2, 174, n. 4, 189 n. 28
Hebrew literature, 1–2, 5–8, 10–21, 23–24, 26, 31, 33–35, 43–44, 49, 55–56, 59, 61–62, 66, 79, 93–94, 100–103, 107–113, 116–118, 123, 126–128, 132–134, 138–140, 143, 145–152, 154–156, 159 n. 1, 162 n. 46, 53, 65, 169 n. 1, 188 n. 2, 4, 14

Hebrew periodicals, 19, 190 n. 45
Hebrew press, 148, 151
Hebron, 145
Ḥedher, 65, 136
Heller, J., 187 n. 28
Henryson, Robert, 119
heroes, 12, 28, 47–48, 50, 60, 81, 108–109, 111, 116, 128–129, 136, 141, 149
heroines, 12, 57, 108–109, 111, 128, 136, 180 n. 5
heroism, 11, 113
Hertzberg, A., 189 n. 30, 36
Herzog, E., 188 n. 13, 189 n. 27
Hess, M., 169 n. 1
Ḥibbath Ṣiyyon, 150
Hirsch, Samson Raphael, 54
historical novels and romances, 11–12, 24–27, 30, 44, 93–94, 103, 128, 130
History of Jonathan Wild, The, 184 n. 22, 185 n. 35
Holdheim, Samuel, 54
Holland, 1
Holocaust, 1
Holtz, A., 159 n. 1, 188 n. 14, 189 n. 30
Homer, 118
House-dog, 191 n. 74
Ḥozei Ḥezyonoth, 93
Hugo, Victor, 120
humor, 14, 40, 46, 52, 77, 109, 112–113, 140–141, 148, 156
hyperbole, 13
Hypocrite, The, 11, 21, 23–24, 26–27, 29–32, 34, 37–39, 44, 56, 93, 102, 128–129, 167 n. 46, 175 n. 62, 181 n. 21, 183 n. 108

'Ikkubh ha-Qeri'ah, 121
Iliad, The, 184 nn. 6, 8
imagery, 152, 155
Inheritance, The, 35, 100, 137
Inspector General, The, 131
intermarriage, 9, 52
Intimations of Immortality, 190 n. 55
intrigue, as theme of novels, 45, 65
In Winter, 189 n. 17
irony, 23, 25–27, 30, 38, 51, 103, 110, 123, 133, 140, 142, 146, 148, 155
Islam, 119
Israel, ancient, 11, 93
State of, 1, 20, 156
Isserles, Moses Israel, 121, 122, 186 n. 44
Italian language, 1
Italy, 1–2
Ivanhoe, 185 n. 23, 33, 35

Jackson, B. S., 184 n. 10, 186 n. 55
Jane Eyre, 185 n. 40
Jannaeus, Alexander, 118, 124, 186 n. 51
Jean Paul, 23
Jerusalem, 53
Jerusalem, 130, 145, 149, 152
Jewish life, 1–12, 14–15, 18, 40, 45, 54–66, 76–78, 93, 101, 102–104, 115–118, 127–133, 135, 138–140, 142–147, 169 n. 24
Job, 118–119,
Jospe, E., 168 n. 1
Jospe, A., 168 n. 2
Joy of the Godless, The, 50, 136
Judgement at Nuremberg, 185 n. 37
Juif errant, Le, 185 n. 27

Kabakoff, J., 188 n. 2
Kabbalah and Kabbalists, 58, 68–69, 73, 88, 90
Kagan, E., 191 n. 71
Karaites, 58,
Katznelson, G., 168 n. 8,20, 184 n. 3
Keeton, G. W., 184 n. 15
Kelebh Bayith, 191 n. 74
Keyser, S. J., 191 n. 71
King of Flesh and Blood, The, 118, 123, 186 nn. 56, 59, 62
Klausner, J., 159 n. 1, 162 n. 38, 170 n. 4, 171 n. 69, 174 n. 3, 181 nn. 15, 18, 22, 42, 188 n. 4
Kleist, Heinrich von, 185 n. 29
Klopstock, F. G., 6
Kochan, L., 159 n. 10
Königsberg, 6
Kovner, A, U., 189 n. 19
Krochmal, Nachman, 54, 169 n. 1

Lachower, 159 n. 1, 188 n. 4
Ladino, 155
Landau, J. L., 23, 161 n. 17
Land Without Shade, A, 154, 190 n. 58
Langer, M. G., 171 n. 37
Latin, 95, 107, 119,
law, Jewish 3, 56–58, 121, 126, 184 n. 1
laws, dietary, 8, 59
Le'an?, 188 n. 48
Ha-Lebhanon, 55
Lebensohn, M. J., 16
Lefin, Menahem, 23
Legend of Good Women, 119
Leiden des jungen Werthers, Die, 22, 50, 162 n. 54
Leinwand, J. I. 35, 42, 44, 47–48, 50, 60, 85, 96, 98, 102
Lemberg, 168 n. 11, 184 n. 1
Lessing, G. E., 114, 119

letters, as a literary device, 11, 23–33, 34–43, 110, 161 n. 4, 162 n. 50, 163 n. 10, 165 n. 87
letter-form, letter-novel, 21–23, 26, 30–35, 38, 41
letter-manuals, 39
Letters of a Turkish Spy, 21
Lettres juives, 23
Lettres portugaises, 22
Levinsohn, Isaac Baer, 54
Life of Glückel of Hameln, The, 159 n. 3
Lilienblum, Moshe Leib, 19, 55–56, 150, 185 n. 42
Lindau, Baruch, 6
Lithuania, 11, 15, 39, 55–56, 59, 76, 89, 104, 106, 118, 121–122, 128–130, 181 n. 8, 184 n. 1
London, 30, 50
Lottery and the Inheritance, The, 103, 106–116, 180 n. 5
Love of the Righteous, The, 36, 96
Love of Zion, The, 11, 24–26, 102, 128, 133, 150, 187 n. 12, 22
Löwisohn, Solomon, 16
Lubavitch, 90, 170 n. 4
Luncz, A. M., 148, 189 n. 23
Luria, Solomon, 186 n. 44
Luzzatto, Moses Chaim, 11
Luzzatto, Solomon David, 54
Lytton, Edward Bulwer, 120, 185 n. 24

MacCann, R. D., 185 n. 37
Ha-Maggidh, 55
Mahler, R., 171 n. 61, 188 n. 3
Maimon, Solomon, 116
Manassah of Ilya, 58
Manassewitz, M., 35, 41, 44, 48, 52, 95, 98, 102, 169 n. 3
Mandelkow, K. R., 161 nn. 24, 59
Mapu, Abraham, 11–12, 21, 23–24, 26–45, 56, 93–95, 100–103, 112, 128–131, 133, 136–137, 140, 149–150, 161 n. 1, 164 n. 54, 167 n. 46, 169 n. 1, 174 n. 4, 175 n. 62 181 nn. 10, 15, 21, 183 n. 90, 108,109
Marana, G. P., 21
marriage, as theme of novels, 45, 52
marriage brokers, 30, 106, 111, 114, 146
Marsden, N., 168 n. 74, 173 n. 36, 175 n. 41, 185 n. 42, 187 n. 18
Martin, B., 159 n. 1
Maskilim, 5–7, 9–10, 12, 55, 65–67, 93, 95, 104, 112, 115–116, 119, 132, 136, 170 n. 7, 172 n. 72, 182 n. 64, 183 n. 109
Mass'oth Binyamin Ha-Šeliši, 140. See also *Travels of Benjamin the Third, The*
Mazor, Y., 160 n. 23
McKillop, A. D., 161 n. 20
Ha-Me'asseph, 6
Measure for Measure, 119
Megalleh Ṭemirin, 10. See also *Revealer of Secrets, The*
Meinkin, S. F., 35–36, 43–44, 96, 98, 102
Melammedhim, 114, 132
Melekh Basar wa-Dham, 184 n. 2. See also *King of Flesh and Blood, The*
Ha-Meliṣ, 55, 174 n. 7
melodrama, 12, 14, 22, 24, 27–29, 33–34, 36–37, 42, 44–45, 49–50, 60, 89, 108, 116, 138–140, 146
Mendel, Menachem, 90, 170 n. 4
Mendele Mokher Sepharim, 13–16, 19, 59, 62, 94, 133–134, 139–142, 144, 147, 160 n. 26, 187 n. 42, 188 n. 15
Mendelssohn, Moses, 53, 58, 64, 132, 138, 168 n. 1, 172 n. 7
Merchant of Venice, The, 119, 184 n. 15
Messias, 6
metaphors 5, 152, 153, 177 n. 142
Meyer, M. A., 186 n. 2
Me'zer, 185 n. 23
Mieses, J. L., 169 n. 1
Mikliszanski, J. K., 188 n. 2
military service, 8, 37, 45, 52. *See also* conscription, military
Milton, J., 119
Minna von Barnhelm, 114
Miron, D. 187 n. 41, 188 n. 12
misfortune, as theme of novels, 28, 45, 47
Mithnaggedhim, 9, 58, 63, 65–66, 69–70, 72–73, 76–77, 81–83, 86–87,104, 129, 132, 170 n. 9, 172 n. 72, 173 n. 60
Montesquieu, C. L., 21, 22, 24, 34
Mosse, G., 159 n. 8
My Mare, 140, 169 n. 39
Mystères de Paris, Les, 185 n. 27

Nameless Journey, 190 n. 56
names, allusive and symbolic, 26, 59, 70, 71, 162 n. 46
narrative, 11, 13, 14, 22–24, 26–27, 29–30, 35–37, 108
Nathan der Weise, 119
nationalism, 1–2, 4, 8, 10–11, 54, 63–64, 128, 131, 138, 149–150, 169 n. 47
Neilson, W. A., 184 n. 12
Neo-orthodoxy, 54
Neqam Berith, 138
Neusner, Jacob, 186 n. 53, 55
Nicholas I, Czar, 8, 9
Nietzsche, Friedrich, 160 n. 34
Nouvelle Héloïse, 22

novels, Hebrew, 11–14, 24, 33–34, 43–44, 56, 59, 61, 66, 79, 93, 102, 107–108, 110–111, 116, 118, 138–139, 162 nn. 46, 53, 65, 185 n. 27. *See also* Hebrew literature

obscurantism, 31, 60–62, 67, 78–79, 95, 114, 134, 136, 182 n. 64
occupations, as social and economic factors, 2, 12, 114, 116
Odessa, 59–60, 71, 78, 81, 86, 152, 169 n. 24
Old Mortality, 185 nn. 23, 32
Oliver Twist, 185 nn. 25, 31
On the Blood, 160 n. 35
On the Threshold of the House of Study, 189 n. 16
Oppenheim, H., 169 n. 32
Origin of Species, The, 137
Outcast, The, 38, 41, 47, 50, 101
Oz, Amos, 152, 190 n. 49

Pagis, Dan, 191 n. 71
Pale of Settlement, 7–9, 54, 57, 62, 103, 132, 140, 143, 145
Palestine, 10, 17, 20, 143, 145, 150–152, 155, 169 n. 47, 188 n. 1. *See also* Israel
Pamela, 21–22, 24, 34, 161 n. 20
Papirna, A. J., 19, 189 n. 19
Paradise Lost, 119
Parents Sin, The, 41, 169 n. 3
Parfitt, T. V., 190 n. 65
Paris, judgement of, 118–119
parody, 23, 43
pathos, 18–19, 48, 113
Patterson, David, 159 nn. 9, 12, 160 nn. 18, 20, 30, 33, 161 nn. 6, 26, 28, 31, 32, 37, 162 nn. 39, 60, 63, 65, 69, 73, 79, 81, 86, 163 n. 22, 164 n. 60, 168 nn. 71, 3, 9, 10, 171 n. 31, 174 nn. 1, 4, 5, 6, 180 n. 2, 184 nn. 2, 3, 185 n. 27, 186 n. 5, 6, 187 n. 12, 188 n. 2, 8, 189 n. 33, 34, 190 n. 48, 54
Paul Clifford, 185 nn. 24, 33
Peele, George, 184 n. 11
Péguy, Charles, 187 n. 12
Pelham, 185 n. 24
Pelli, M., 159 n. 7
People's Court, 185 n. 37
Perl, Joseph, 10–11, 23–24, 31, 33–35, 38–39, 43, 169 n. 1
Perry, M., 160 n. 27, 187 nn. 42, 43, 188 n. 12
Perry Mason, 185 n. 37
Persian Letters, 21–24, 34
Peveril of the Peak, 185 nn. 23, 34, 35
Pickwick Papers, The, 185 nn. 25, 33
plots, plot construction, 11–13, 24–27, 29–31, 33–35, 39, 43–47, 49, 56–57, 59–60, 69, 84, 103–107, 110–111, 114, 118, 121, 137–140, 161 n. 4, 165 n. 87, 168 n. 13, 169 n. 23, 180 n. 5, 181 n. 6
poetry, Hebrew, 5–7, 10, 16–19, 26, 146–148, 153–154, 156, 180 n. 1, 191 nn. 71, 74
pogroms, 10, 50, 143, 147, 150
Poland, 8, 15, 23, 76, 90, 116
Polish language, 114–115
  revolts, 38
Poles, 89, 104–106, 112, 114, 116, 183 n. 99
Positivist School, Russian, 13, 55, 137, 139
poverty, as a social factor, 10, 44, 51, 57, 59, 62, 87, 116, 140, 146, 148
Price, L. M., 185 n. 23, 24
Pride and Fall, 75
Processus Belial, 119,

Qinath ha-'Emeth, 176 n. 88

Rabelais, 23
Rabin, C., 159 n. 2
Rabinowitz, A. S., 44, 52, 61, 89–90, 95, 97, 98, 102, 109, 150, 169 n. 34, 47, 172 n. 2, 177 n. 161
Ragoler, Elijah, 181 n. 15
Raisin, J. S., 183 n. 109
Rapoport, Solomon Judah, 54
Rea, J. D., 184 n. 15
realism, 12, 138, 45
reform, religious 4, 9, 13, 37, 39, 54–59, 61–62, 64, 118, 120, 122, 139, 185 n. 42
  secular and social, 10, 13, 16, 32, 39, 66, 132–133, 137
Reform movement, 55, 57, 59
religion, 8, 38, 56–58, 60–61, 116, 122, 137, 156, 184 n. 1
Religion and Life, 13, 35, 37, 39, 42–43, 56, 59, 78, 102, 118, 121, 132, 134, 137, 139, 169 n. 3
religious problems, 16
  life, 65, 132
remedies, superstitious, 52, 84, 86, 168 n. 74
remorse, as theme of novels, 45
Revealer of Secrets, The, 10, 23–24, 34
revenge, as theme of novels, 36, 45, 108
revival of Hebrew, 1, 6, 15, 94, 111, 150, 155
Reward of the Righteous, The, 38, 100
Richardson, S., 21–22, 24, 34, 161 n. 20
Rivlin, A. A., 160 n. 37, 189 n. 18
Ro'i, Y., 189 n. 37
Rola, 116
Roosbroek, G. L. van, 161 n. 7, 165 n. 67
Rosenberg, E., 184 n. 15
Roth, C., 159 n. 4
Roumania, 64, 89, 138
Rousseau, 22

Rubianus, 10
Ruppin, A., 188 n. 7
Russia, 7–8, 10–12, 17, 54–55, 59, 76, 103, 120, 129, 131–132, 140, 142–145, 147, 156, 159 n. 10, 185 n. 25
Russian language 1, 8, 95–97, 114–115, 131–132
 government, 9–10, 54, 132
 literature, 15, 55, 120, 135, 137
Ruth, 112

Sabbatai Zevi, 2
Sabbath, 57, 58, 78, 87, 96, 108, 109, 113, 121, 133, 146
Sachs, A. S., 185 n. 39
Ṣaddiq, Ṣaddiqim, see Hasidism
Safed, 145
Ha-Šaḥar, 169 n. 40, 170 n. 4
Saphiaḥ, 17, 190 n. 54
Satanow, Isaac, 6
satire, 10–12, 14, 21, 23–24, 33–35, 39, 43, 45, 50, 52, 55, 62–63, 67, 69, 73, 77, 79, 80, 85, 87, 91–92, 109–110, 112–115, 134, 138, 142, 162 n. 51, 169 n. 34, 176 n. 89, 188 n. 15
Scharfstein, Z., 189 n. 27
Scholem, G., 186 n. 3, 187 n. 12
schools, *see* education.
Schulman, K., 185 n. 27
Scott, W., 120, 185 n. 23, 36
Ṣe'ena u-Re'ena, 75
secular knowledge and study, 4, 9, 12, 32, 41, 60–61, 63, 66, 73, 79, 114, 115, 129, 134, 155, 171 n. 42, 190 n. 66
Sened, Yonat and Alexander, 154
Sepher ha-Qabbṣanim, 140. See also *Book of the Beggars, The*
Šetei ha-Qeṣawoth, 13, 169 n. 22. See also *Two Extremes, The*
Shaanan, A., 159 n. 1, 188 n. 4
Shaked, G., 159 n. 1, 187 n. 42, 190 n. 58
Shakespeare, W., 119, 136, 191 n. 71
Shamir, M., 118, 123–124, 190 n. 68
Shapiro, I., 184 n. 17, 18
Shavit, Z., 189 n. 20
Sheikewitz, N. M., 35, 41–42, 44, 47–49, 50, 61, 90, 95, 96, 98, 101, 102, 172 n. 2, 177 n. 167
Shentukh, Y., 187 n. 43
Shimoni, 153–154
Shimoni, D., 190 n. 57,62
Shirei Tiph'ereth, 6
Shmeruk, C., 187 n. 43
Shneur, Z., 147
Shofman, G., 15, 147
Silberschlag, E., 159 n. 1, 160 n. 33, 160 n. 35, 174 n. 2, 187 n. 12, 188 n. 2, 189 n. 23
Ha-Šiloaḥ, 20
Sirkis, I. J., 44, 52, 69, 82, 95, 97, 98, 102
Ṣitron, S. L., 163 n. 77
Sketches by Boz, 185 n. 25
Smolenskin, Peretz, 12–13, 34–35, 39, 41–52, 61–64, 67–71, 73, 75–78, 80, 82, 85, 87–89, 95, 97–102, 129, 136, 137–139, 150, 160 n. 21, 164 n. 54, 168 n. 71, 169 n. 36, 40, 45, 47, 170 n. 4, 7, 9, 172 n. 3, 174 n. 8, 177 n. 171, 181 n. 10, 182 n. 51, 83
social conditions, 33, 55, 101, 103, 107, 114
 conflict, 8
 criticism, 13, 14, 16, 21, 31, 43, 45, 71
 problems, 12, 16, 44, 51, 120
 purpose, 2, 138–139
socialism, 4, 128, 144, 190 n. 51
Songs of Glory, 6
Ha-Ṣopheh le-Bheith Yisrael, 10
Speake, Mrs J., 184 n. 11
Spenser, 119
Spicehandler, E., 159 n. 2, 191 n. 70
Stanislawski, M., 159 n. 11
Sterne, 23
Sturm-und-Drang, 22
style, 11–12, 16, 20, 26, 31–32, 36, 39, 41, 43, 93, 103, 110, 112, 113, 118, 127, 130, 139, 141, 146, 190 n. 49
Sue, Eugène, 11, 120, 185 n. 27
suicide, 29, 37, 50
Šulḥan 'Arukh, 56–58, 121–122, 184 n. 1, 185 n. 43–44
superstition, 4, 10, 52, 60, 65, 67, 69, 75, 77–78, 86, 111, 134, 168 n. 74
Susanna, 118, 120, 124, 184 n. 14
Susathi, 140, 169 n. 39
Swift, 23

Tale of Two Cities, A, 185 nn. 25, 32, 35
Talmon, S., 190 n. 66
Talmud, 1, 6, 7, 8, 42, 56–59, 67–68, 72–73, 121–122, 142, 147, 173 nn. 55, 59, 186 nn. 51, 55
teachers, 8, 18, 111, 125, 131–132, 136
Testament of Cresseid, The, 119
Test of the Righteous, The, 10, 23, 24, 34
theft, as theme of novels, 45, 108
Tiberias, 145
Time to Plant, 169 n. 45
Ṭobh, as alternative term for *Ṣaddiq*, 172 n. 1
Tom Jones, 184 n. 22, 185 n. 31, 35
Tosefta, 186 n. 52
Touch the Water, Touch the Wind, 152

translation into Hebrew, 5, 8, 119, 140
transliteration of foreign words, 95, 98, 112, 180 n. 1
Transmigration of Souls, 174 n. 16
Travels of Benjamin the Third, The, 140, 188 n. 15
Troilus and Criseyde, 119
Truth from 'Ereṣ Yisrael, 150
Tschernichowsky, Saul, 18, 147
Tulipe Noire, La, 185 n. 28
Twelve Angry Men, 185 n. 37
Two Extremes, The, 13, 36, 38, 39, 42–43, 50, 59–60, 70, 78, 81, 86, 139, 172 n. 4
Two Masters, 190 n. 42

Ukraine, 15, 76
United States, 10, 143, 147, 149, 151, 188 n. 2, 189 n. 28

villainy, as theme of novels, 28, 36, 46, 48–49, 70, 89, 115
Vilna, 60, 86
  Gaon *see* Elijah, Gaon of Vilna
violence, as theme of novels, 45, 49–50, 77, 108
Vision, 180 n. 5
Visionaries, The, 93
Vitebsk, 170 n. 4
vocabulary, biblical, 5, 12, 16, 94, 112
  insufficiency of Hebrew for modern terms, 6, 13, 16, 113, 139, 155
  post-biblical, 6, 13
Volhynia, 71, 76, 90

Wagoners Jubilee, The, 153
Wahlverwandtschaften, Die, 59
Waidson, H. M., 162 n. 65
Wanderer in the Paths of Life, The, 34–35, 39, 41–43, 45–46, 48, 50, 64, 67, 75, 81–82, 100, 102, 129, 168 n. 71, 170 n. 4
Warsaw, 103, 161 n. 2, 169 n. 22, 180 nn. 1, 5
Watchman of the House of Israel, The, 10, 174 n. 16
Waverley, 185 n. 23
Waxman, M., 159 n. 1, 188 nn. 2, 4
Weinfeld, D., 160 n. 21
Weingreen, J., 174 n. 9
Weisbrem, Israel, 35, 39, 41–44, 46–49, 84, 95, 97–99, 101–104, 107, 110–116, 169 n. 47, 180 nn. 1, 5, 6
Werblowsky, R. J. Z., 171 n. 37
Werses, S., 23, 159 n. 1, 161 nn. 16, 18, 19, 22, 24, 162 n. 63, 163 nn. 75, 10, 164 nn. 59, 61, 165 nn. 63, 68, 165 n. 75, 166 n. 103, 187 n. 40
Wessely, Naphtali Hartwig, 6, 16
Wiek, 116
Wieland, 23
Winter's Tale, The, 184 n. 14
Wordsworth, William, 190 n. 55

Yabham, 57
Yahrblum, M., 160 n. 21
Yardeni, G., 188 n. 6, 189 n. 23
Ha-Yašiš, as alternative title for Ṣaddiq, 172 n. 1
Yemei Ṣiqlagh, 154. See also *Days of Ziklag*
Yešibhah, 7–8, 65, 69, 135–136
Yiddish language, 4, 95, 97, 141, 149, 155, 176 n. 85
  literature, 1, 13, 61, 94, 102, 140, 144, 156, 187 n. 17
Yizhar, S., 154, 189 n. 21, 190 n. 59
Yobhel ha-'Eghlonim, 153
Yudkin, L., 190 n. 61

Zalman of Ladi, 58
Zborowski, M., 188 n. 13, 189 n. 27
Zederbaum, A., 174 n. 7
Zinberg, I., 159 n. 1
Zionism, Zionist movement, 1, 11, 115, 130, 143, 149, 151–152, 190 n. 66
Zipperstein, S. J., 169 n. 24
Zobeizensky, B. I., 43–44, 50, 60–61, 83, 89, 95, 96, 98–99, 102, 169 n. 36, 172 n. 3
Zohar, The, 68, 70, 72–73, 137
Zunz, Leopold, 54
Zweifel, E. Z., 169 n. 1